NEW ORLEANS *fabulous* STREETCARS

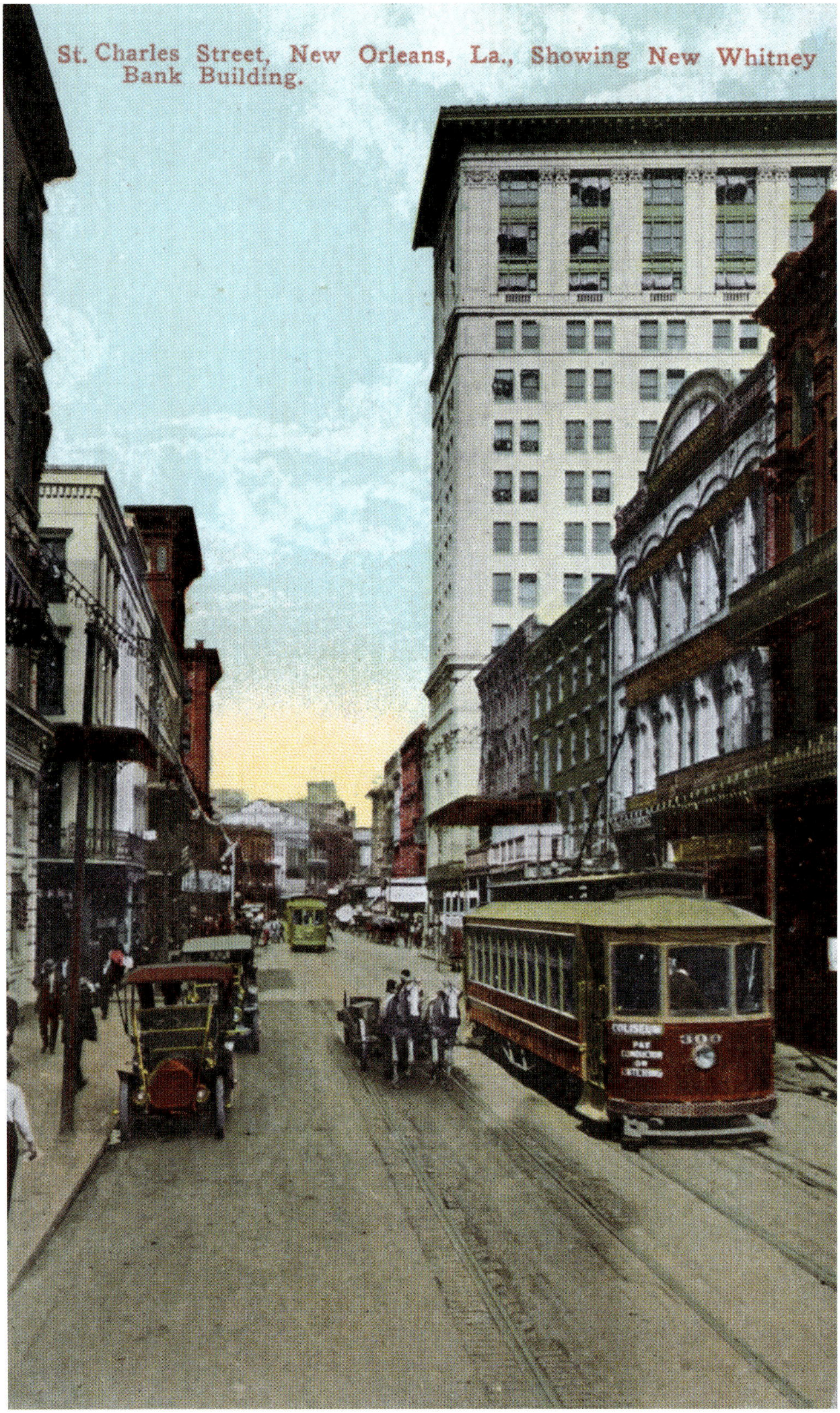

Streetcars are on St. Charles Street (later Avenue) looking towards Canal Street in this early postcard scene of the Central Business District of New Orleans around 1910. The fourteen-story Whitney Bank Building opened in 1909 and was the tallest building in Louisiana from 1909 until 1921. St. Charles Street was used by the Dryades line, which was electrified on January 14, 1896, and discontinued on July 2, 1929. When the St. Charles and Tulane Belt streetcars were discontinued on January 8, 1951, the St. Charles streetcars operated from Canal and St. Charles via St. Charles and Carrollton to Dixon. On August 10, 1952, the St. Charles line was cut back from Dixon to South Claiborne.

NEW ORLEANS *fabulous* STREETCARS

KENNETH C. SPRINGIRTH

FONTHILL

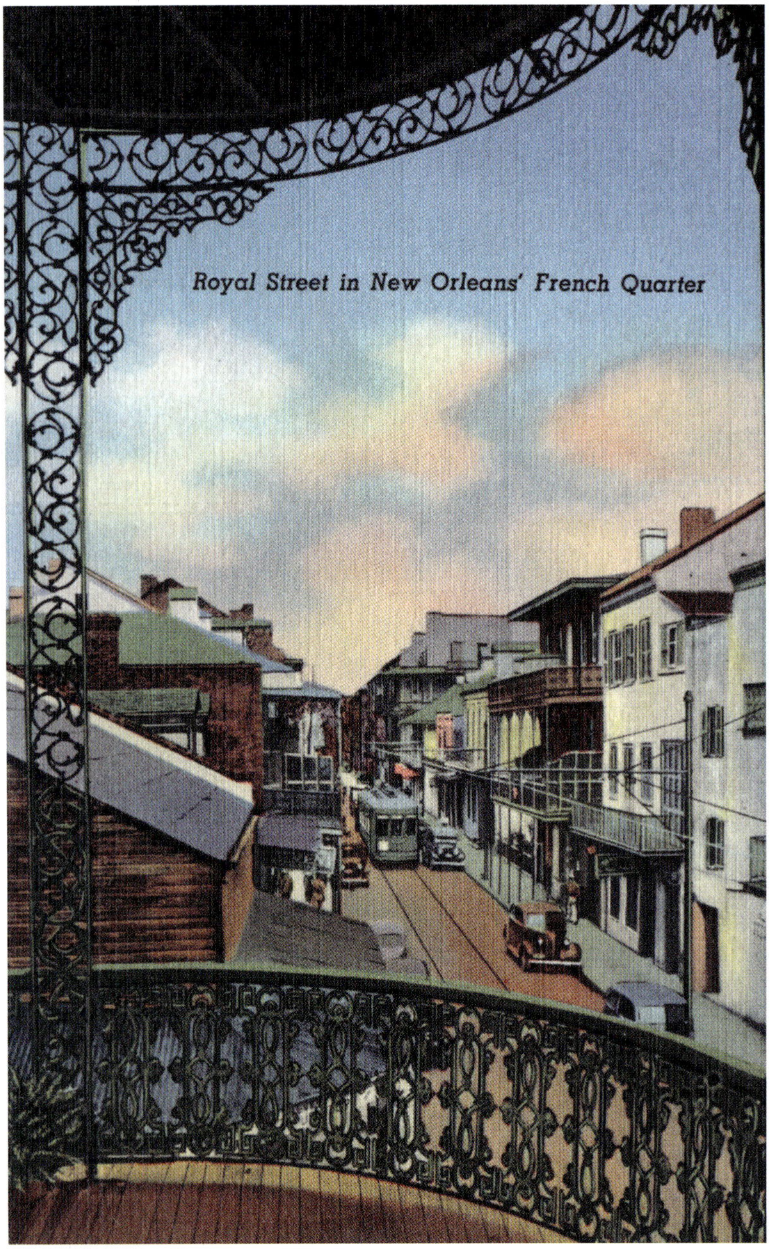

A streetcar makes its way along Royal Street in the French Quarter of New Orleans in this postcard view around the 1930s, with its buildings featuring picturesque wrought iron railings. This was used by the Desire streetcar line which opened on October 17, 1920 and was converted to bus operation on May 30, 1948. The line was featured in the Tennessee Williams play *A Streetcar Named Desire*. Royal Street, one of the oldest streets in the city, was famous for its antique shops, art galleries, and stately hotels.

On the cover: New Orleans Regional Transit Authority (RTA) streetcar No. 2002 is passing by the United States Custom House on Canal Street at Magazine Street in New Orleans on April 21, 2013. The United States Custom House, a monumental four-story granite building featuring round fluted Egyptian architectural style columns, was completed in 1881 and was designated a National Historic Landmark in 1974. With the opening of the Loyola streetcar line on January 28, 2013, the RTA operated 66 streetcars on four routes and 206 buses on thirty routes.

Fonthill Media Limited
Fonthill Media LLC
www.fonthillmedia.com
office@fonthillmedia.com

First published in 2014

Copyright © 2014 by Kenneth C. Springirth

ISBN 978-1-62545-039-5

All rights reserved. No part of this publication may be reproduced, stored in a retrieval system or transmitted in any form or by any means, electronic, mechanical, photocopying, recording or otherwise, without prior permission in writing from Fonthill Media LLC

Typeset in Utopia Std

Contents

Acknowledgments

Thanks to the Erie County, Pennsylvania Public Library for its internet access, reference books, interlibrary loan system and dedicated staff. The New Orleans Public Library was also a valuable source for information. Postcards are from the author's collection, and all the photographs were taken by the author on numerous trips to New Orleans between 1963 and 2013.

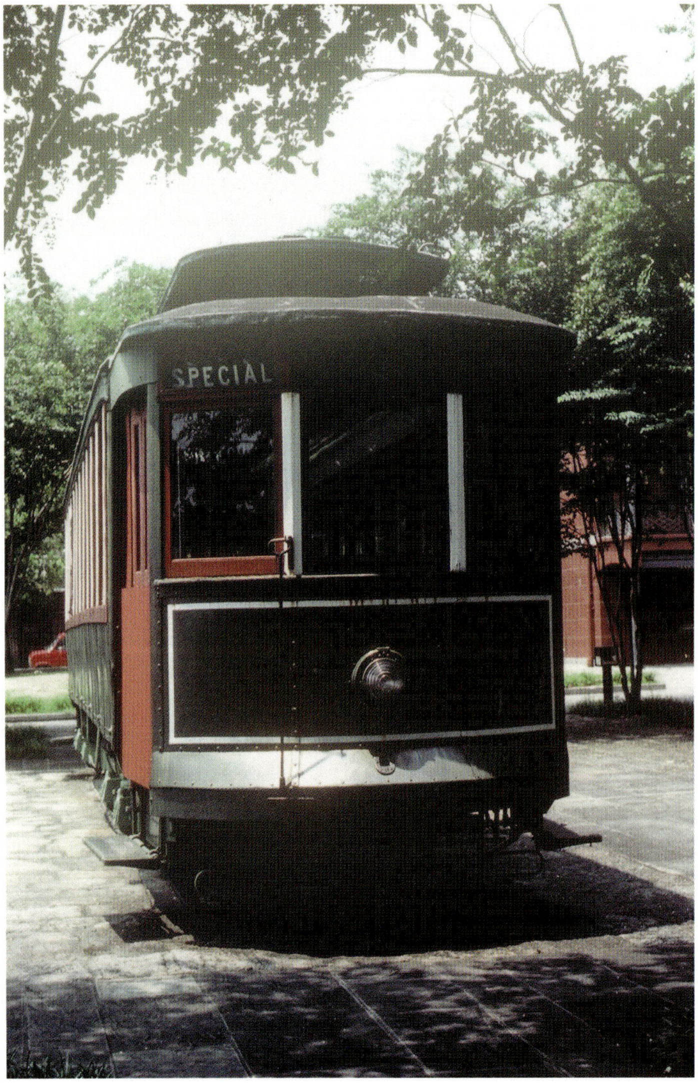

New Orleans streetcar No. 453 is on display, on July 27, 1989, at the Old United States Mint in New Orleans. This was one of twenty-five streetcars numbered 300 to 324 built by the American Car Company in 1906 for the New Orleans Railway and Light Company. During 1917, these streetcars were rebuilt and renumbered 450 to 474. Streetcar No. 453 was retained as a training car, and the other twenty-four cars were scrapped during 1935. In 1967, this car was placed in the French Market where it served as a tourist office. The car was moved over to the United States Mint property on Esplanade Avenue and was repainted. After deterioration again occurred, the car was returned in the early 1990s to the shelter of the Carrollton Station carbarn.

Introduction

In the first week of 1835, the New Orleans and Carrollton Railroad opened the first horse-drawn street railway line in New Orleans – the Poydras-Magazine line. Soon after, on September 26, 1835, the 4 foot 8.5 inch standard gauge 4.5 mile Carrollton line, later to become the St. Charles line, opened with steam-powered passenger trains. At the end of the Civil War, the New Orleans and Carrollton Railroad was near bankruptcy and was leased to General Pierre Gustave Toutant Beauregard and others for twenty-five years. Objections to the soot and noise produced by the steam locomotives resulted in switching to cars that were pulled by horses and mules in 1867, with 226 head of stock and 61 horse cars on the roster. Horse-drawn service on Canal Street began on June 1, 1861.

In the next few years, there were many short-lived attempts at innovation in street railways. On November 30, 1869, General Beauregard was issued a United States patent for an overhead cable traction system, and formed the New Orleans Improved Car Traction Company in 1870 to try cable cars on a 2,400 foot section of track on the St. Charles line. Cars featured a device mounted on the roof to grip or release the cable as needed. The idea was soon abandoned, because it was too expensive. During June 1870, an ammonia engine – similar to a fireless stored steam engine, except that a solution of water and ammonia provided the motive power – was tested on a trial run on the Canal line. Unfortunately, the new engine was not successful. In 1874, Dr. Emile Lamm and Sylvester Langdon formed the Lamm Fireless Engine Company to build fireless locomotives that were used on the New Orleans and Carrollton Railroad. On May 1, 1889, the use of steam dummies was discontinued, because it was too expensive. During that period of trying to make operational improvements, freight service on the St. Charles line was discontinued on February 1, 1871.

Horse-drawn service hit a snag in December 1872, when an animal epidemic struck town. So many horses became sick that service on the St. Charles line had to be suspended. Car drivers of the New Orleans and Carrollton Railroad requested permission to propel the cars by hand, and permission was granted. The car was pulled by four men and pushed by two men. Within a day, the horse disease had run its course, and horses were again used to pull the cars. Despite recovering from this short-term set-back, the use of horses to pull cars was on the decline, as New Orleans, and the nation, moved towards electrification. The last horse-drawn line built in New Orleans was the South Peters line which opened on April 26, 1890.

Work to electrify the Carrollton line began on July 13, 1890, and construction began to extend the line from St. Charles and Carrollton, via Carrollton to Jeanette, with new shops and a carbarn built at the corner of Jeanette and Dublin. Renamed "St. Charles," the extended, electrified line opened for service with each car powered by a pole contacting an overhead power system, on February 1, 1893. Car No. 21, operated by motorman William Moseley with conductor A.S. Roos, made the first trip leading a procession of seven cars leaving Carrollton Avenue at 10:15 a.m. and was greeted by large crowds of enthusiastic people from Baronne and Howard Streets to Canal Street. There were fifty-two cars built by the St. Louis Car Company at a cost of $2,949 per car. In addition to handling basic transportation needs, the new electrified "streetcars" were rented for private parties. While many cities use the term "trolley car," in New Orleans these vehicles are known as "streetcars," because the device that transmits electric current to the motor – the trolley – was developed many years after New Orleans streetcars were in use.

The New Orleans Traction Company was the second company to electrify its lines, with the Canal line electrified on July 28, 1894. Electric service was started by the Canal and Claiborne Railroad Company on the Claiborne and Tulane lines on October 10, 1896. During 1899, the New Orleans and Carrollton Railroad acquired the Canal and Claiborne Railroad Company and adopted an olive green and cream paint scheme for its streetcars which became standard for New Orleans streetcars. On September 26, 1901, the New Orleans and Carrollton Railroad was sold and became the New Orleans and Carrollton Railroad Light and Power Company.

By 1902, the four streetcar companies operating in New Orleans (New Orleans and Carrollton Railroad Light and Power Company, New Orleans City Railroad Company, Orleans Railroad Company, and St. Charles Street Railroad Company) were consolidated into the New Orleans Railway Company, which went into receivership in 1905 and was reorganized as the New Orleans Railway and Light Company. The New Orleans Railway and Light Company – operating 555 motor streetcars, forty-two passenger trailers, one baggage trailer, and sixty-eight work/service cars on its 219 miles of track – went into receivership in 1918. On September 27, 1922, the company reorganized as the New Orleans Public Service Inc. providing street railway, power, and natural gas service in New Orleans.

Immortalized in Tennessee Williams' play *A Streetcar Named Desire,* that was first staged in 1947, the Desire streetcar line opened on October 17, 1920 operating from Canal and Bourbon via Bourbon, Esplanade, Decatur, Elysian Fields, Chartres, Desire, Tonti, France, and Royal to Canal. On May 6, 1923, the Desire line was changed to operate from Canal and Bourbon via Bourbon, Pauger, Dauphine, Desire, Tonti, France, and Royal to Canal. After nearly three decades of streetcar service, the Desire line was converted to bus operation on May 30, 1948.

During this time, New Orleans Public Service Inc. was actively maintaining and modernizing the city's streetcar routes, but buses were coming. Seventy-three streetcars were built from 1923 to 1924 by the Perley A. Thomas Car Company of High Point, North Carolina, each costing $15,144, and numbered 900 to 972. As well, during 1924, New Orleans Public Service Inc. established its first motor bus line on the newly created North Carrollton line – from Tulane to the main entrance of City Park. The last two streetcar lines created by this company were St. Claude Avenue and Gentilly, opened on February 21, 1926. By that year, there were twenty-six streetcar and five bus lines operated by New Orleans Public Service Inc. Some duplicate track had been eliminated, and three streetcar lines had been abandoned in 1925, without bus replacement (Ferry, Bayou St. John, and Peters Avenue). These changes by the New Orleans Public Service Inc. resulted in the trackage being reduced from its peak of 225 miles in 1922, to 209 miles by 1926. Most of the streetcar lines in New Orleans were built to the broad gauge of 5 foot 2.5 inches; the standard gauge lines, including the St. Charles line, were converted to broad gauge by 1929.

On July 1, 1929, a strike of operating personnel occurred over New Orleans Public Service Incorporated's power to discharge employees, and because the company refused to accept a closed shop provision. Gradual restoration of service began on August 15, 1929, but the strike was not settled until workers voted on October 10, 1929 to accept an agreement worked out by company president A. B. Paterson and union president Green. The strike resulted in a severe ridership decline (from 148,488,286 in 1926 to 96,898,277 in 1929) and elimination of five streetcar routes: Coliseum on May 11, 1929; Dryades on July 2, 1929; Tchoupitoulas on July 2, 1929; Oak Street shuttle on July 2, 1929, converted several weeks later to trackless trolley; and St. Bernard on July 2, 1929, converted to bus operation at the end of the strike.

By 1930, the din of the strike had subsided and it was back to business for New Orleans Public Service Inc. That year, the company paid fifty percent of the $3.5 million cost to beautify almost two miles of Canal Street, from the loop north of the Mississippi River to North Claiborne Avenue. By 1940, they were operating 109 miles of streetcar track, 117 miles of motor bus and trackless trolley lines, 243 motor streetcars, 17 work cars, and 168 motor bus/trackless trolleys.

The Second World War resulted in a gigantic ridership increase in New Orleans – up from 124,000,000 in 1940, to 246,668,635 in 1945. No streetcar lines were abandoned during these years due to the United States Office of Defense Transportation ban on the substitution of buses for streetcars from 1942 to 1945. However, after the end of the Second World War in 1945, transit ridership declined, falling to to 164,075,000 by 1960. On December 1, 1946, the Freret line was converted to bus operation, trackless trolley operation on September 4, 1947, and bus operation on June 10, 1963. The Jackson line was converted to bus operation on May 19, 1947 and trackless trolley operation on October 2, 1947. The Magazine line was converted to bus operation on February 11, 1948 and trackless trolley operation on July 7, 1948. The Gentilly line was converted to bus operation on July 17, 1948. The Desire line was converted to bus operation on May 30, 1948, as noted above. The St. Claude line was converted to bus operation on January 1, 1949, to trackless trolley operation on November 6, 1949, and back to bus operation on July 22, 1962. The West End line was converted to bus operation on January 15, 1950. The St. Charles line was cut back to South Carrollton and South Claiborne Avenues on August 10, 1952.

In early 1953, there were 193 miles of motor bus lines with 349 buses, 48 miles of trackless trolley lines with 212 trackless trolleys, and 36 miles of streetcar lines with 141 streetcars. With the conversion to bus operation of the South Claiborne line on January 5, 1953, and the Napoleon line on February 18, 1953, only the St. Charles and Canal lines remained. By 1958, the system had 363 buses for thirty-two routes, 176 trackless trolleys for seven routes, and 85 streetcars for two routes. Rehabilitation of the streetcar fleet began in 1962, with cars Nos. 900, 914, and 915 receiving rubber sealed blue-tinted glass standee windows that were rounded at the corners, new metal leaf doors, and a refurbished interior. Car No. 900 received the first all-aluminum roof.

During 1963, New Orleans Public Service Inc. was seeking permission to convert the Canal streetcar line (which operated on reserved track except for the loop at the river end of Canal Street) to bus operation. Despite significant public opposition, the Canal line was converted to bus operation on May 31, 1964. The next to last car, No. 958, left Canal Street near the Mississippi River about 4 a.m. and journeyed to the Canal Station carbarn where passengers transferred to remodeled and decorated car No. 972. The car travelled to the Cemeteries terminus and went back via Canal Street to St. Charles Avenue. Around 5 a.m., the last Canal streetcar met the first Canal bus. Power for the Canal Street line was turned off immediately, and the overhead wire was torn down that morning by New Orleans Public Service, Inc. crews. Rail was quickly removed at the Canal Street loop near the Mississippi River and at the Cemeteries end of the line.

It is significant to note that New Orleans Public Service, Inc., in its *Transit Rider's Digest,* stated, "The changes on Canal Street will have no effect on the operation of the St. Charles streetcar line. Public Service does not intend now or in the foreseeable future to recommend any changes in the St. Charles streetcar operation." The City Council ordinance that permitted the replacement of the Canal streetcar line required that the entire project had to be completed by October 1, 1964. This included widening of Canal Street from North Anthony Street to North Claiborne Avenue allowing three traffic lanes on both sides of the 32.5 foot median strip or neutral zone (the landscaped area in the middle of the roadway), with all streetcar track, poles, and wires removed. As well, the former concrete paved streetcar right of way between North Claiborne Avenue and the Mississippi River was repaved for bus use. Three bus routes served by fifty-one new air conditioned buses manufactured by Flxible were operated: Canal–Lake Vista via Canal Boulevard, Canal–Lake Shore via Pontchartrain Boulevard, and Canal–Cemeteries operated over the former streetcar line. New Orleans Public Service, Inc. donated eleven streetcars to various museums and the remaining Canal streetcars were either stripped of parts for the St. Charles streetcars or were sold to scrap dealers.

After the Canal Street line conversion to bus in 1964, streetcars were now only in use on the St. Charles line. That year, the renovation of car No. 945 marked the completion of the rebuilding of thirty-five streetcars used on this line by New Orleans Public Service, Inc. These cars received new gears, all steel wheels and axles with roller bearings, and overhauled motors. Inside illumination was increased, car roofs were covered with aluminum sheeting, floors were rebuilt, new metal doors added, and new rounded standee windows were installed. With the installation of automatic fareboxes on June 4, 1972, the job of conductor was eliminated, and one-man operation was introduced on the streetcars.

The New Orleans Regional Transit Authority (RTA) took over the public transit operation from New Orleans Public Service Inc. on July 1, 1983. During 1990, the track was completely rebuilt. In December 1990, the Carrollton Station carbarn and shop were renovated. The thirty-five St. Charles streetcars were rebuilt, replacing the rounded standee and door windows that had been installed during the 1962-64 rebuilding, with rectangular windows similar the original 1923 design. Car No. 937 was the first car completed on June 24, 1991. Opening of the Riverfront streetcar line on August 14, 1988 marked the first new streetcar line in New Orleans in sixty-two years. Then, on April 18, 2004, streetcar service returned to Canal Street, almost forty years after the line had been converted to bus operation. From the foot of Canal Street, this line operates on Canal Street and, at Carrollton Avenue, splits into two branches. One branch continues on Canal Street to an area of historic cemeteries. The other branch (which never had streetcar service) turns onto North Carrollton Avenue to City Park.

Hurricane Katrina hit New Orleans on August 29, 2005, causing severe destruction to most of the city, along with its bus and streetcar system. Tragically, many residents, including RTA employees, lost their homes. However, in the sixty days after the storm, public transit began operation again. The RTA assembled a handful of buses that survived the flood, and other transit agencies donated buses. Over time, the bus fleet has been replaced with new vehicles. The red streetcars flooded by water containing corrosive oil and diesel fuel were decontaminated and rebuilt, with the first of the red cars back in service on Canal Street on December 12, 2008. In October 2008, Veolia Transportation, a private public transit operator that is a subsidiary of Veolia Environment in France, began operating the RTA. On July 1, 2009, the RTA Board of Commissioners approved a five-year management contract with Veolia that went into effect on September 1, 2009.

As a testament to the resilience of the New Orleans transit system, according to the American Public Transportation Association's "Light Rail (Streetcar) Public Transportation Ridership Report" for the fourth quarter of 2012, the New Orleans RTA streetcars had an average weekday ridership of 10,000. In addition, a new Loyola streetcar line opened on January 28, 2013, proving that the citizens of New Orleans continue to value the service these fabulous streetcars provide.

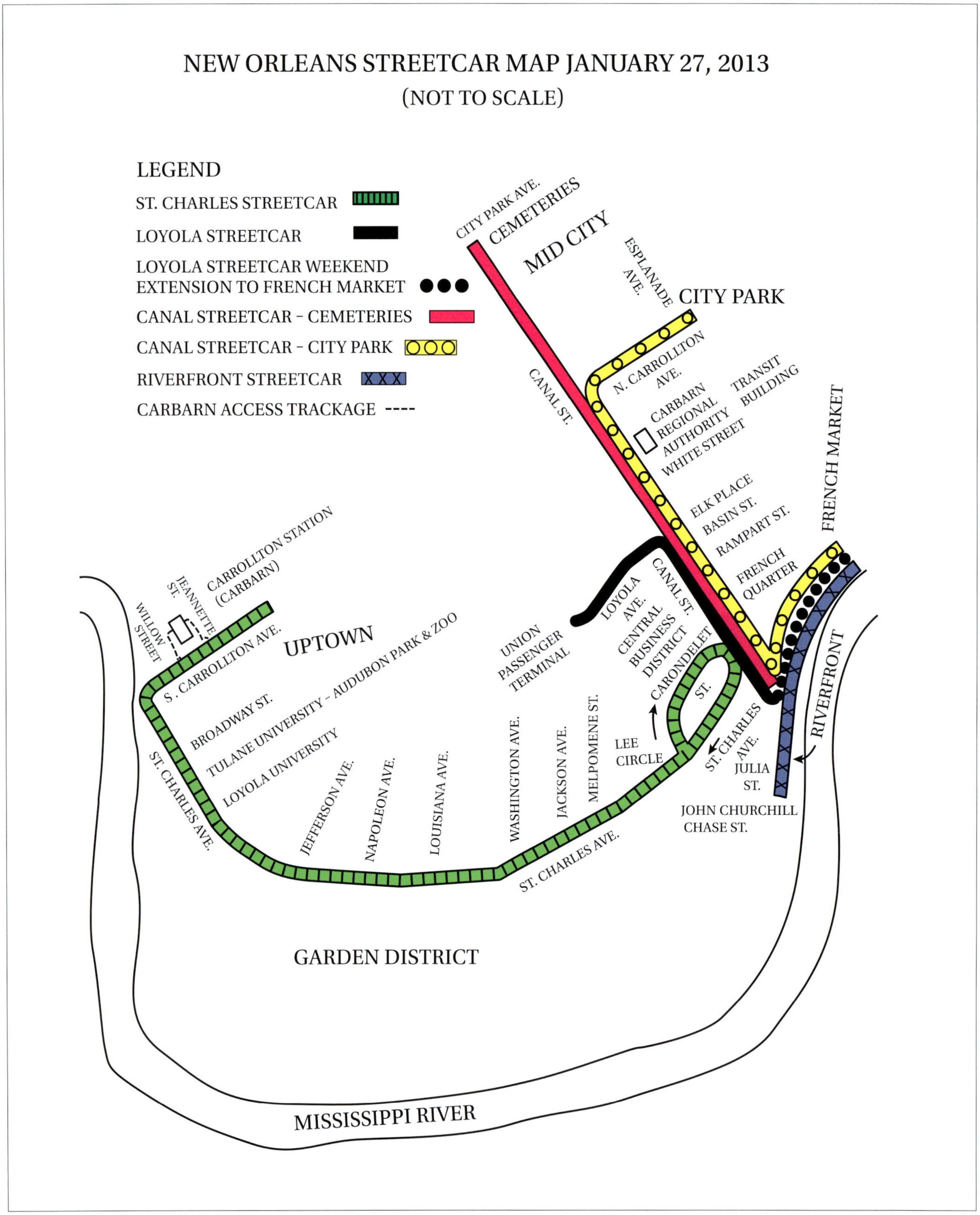

The map of the New Orleans Regional Transit Authority streetcar lines shows the service that was in effect on January 27, 2013. However, the August 25, 2013 schedule no longer shows the City Park line serving the French Market. According to the RTA, due to system maintenance, the Loyola and City Park lines no longer serve the French Market, necessitating a transfer to the Riverfront streetcar line at the Canal Street Station.

Chapter 1

Canal Streetcar Line

At one time, Canal Street had as many as eight streetcar tracks in the heart of downtown New Orleans (nine tracks for the loop at the foot of Canal Street), which was cut back to four tracks by 1930, and, later, to two with the exception of the third track used by St. Charles streetcars for one block between Carondelet Street and St. Charles Avenue. Opening on June 15, 1861 as a horse-drawn street railway, the Canal line was electrified on August 1, 1894 and, for much of its existence, operated from the foot of Canal Street to the Cemeteries. Beginning July 17, 1898, West End cars operated from Carondelet and Canal via Canal to City Park Avenue, turning left and along the bank of the New Basin Canal to West End on Lake Pontchartrain. This line was converted to bus operation on January 15, 1950. On June 1, 1901, a Canal Belt line operated as a loop using Canal Street, City Park Avenue, Moss Street, Esplanade Avenue, Rampart, and back to Canal Street. Esplanade became a bus line on December 27, 1934, and Canal cars operated only on Canal Street. Converted to bus operation on May 31, 1964, the Canal line was combined with the West End bus line.

Canal Street returned to streetcar operation with the first six-block long section opened to connect the Riverfront line with the St. Charles line, in 1999. Ground breaking for the next phase of the Canal Street project took place on July 20, 2001, and on July 24, 2001 the construction contract of the 1.5 mile portion between Baronne and Salcedo Streets was approved by the RTA. By November 30, 2001, assembly was in process on five replica Canal streetcars at the Carrollton Station shop. On December 18, 2001, the RTA awarded the contract to erect the carbarn for the new Canal streetcar line behind the RTA's existing A. Philip Randolph operations center. There were twenty-four streetcars built at the Carrollton Station shop for this line, retaining some of the classic lines of the St. Charles streetcars, while adding air conditioning plus modern control and braking equipment. On October 17, 2003, RTA superintendent for vehicle assembly, Elmer Von Dullen, operated, at a slow speed, new streetcar No. 2017 on Canal Street from Baronne Street to the Cemeteries terminus, testing clearances, track, switches, and power. Shortly after 3 a.m. on April 18, 2004, over 150 people (students of transportation, history buffs, and people who like early morning events) were on hand to board the first revenue streetcar at Canal and Salcedo Streets, marking the opening of the 3.6 mile line on Canal Street connecting the Riverfront to a terminal at Cemeteries with a 0.9 mile branch line on North Carrollton Avenue from Canal Street to the City Park. A formal dedication of the line took place on Memorial Day weekend of 2004 to mark the 40th anniversary of the May 31, 1964 date the last streetcar operated on Canal Street.

On August 29, 2005, Hurricane Katrina caused major flooding of the Canal Street carbarn with extensive damage to the twenty-four Canal and six of the seven Riverfront streetcars (car No. 461 was the only surviving Riverfront car). Brookville Equipment Company was awarded the contract to provide new trucks and power systems to the damaged streetcars that had been submerged in five feet of water at the Canal Station carbarn. Body work, painting, and final assembly of the restored streetcars was performed by RTA craftsman at the Carrolton Station shop. While the Carrollton Station carbarn and its thirty-five St. Charles streetcars escaped the flood, the damage to the overhead wire for the St. Charles streetcar line was extensive. On December 12, 2005, streetcar No. 930 – towed from the Carrollton Station shop – made a series of test runs on Canal Street. After the Canal Station carbarn had dried out enough for streetcars to be stored there, partial streetcar service was restored using cars from the St. Charles line operating on the Riverfront line from the French Market at Esplanade Avenue to Canal Street station, and then on Canal Street to Crozat Street on December 18, 2005. A portable substation, on loan from the Massachusetts Bay Transportation Authority in Boston, was placed in service, and streetcar service was restored on April 2, 2006 to the full length of the Canal Street line and the Carrollton Avenue branch line to City Park, using cars from the St. Charles line. By March 2009, enough of the red streetcars had been restored to handle the service on the Canal and Riverfront lines. The seven Riverfront streetcars were worked on and began to return to service in early 2010.

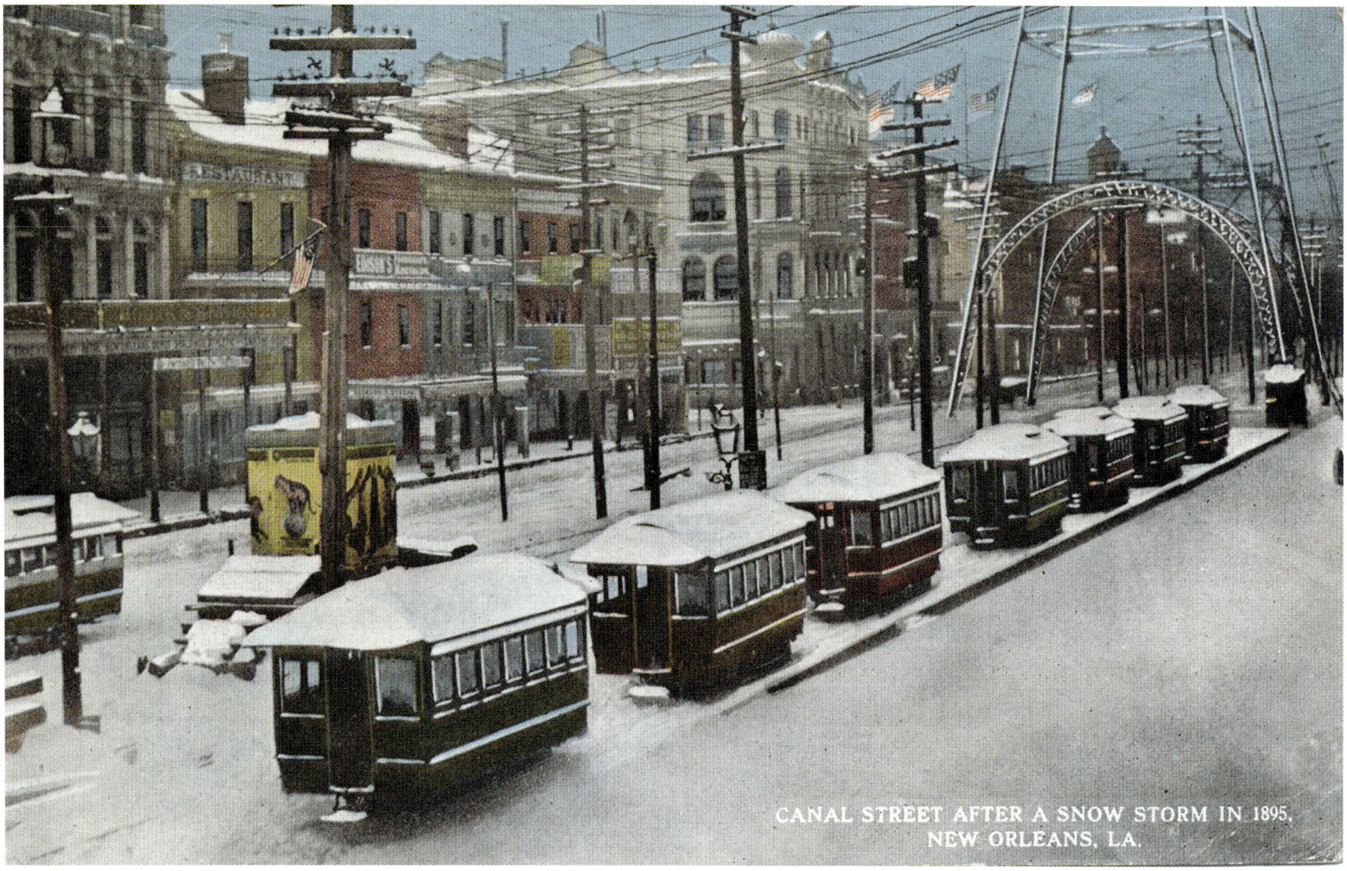

Canal Street in New Orleans is covered in a blanket of snow during 1895 in this postcard postmarked December 27, 1916. The electric streetcars – the new vehicle that eliminated the animal waste problem – were replaced by the old mule-drawn cars, because the lack of equipment to remove ice from the overhead wire kept the electric streetcars in the carbarn.

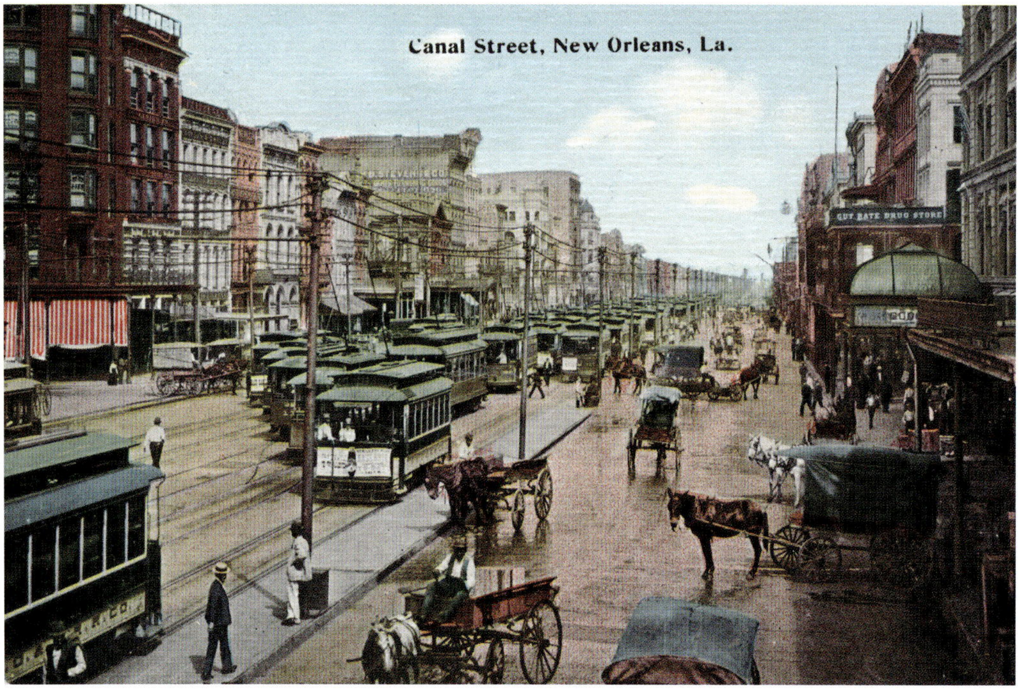

Canal Street in New Orleans is busy with an amazing number of streetcars on five streetcar tracks in this postcard scene around 1902. The original plan to build a canal in the middle of Canal Street never happened, but it resulted in an over 170 foot wide street that became the Broadway of New Orleans where the principal department stores were located. The median of the street became known as neutral ground as it separated the "American sector" from the French Quarter. Even today, all medians of streets in New Orleans are referred to as neutral ground.

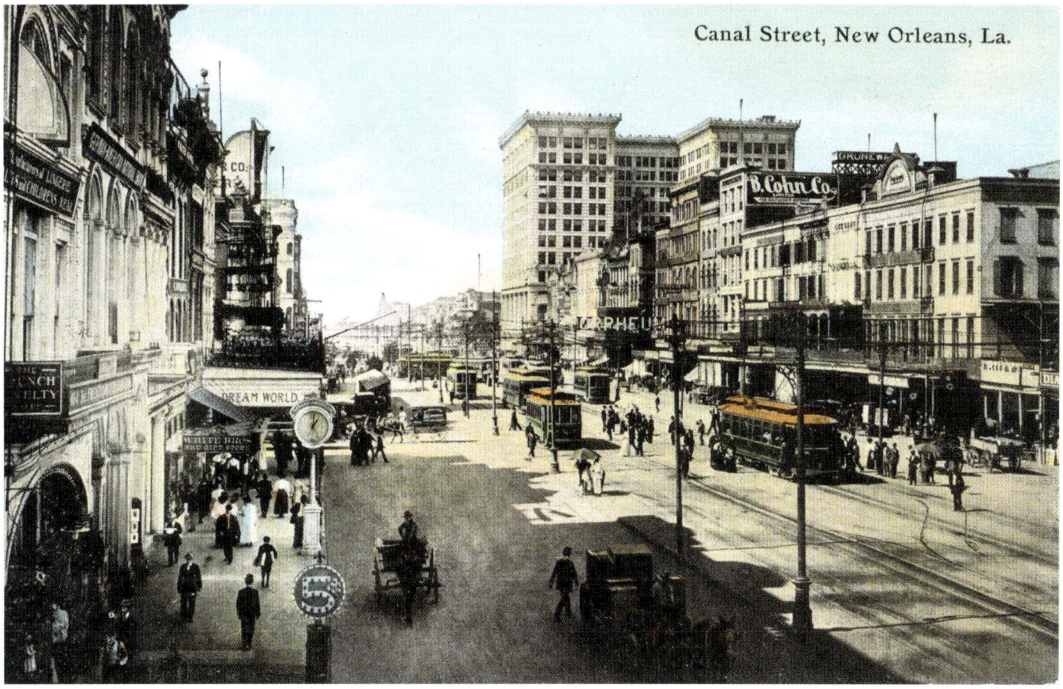

Canal Street is the shopping center hub of New Orleans in this 1902 postcard view. The twelve-story building in the center of the picture was the noted southern department store Maison Blanche that was a direct beneficiary of the numerous streetcars bringing potential customers into downtown New Orleans. Located at the corner of Canal and Dauphine Streets, the Maison Blanche department store, founded by German immigrant, Isidore Newman, opened on October 30, 1897.

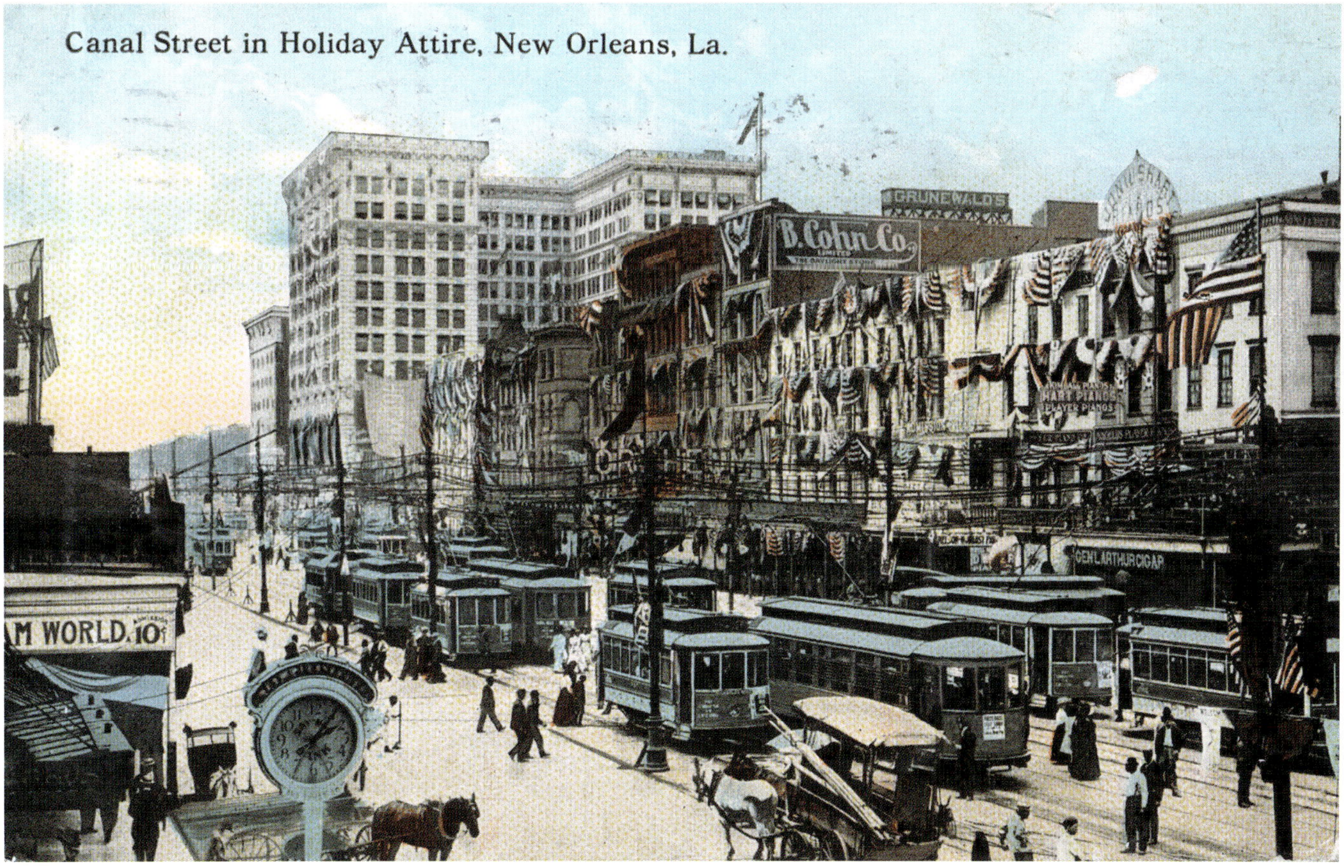

In this1902 postcard view, the decorations on the buildings along Canal Street, according to the postcard, "are in honor of one of the numerous conventions which are held in the WINTER CAPITAL OF AMERICA each year." Canal Street was filled with streetcars as far as the eye could see. The twelve-story Maison Blanche department store (highest in the picture) was demolished around 1908 and was replaced by a distinctive new building in 1909.

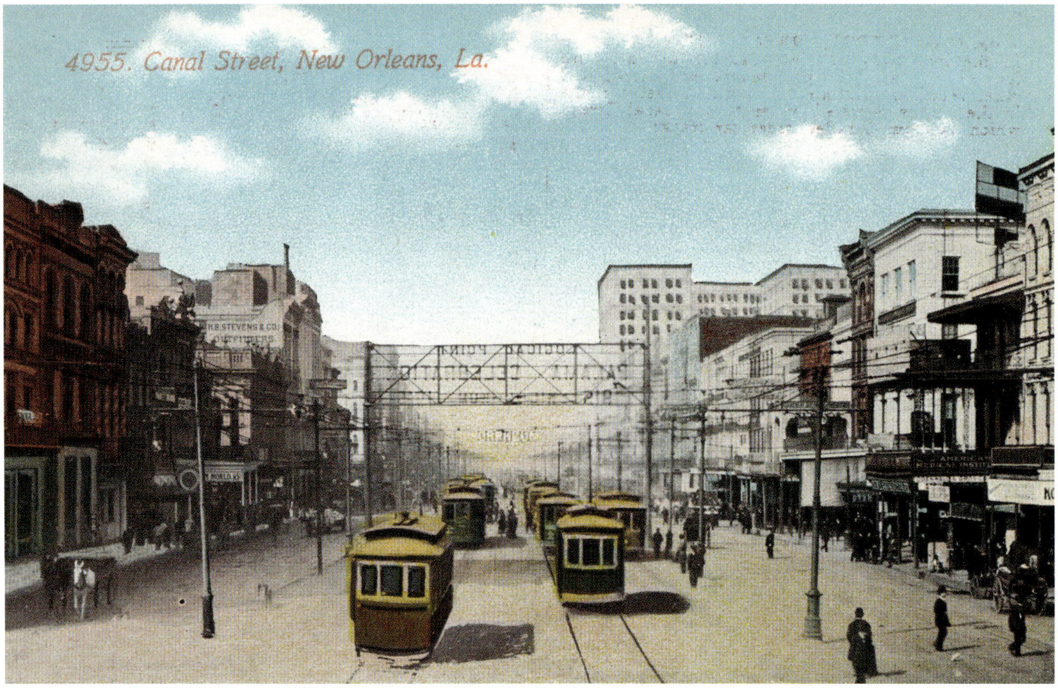

Automobiles are not in the picture of Canal Street in this postcard scene of around 1910. Every street car line in New Orleans operated on or across Canal Street. All of the major department stores and other retail establishments were located on Canal Street. At the foot of Canal Street, near the Mississippi River, there were nine tracks at the layover area, which was reduced to four tracks, and remained at four tracks up to the conversion of the Canal streetcar line to bus operation on May 31, 1964.

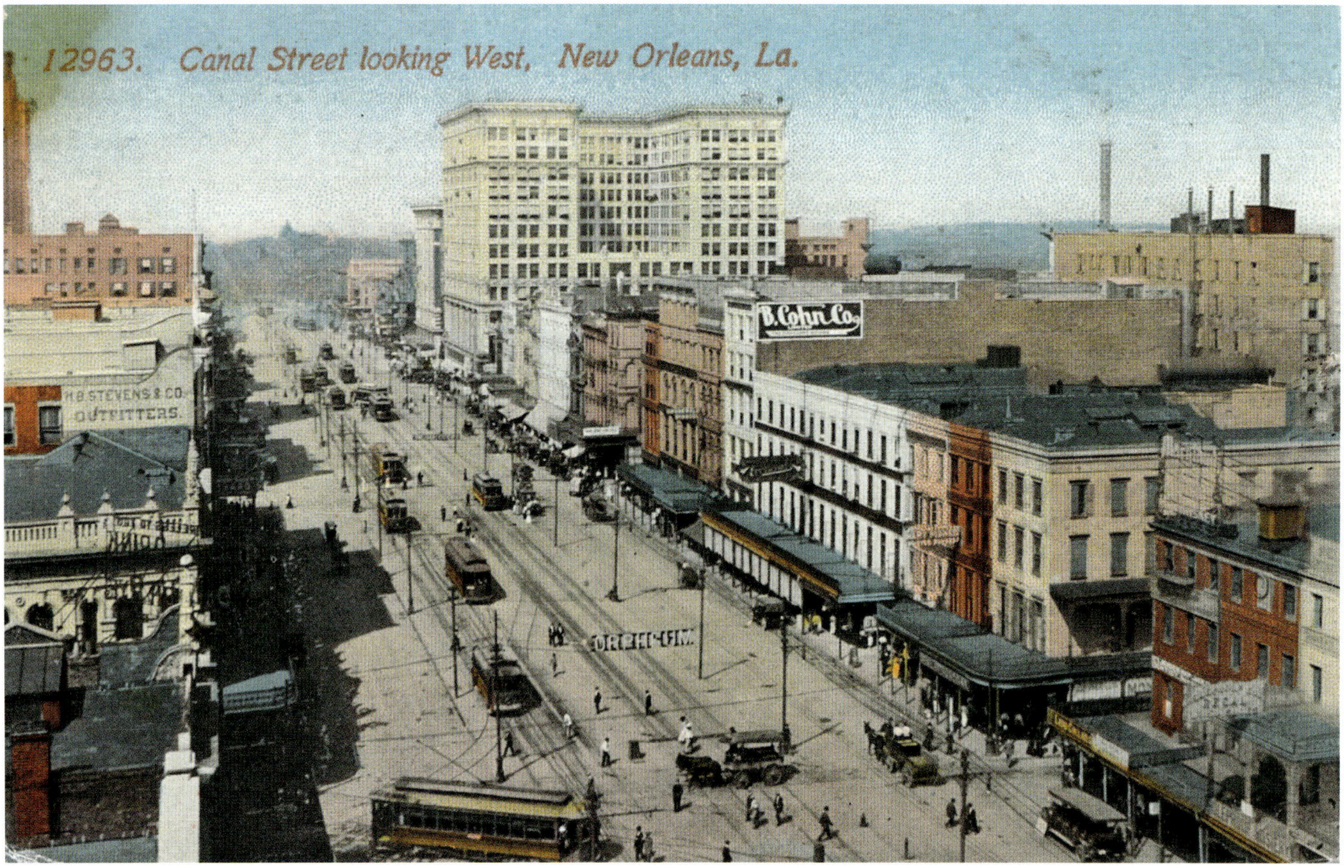

Looking down Canal Street, with the twelve-story Maison Blanche department store in the upper center of the picture, finds many streetcars in this postcard scene around 1910. New Orleans was the first city west of the Allegheny Mountains to have street railway passenger service. In New Orleans, the term "streetcar" is used instead of "trolley car," because they had horse-drawn streetcars long before the electric trolley car was developed.

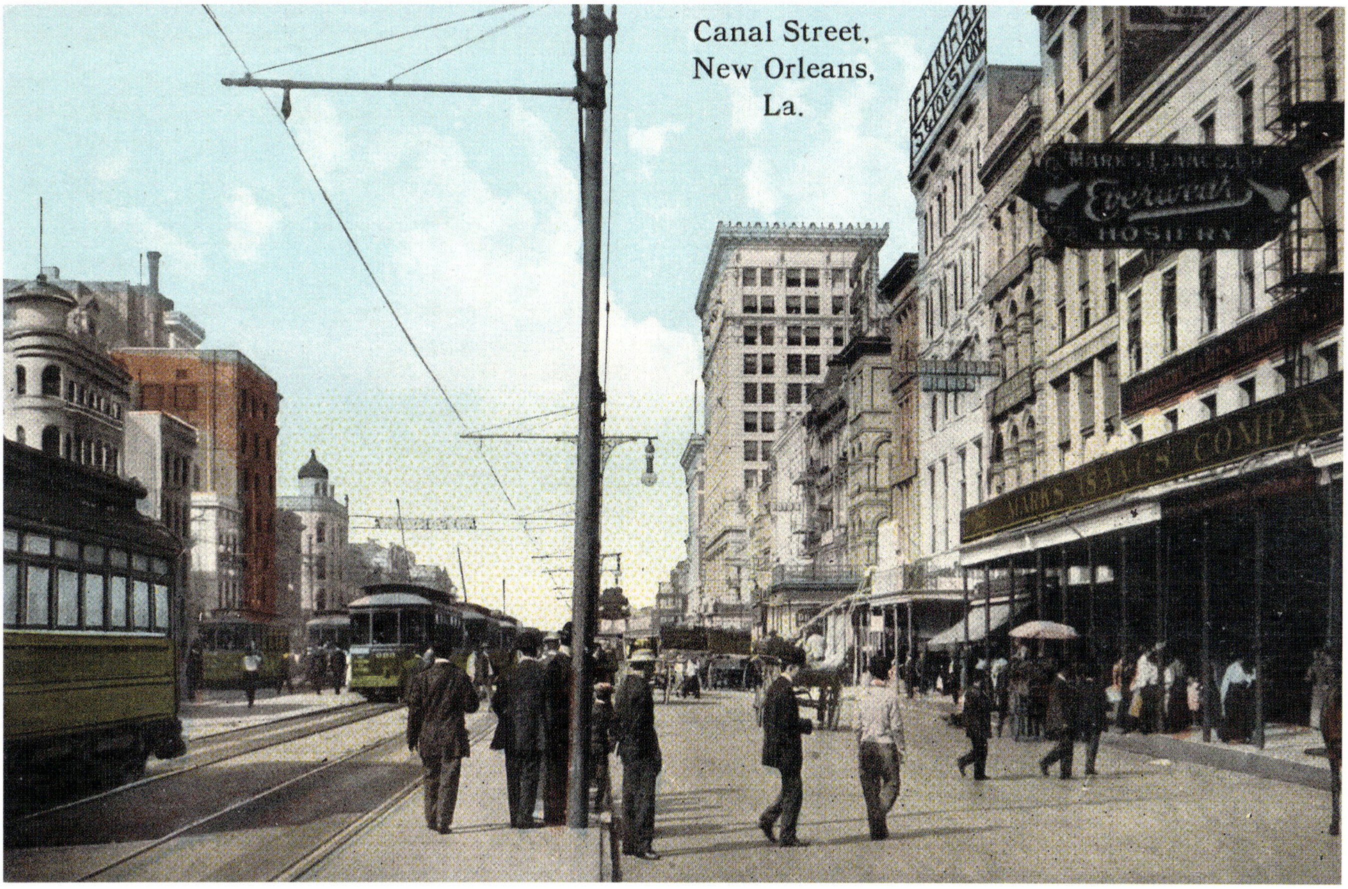

Canal Street is alive with a large number of streetcars and pedestrians in this 1910 postcard scene. Streetcars came from almost all the neighborhoods of New Orleans to Canal Street. Americans began to settle on the other side of Canal Street from the French Quarter. The median of the wide Canal Street became a place where the two cultures could meet and do business. It became known as "neutral ground" in modern New Orleans.

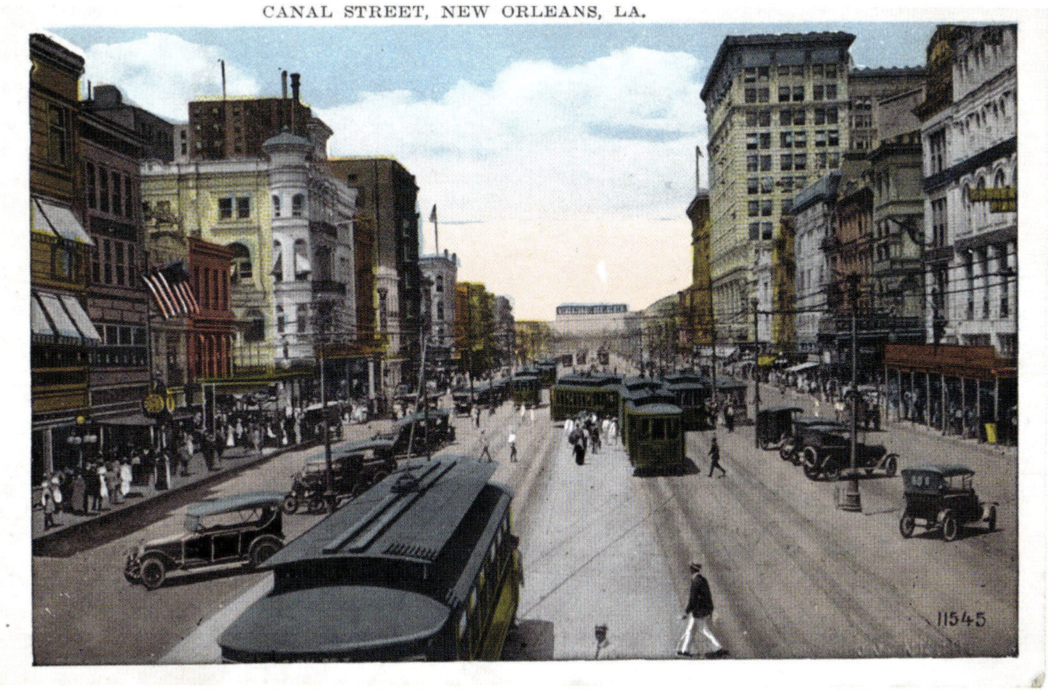

Automobiles are plentiful along with streetcars on Canal Street in this postcard scene around 1920. Canal Street was the main retail district of New Orleans, with the streetcars bringing people into the downtown area. The 1929 strike resulted in a severe ridership decline, and elimination of five streetcar routes marked the beginning of the decline of the streetcar in New Orleans.

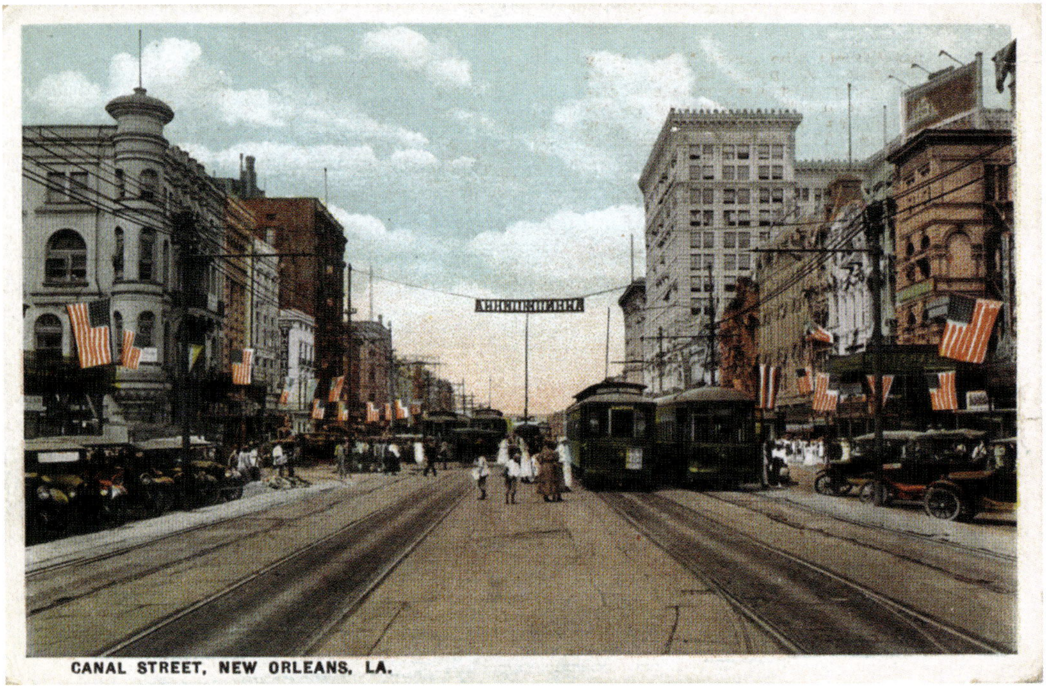

Automobiles line both sides of Canal Street with four busy streetcar tracks on a reserved right of way in this 1920 postcard view. From 1899 to 1930, at the foot of Canal Street - from Wells Street to Peters Street - there were nine tracks in the layover area. The layover area was then reduced to eight and, finally, four tracks, which remained in place until the Canal line converted to bus operation on May 31, 1964.

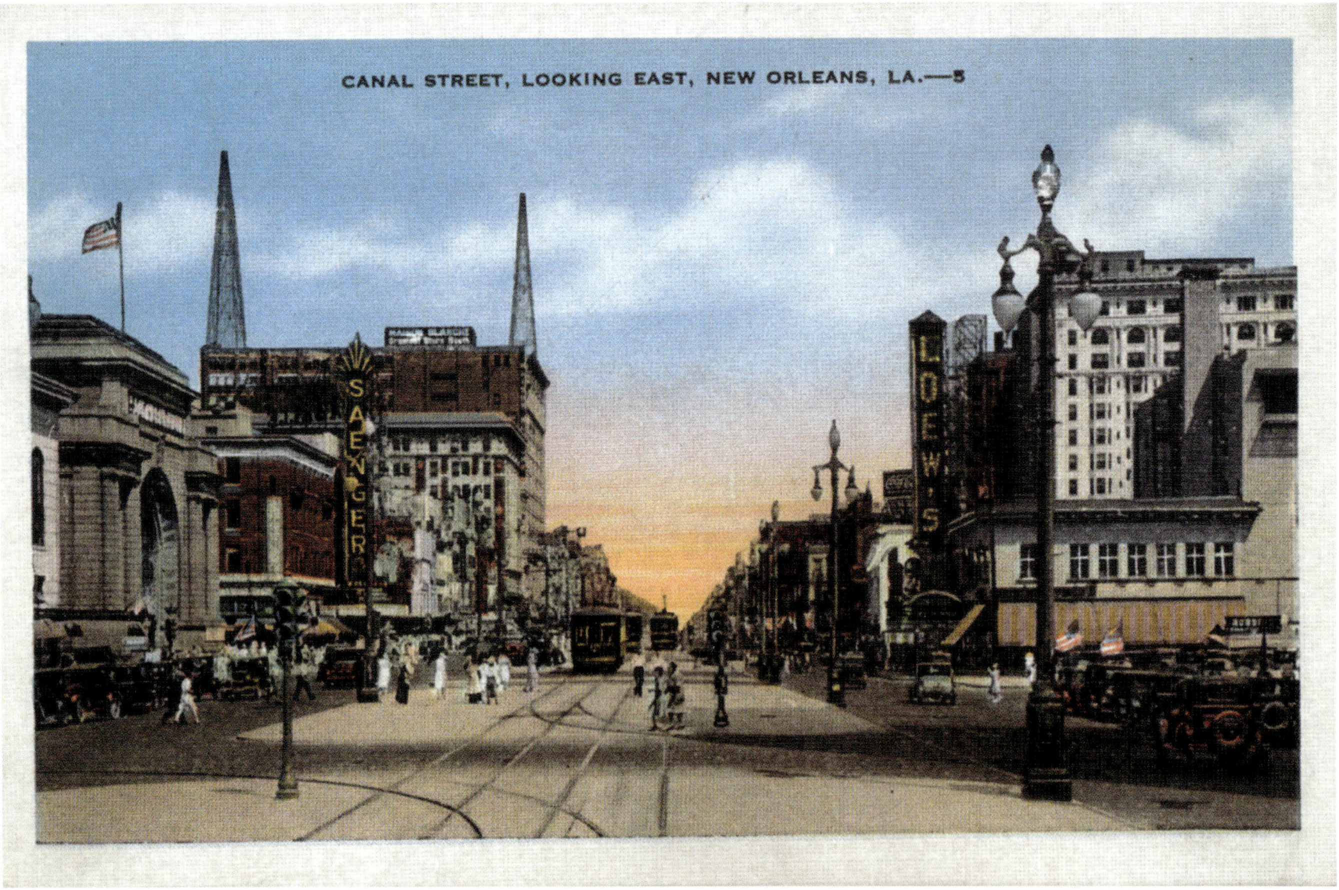

In this 1930 postcard view, Canal Street features two streetcar tracks on a paved reserved right of way and was one of the widest central business thoroughfares in the world. The Saenger Theatre marquee is on the left, the Loew's State Theatre marquee is on the right, and the two towers were for radio station WSMB. Greater use of automobiles and the Depression contributed to the conversion to bus operation which eliminated costly track and overhead wire.

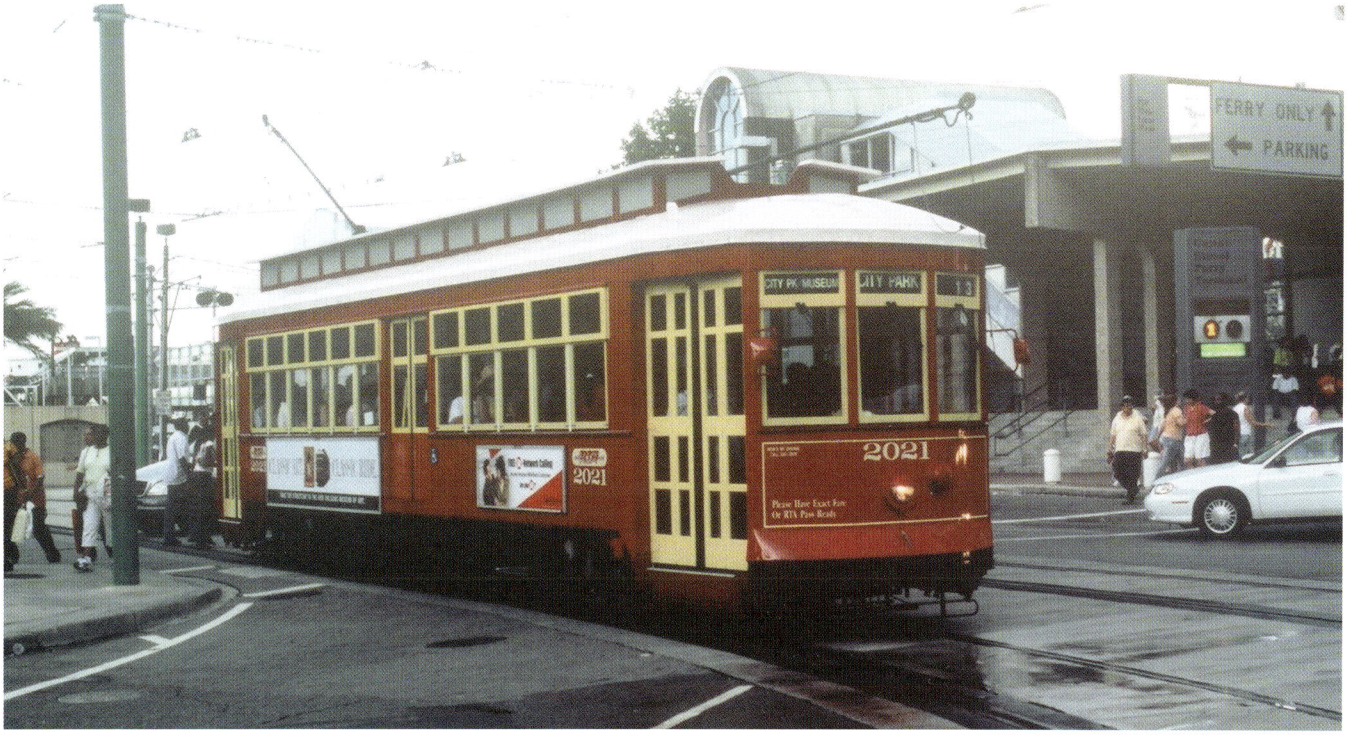

New Orleans Regional Transit Authority (RTA) streetcar No. 2021 has left the Riverfront streetcar line and is turning onto Canal Street for a trip to City Park on July 3, 2004. The twenty-four streetcars for Canal Street Nos. 2001 to 2024 were built at the Carrollton Station shop with many local industries involved in the manufacturing process, such as doors made in Chalmette, Louisiana and seats constructed in Slidell, Louisiana.

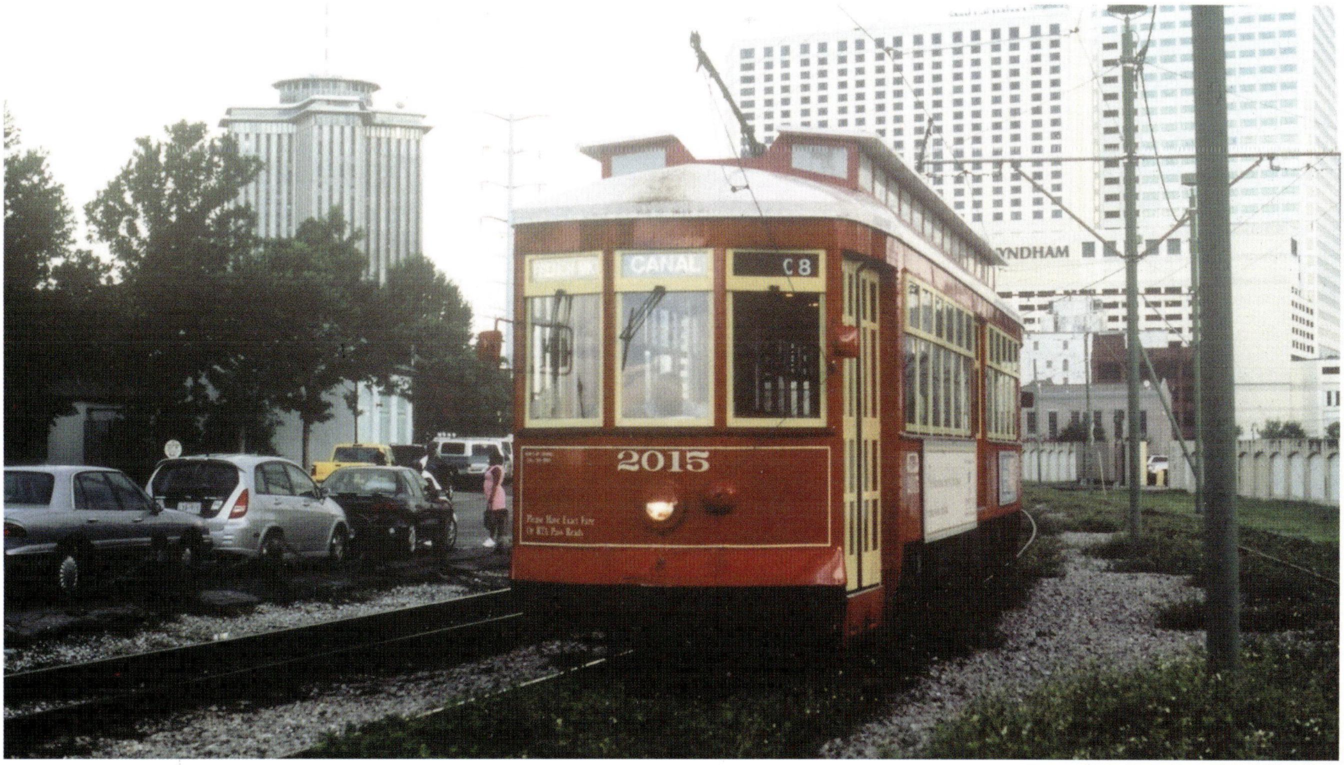

RTA streetcar No. 2015 is on the Riverfront line heading for the French Market at Esplanade Avenue on July 3, 2004. The New Orleans Public Belt Railroad track is on the left side of the streetcar. The trucks, motors, and controls for prototype streetcar No. 2001 were from CKD (Ceskomoravska Kolben-Danek) Tatra of the Czech Republic. Streetcars No. 2002 to 2024 had trucks, motors, and controls provided by the Brookville Equipment Company.

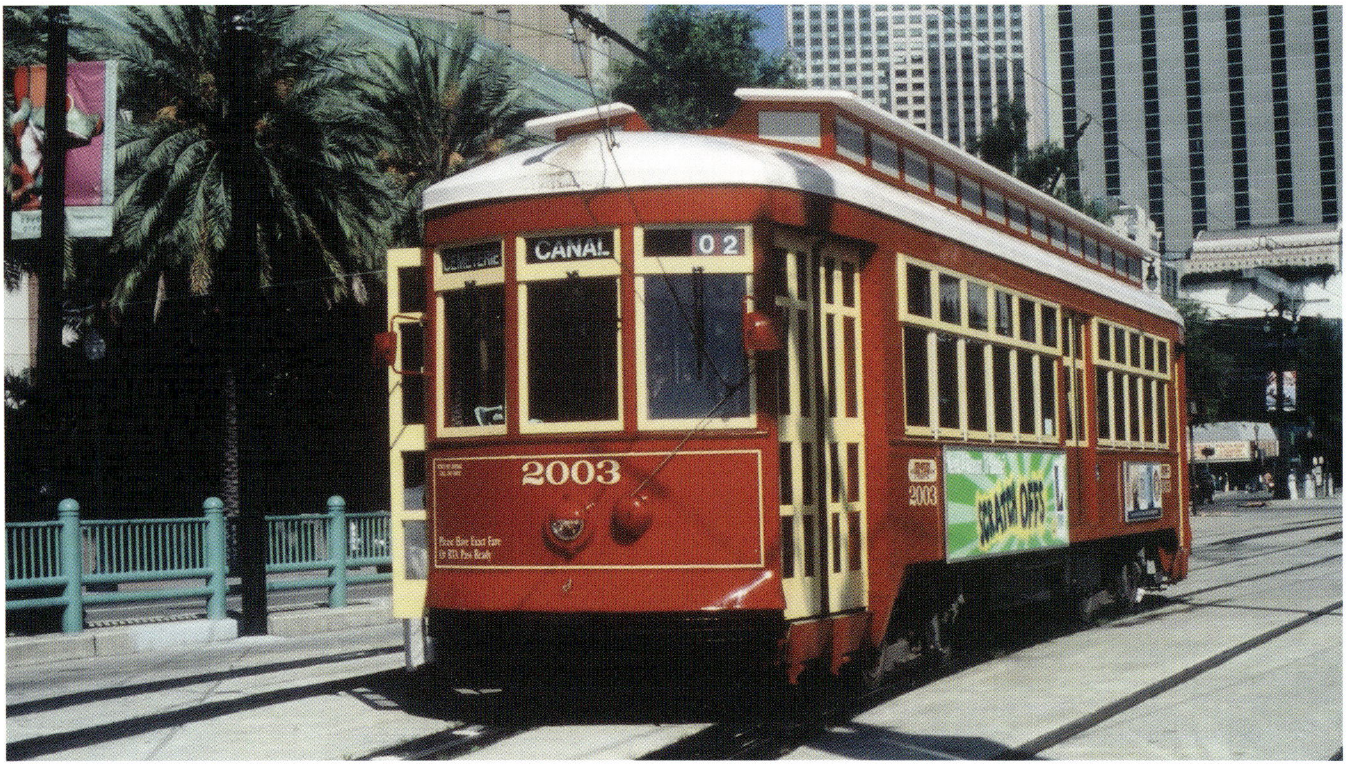

Canal Street and Wells Street finds RTA streetcar No. 2003 at the terminus of the Canal line near the Mississippi River on July 4, 2004. This end of Canal Street near the Mississippi River is often called "the foot of Canal Street." The Canal streetcar to the Cemeteries is officially route 47, but that number is not displayed on the streetcar.

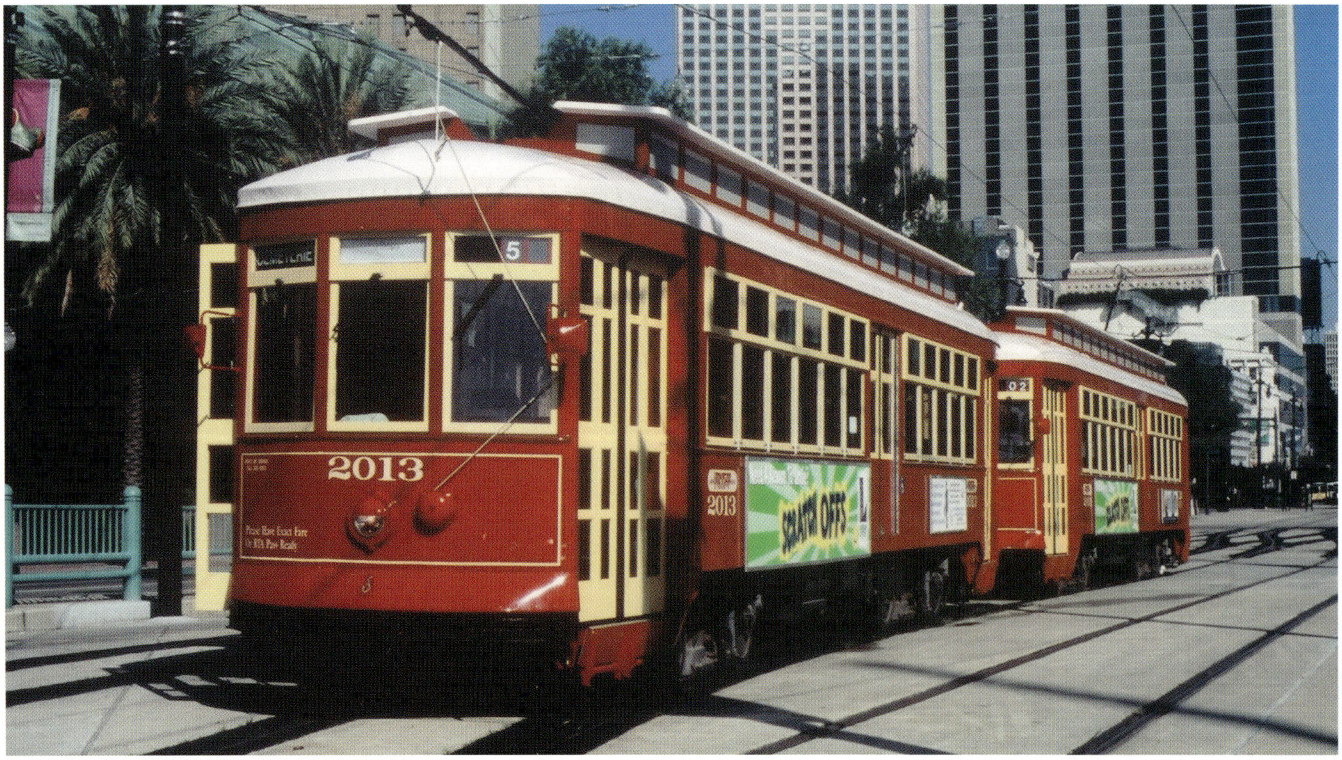

At the foot of Canal Street at Wells Street on July 4, 2004, two RTA streetcars headed by No. 2013 are on a layover. Streetcar No. 2013 was the second streetcar to go in service on the new Canal streetcar line on April 18, 2004. The return of Canal Street to streetcar operation began in 1999 with the opening of a six block section on Canal Street connecting the St. Charles and Riverfront lines.

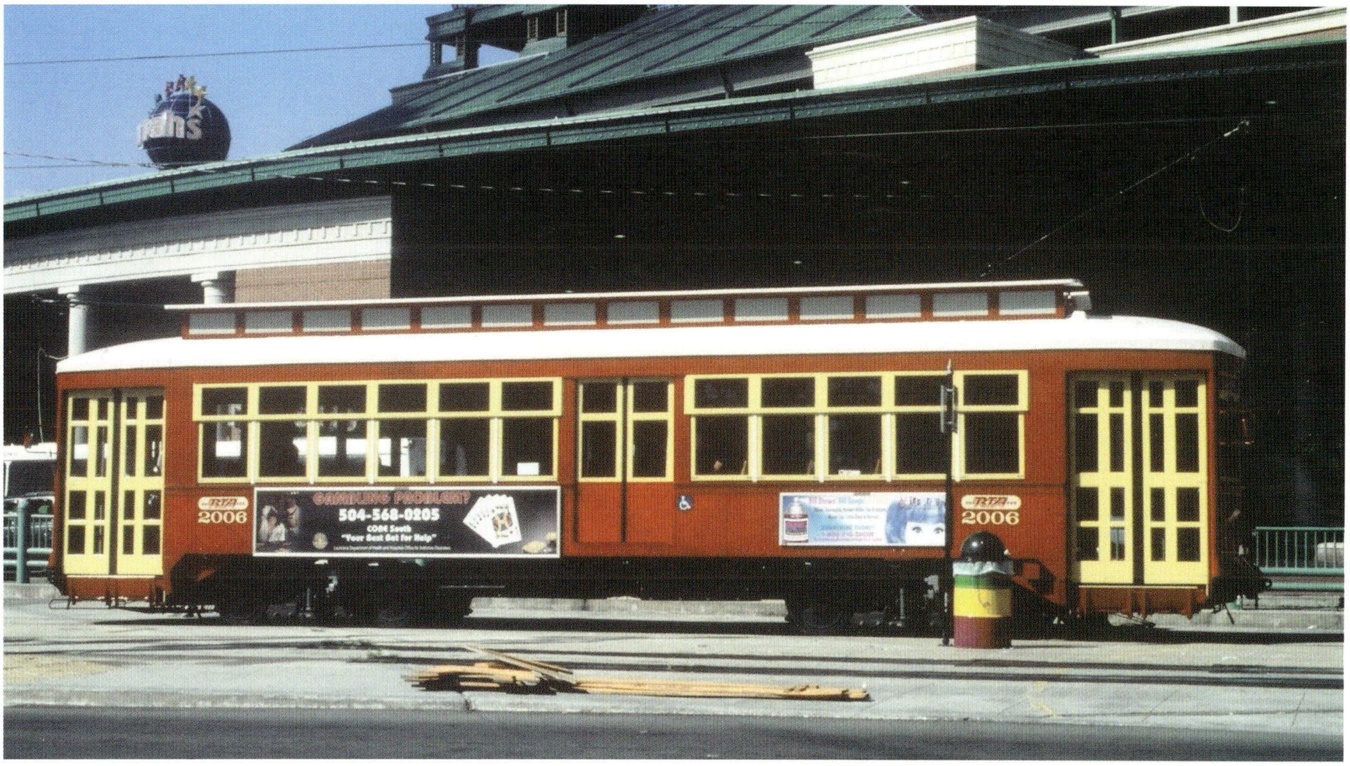

RTA streetcar No. 2006 is at Canal Street at Wells Street, ready for departure on July 4, 2004. For many years, Canal Street was where the biggest, finest, and greatest variety of stores were located in New Orleans. The streetcar contributes to bringing riders into the Canal business area, which enhances the shopping district. Even with the development of shopping malls, Canal Street is still a retail destination for New Orleans residents and visitors.

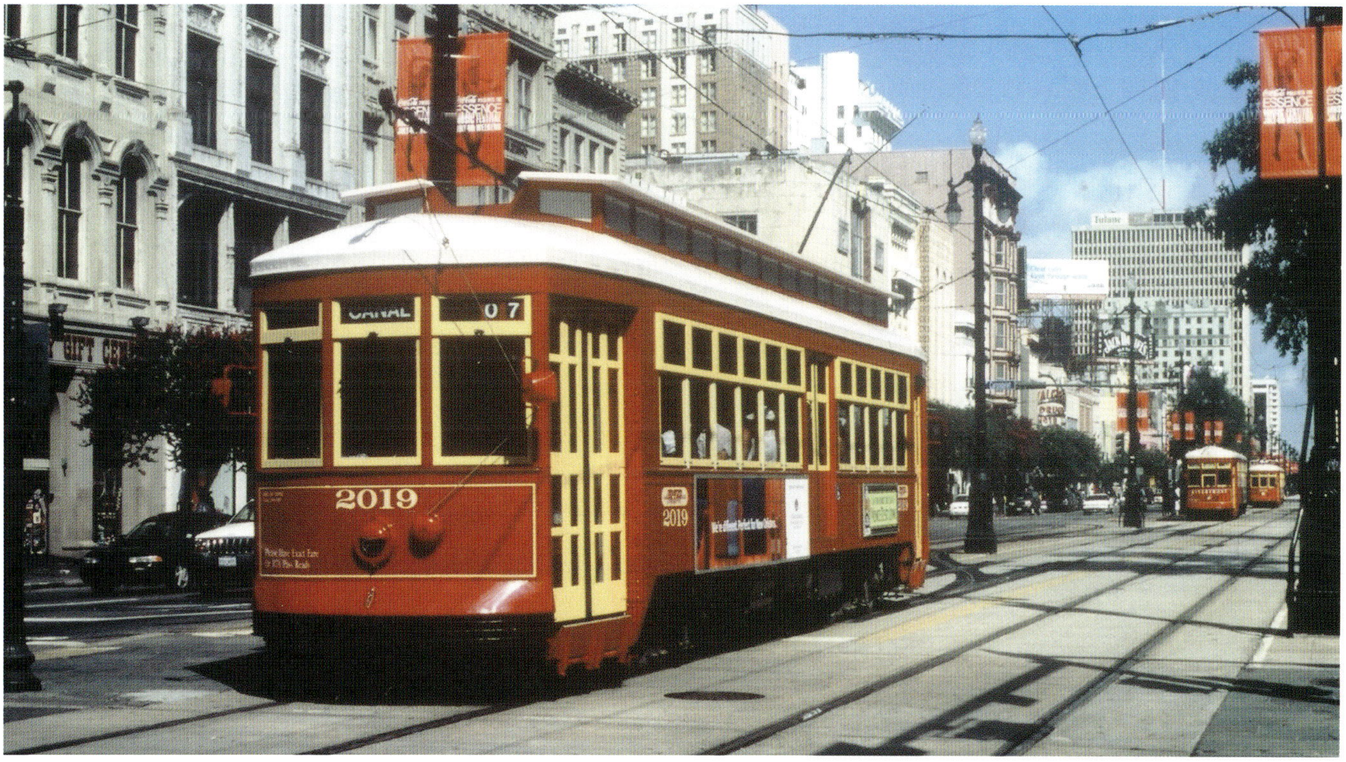

A bright summer July 4, 2004 finds RTA Canal Streetcar No. 2019 on Canal Street at St. Charles Avenue. New Orleans streetcars are a distinguishing characteristic of this unique city. Streetcars are an attraction by themselves, and are an economical way to travel around the areas they serve.

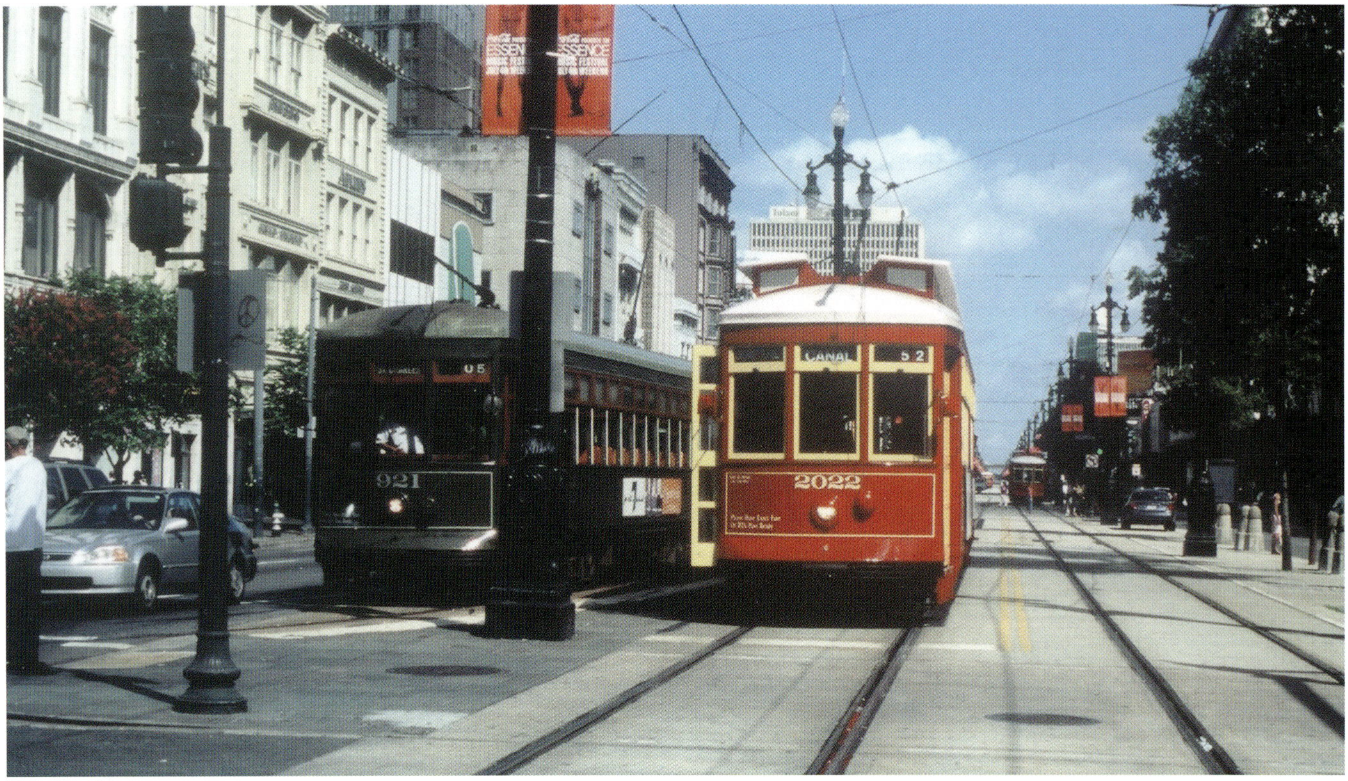

St. Charles streetcar No. 921 and Canal streetcar No. 2022 are on Canal Street at St. Charles Avenue on July 4, 2004. New Orleans streetcars are used by tourists as a fun way to get from one attraction to another. Residents use the streetcars for a number of reasons, including transportation to work, school, medical appointments, shopping, and attractions.

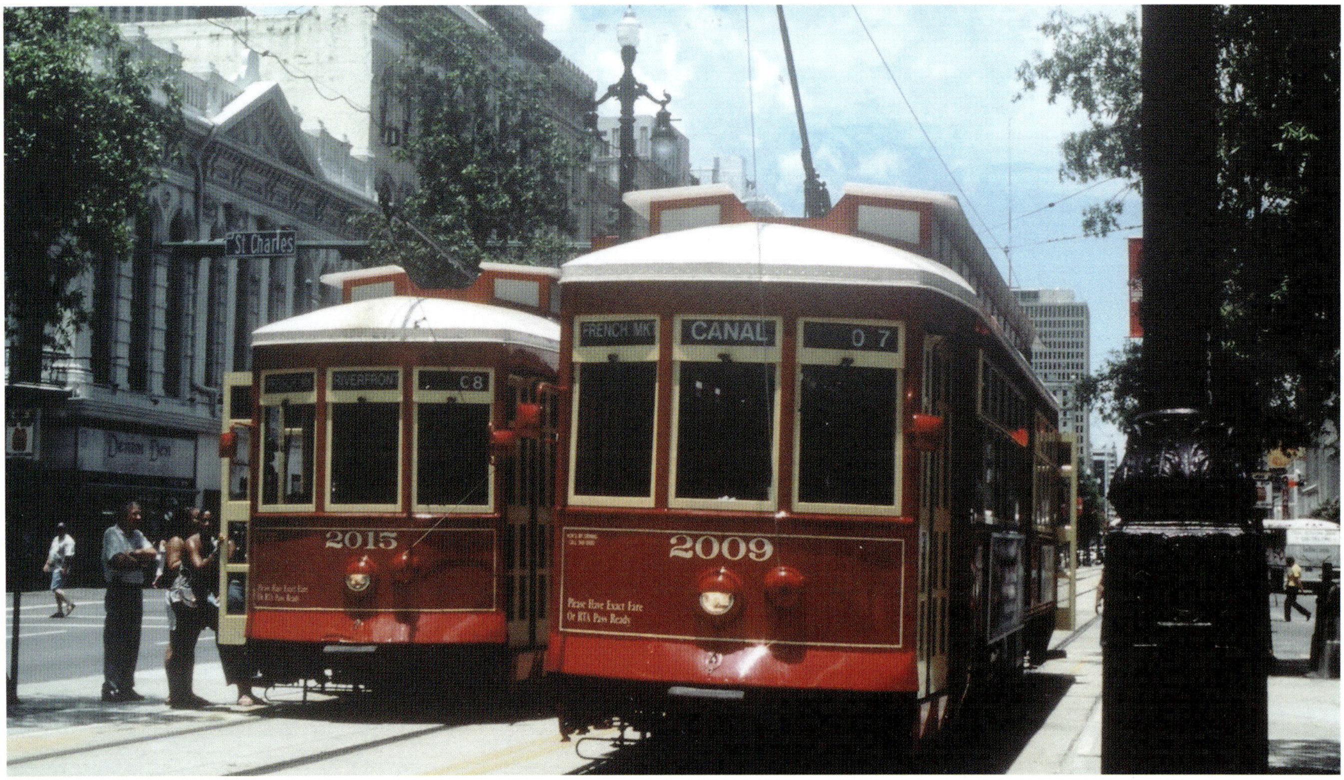

On Canal Street at St. Charles Avenue on July 3, 2004, RTA streetcars Nos. 2015 and 2009 are at a passenger stop. This is one block south of Carondelet Street, which is a transfer point to the St. Charles streetcar line. Some of the vintage buildings still show ornamentation at the top. Canal Street, in the Central Business District, has served as a hub for many of the streetcar and bus routes of the RTA.

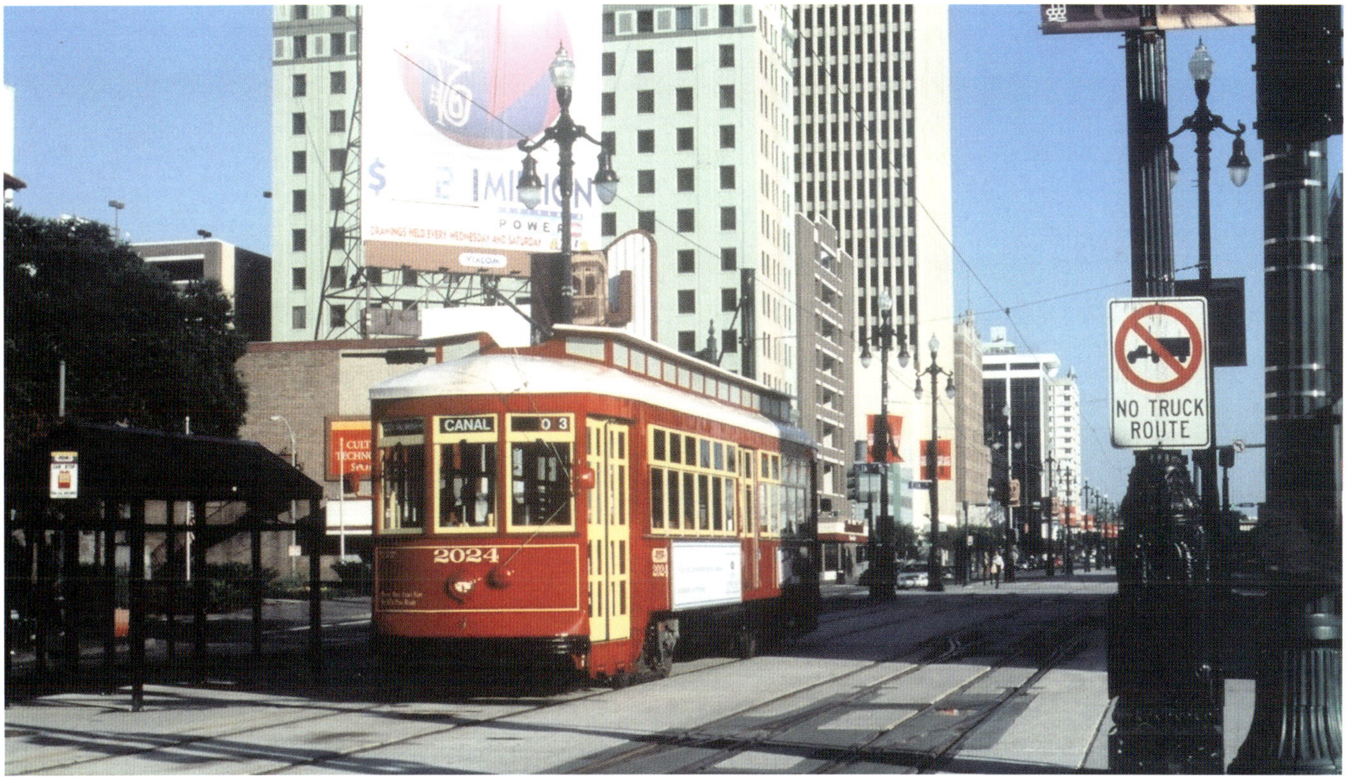

On July 4, 2004, RTA streetcar No. 2024 is on Canal Street ready to cross Rampart Street. The bright red Canal streetcars are modeled after the historic Perley A. Thomas Car Company streetcars used on the St. Charles line, but the newer Canal streetcars include modern features such as air conditioning and wheelchair access.

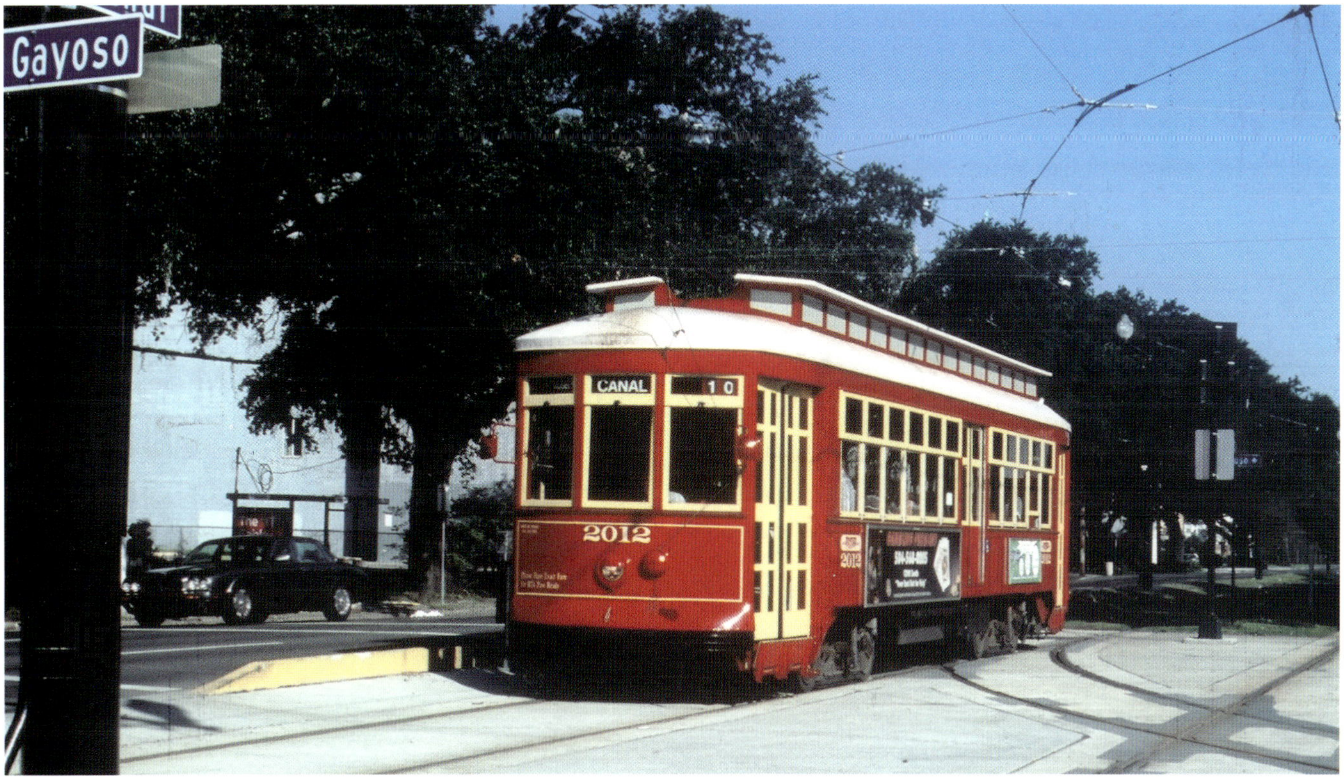

On Canal Street at North Gayoso Street in the Mid-City neighborhood of New Orleans, RTA streetcar No. 2012 is passing the track leading to the Canal Station carbarn on July 4, 2004. As you head away from the Mississippi River on Canal Street, where the street name remains the same, the streets on the left side of Canal Street are marked south, and on the right side of Canal Street are marked north.

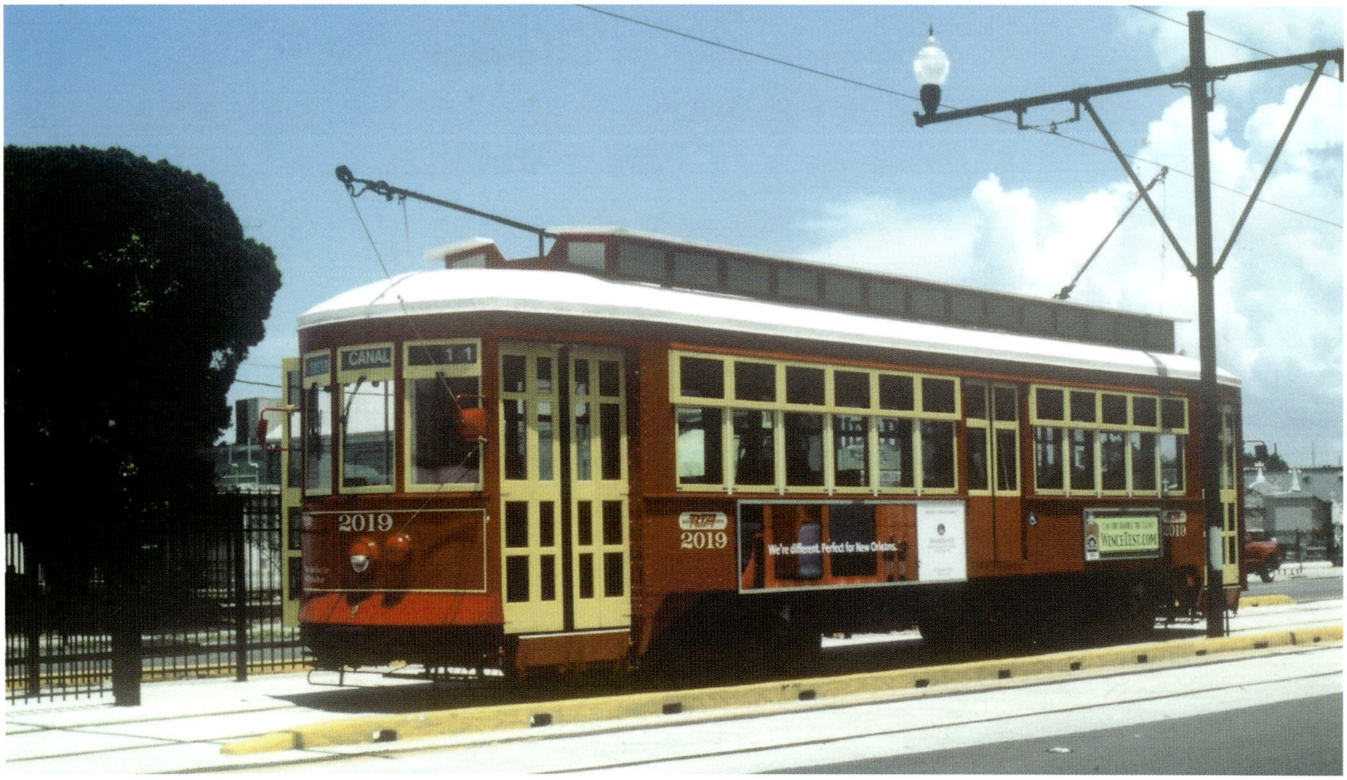

The Canal streetcar line ends at an area of historic cemeteries that have row after row of granite tombs and magnificent statues. Streetcars serving this line display "Cemeteries" on exterior destination signs. On July 3, 2004, RTA streetcar No. 2019 awaits departure time at Canal Street near City Park Avenue for the next trip to the downtown business district.

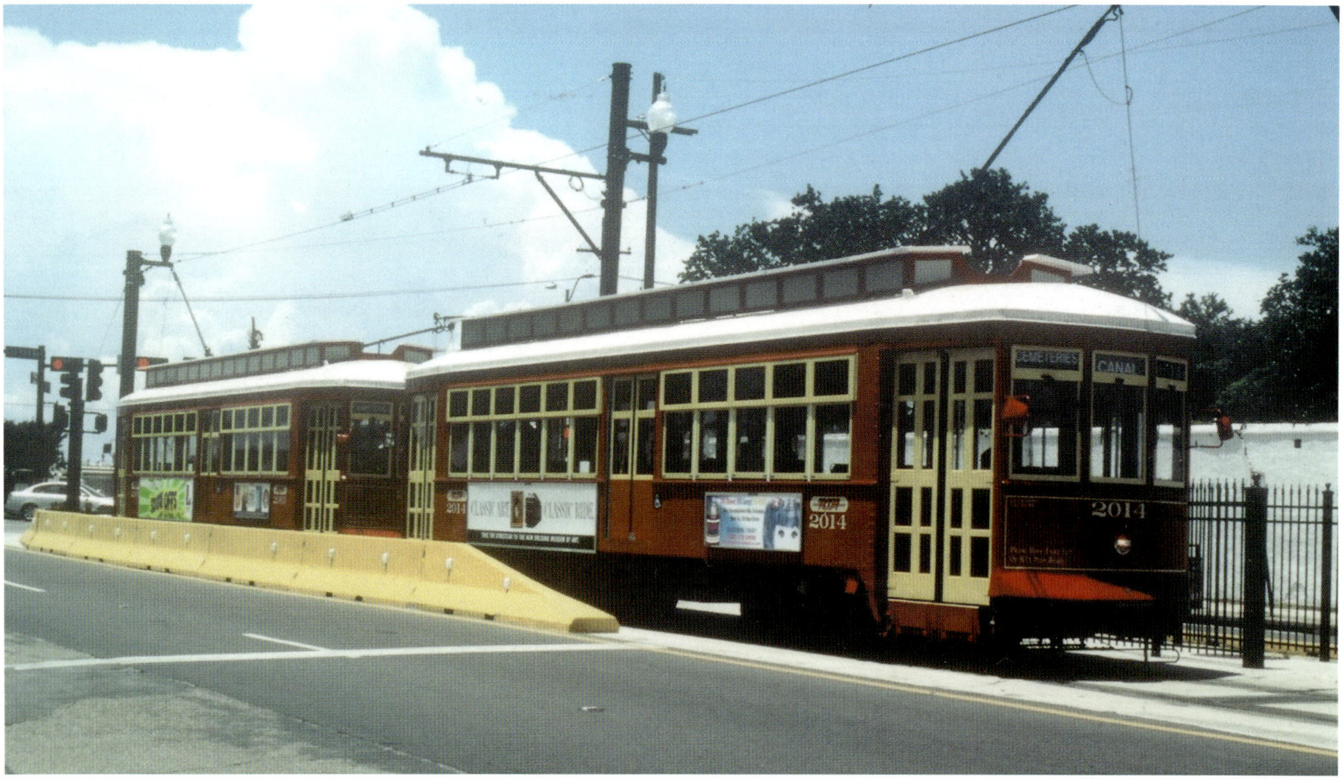

Two Canal Street streetcars, Nos. 2014 and 2003, are at the Cemeteries terminus on July 3, 2004. This is a transfer point to a number of bus lines serving City Park Avenue. Cemeteries are a tourist attraction in New Orleans, because the city is built on a swamp, so the deceased have to be buried above ground, with many in elaborate stone burial vaults and mausoleums.

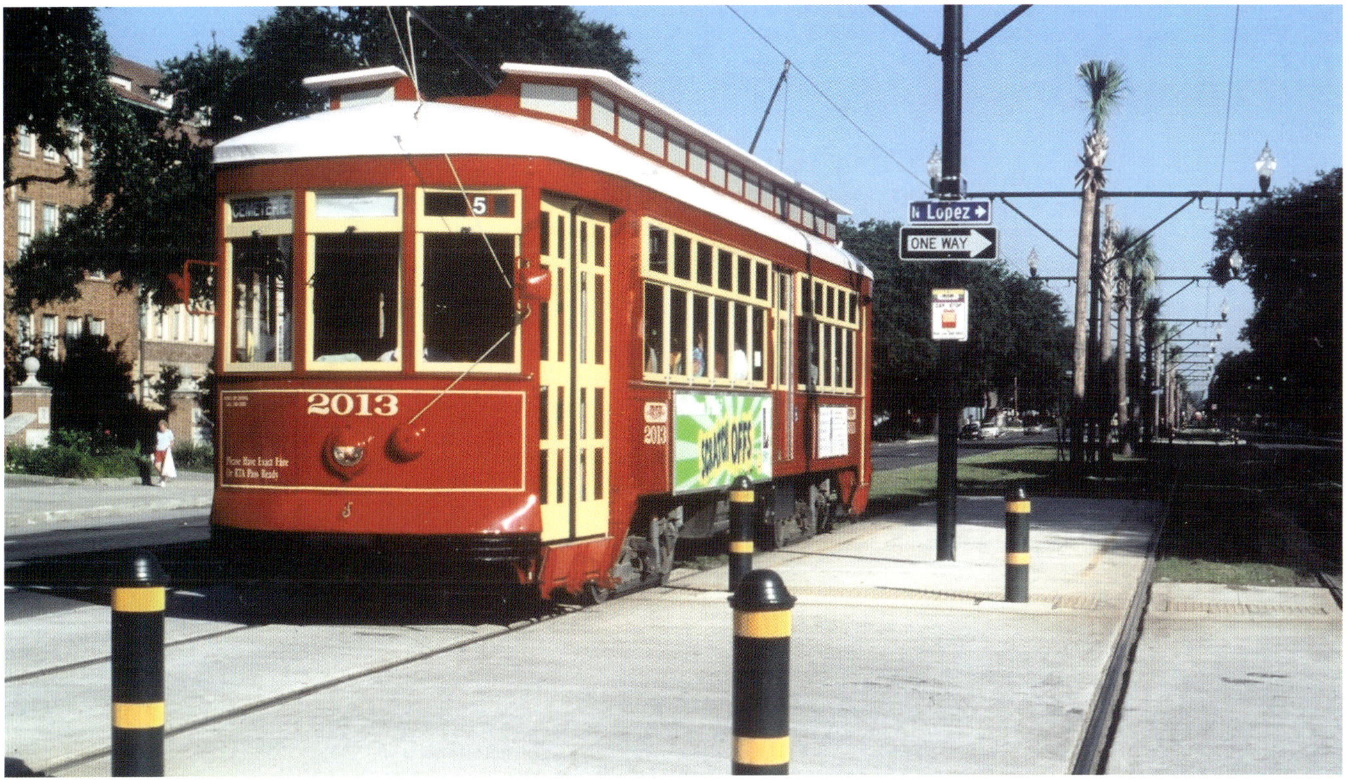

Canal Street streetcar No. 2013 is crossing North Lopez Street in the Mid-City neighborhood of New Orleans on July 4, 2013. Mid-City is one of the largest neighborhoods in New Orleans and features a great mix of historic residences.

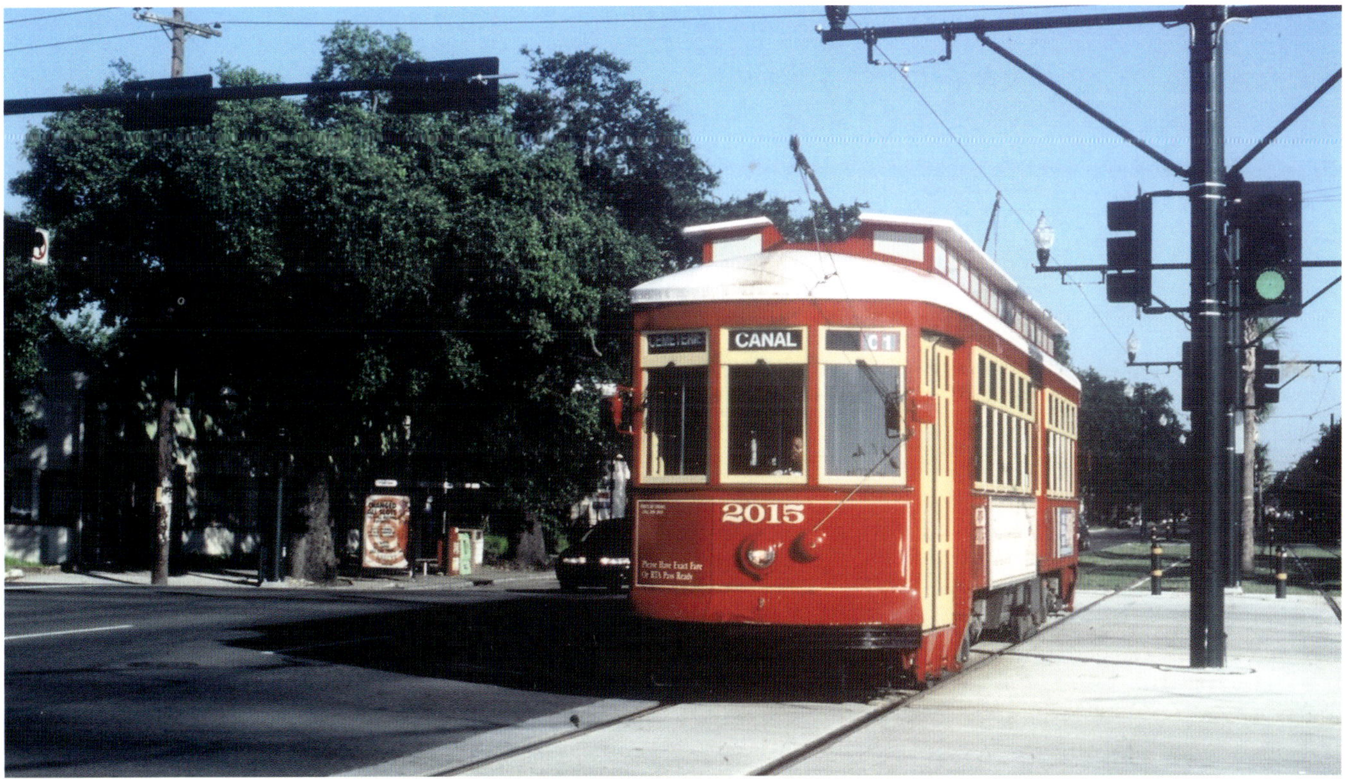

RTA streetcar No. 2015 has just left the median reserved right of way of Canal Street to cross North Carrollton Avenue on July 4, 2004. This is also the junction point for the streetcar line that uses North Carrollton Avenue to the City Park and Museum of Art.

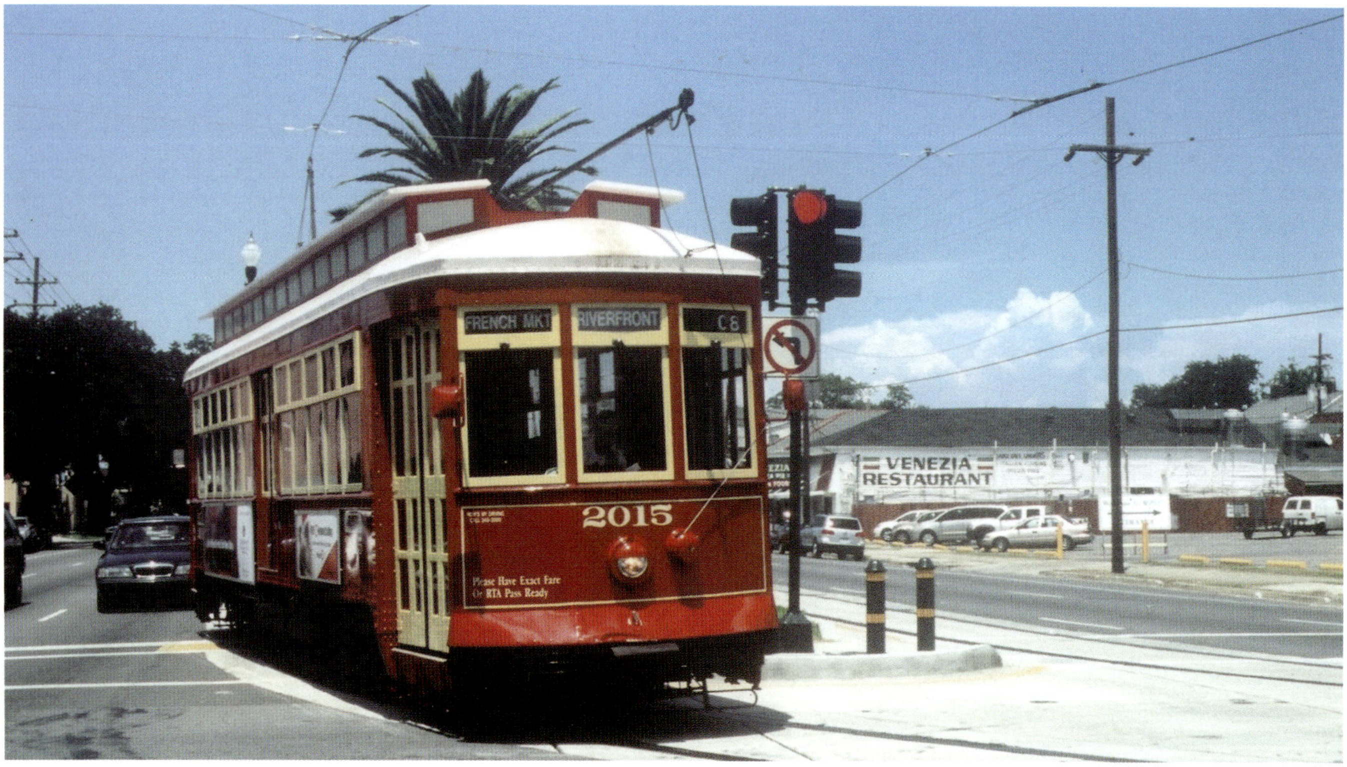

On July 3, 2004, RTA streetcar No. 2015 is carefully turning from North Carrollton Avenue onto Canal Street. The trackage on North Carrollton Avenue links the City Park and Museum of Art to the Canal Street line. The Canal streetcar to the City Park/Museum is officially route 48, but that number is not displayed on the streetcar.

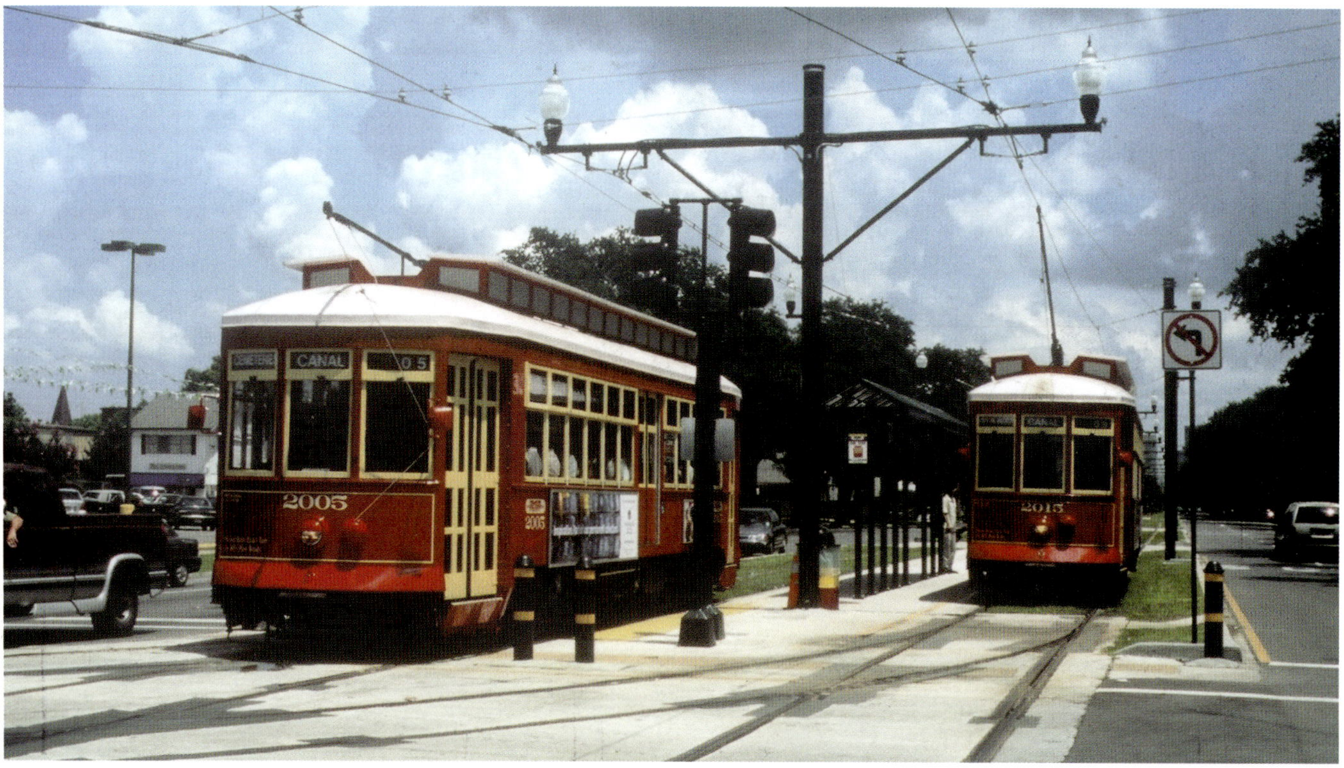

RTA streetcar No. 2015 has completed turning from North Carrollton Avenue onto Canal Street for its trip to the French Market, as streetcar No. 2005 prepares to continue its run on Canal Street to the Cemeteries terminus on July 3, 2004. Streetcars that turn from Canal Street to North Carrollton Avenue for City Park display "City Park/Museum" on the exterior destination signs. A one way trip on this line takes about thirty minutes.

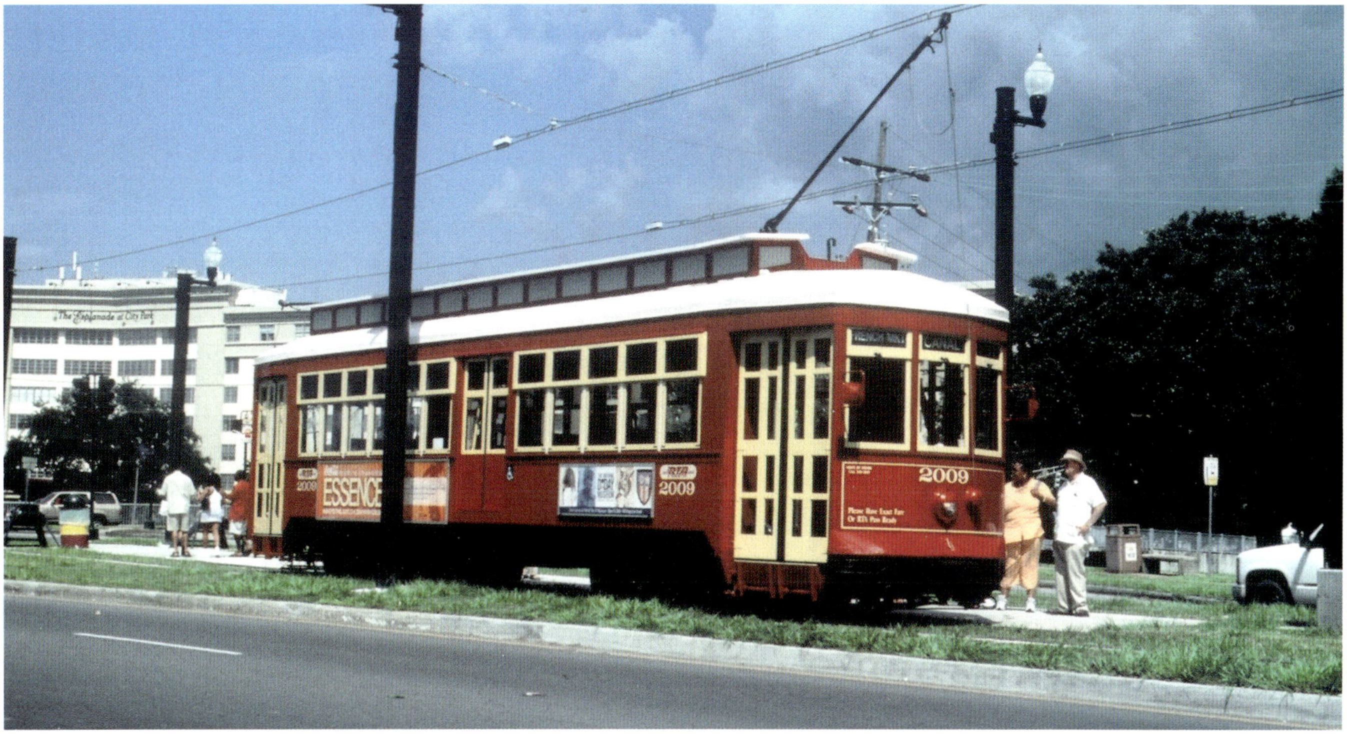

North Carrollton Avenue at Beauregard Circle is the location of RTA streetcar No. 2009, pictured on July 3, 2004. Beauregard Circle, where Esplanade Avenue and City Park meet, features a statue of General Pierre Gustave Toutant Beauregard who was a general in the Confederate States Army during the American Civil War, and was president of the New Orleans and Carrollton Street Railway from 1866 to 1876. Streetcar No. 2009 made the first public revenue run on April 18, 2004 on North Carrollton Avenue to City Park. For the first time, North Carrollton Avenue had a streetcar line.

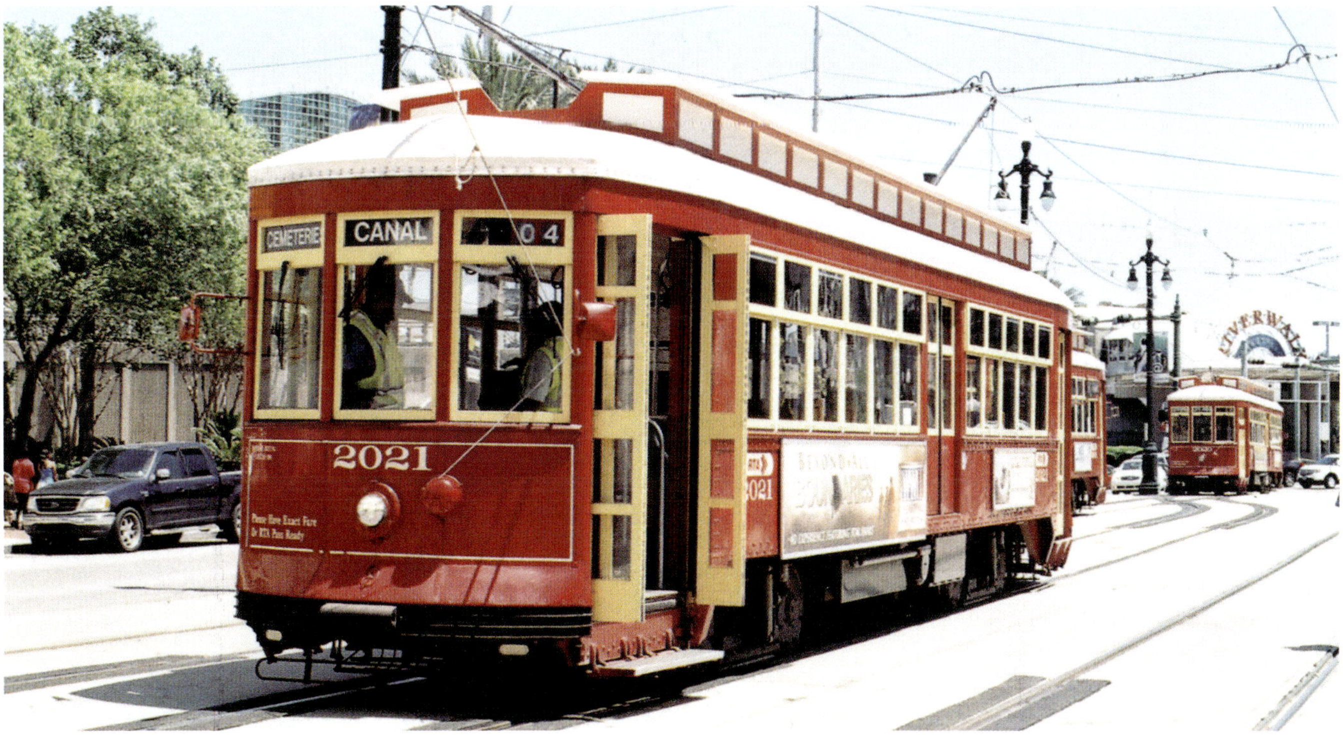

At the foot of Canal Street near the Mississippi River, on April 21, 2013, RTA streetcar No. 2021 leaves for its next trip to the Cemeteries terminus at City Park Avenue. A one way trip on this line takes about thirty minutes. In 2008, the Brookville Equipment Company began the project of providing the components needed to rebuild the Canal and Riverfront streetcars that had been damaged by the floodwaters of Hurricane Katrina with completion in 2010.

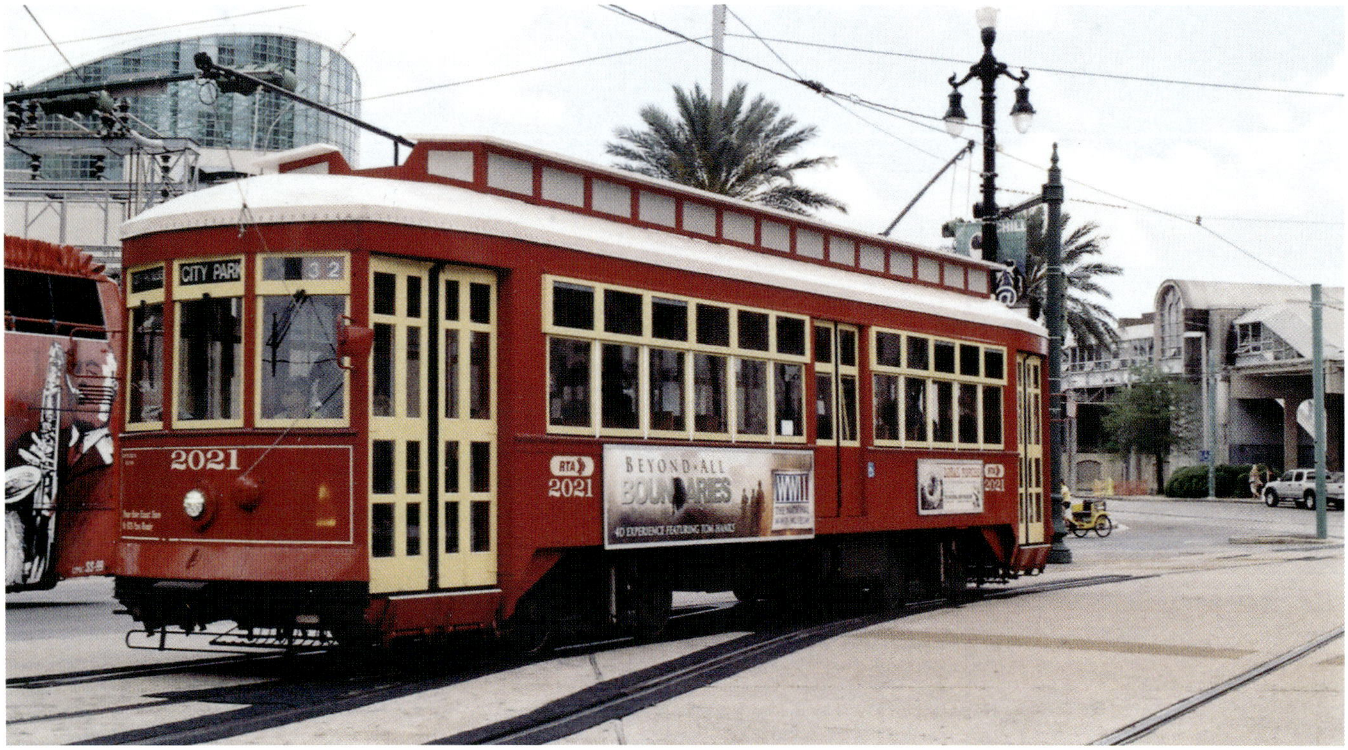

RTA streetcar No. 2021 is on Canal Street at Convention Center Boulevard, on April 23, 2013, heading for City Park. New Orleans has a po-boy or poor boy sandwich, which reportedly originated in a restaurant owned by former streetcar conductors. It is said that, during a four month strike in 1929 against the streetcar company, they created and served these free-of-charge to their former colleagues. The sandwiches - usually roast beef and lettuce on French bread - came to be known as "po-boy sandwiches."

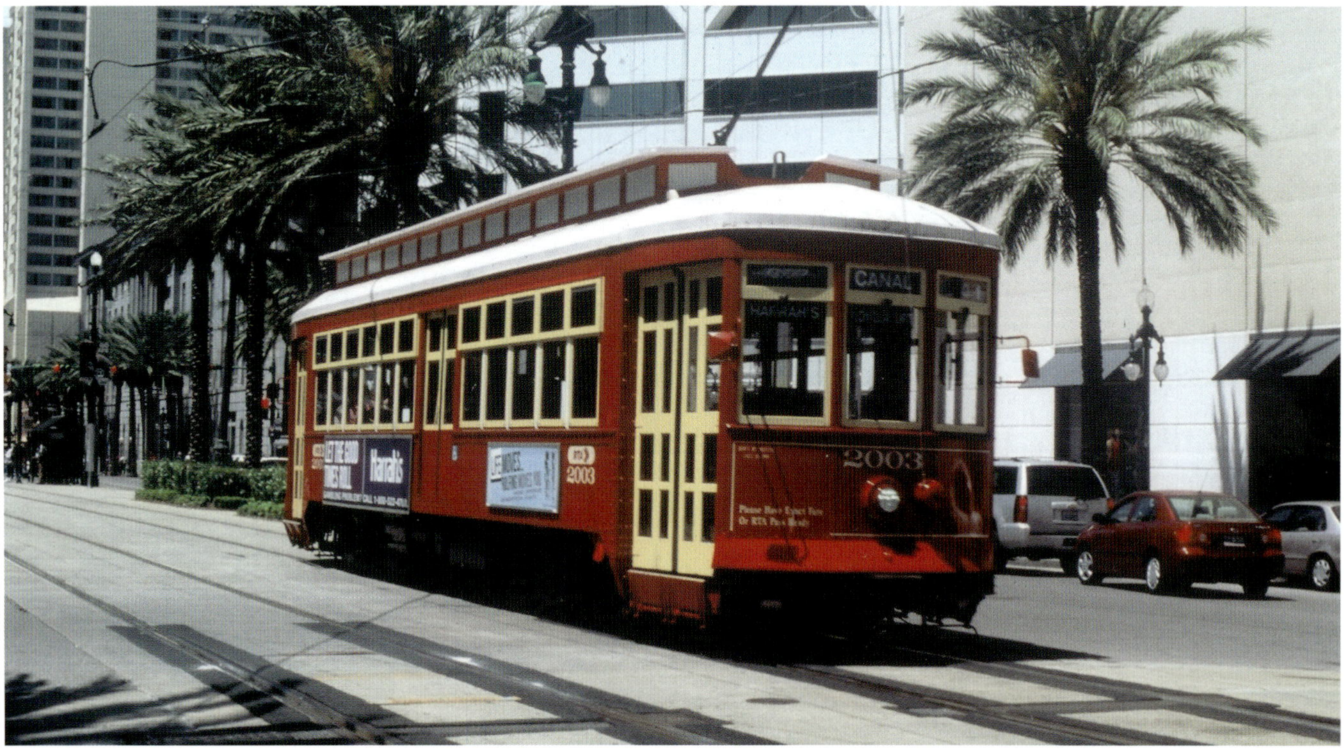

Canal Street near Convention Center Boulevard, on April 21, 2013, is the location of beautiful RTA streetcar No. 2003. When Hurricane Katrina hit New Orleans on August 29, 2005, many of the levees (concrete floodwalls) had been breached and within two days, eighty percent of the city was under water. It was a slow and arduous process, but the streetcar system was restored. Streetcar No. 2003 shows the work that was done at the Carrollton Station shop.

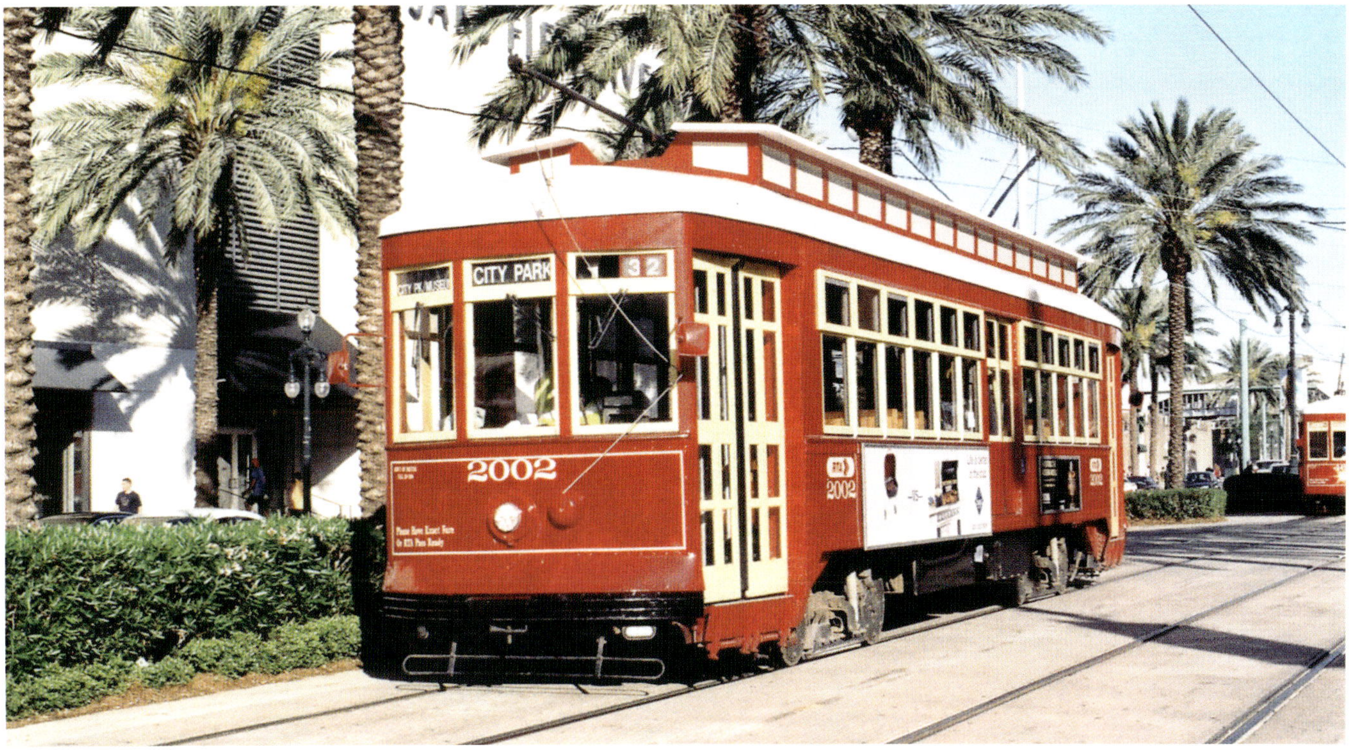

The reserved median of Canal Street near North Peters Street gives RTA streetcar No. 2002 a traffic-free right of way in the heart of the Central Business District, shown on April 21, 2003. On the left is the Canal Place Shopping Mall with over forty stores, including Saks Fifth Avenue.

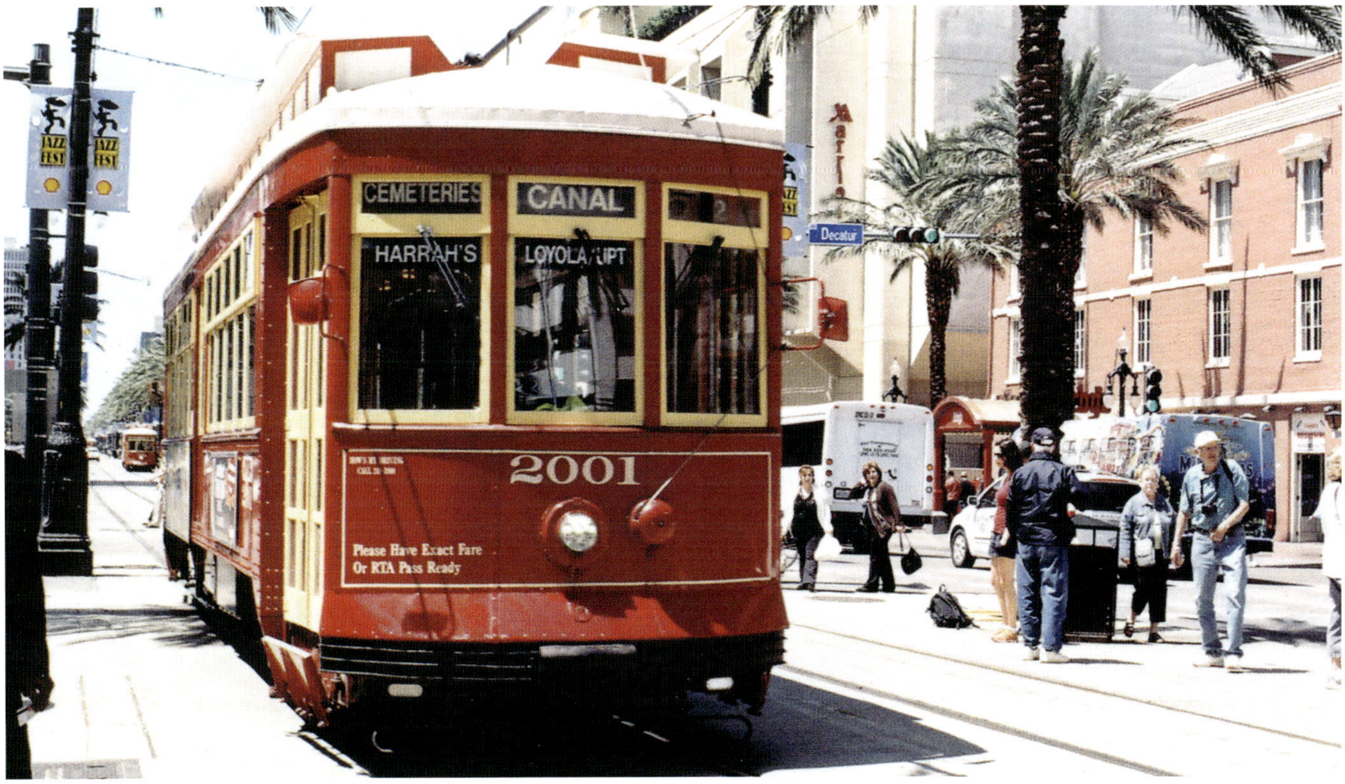

RTA streetcar No. 2001 is on Canal Street at Decatur Street on April 21, 2013. With an all-day pass costing three dollars during 2013, riding the streetcars and buses was an inexpensive way to see New Orleans. Although on August 29, 2005 Hurricane Katrina hit New Orleans with massive destruction, the areas along the streetcar lines have made a dramatic recovery.

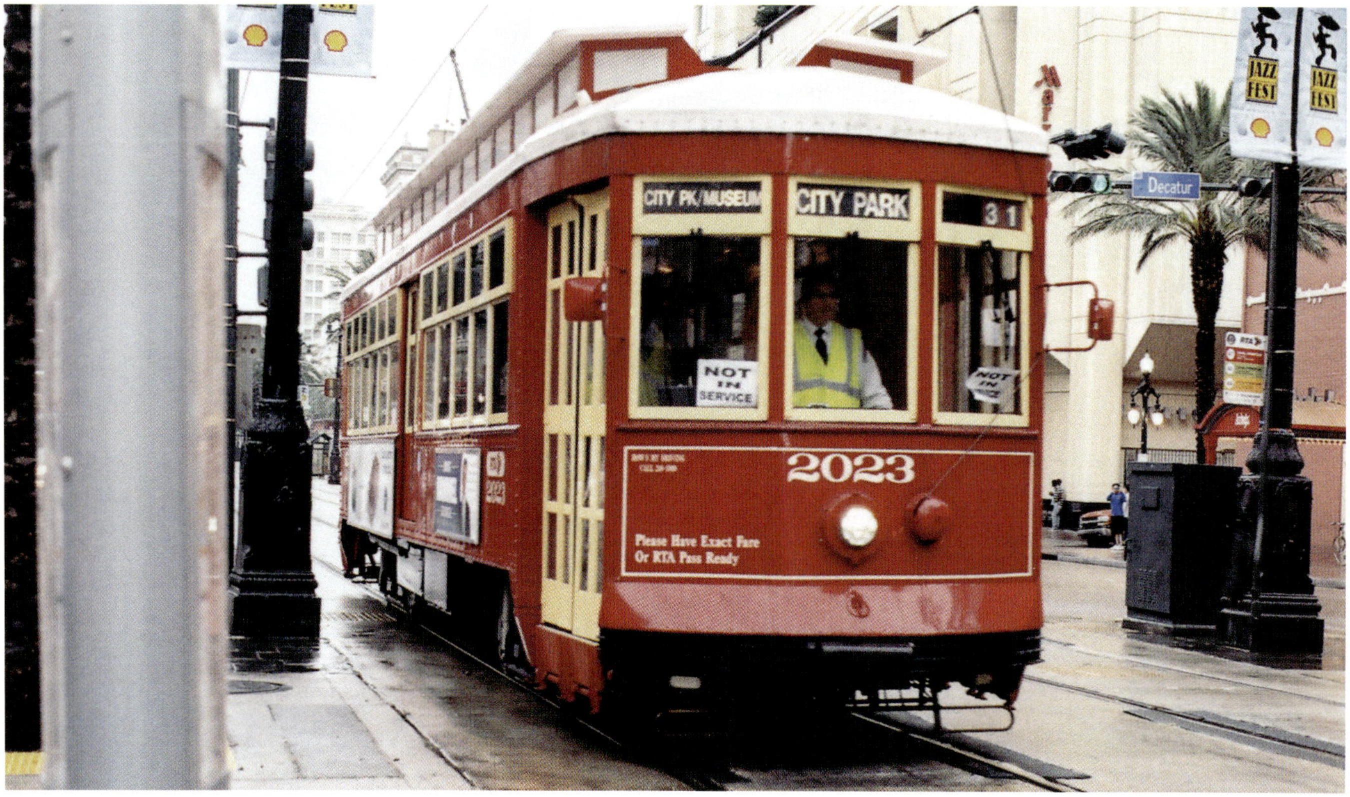

On an April 24, 2013 operator training run, RTA streetcar No. 2023 is on Canal Street at Decatur Street. Learning to properly operate a streetcar requires a skilled instructor that guides the student to pay careful attention to details, be alert at all times, and adhere to the safety rules.

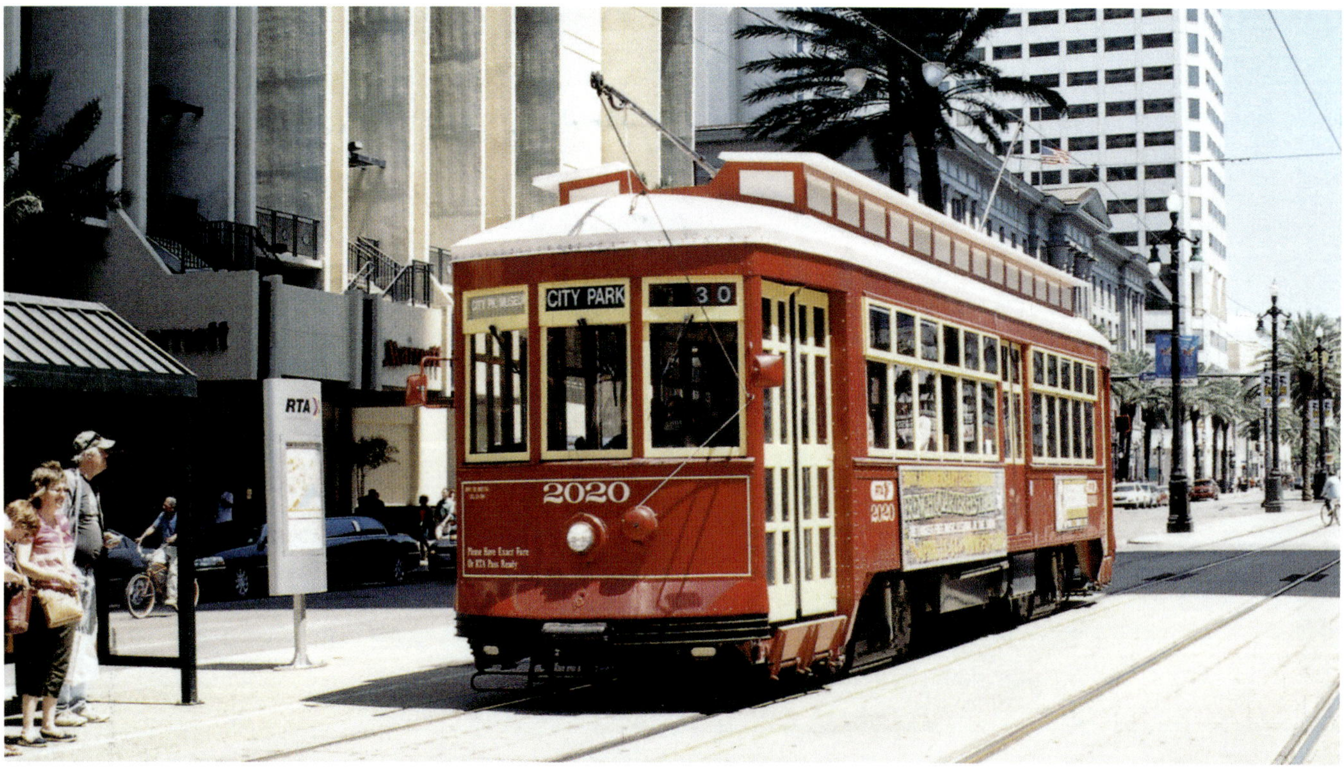

Canal Street at Decatur Street finds RTA streetcar No. 2020 coming to the passenger stop, on April 21, 2013. The Central Business District is the main economic hub for the region and offers new opportunities as people rediscover downtown living with its attractive streetcar service.

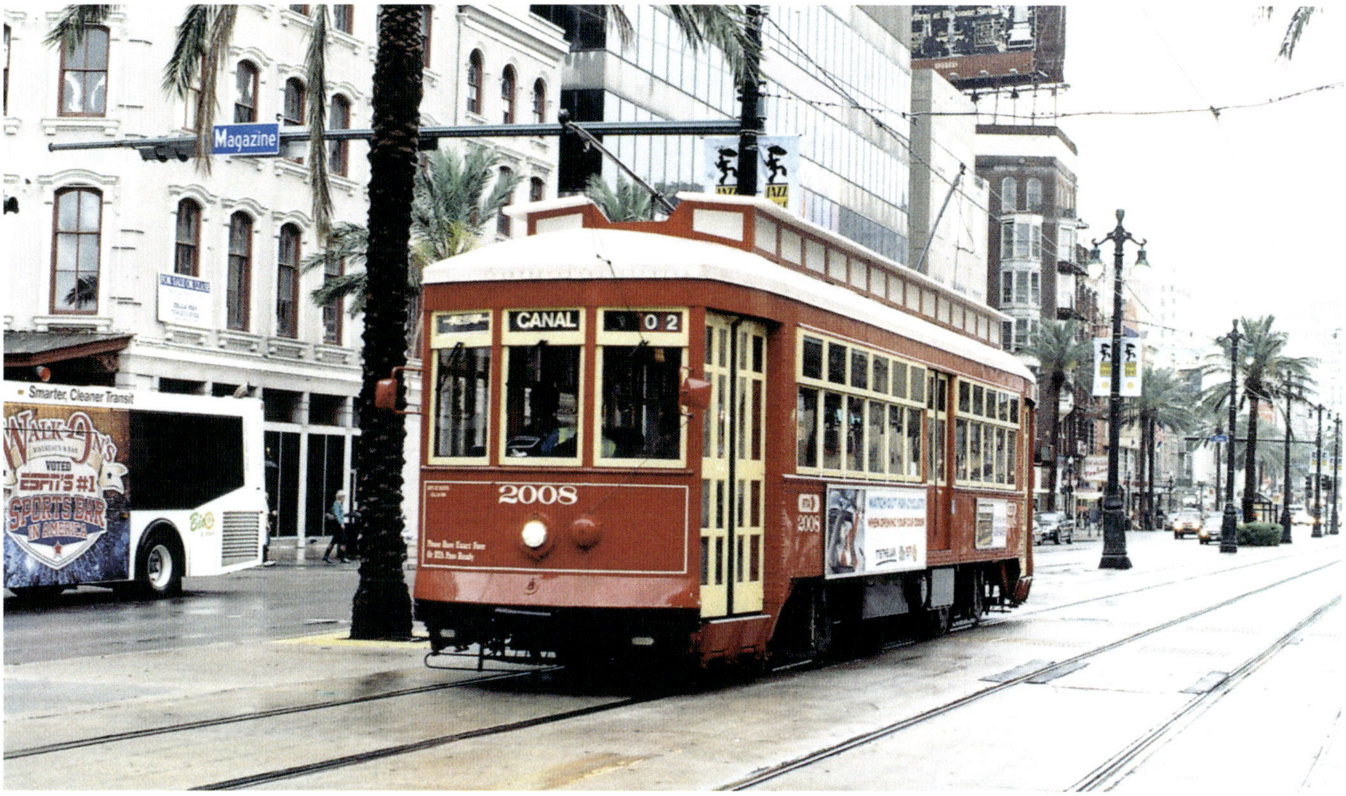

Heading for its terminus at the foot of Canal Street near the Mississippi River, RTA streetcar No. 2008 is on the reserved paved right of way of Canal Street at Magazine Street on April 24, 2013. Canal Street has often been noted as the widest roadway in the United States to have been classified as a street instead of an avenue or boulevard.

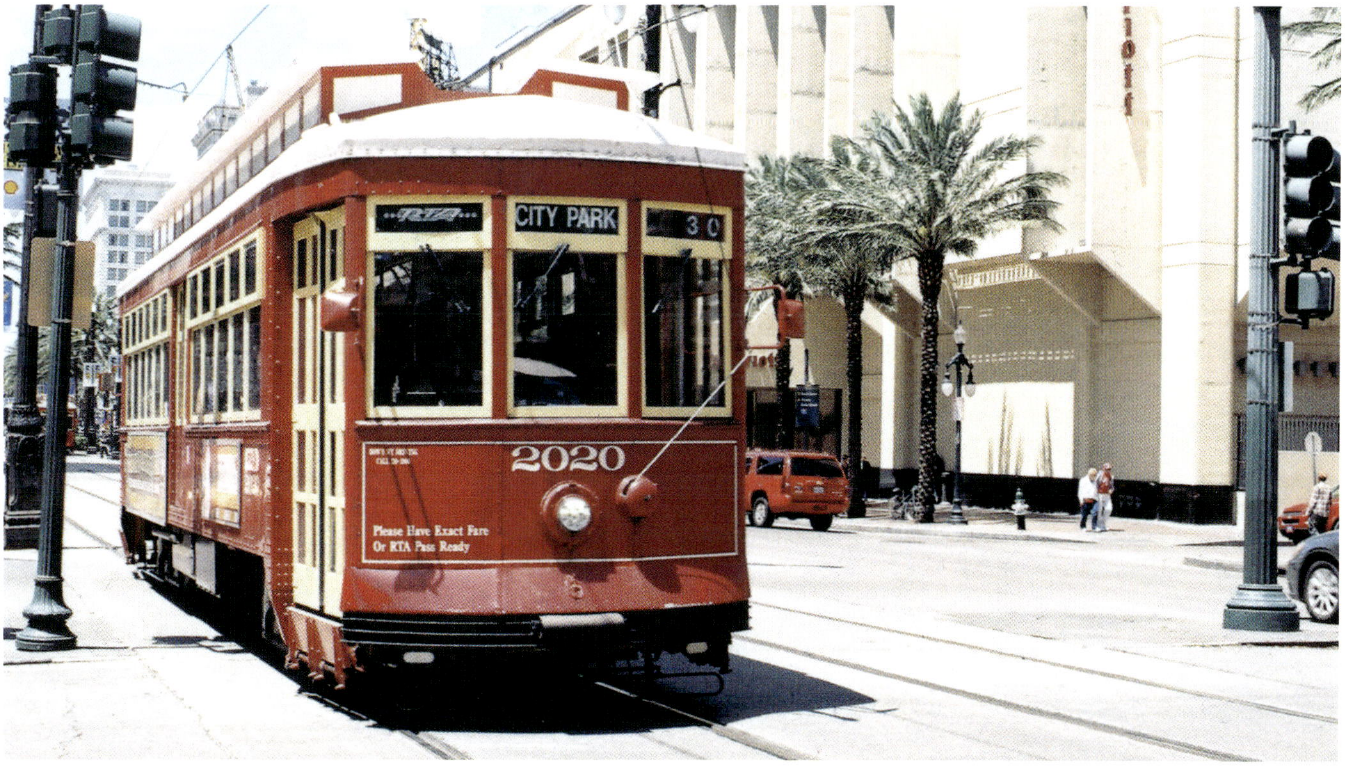

RTA streetcar No. 2020 is on Canal Street ready to cross Magazine Street on April 21, 2013. On the right side of the streetcar is the 42-story (449 foot tall) Marriott Hotel.

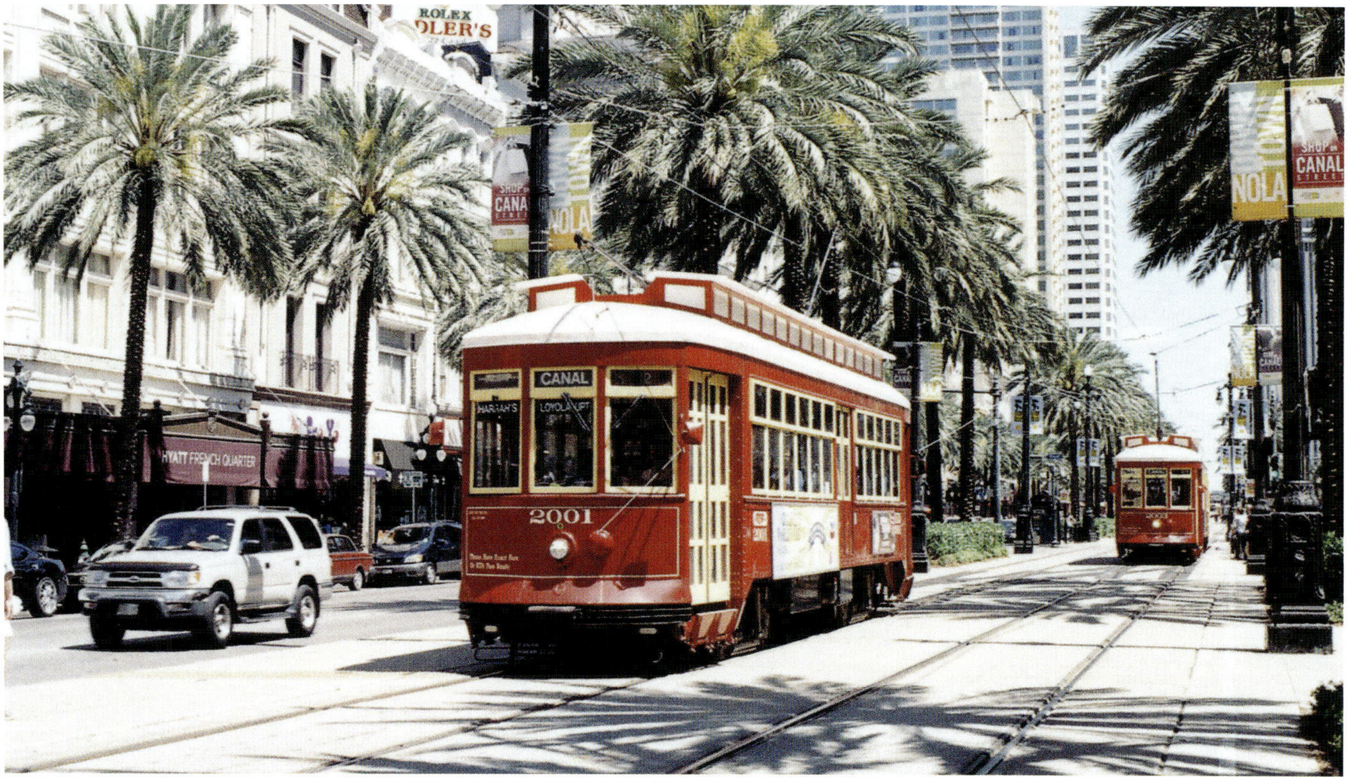

On Canal Street at Chartres Street, on April 21, 2013, RTA streetcar No. 2001 blends nicely with the Central Business District environment. Over the years, while there have been challenging times for many businesses, Canal Street has remained the main street of New Orleans.

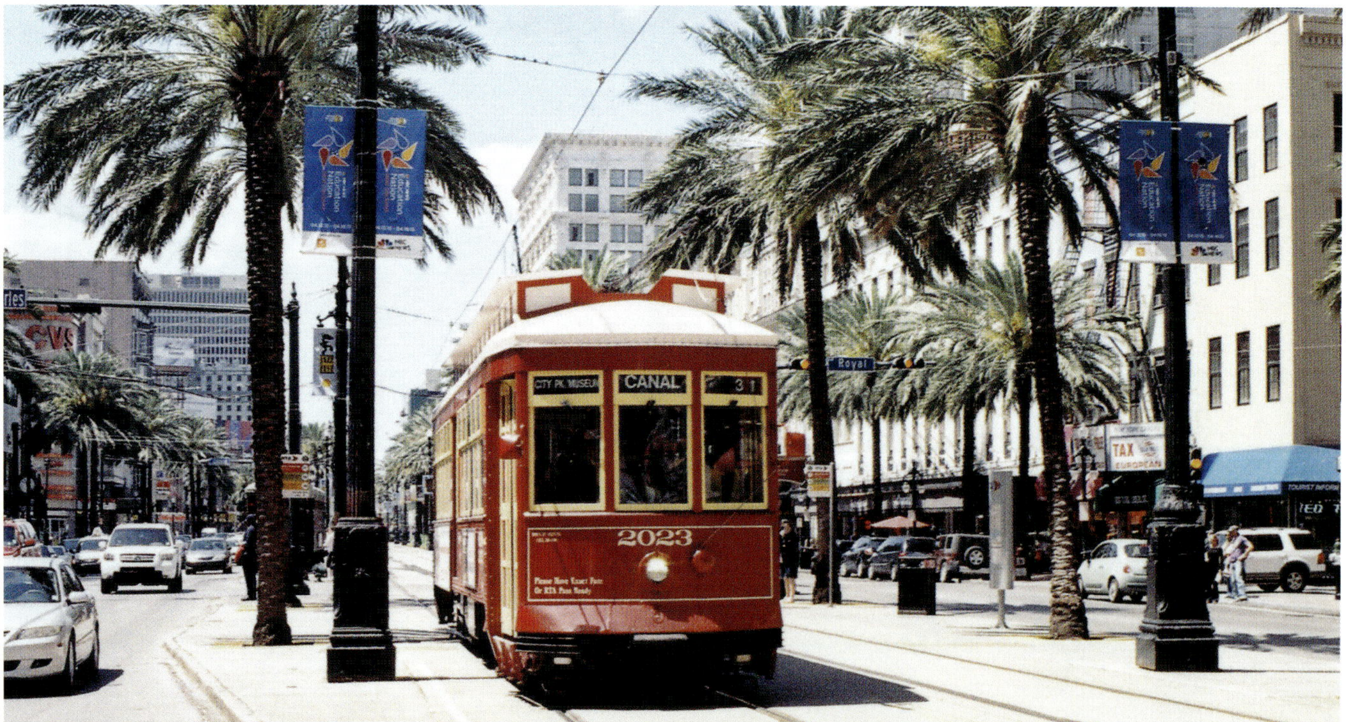

Adorned by palm trees on both sides of the median strip of Canal Street, RTA streetcar No. 2023 is passing Royal Street, on April 21, 2013. The white twelve-story building that can be seen in the center of the picture above the streetcar roof line is the Ritz-Carlton Hotel. Constructed in 1908-09 for the Maison Blanche department store, which closed in 1982, the store reopened in 1984 under new owners, but since October 6, 2000 has been the Ritz-Carlton Hotel.

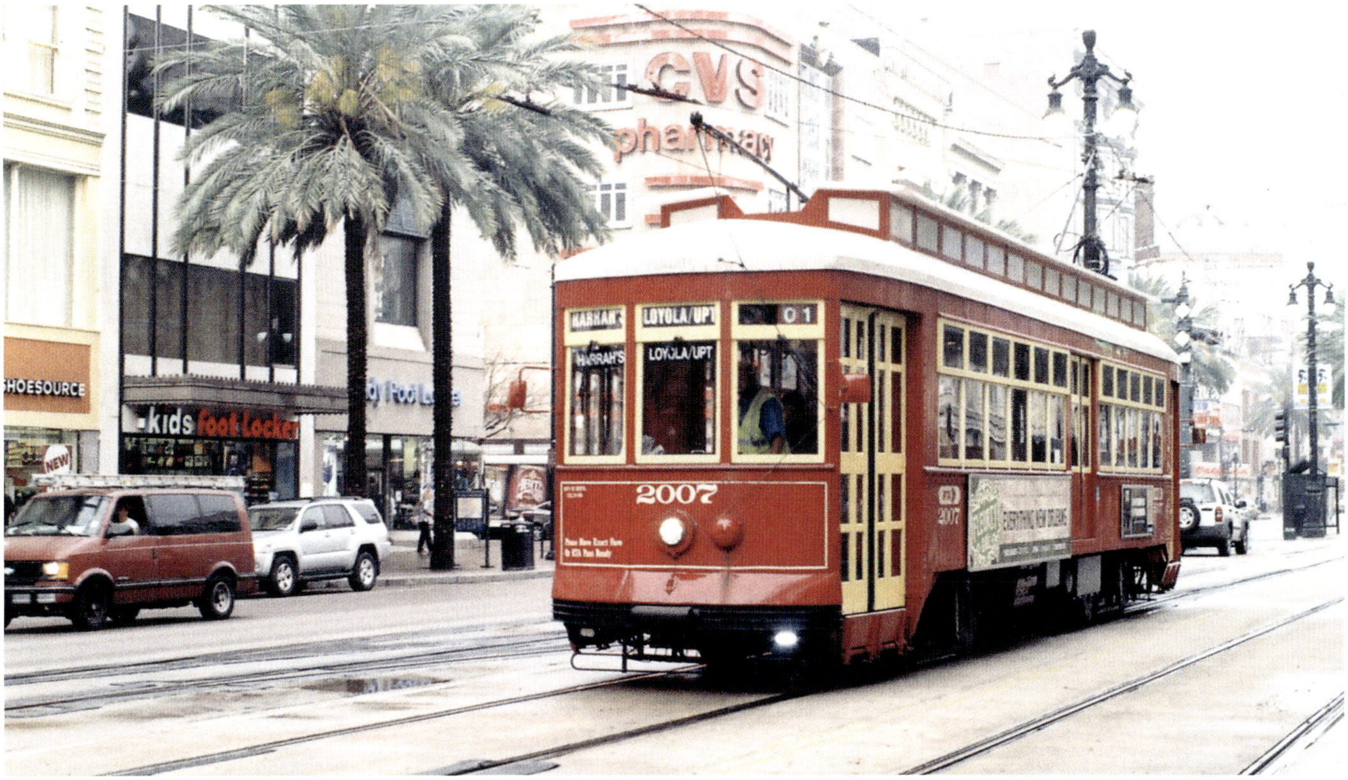

On April 24, 2013, RTA streetcar No. 2007 is on Canal Street at Carondelet Street and operates to the foot of Canal Street. The building housing the CVS Pharmacy was once the Gus Mayer department store. Many of the older buildings that once housed department stores, such as Maison Blanche, have been converted into hotels.

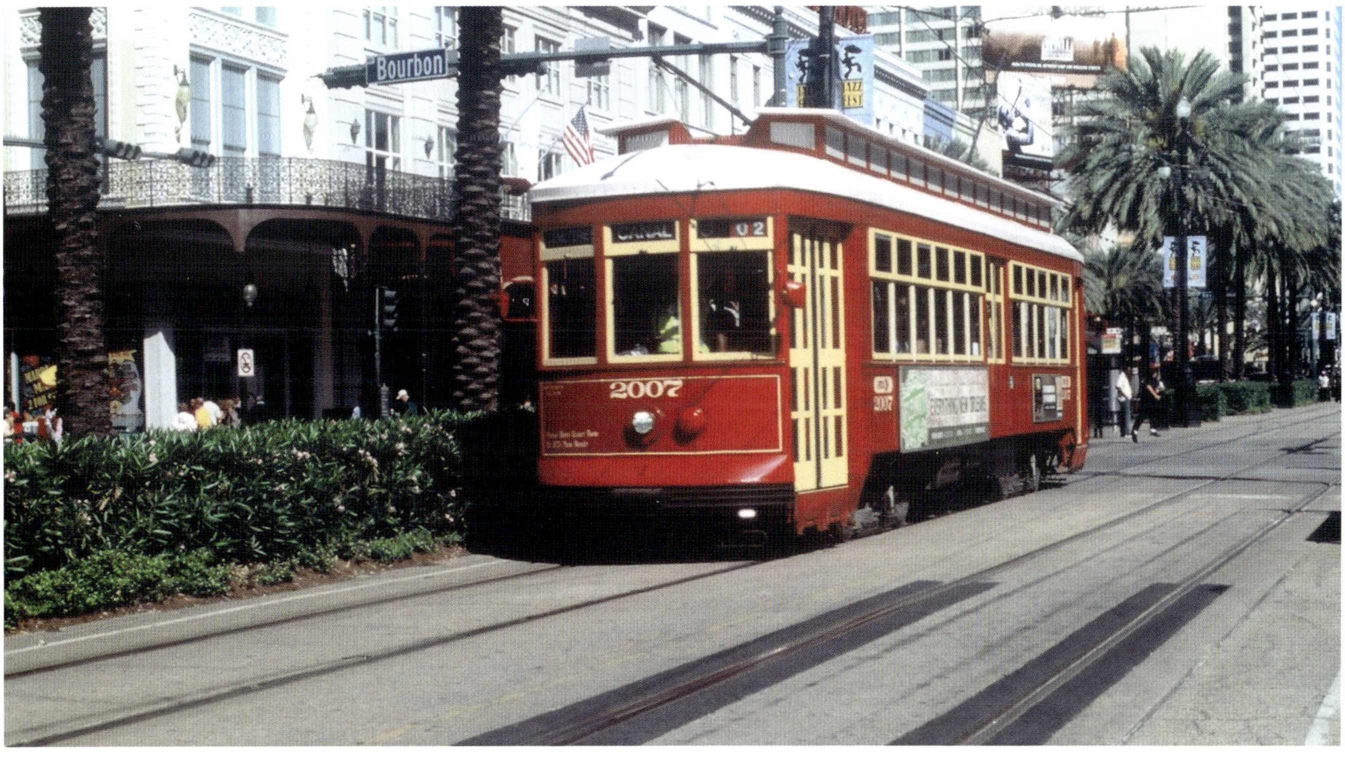

On April 21, 2013, RTA streetcar No. 2007 is on Canal ready to cross Bourbon Street. Canal Street is the starting point for every major street that runs the length of the French Quarter. It is also the starting point for all the major avenues that run from Downtown to Uptown, and is the street that divides north from south in the city street system. Although national trends have not favored downtown retail businesses, Canal Street has seen a steady rebirth.

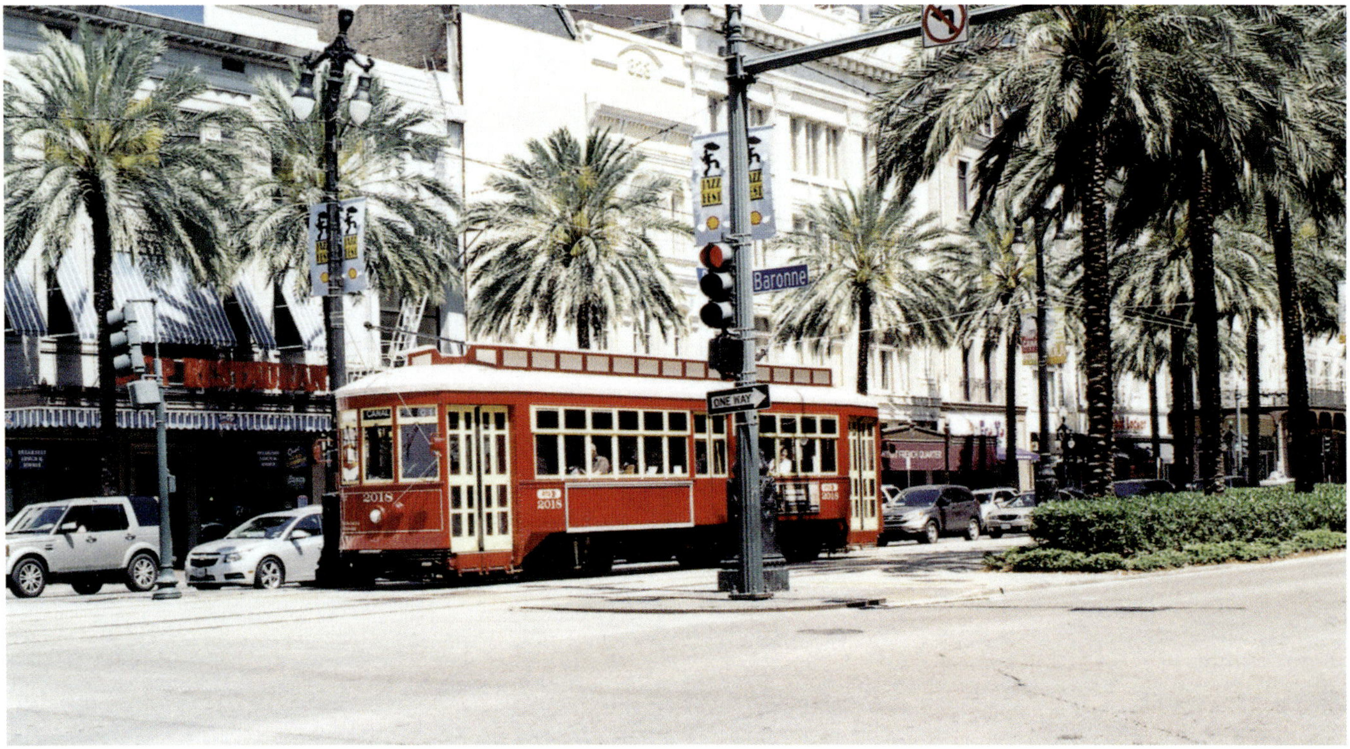

RTA streetcar No. 2018 is on Canal Street pausing for a red light at Baronne Street on April 21, 2013. Canal Street began as a country street; by the 1850s, it had two- and three-story buildings and, by the 1900s, skyscrapers were constructed. In the top right hand side of the picture, some of the ornamentation of the original building can be seen.

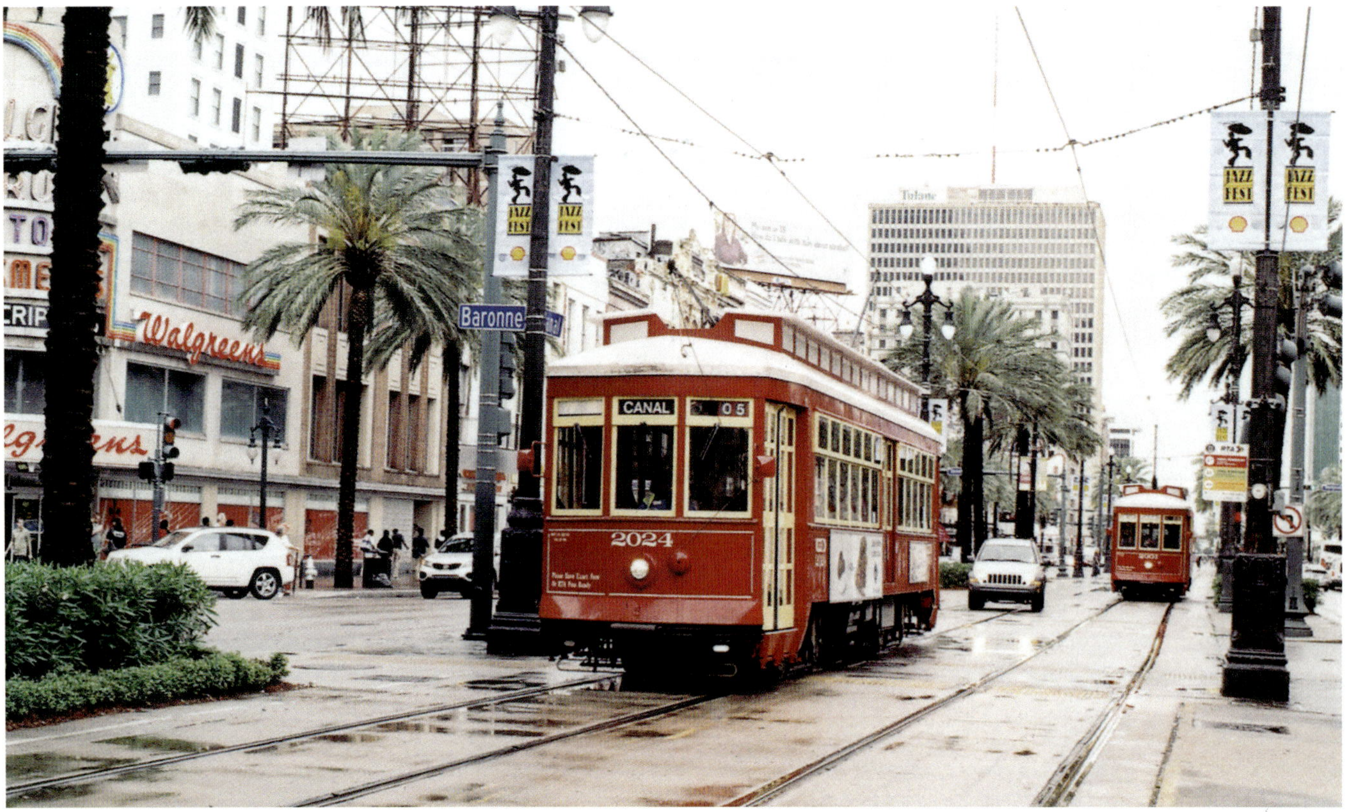

On April 24, 2013, RTA streetcar No. 2024 has already passed streetcar No. 2001 (in the distance on the right) on Canal Street at Baronne Street. The Walgreens drugstore has an Art Deco façade of the 1940s with stylish neon lighting.

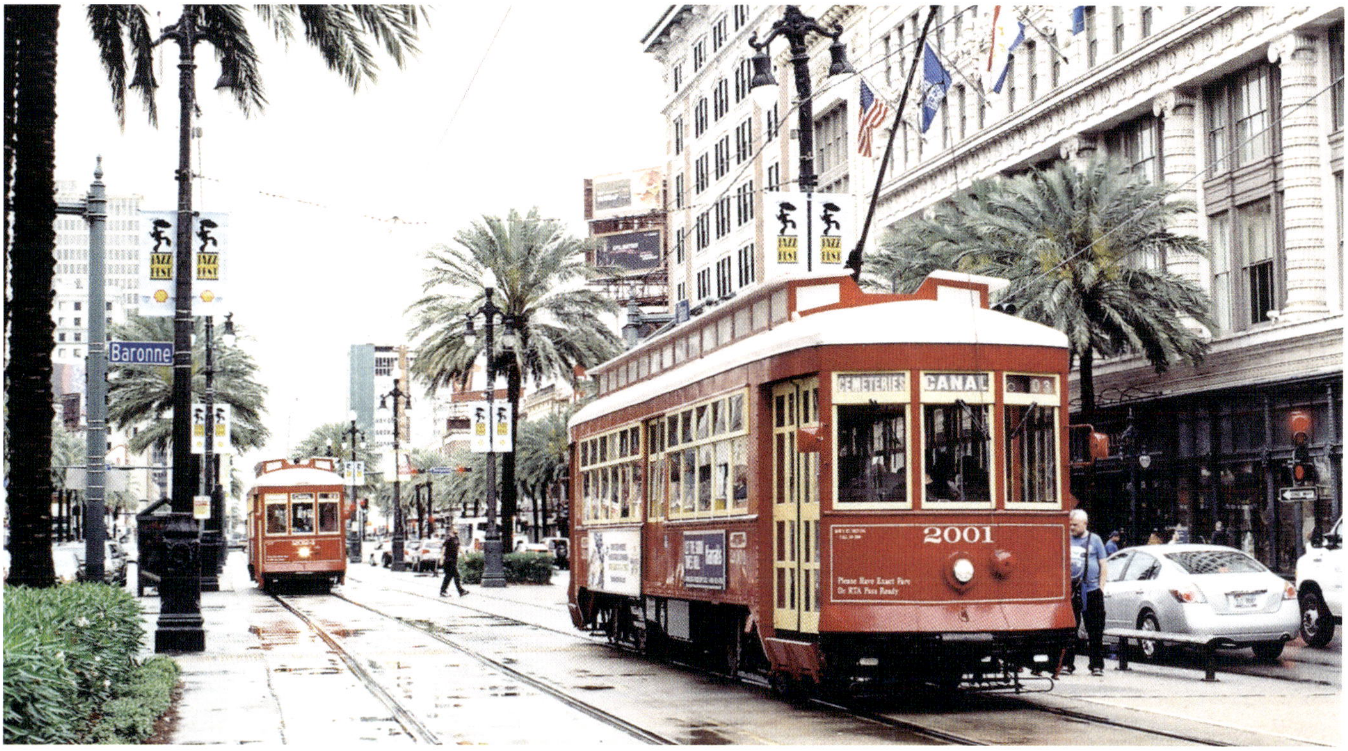

On the left, on April 24, 2013, RTA streetcar No. 2004 will soon pass streetcar No. 2001 on Canal Street at Baronne Street. On Sunday, April 18, 2004, RTA streetcar No. 2004 made the first public revenue trip on the new Canal streetcar line from the Canal Station carbarn to the cemeteries on Canal Street at City Park Avenue.

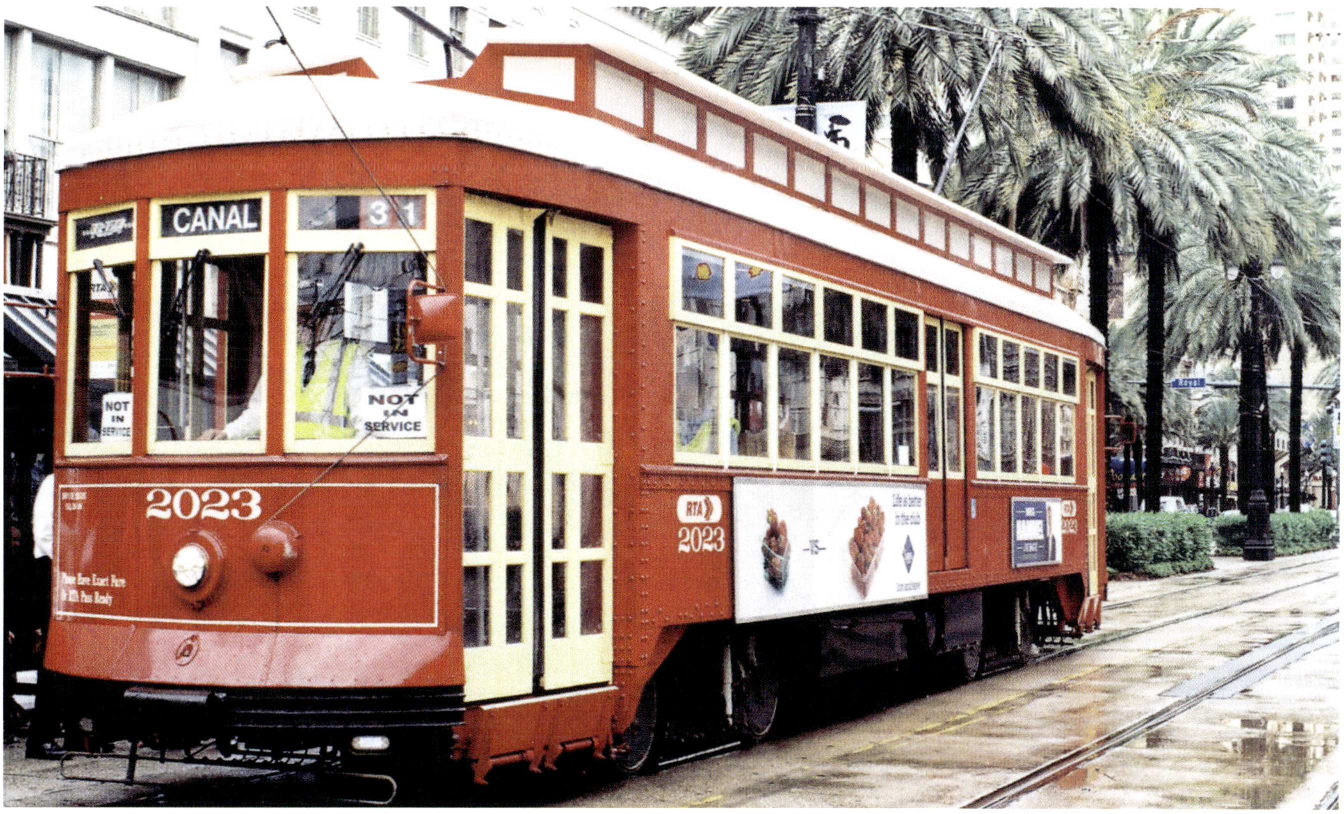

In the gentle afternoon rain of April 24, 2013, RTA streetcar No. 2023 is on Canal Street at Bourbon Street on an operator training run. In addition to operating the streetcar, the operator serves as a tour guide, policeman, problem solver, and supervisor in the course of navigating through city traffic. Earlier in the day, New Orleans had been hit with a significant rain storm.

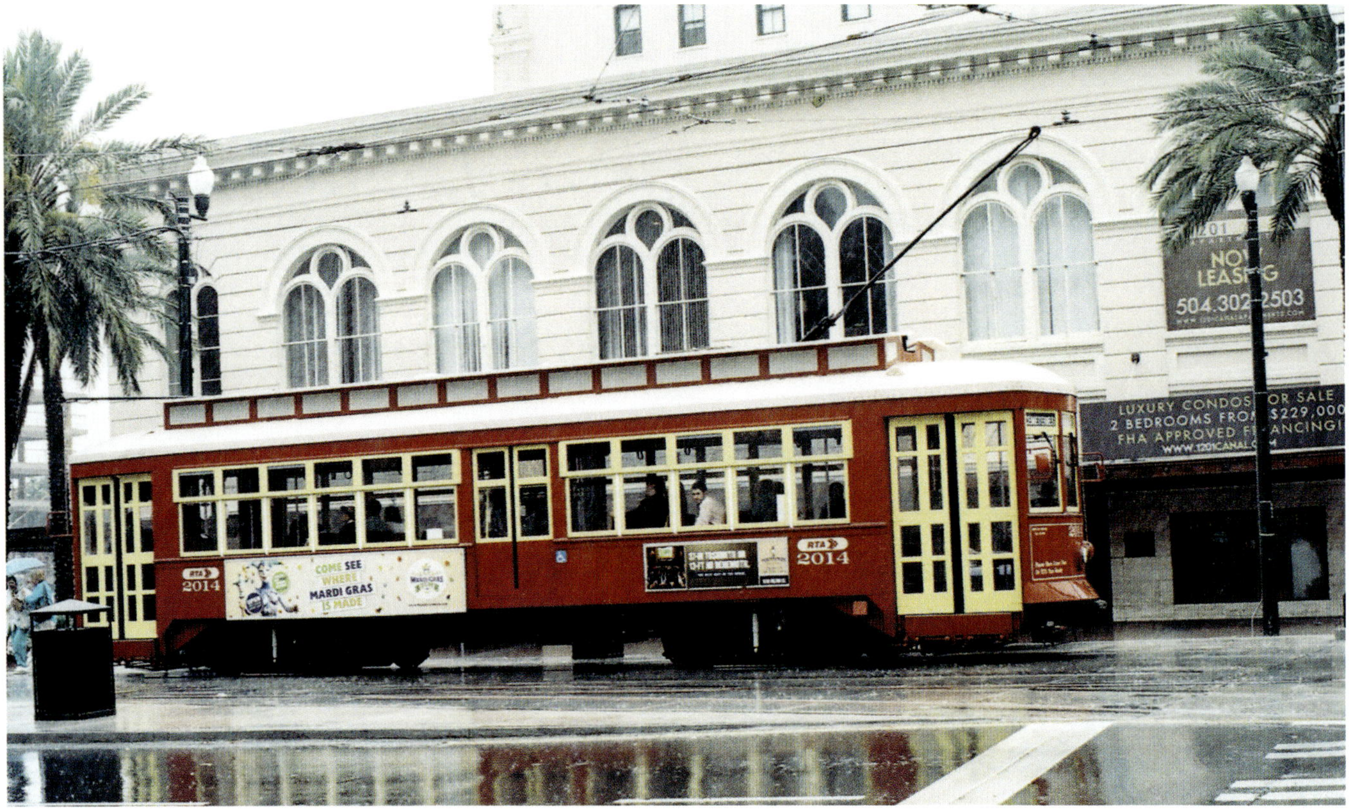

The rain has created a reflection of RTA streetcar No. 2014 on Canal Street at Elk Place on April 24, 2013. This intersection features the nearby Joy Theater and Saenger Theatre. The entire length of Canal Street is served by the Canal streetcar line.

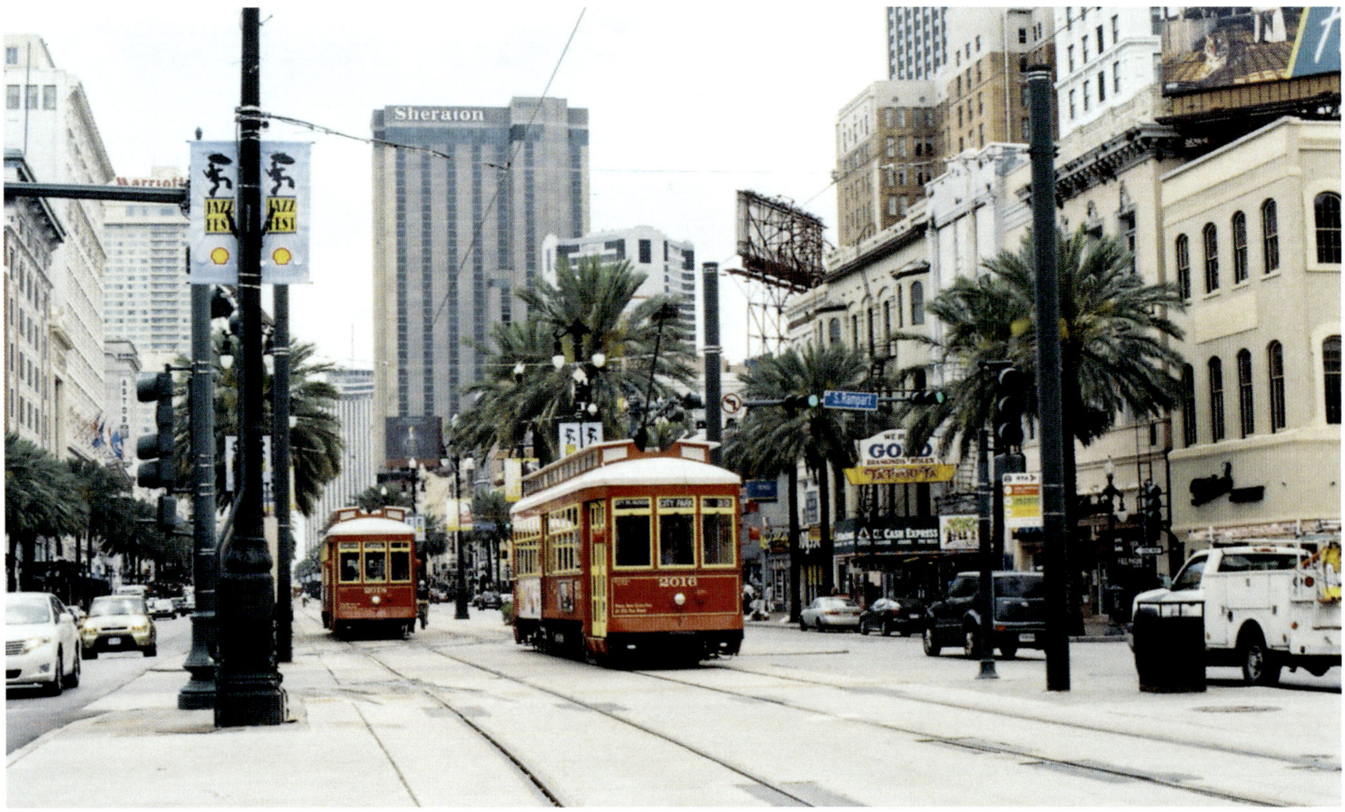

On the left, RTA streetcar No. 2018 will soon be passing streetcar No. 2016 on Canal Street at South Rampart Street, on April 23, 2013. Canal Street is still the place to go in New Orleans for shopping, dining, and entertainment with a unique music heritage.

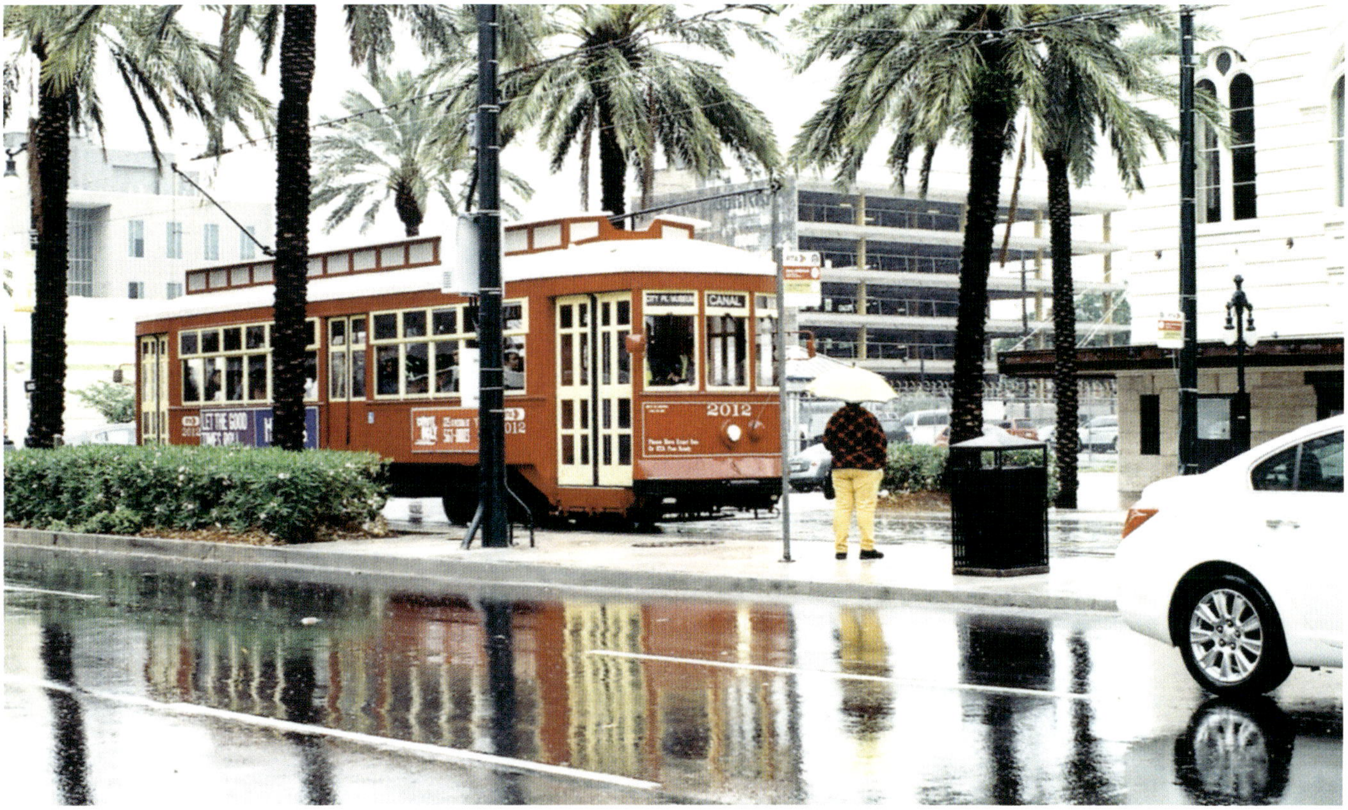

RTA streetcar No. 2012 is pulling up to the transit stop on Canal Street at Basin Street, on April 24, 2013. The light afternoon rain has produced this scenic reflection of the streetcar on the roadway. Canal Street continues to be the main street of New Orleans.

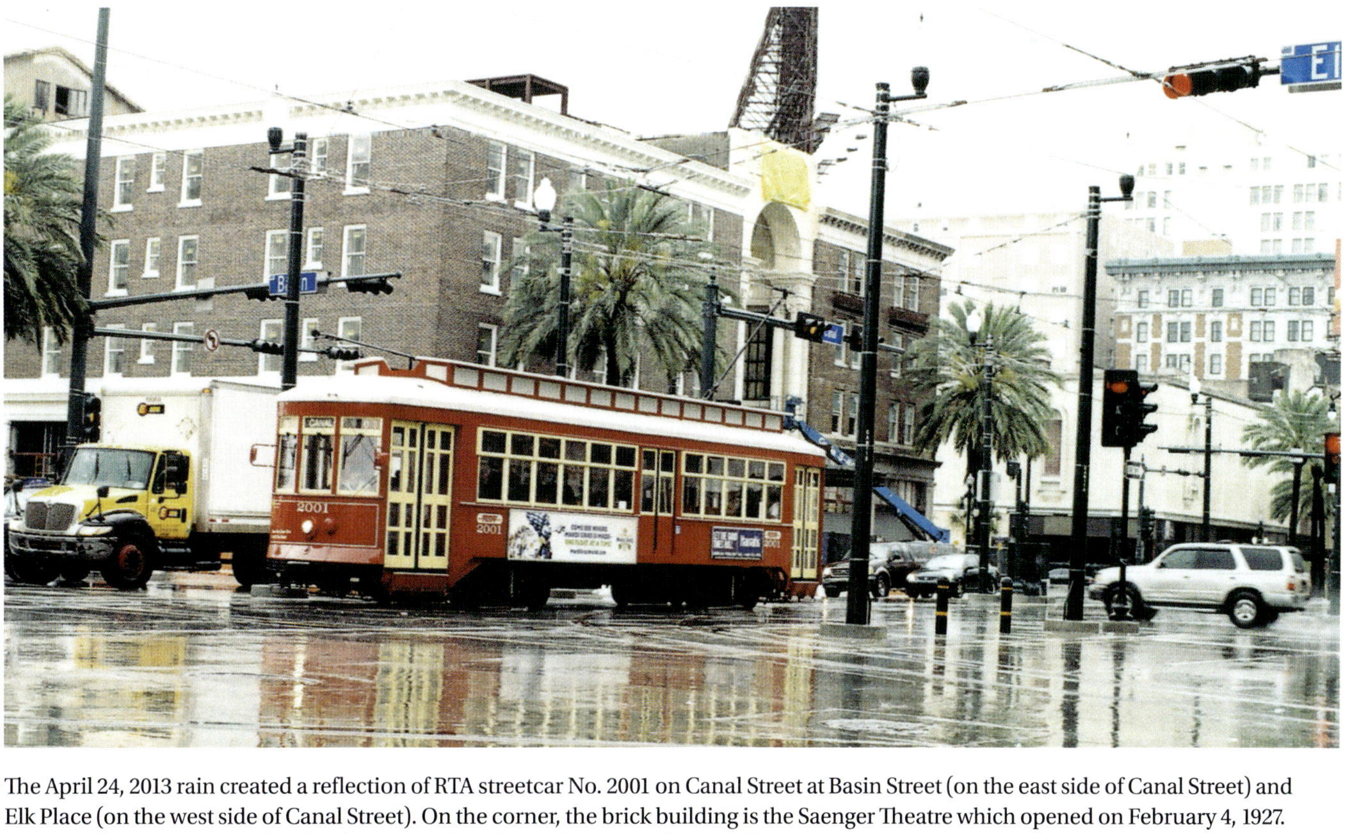

The April 24, 2013 rain created a reflection of RTA streetcar No. 2001 on Canal Street at Basin Street (on the east side of Canal Street) and Elk Place (on the west side of Canal Street). On the corner, the brick building is the Saenger Theatre which opened on February 4, 1927. In December 1977, it was added to the National Register of Historic Places. Following renovations in 1980, Johnny Carson made a gala performance at the theater's reopening.

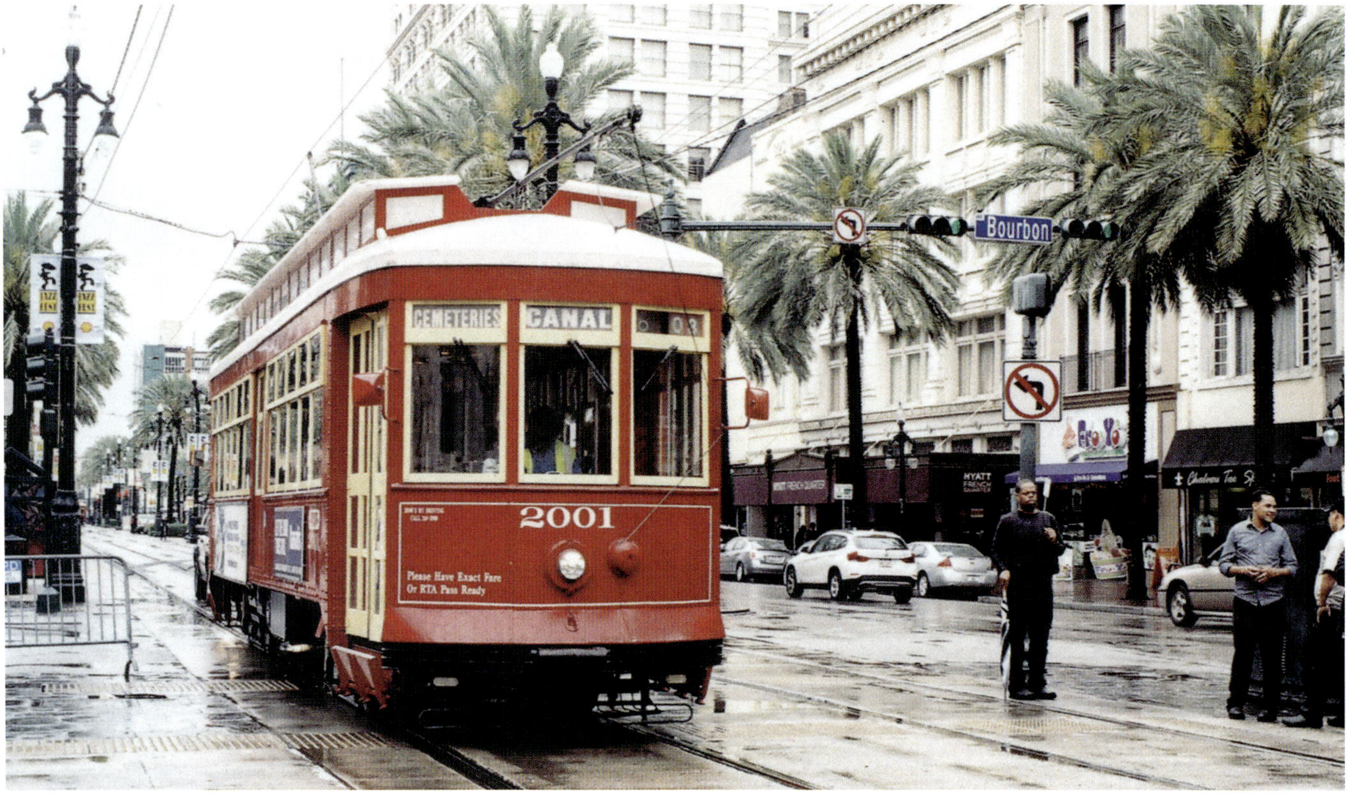

RTA streetcar No. 2001 on April 24, 2013, is on Canal Street at Bourbon Street in the Central Business District. In the top center of the picture is the former Maison Blanche department store (highest in the picture), now a Ritz-Carlton Hotel.

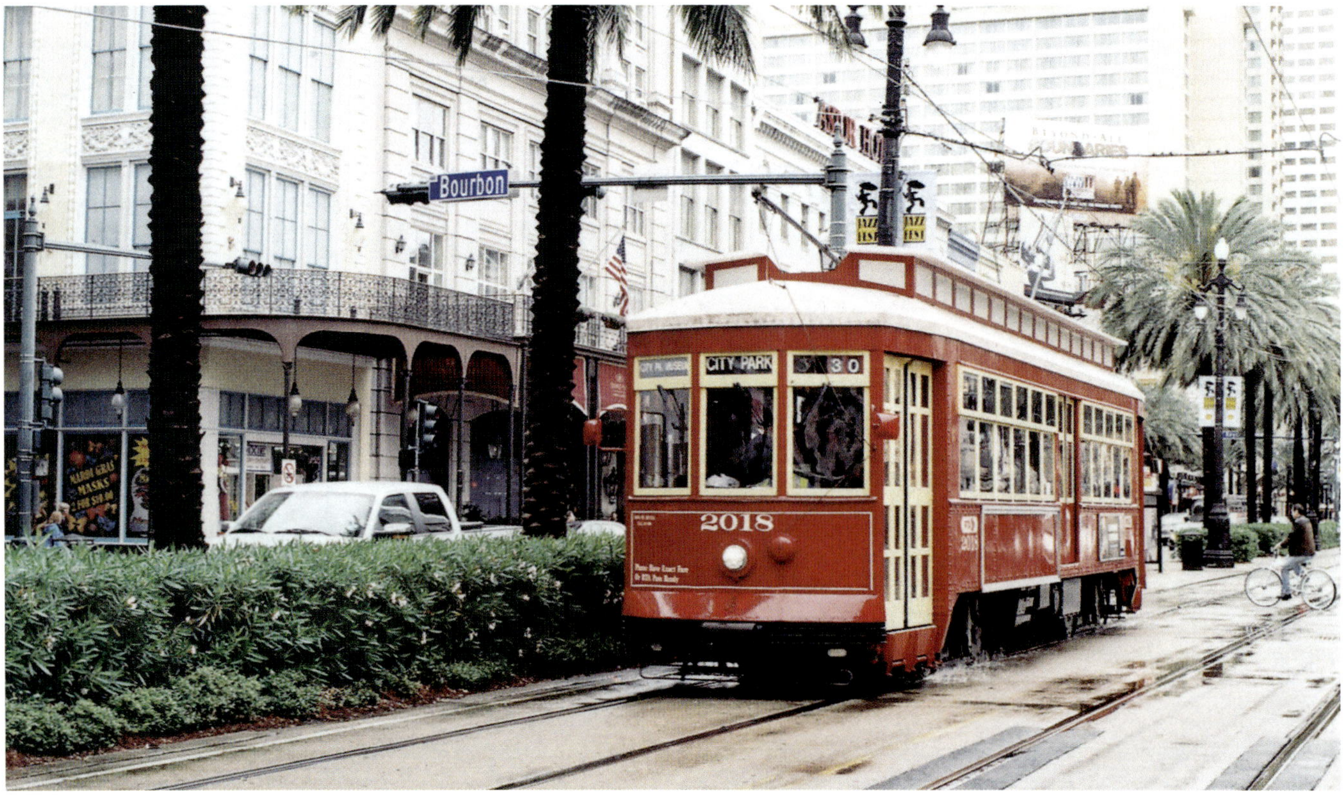

With City Park as the destination, RTA streetcar No. 2018 is making its way along Canal Street at Bourbon Street, on April 24, 2013. The downtown segment of Canal Street has been undergoing redevelopment which has included new hotels, apartments, and the renovated Joy Theater.

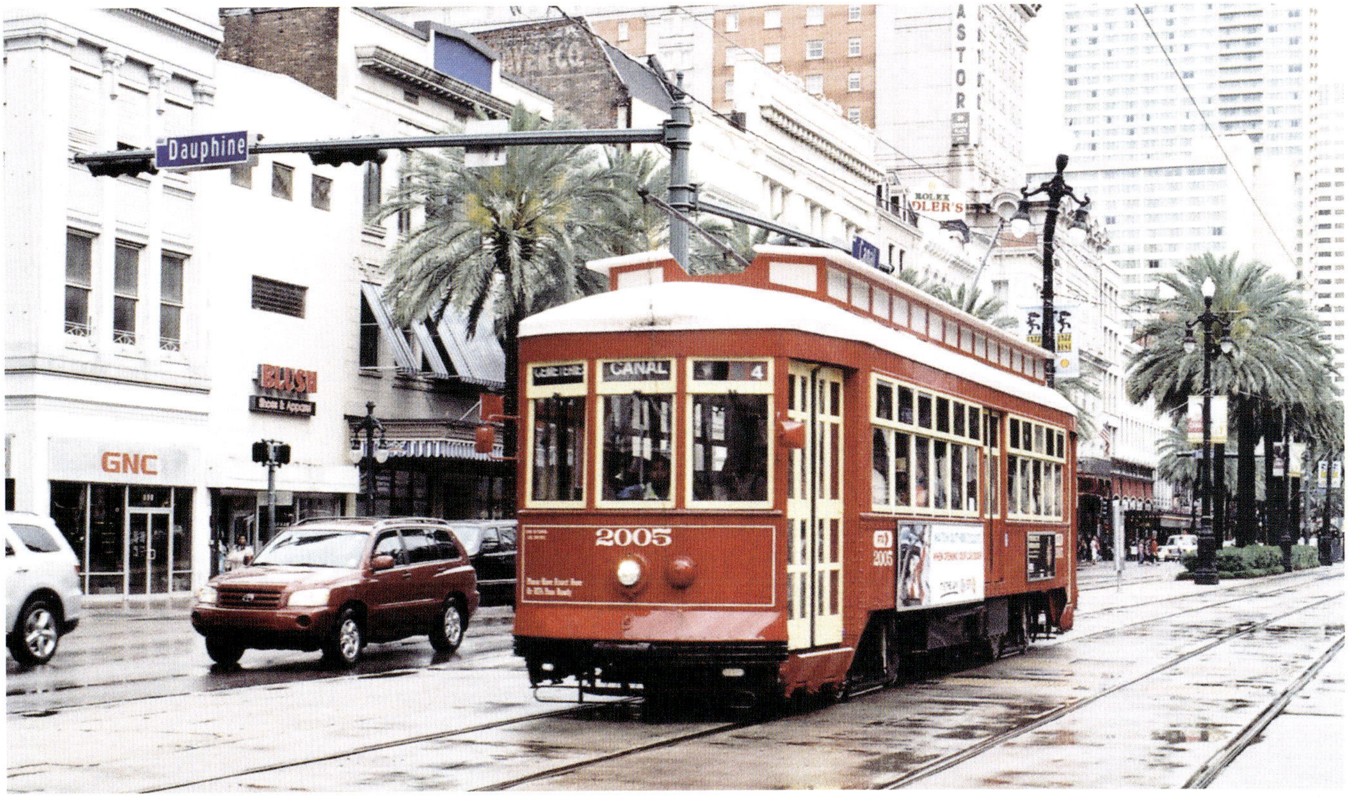

On April 24, 2013, RTA streetcar No. 2005 is on the paved reserved right of way of Canal Street at Dauphine Street. Many former Canal Street stores have been converted to hotels.

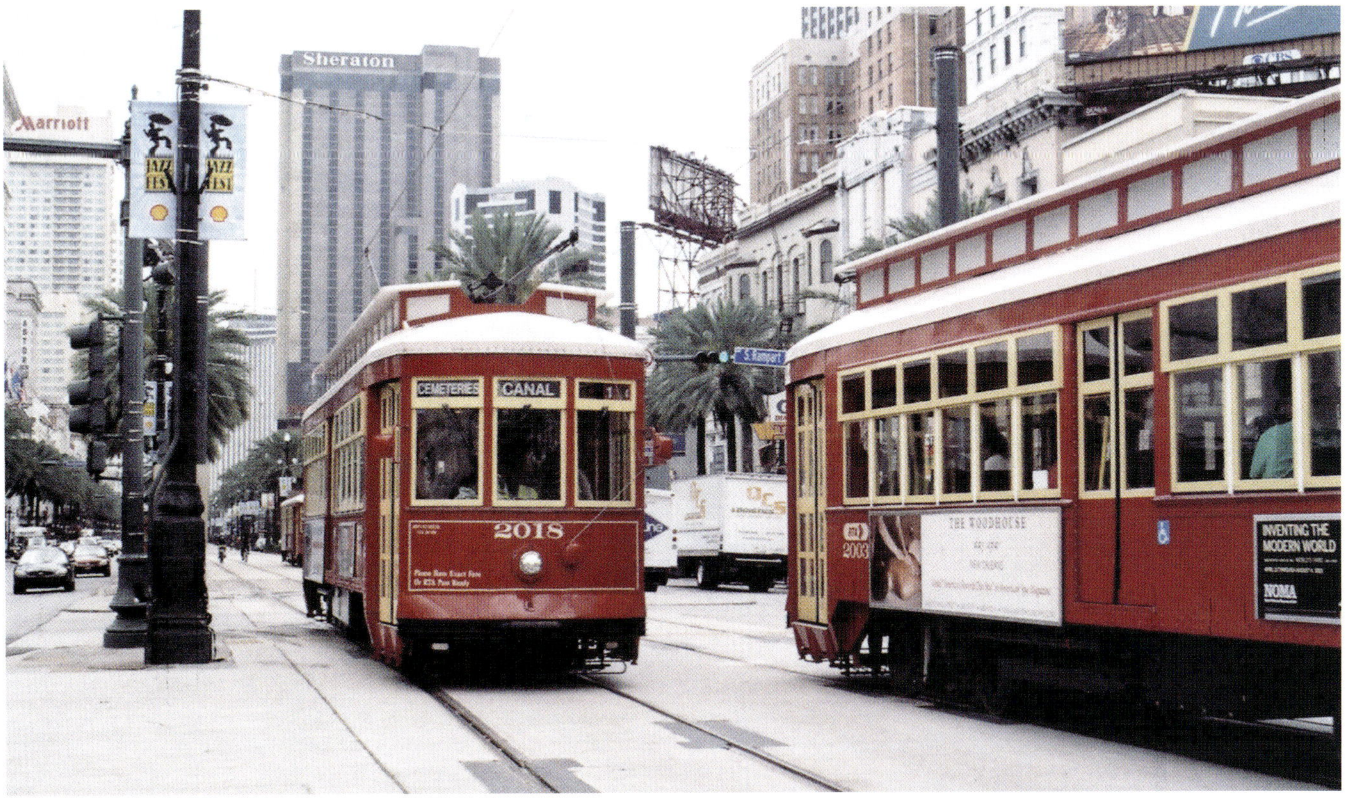

On Canal Street at South Rampart Street, RTA streetcar No. 2018 is about to pass streetcar No. 2003 on April 23, 2013. The Sheraton Hotel and Marriott Hotel are in the background.

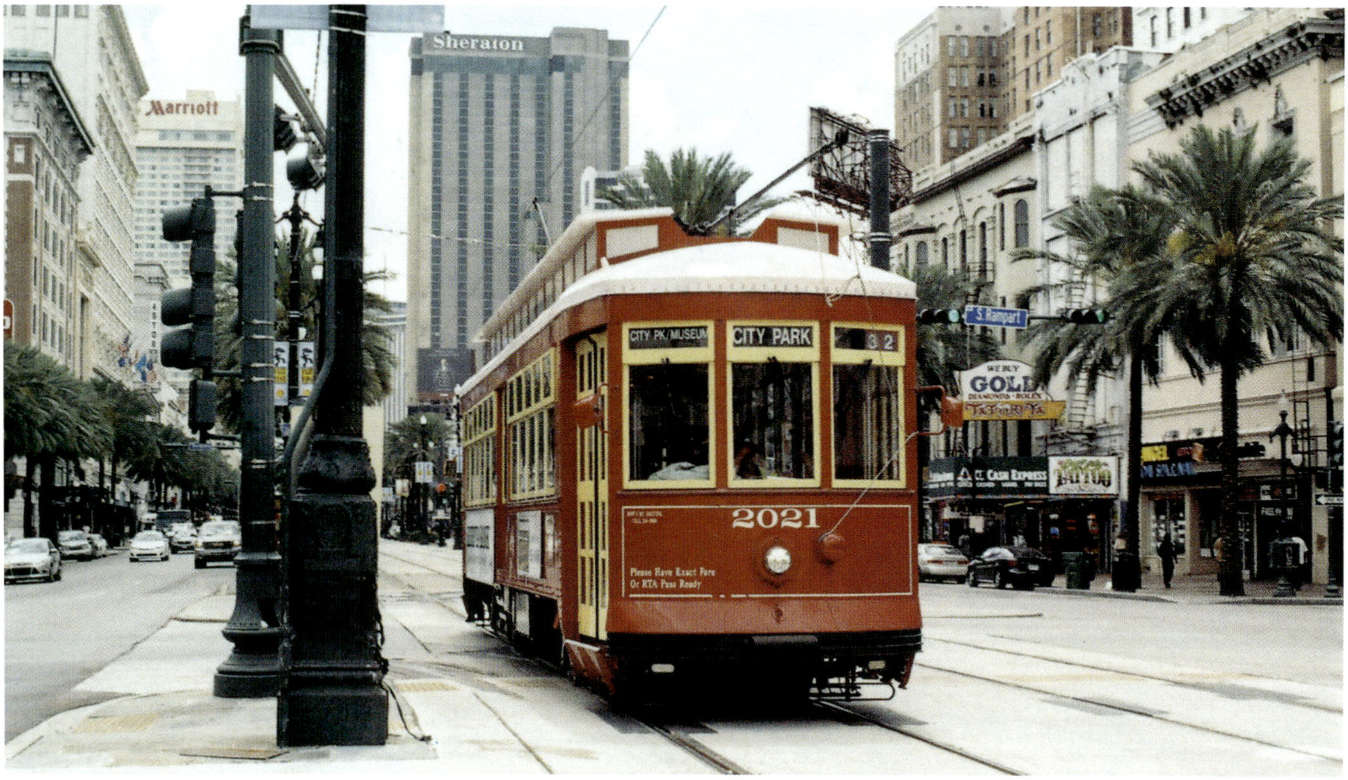

Quietly coming along Canal Street, RTA streetcar No. 2021 is crossing South Rampart Street on its trip to City Park on April 23, 2013. The three high-rise buildings from left to right are the Marriott Hotel, World Trade Center, which is further away at the foot of Canal Street, and the Sheraton Hotel.

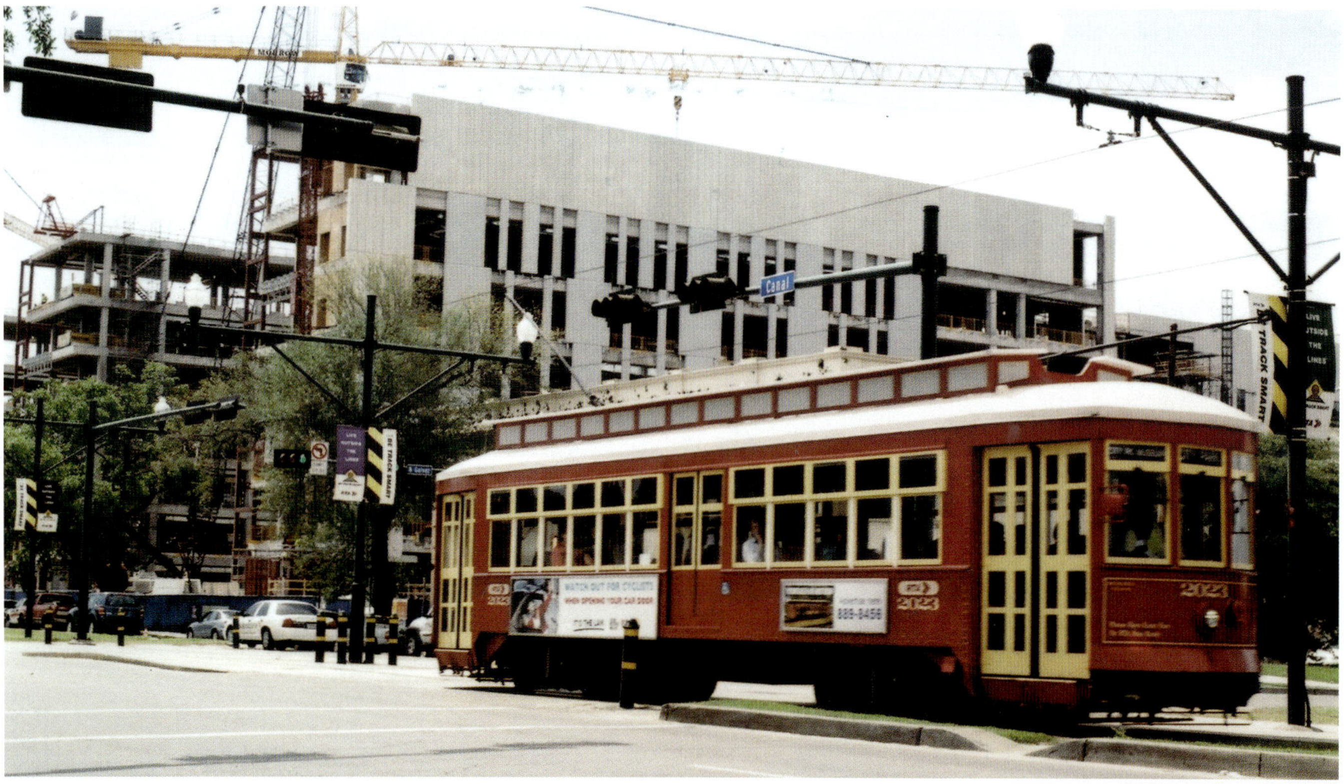

Passing by massive construction projects on Canal Street, RTA streetcar No. 2023 is crossing North Galvez Street on April 22, 2013. Impressive new medical facilities for research and health care delivery are under construction on this portion of Canal Street, which should position New Orleans to become a health care hub.

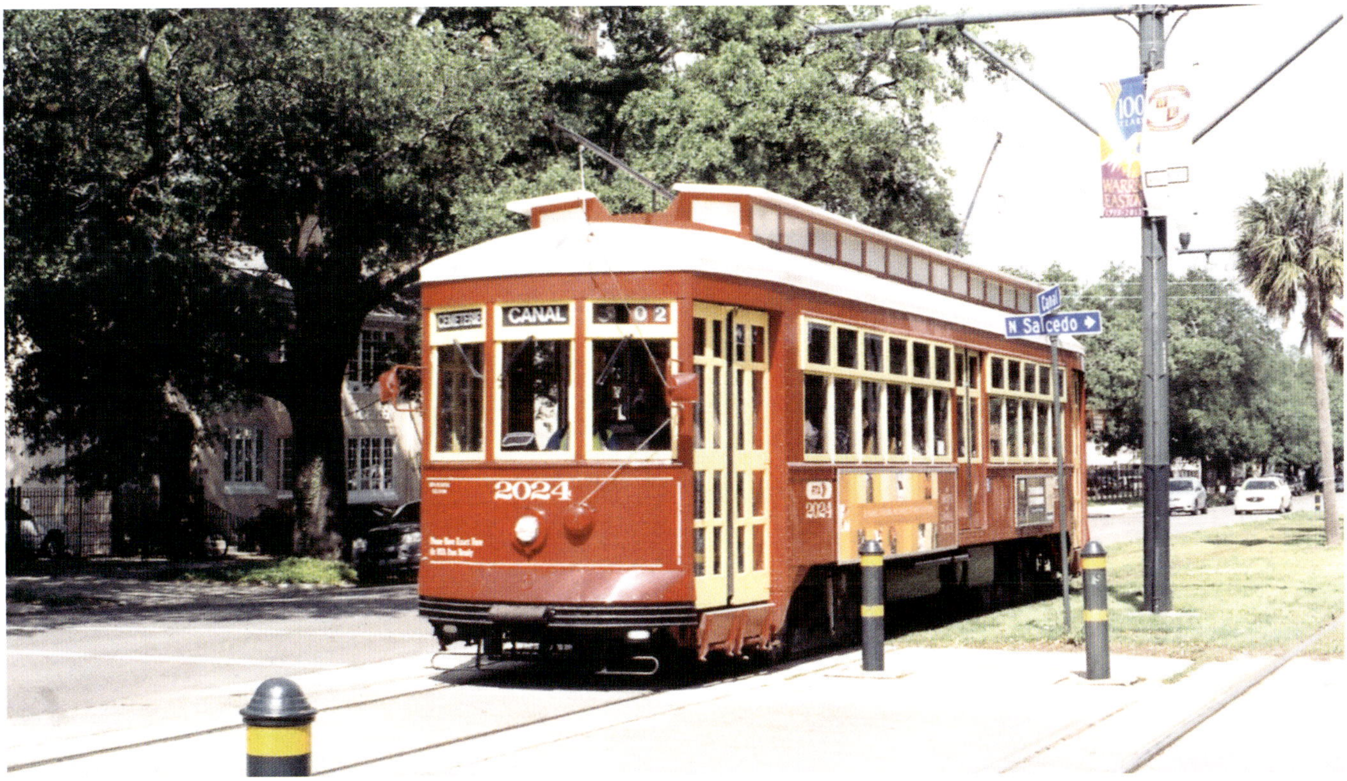

On April 22, 2013, RTA streetcar No. 2024 is on the scenic reserved right of way in the center of Canal Street crossing North Salcedo Street.

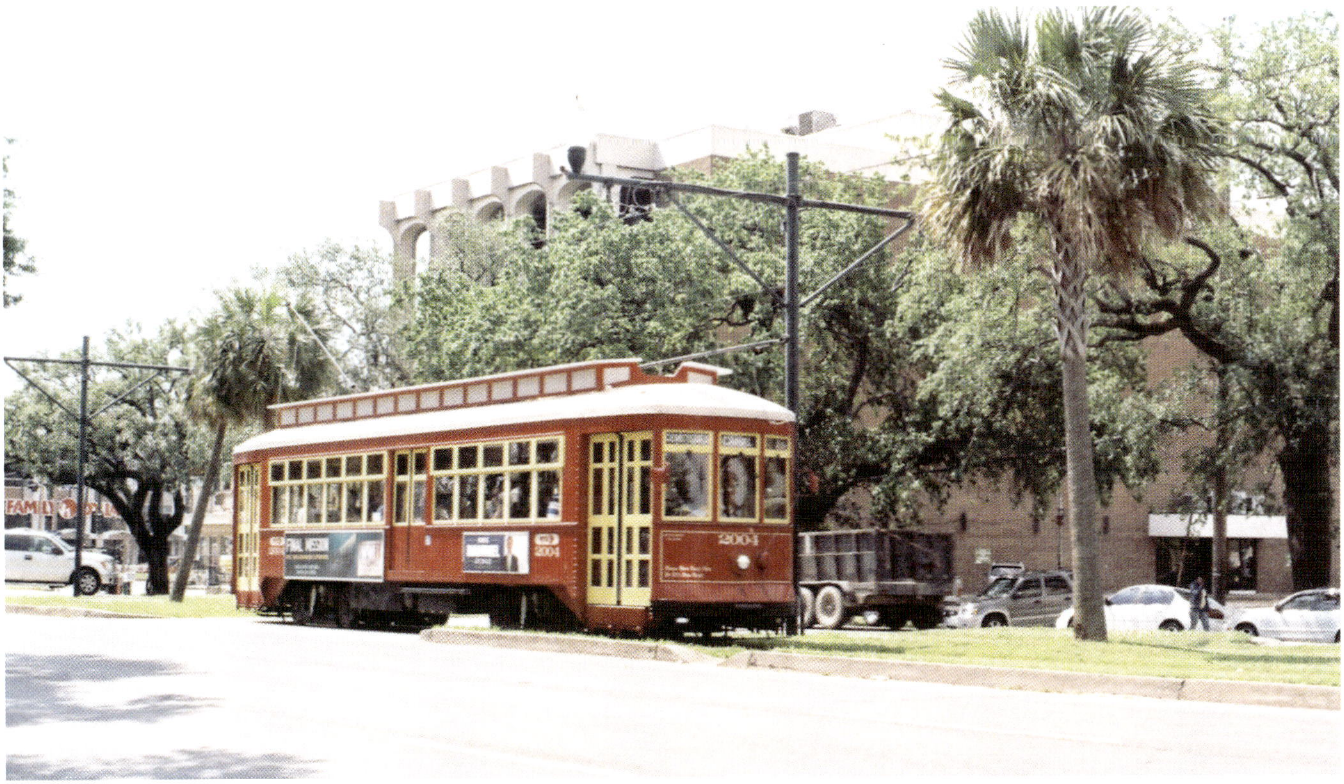

Canal Street at White Street in the Mid-City neighborhood of New Orleans on April 22, 2013 finds RTA streetcar No. 2004 proceeding quickly along the private right of way in the center of Canal Street.

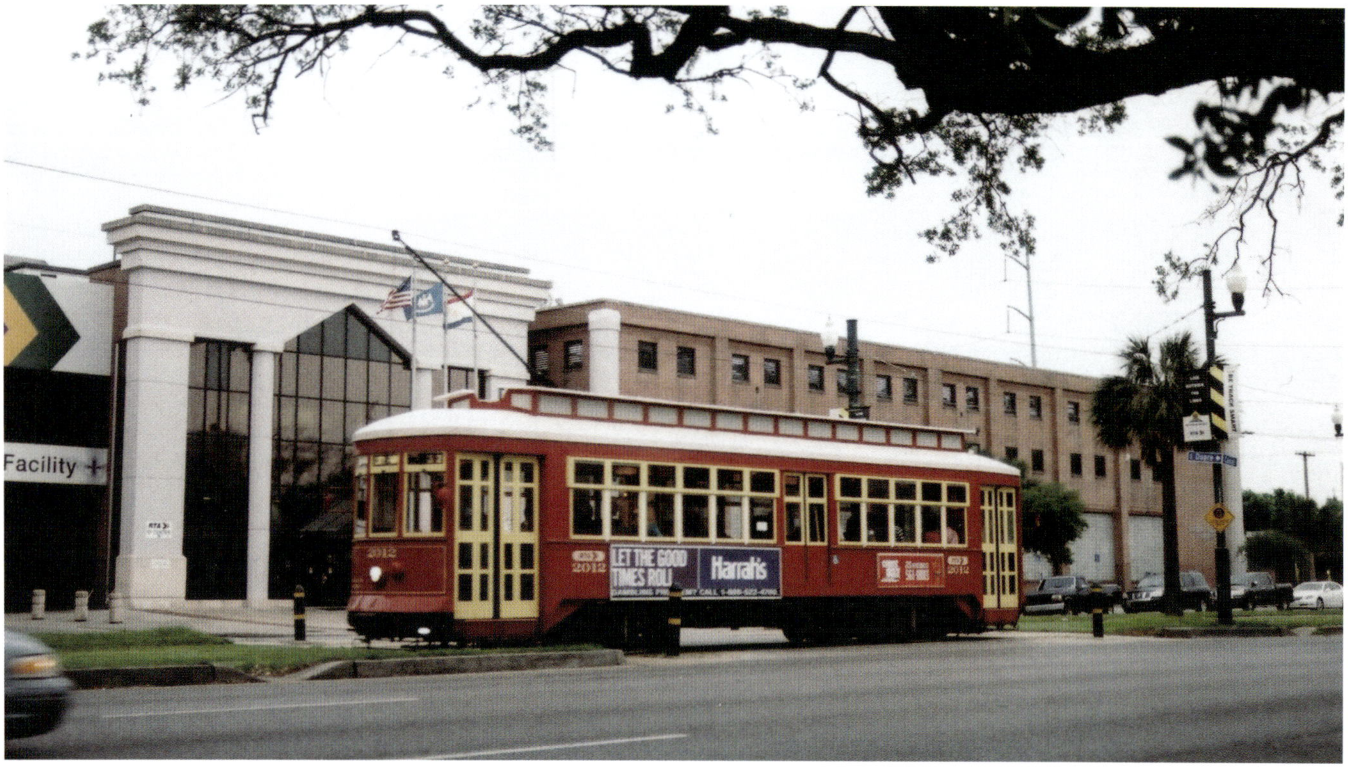

RTA streetcar No. 2012 is passing by the RTA Administration Building on Canal Street at North Gayoso Street on April 24, 2013. The Canal Station carbarn is also located at this site.

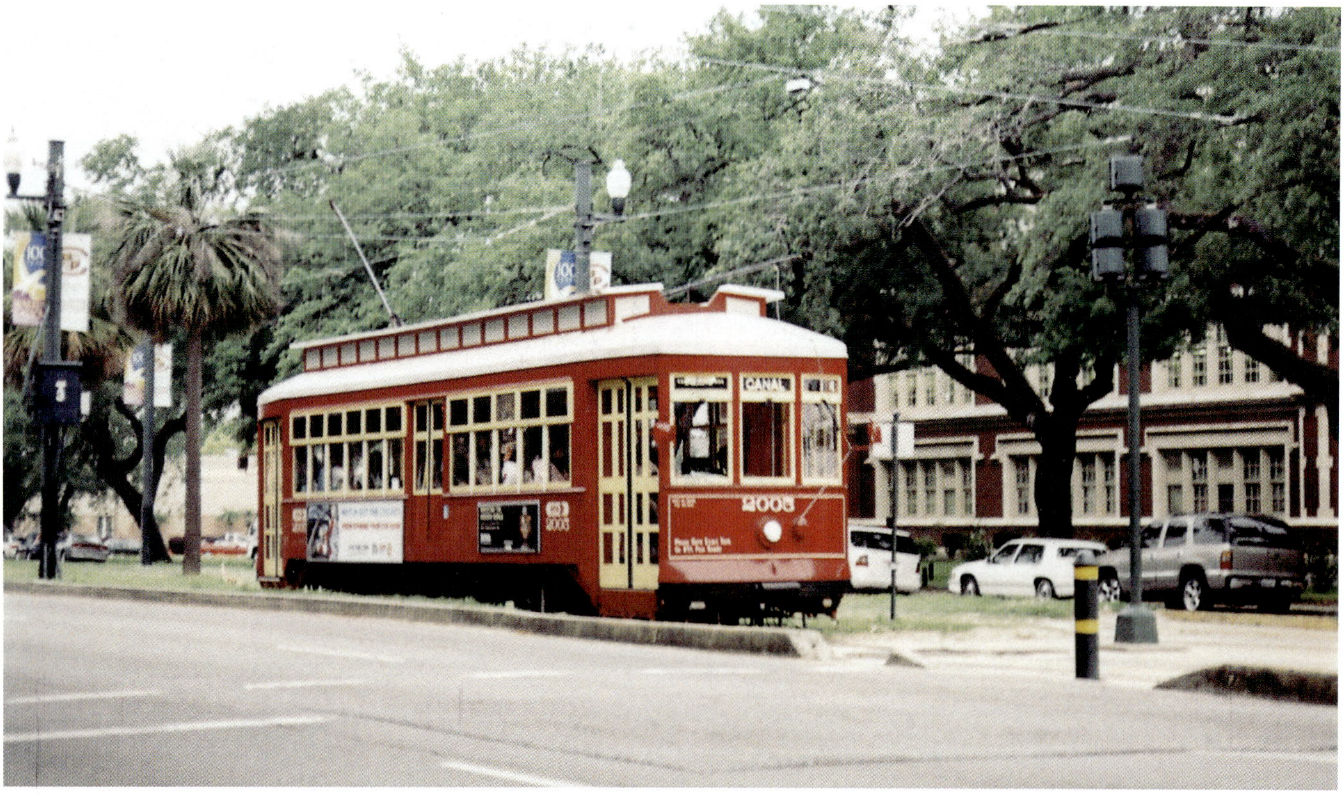

On April 24, 2013, RTA streetcar No. 2005 is on Canal Street at North Gayoso Street. On the right side of the streetcar is the Warren Easton High School, which was named for Warren Easton, the first Supervisor of Education for the city of New Orleans and state of Louisiana. During 2006, the school was closed for one year, due to Hurricane Katrina, and reopened as a charter school.

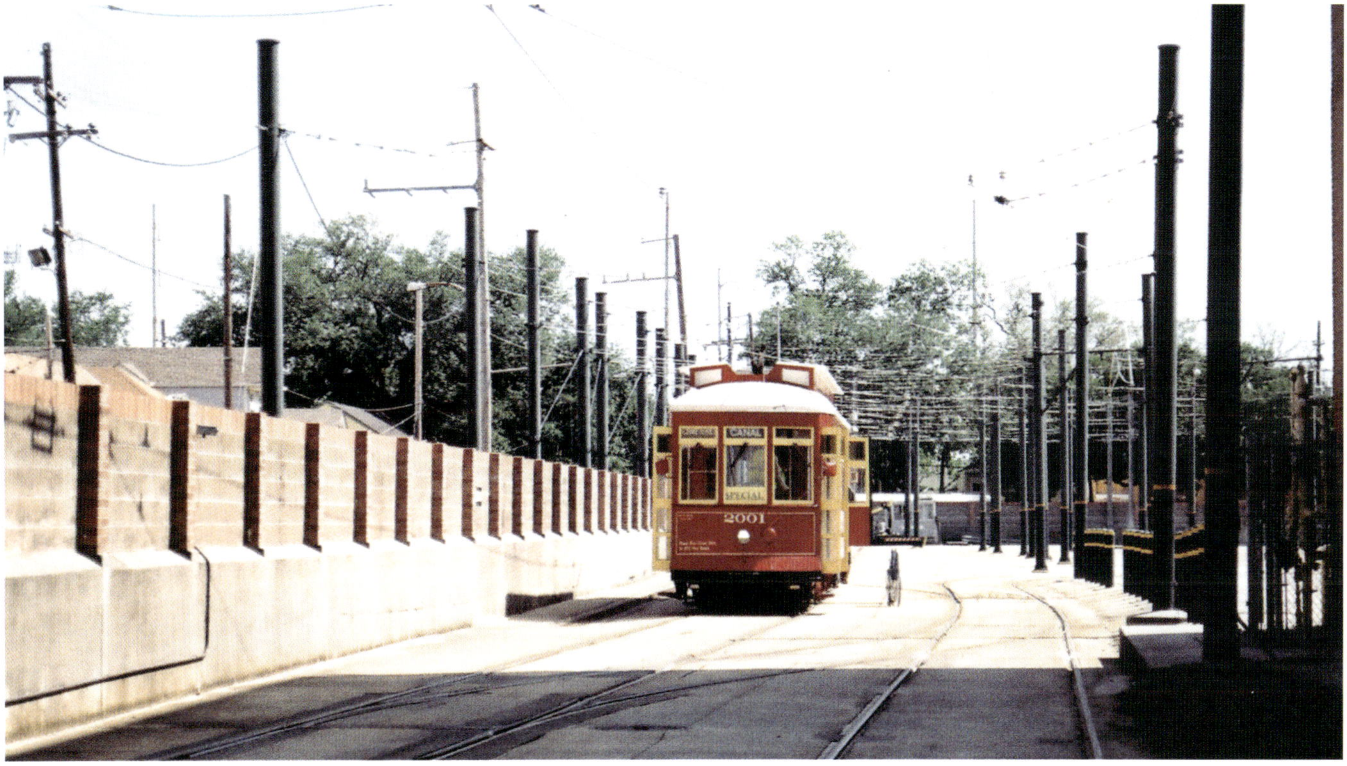

At the Canal Station carbarn on April 22, 2013, RTA streetcar No. 2001 is signed "Special." This carbarn was established in 1861 by the New Orleans City Railroad Company. It became a bus garage after the Canal Street line was converted to bus operation on May 31, 1964. With the return of streetcars on Canal Street on April 18, 2004, the Canal Station carbarn has been restored.

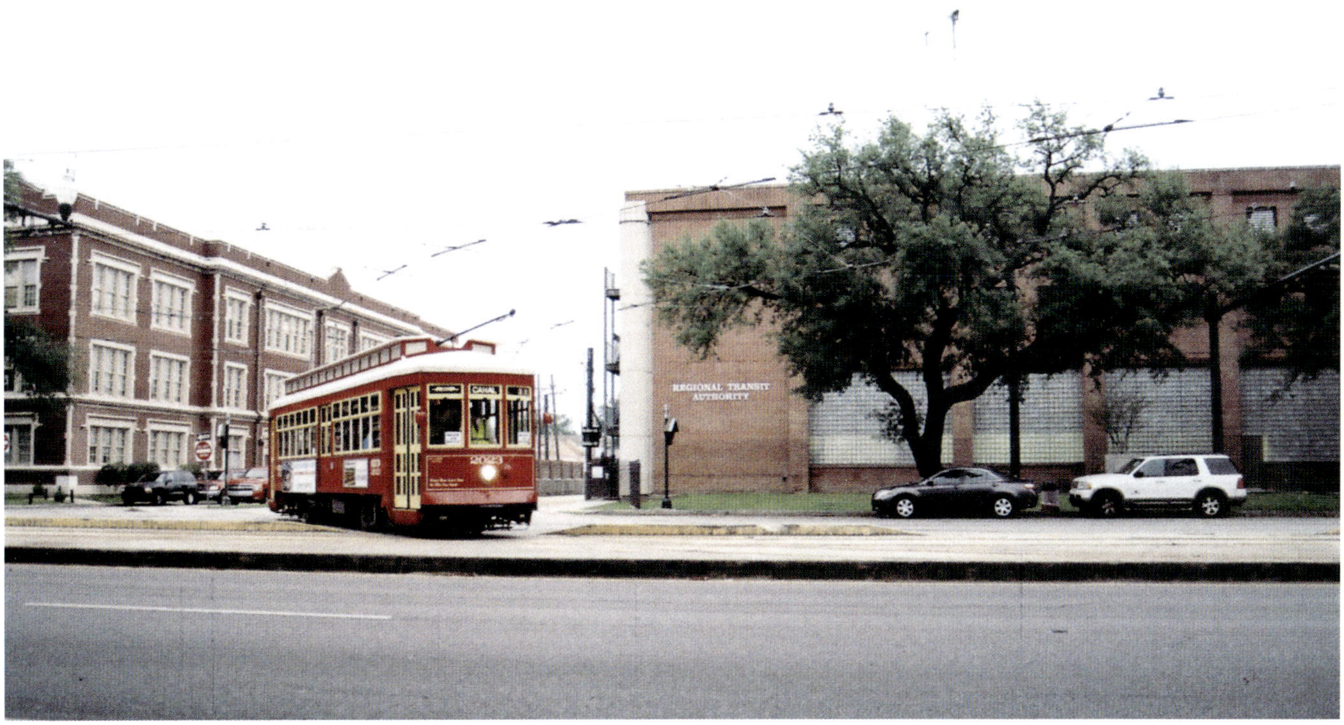

On April 24, 2013, RTA streetcar No. 2023 has pulled out of the Canal Station carbarn yard onto Canal Street, commencing regular service. To the right of the streetcar is the RTA administration building. To the left of the streetcar is the Warren Easton Senior High School.

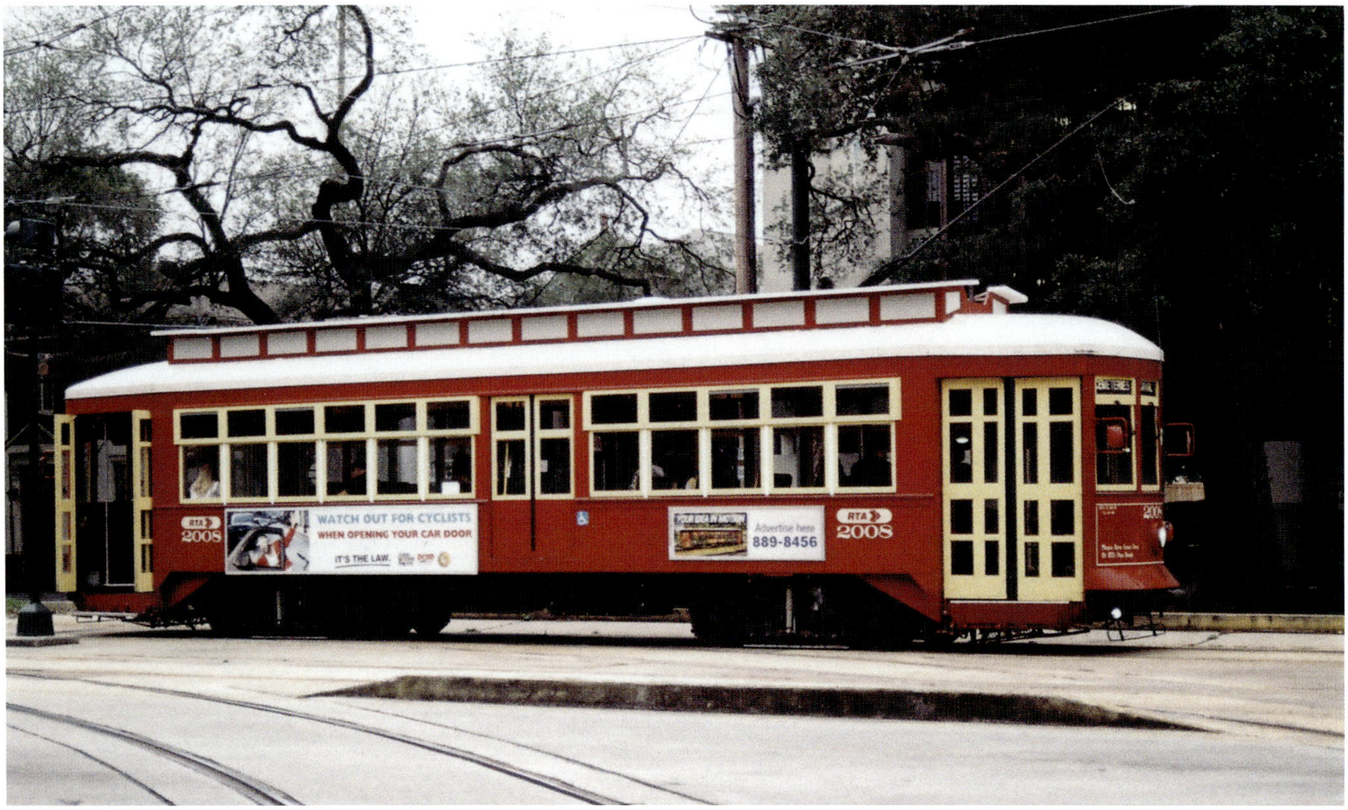

RTA streetcar No. 2008 is on Canal Street passing the access trackage into the Canal Station carbarn near North Gayoso Street on April 24, 2013.

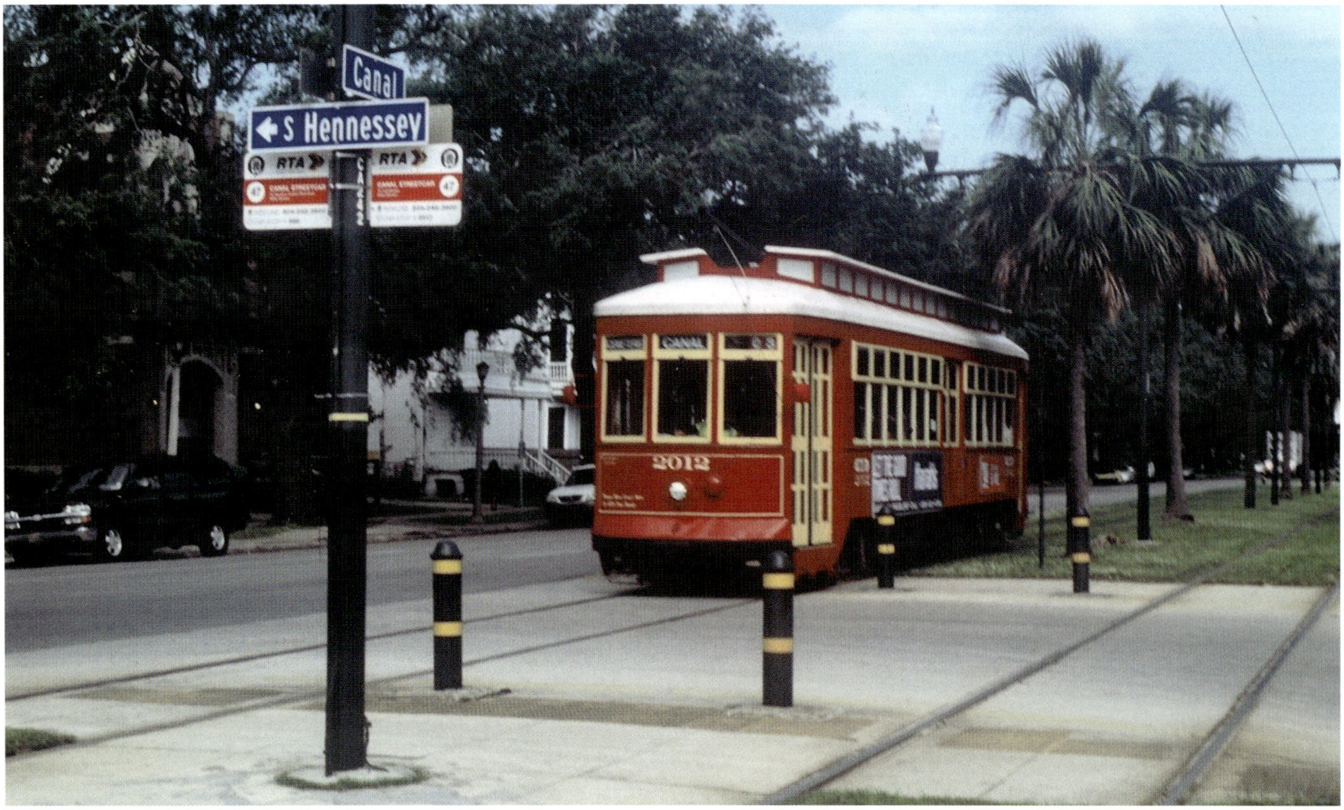

Along the picturesque reserved right of way of Canal Street, RTA streetcar No. 2012 is crossing South Hennessey Street in the Mid-City neighbourhood of New Orleans on April 21, 2013. To the left is South Hennessey Street and to the right is North Hennessey Street.

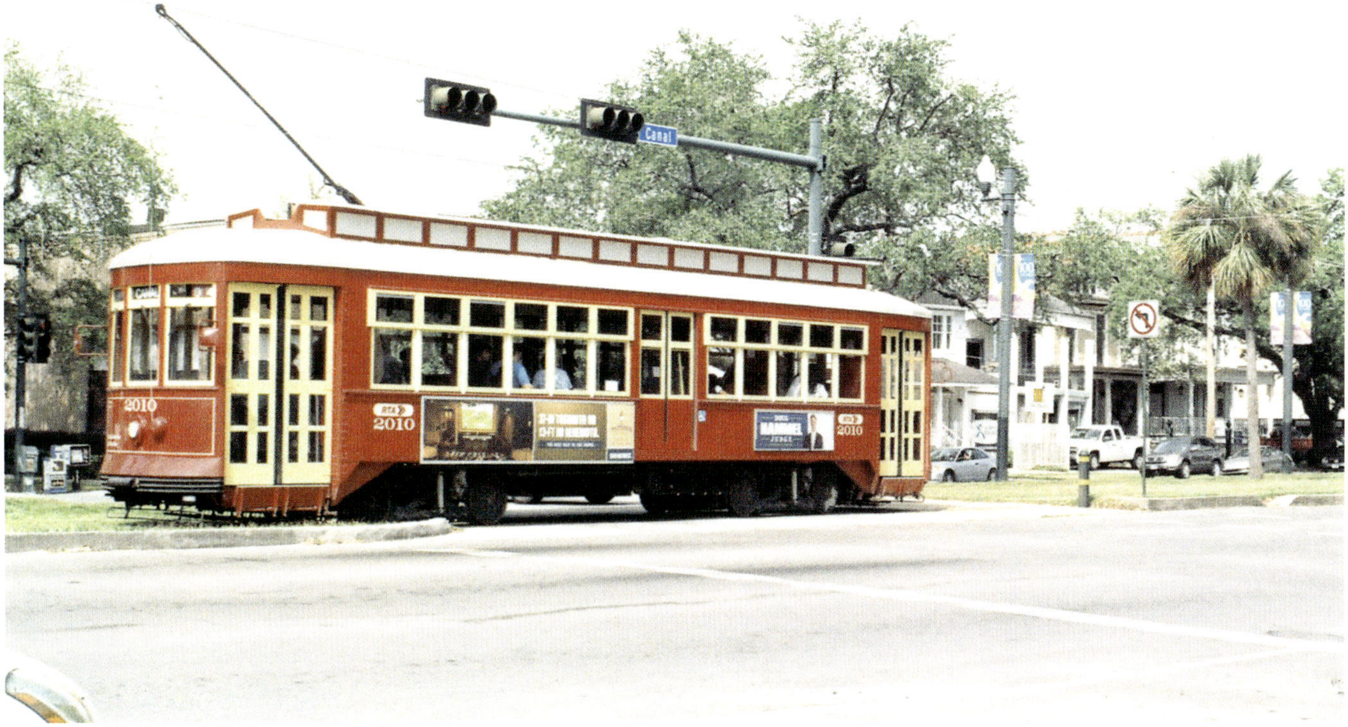

Amid the grass-covered private right of way in the center of Canal Street, on April 22, 2013, RTA streetcar No. 2010 is in the Mid-City center of New Orleans crossing Jefferson Davis Parkway. The Parkway was named for Jefferson Davis who served as the United States Secretary of War under President Franklin Pierce, and was President of the Confederate States of America from 1861 until its collapse in 1865. Davis died in the Garden District of New Orleans during a visit in 1889.

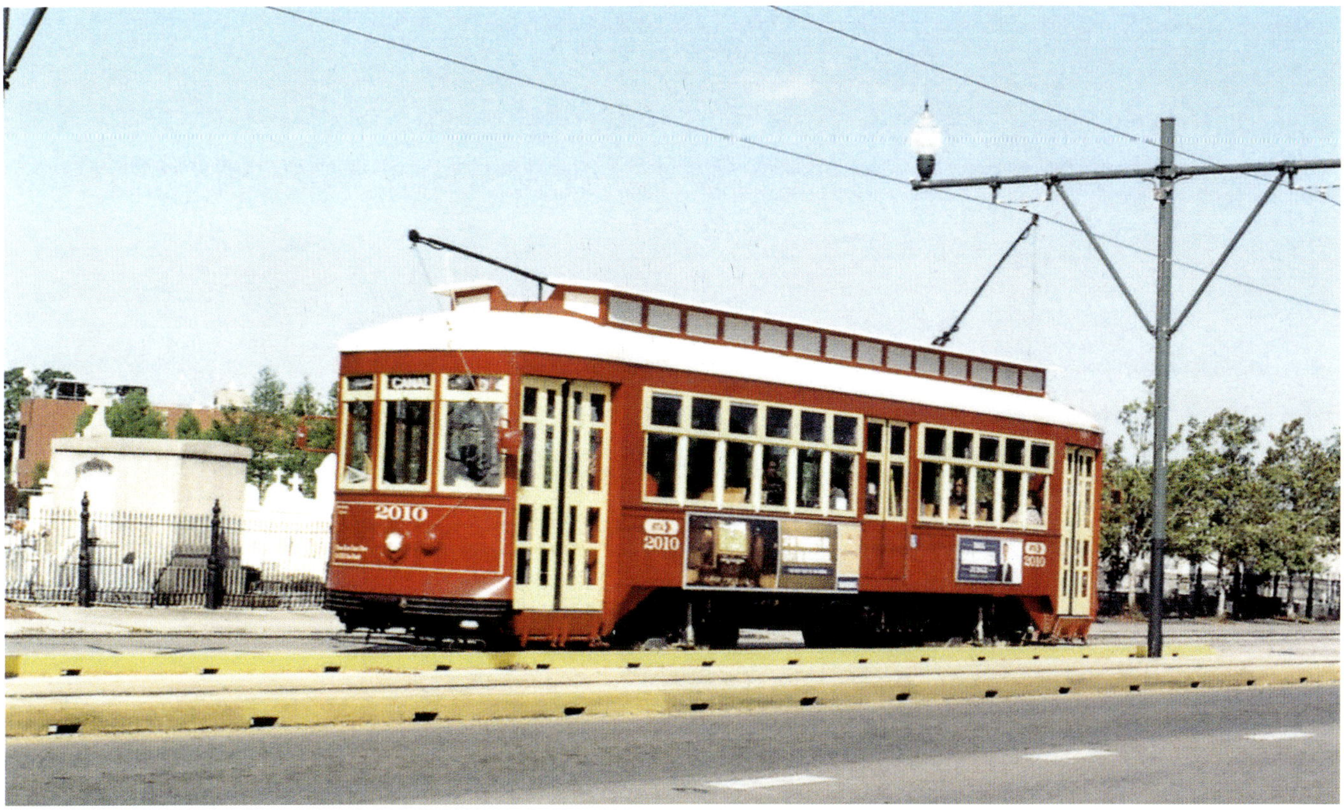

On the reserved private right of way in Canal Street, on April 22, 2013, RTA streetcar No. 2010 has just left the Cemeteries terminus at City Park Avenue heading for the Central Business District. Towards the left are the above-ground cemetery tombs.

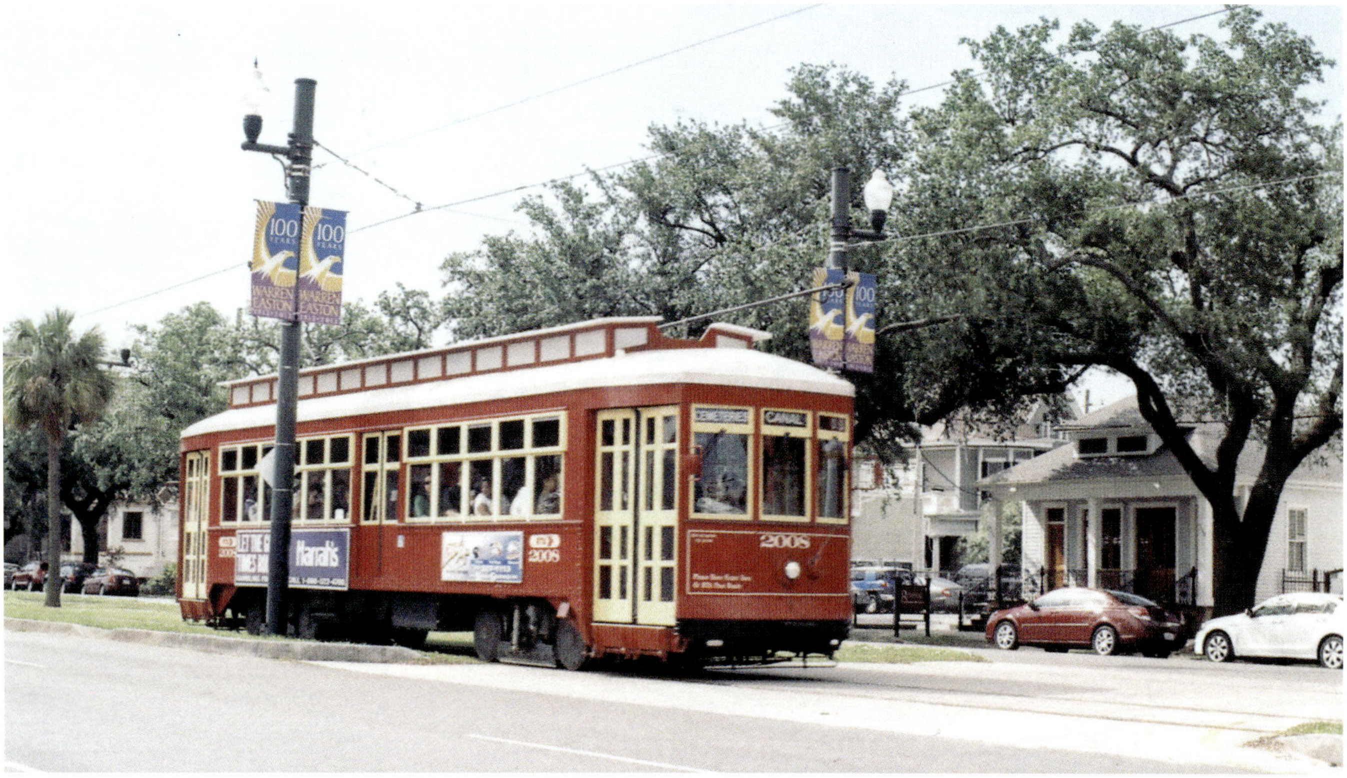

RTA streetcar No. 2008 is on Canal Street near South Carrollton Avenue handling a trip to the Cemeteries terminus near City Park Avenue on April 22, 2013. The pole that serves to support the overhead streetcar wire and lamp post has a banner proclaiming the 100-year anniversary of the Warren Easton Senior High School, which opened on September 16, 1913 on Canal Street at Gayoso Street (next to the Canal streetcar barn).

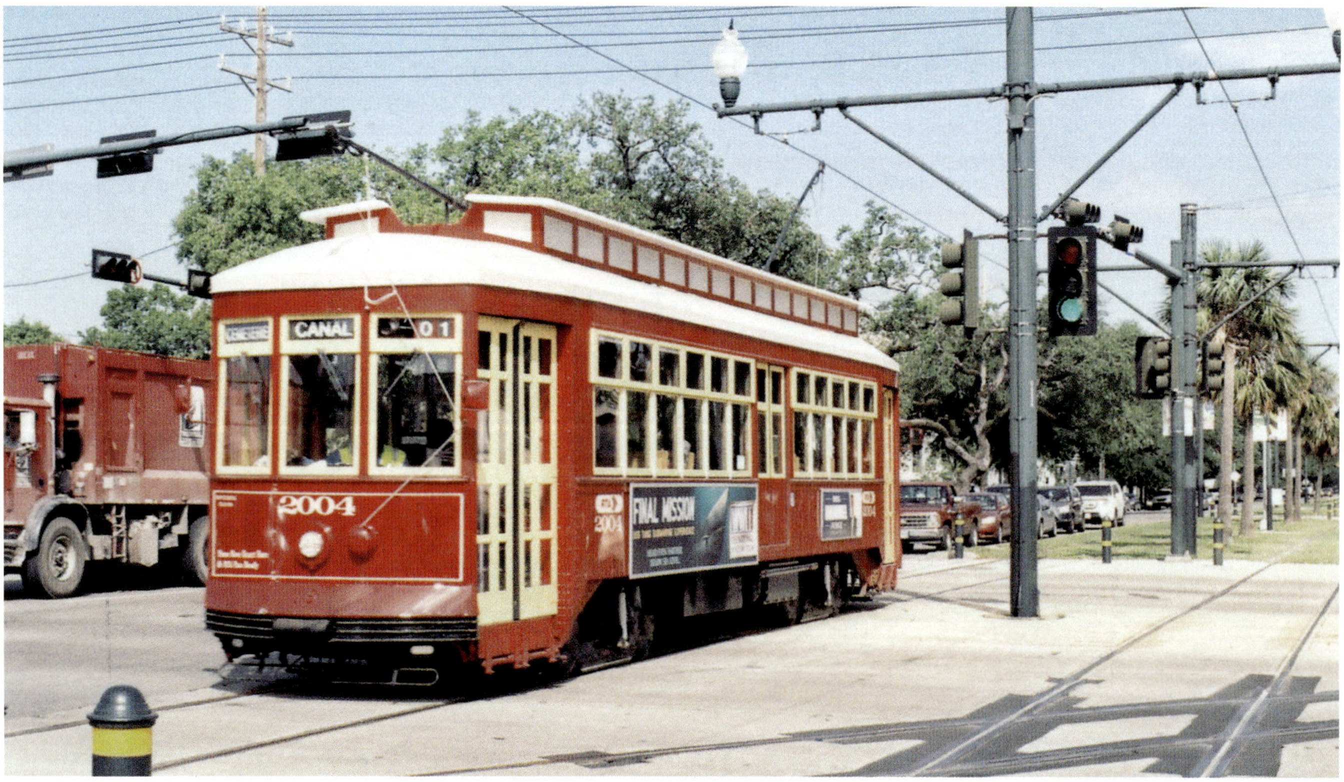

RTA streetcar No. 2004 on April 22, 2013 is on Canal Street crossing North Carrollton Avenue, which is a junction point with the line that runs via North Carrollton Avenue to City Park and the Museum of Art.

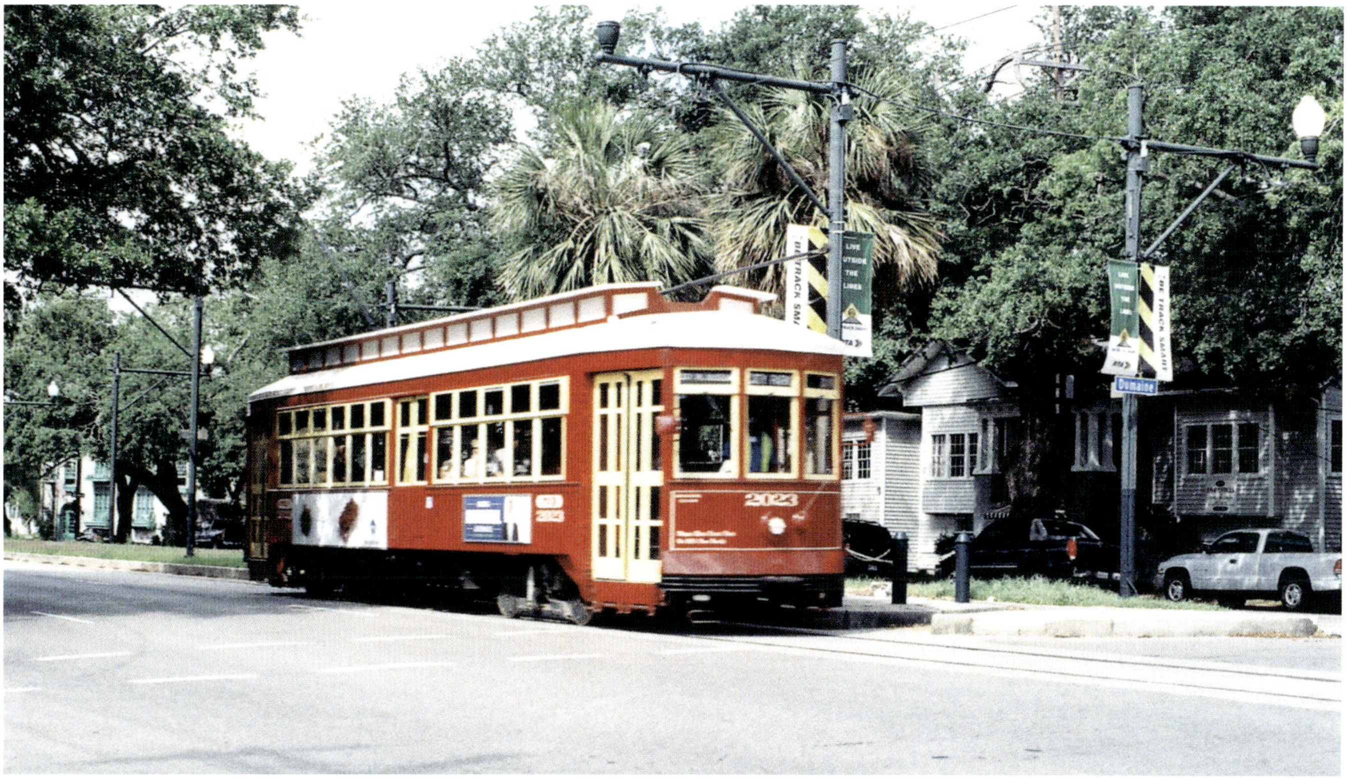

RTA streetcar No. 2023 is on North Carrollton Avenue at Dumaine Street on April 23, 2013 heading for the City Park terminus.

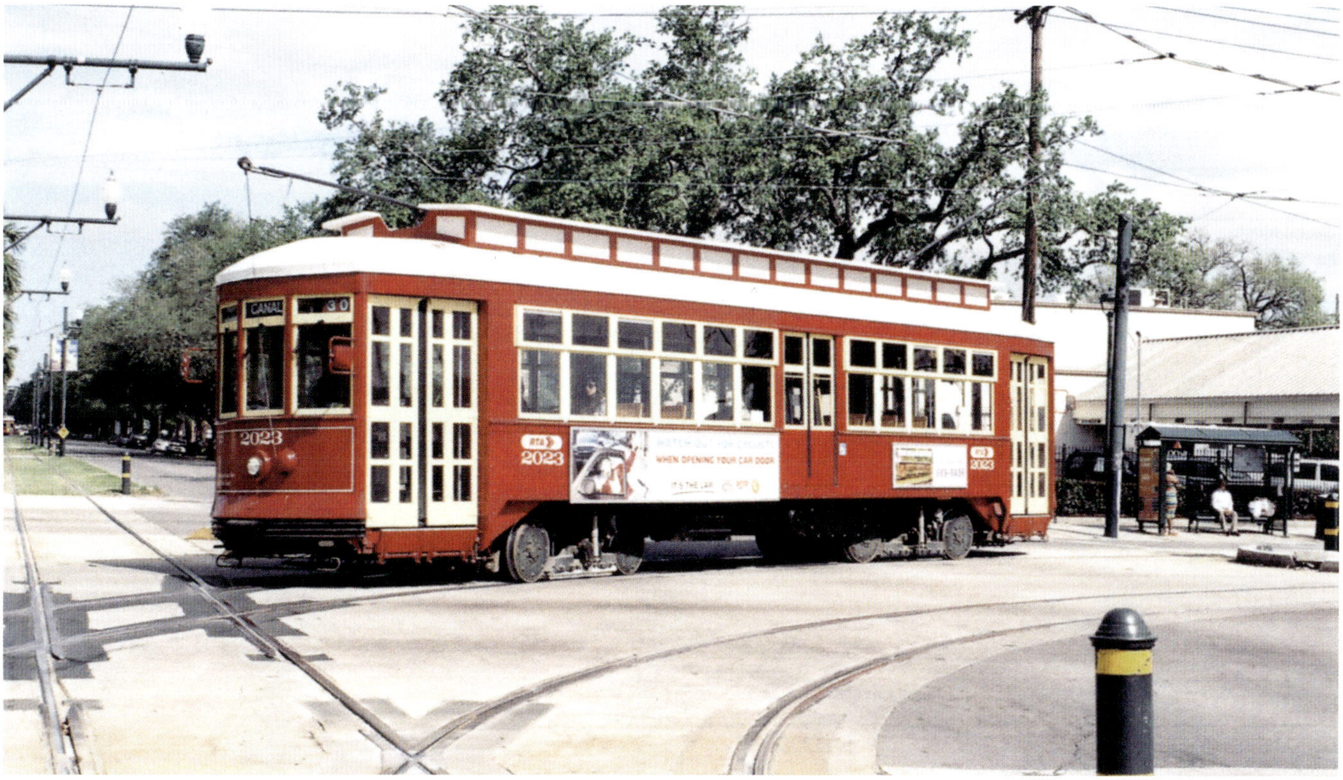

On April 22, 2013, RTA streetcar No. 2023 is turning from North Carrollton Avenue onto Canal Street. North Carrollton Avenue from Canal Street to City Park never had streetcar service until Canal streetcar service was restored on April 18, 2004.

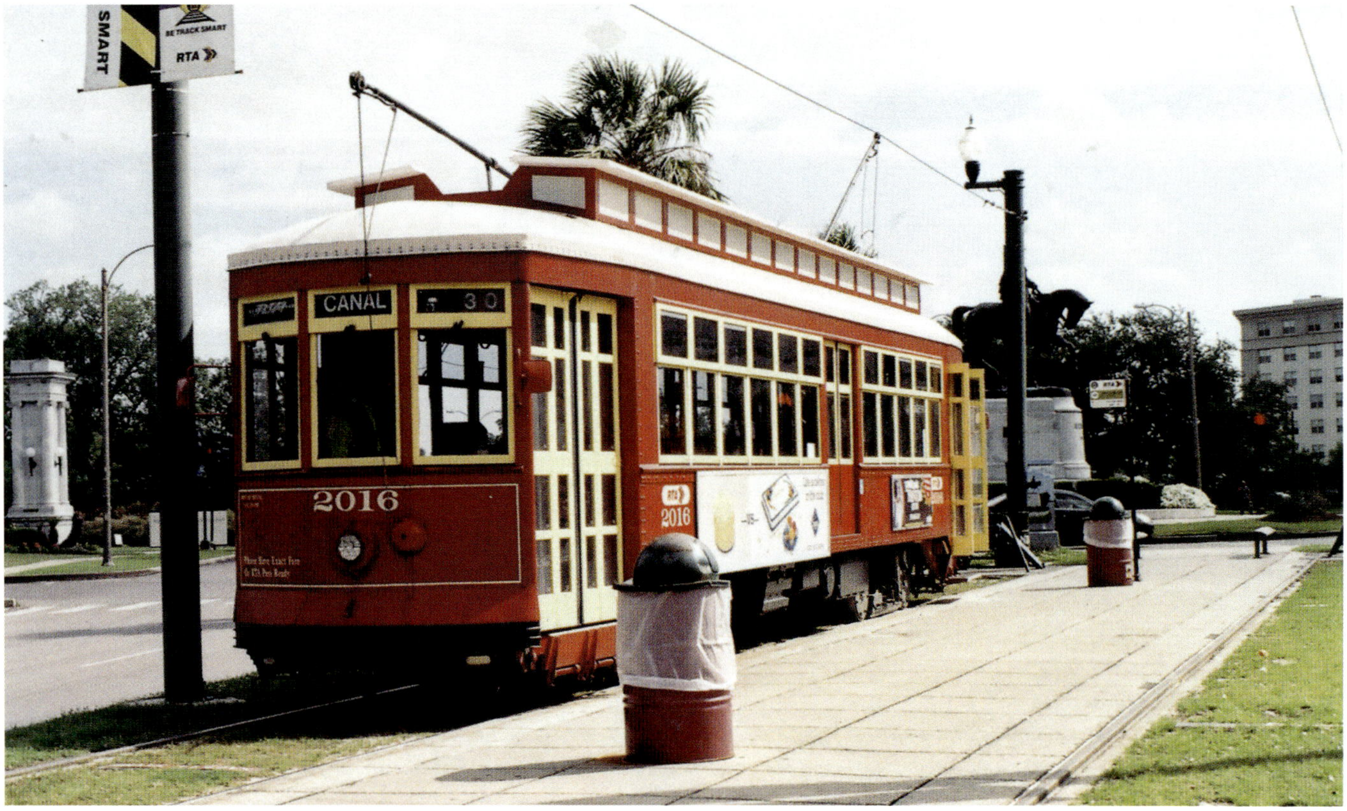

On North Carrollton Avenue at the City Park Avenue terminus in the City Park neighborhood of New Orleans, RTA streetcar No. 2016 is awaiting departure time, as shown on April 23, 2013.

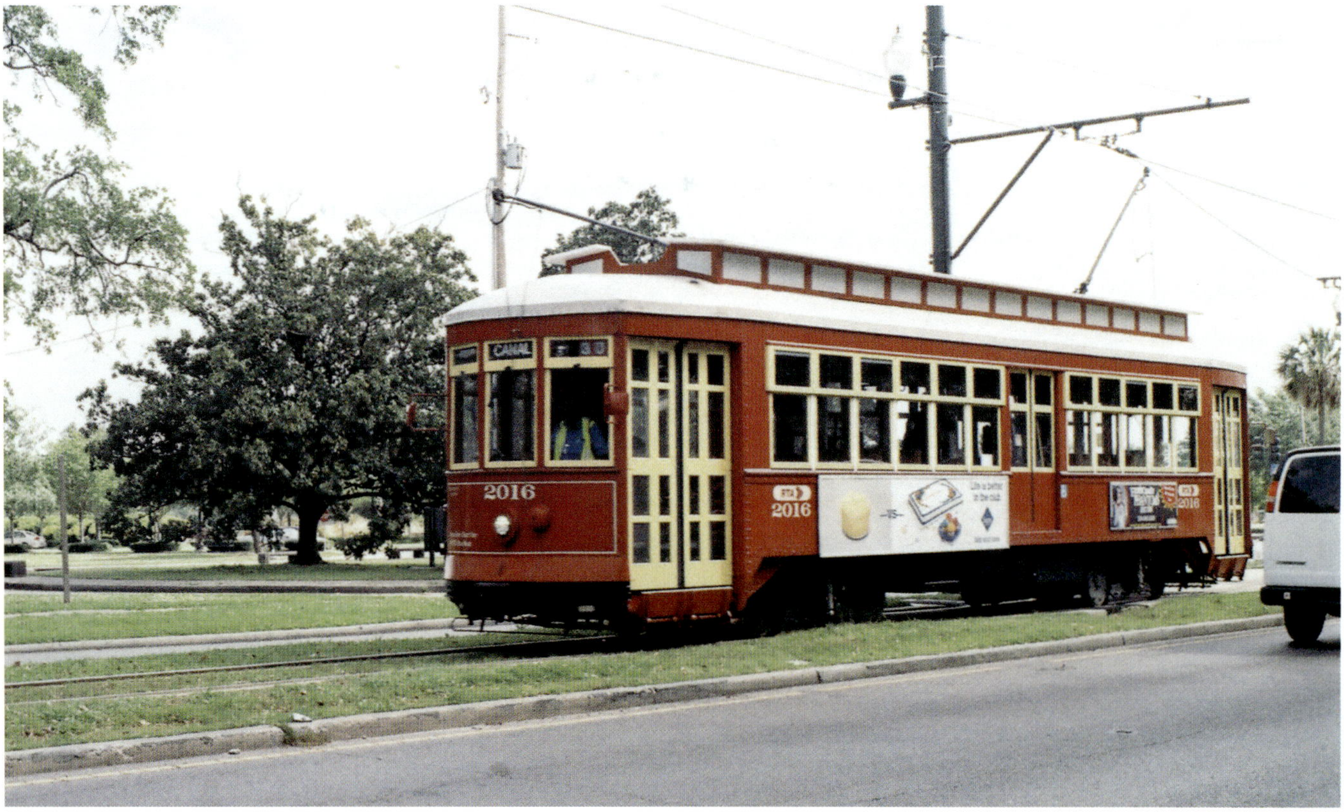

On April 23, 2013, RTA streetcar No. 2016 is on the grass-covered reserved right of way on North Carrollton Avenue, having just left the City Park Avenue terminus, which also serves the New Orleans Museum of Art.

Chapter 2

St. Charles Streetcar Line

The 6.6 mile St. Charles line has streetcars running on ten blocks of Carondelet Street, one block of Canal Street, and ten blocks of St. Charles Avenue in the Central Business District. After it passes Lee Circle, it operates on the grass-covered center median known as the "neutral ground" of St. Charles Avenue and continues through the Garden District passing Loyola University, Tulane University, and Audubon Park. As it nears the Mississippi River, it turns onto the "neutral ground" of South Carrollton Avenue and ends at South Claiborne Avenue. Starting February 19, 1900, the St. Charles line operated as a belt line from the foot of Canal Street using Canal, Baronne, Howard, St. Charles, Carrolton, Tulane, South Rampart and Canal to the foot of Canal.

Beginning in 1930, the line no longer operated to the foot of Canal Street. On March 6, 1947, St. Charles Belt cars turned from Tulane to South Liberty to reach Canal Street. Effective January 8, 1951, the St. Charles line reverted to operate from Canal to St. Charles and Carrollton to Dixon Street. On August 10, 1952, the line was cut back to South Carrollton and South Claiborne, which is still the same terminus in 2013. In April 1960, the fare was increased from seven to ten cents and, on January 26, 1970, it was increased from ten to fifteen cents.

The St. Charles line was added to the United States National Register of Historic Places on August 4, 1973. The New Orleans Regional Transit Authority (RTA) on July 1, 1983 acquired the New Orleans Public Service Inc. bus and streetcar system. On December 9, 1984, the St. Charles line was designated a National Historic Mechanical Engineering Landmark by the American Society of Mechanical Engineers.

Between 1988 and 1992, the RTA completed a $47 million renovation of the St. Charles line, plus a complete rebuilding of the thirty-five streetcars and the Carrollton Station carbarn and shop. While the streetcars built in 1924 by Perley A. Thomas Car Company have had numerous modifications made over the years, such as installation of roller bearings and an aluminum roof in place of the original canvas roof, they have retained their dark green painted car body and operate true to their original design. The rebuilt cars are better than new and have been well maintained. This is not a museum operation; it is a real transit line handling thousands of daily commuters and visitors.

On August 29, 2005, Hurricane Katrina caused severe wind damage, with falling trees taking out many sections of trolley wire along St. Charles Avenue. Fortunately, the cars stored for this line at the Carrollton Station carbarn escaped flood damage. A 1.2 mile section of the St. Charles line opened from Canal Street to Lee Circle on December 19, 2007, using two cars that operated from 9 a.m. to 6 p.m. every thirteen to twenty-six minutes. Beginning November 11, 2007, St. Charles cars operated from Canal Street to Napoleon Street. Streetcar service was restored for the full length of St. Charles Avenue to the Riverbend on December 23, 2007, and was restored to the end of the line at South Carrollton Avenue and South Claiborne Avenue on June 22, 2008. Given its role in the heritage of New Orleans, the return of the St. Charles line was important, as it helped to return a sense of normalcy to the city for residents and visitors.

As a result of the need to replace the wooden crossties that hold the rails in place, the St. Charles line was shut down in phases, beginning in 2011. During April 2013, St. Charles streetcars operated between Canal Street and Jefferson Avenue, with bus service between Jefferson Avenue and the terminus at South Carrollton Avenue and South Claiborne Avenue. The wooden ties were last replaced during 1988 when the RTA renovated the St. Charles line's streetcars and track. A tropical hardwood known as azobe (coarse textured wood that is resistant to decay) was used for the ties, but a combination of weather and termite damage has contributed to signs of rot, which could result in a safety issue, as the ties serve to support the rails and maintain the track gauge.

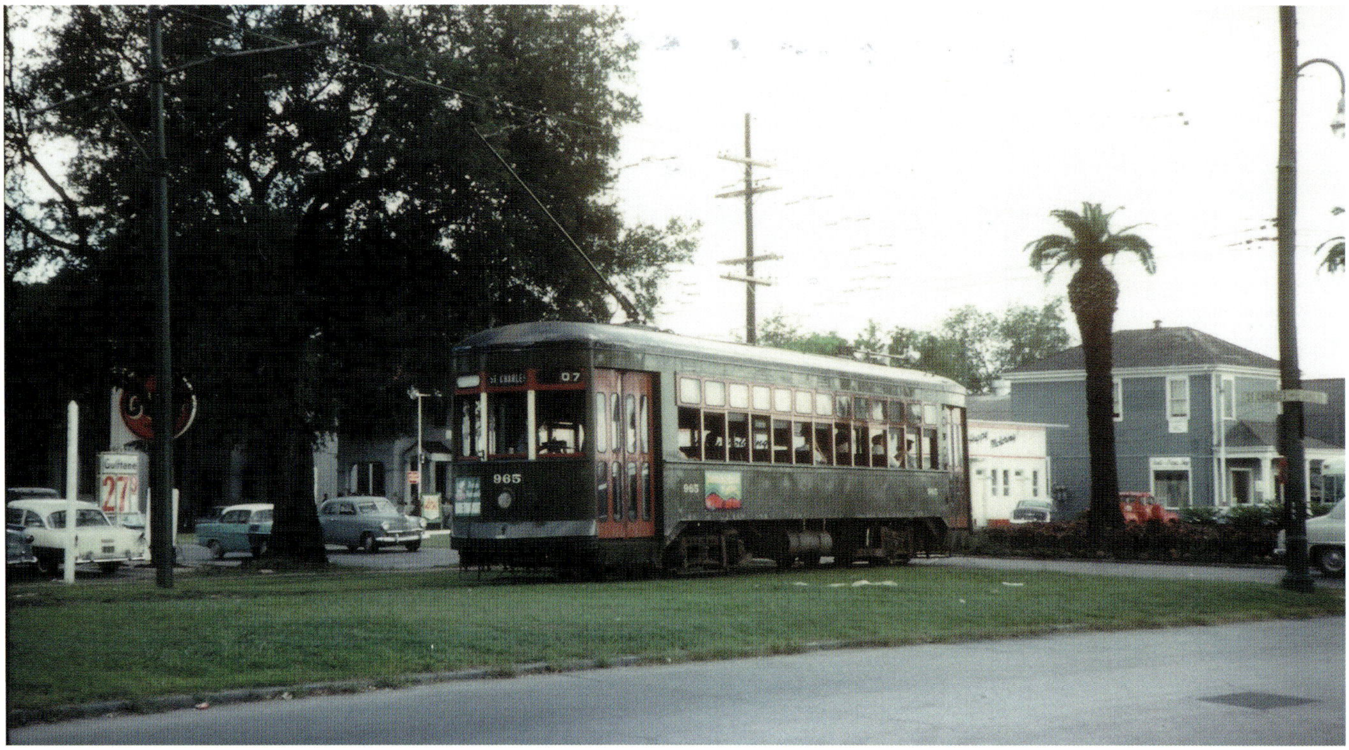

New Orleans Public Service Inc. streetcar No. 965 (weighing 42,036 pounds and powered by two General Electric type 263A motors) is on South Carrollton Avenue ready to make the turn onto St. Charles Avenue, on July 16, 1963. The center median - known locally as "neutral ground" - on St. Charles Avenue and South Carrolton Avenue, is covered with grass flush with the top of the rails. The overhead contact system is trolley wire, powered at 600 volts direct current, suspended primarily by bracket arm construction using center poles.

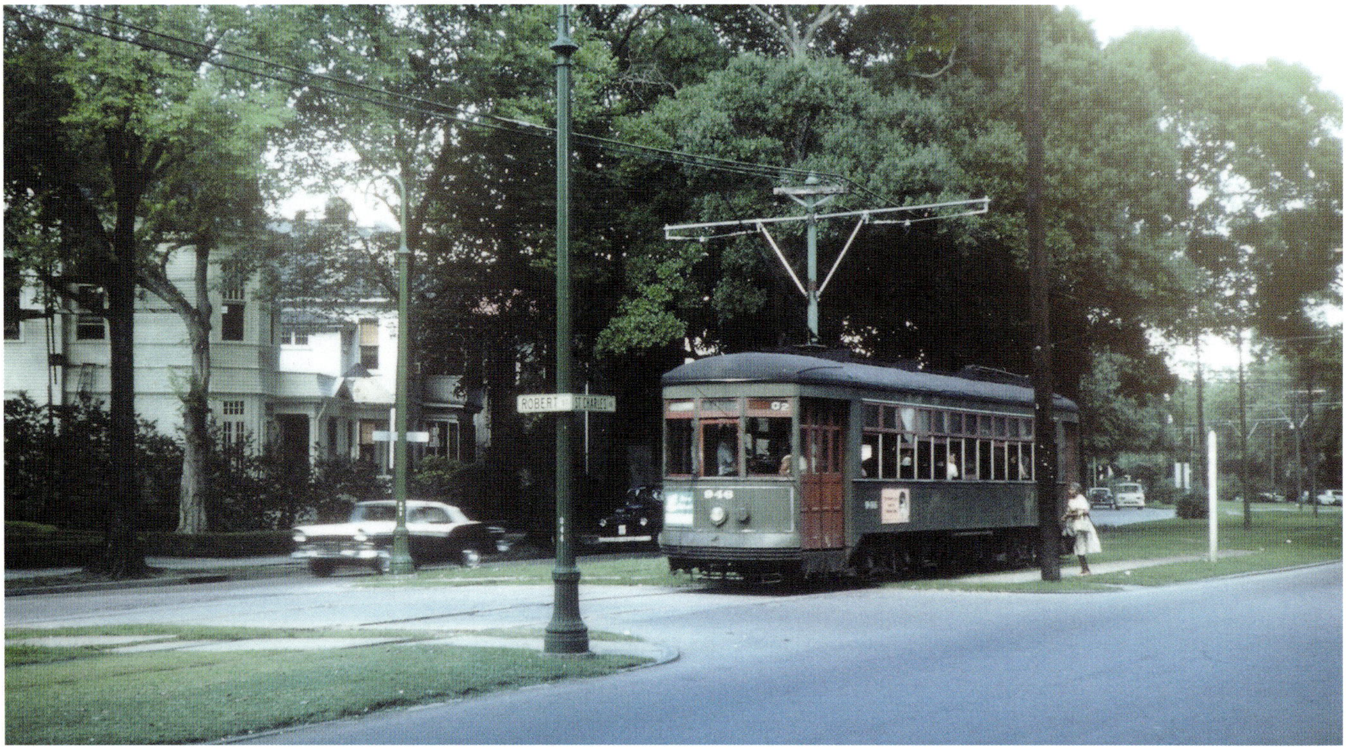

On July 16, 1963, New Orleans Public Service Inc. streetcar No. 946 (weighing 41,148 pounds and powered by two Westinghouse type 306-CV4 motors) is on the grass-covered reserved right of way on St. Charles Avenue at Robert Street, which is in the Uptown neighborhood of New Orleans about five blocks east of Jefferson Avenue. Track gauge (the distance between the inside face of the rails measured 5/8 inch from the top of the rail) is 5 foot 2.5 inches.

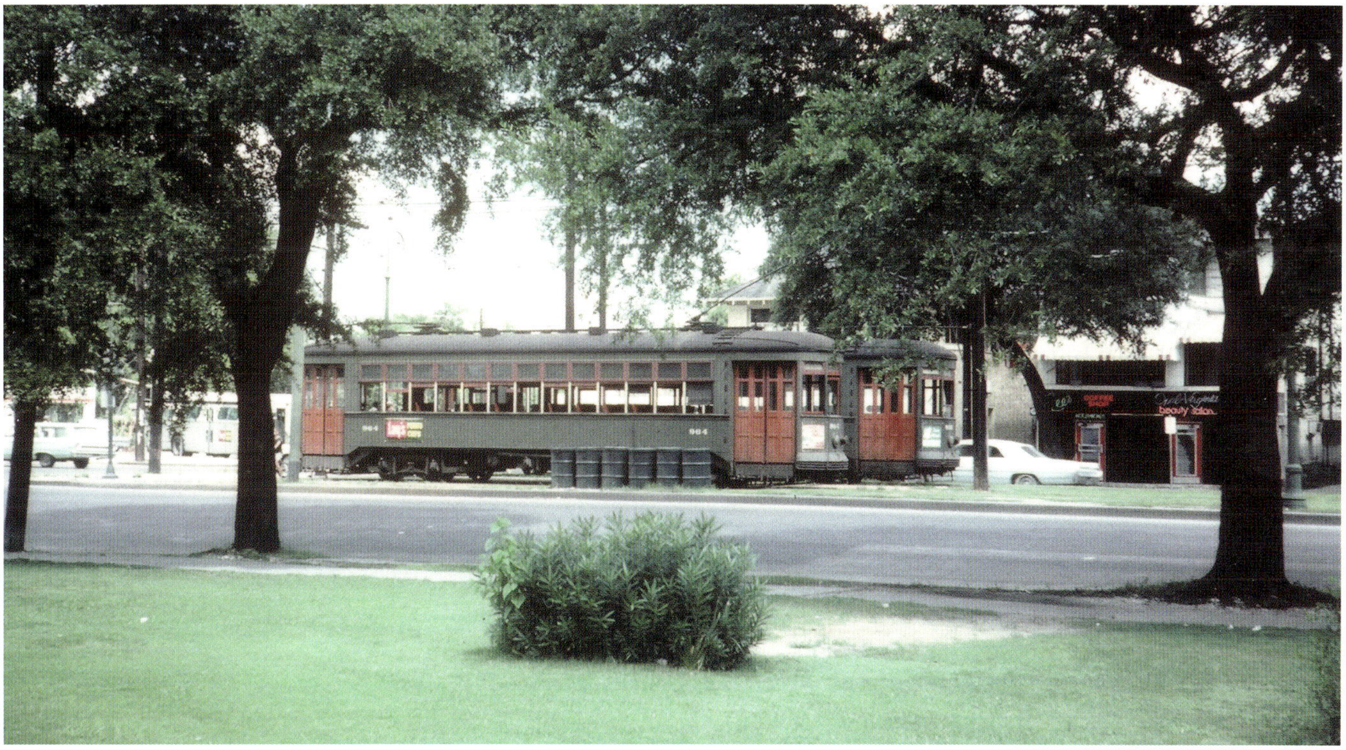

Amid the trees of Lafayette Square, New Orleans Public Service Inc. streetcar No. 964 (weighing 42,036 pounds and powered by two General Electric type 263A motors) is passing by on St. Charles Avenue, July 16, 1963. Lafayette Square was named after Gilbert du Motier, marquis de La Fayette, a French general who fought on the American side in the American Revolutionary War. The square was designed in 1788 by Charles Laveau Trudeau, general surveyor of Louisiana under the Spanish government.

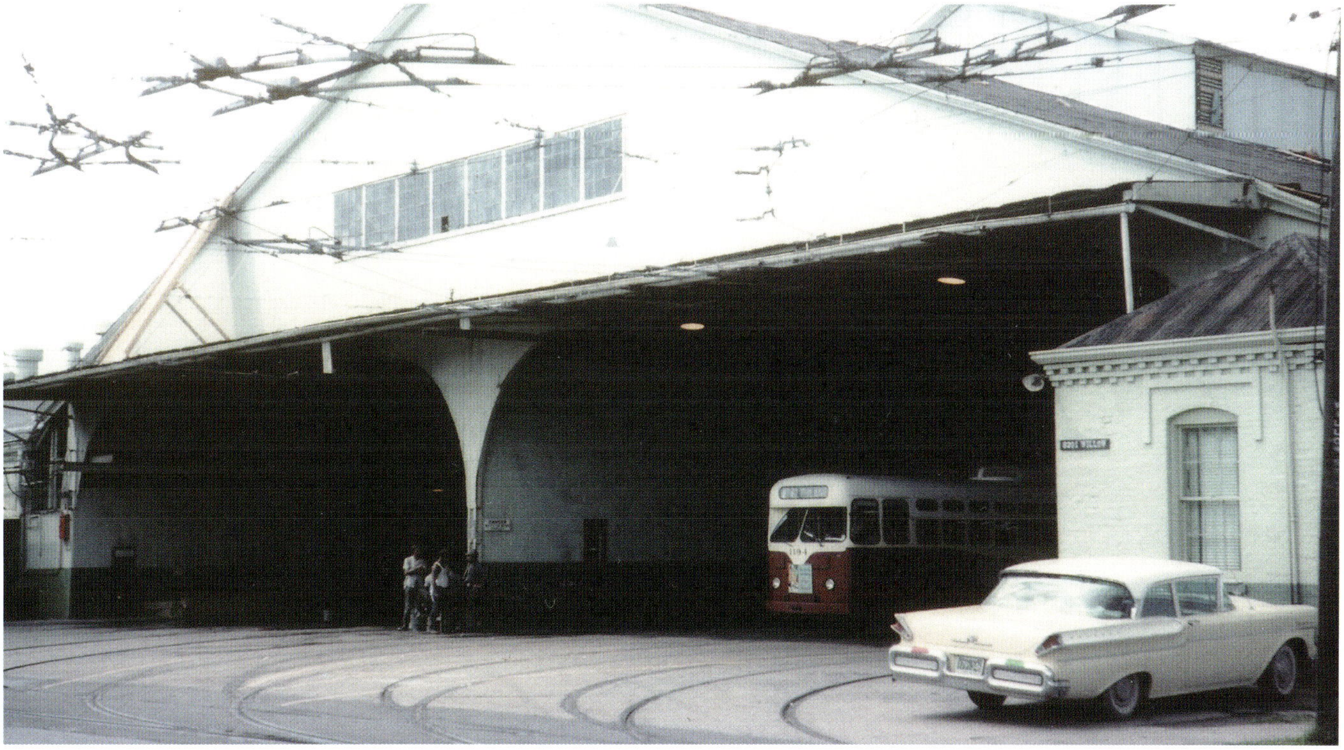

Trackless trolley No. 1194 is at the Willow Street also known as Carrollton Station carbarn on July 16, 1963. A trackless trolley is an electric bus that does not run on track but has two poles, each contacting one of the two parallel overhead wires. The last trackless trolley routes in New Orleans were: St. Claude, converted to bus July 22, 1962; Freret, converted to bus June 10, 1963; City Park, converted to bus December 13, 1964; and Tulane, converted to bus December 27, 1964.

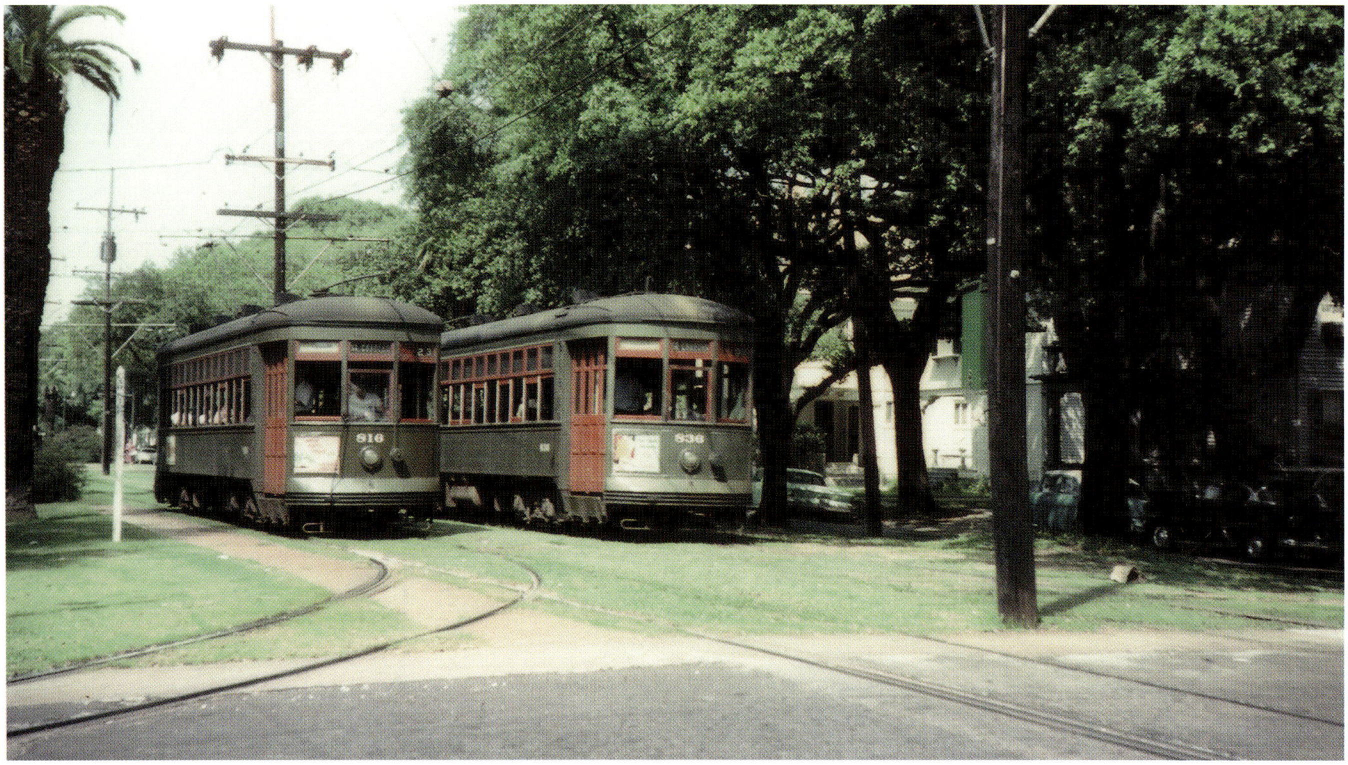

On July 16, 1963, New Orleans Public Service Inc. streetcar No. 816 is passing streetcar No. 836 on South Carrollton Avenue. The track going off to the left is for access to the Carrollton Station carbarn. Streetcars numbered 800 to 831 and 852 to 894 were built by the J.G. Brill Car Company in 1922. Streetcars numbered 832 to 851 and 895 to 899 were built by Perley A. Thomas Car Company in 1922 followed, by streetcars numbered 900 to 972 during 1923-24.

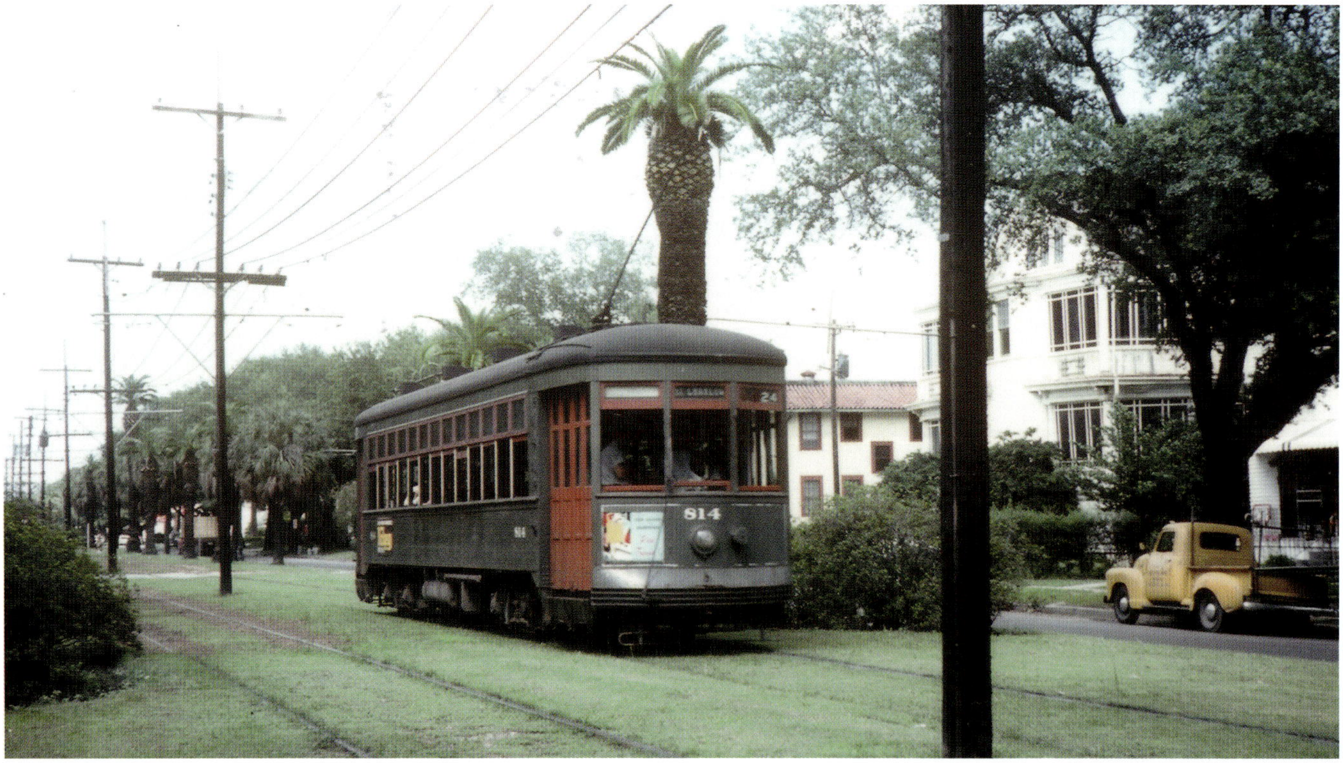

New Orleans Public Service Inc. streetcar No. 814 is on the wide, grass-covered median strip of South Carrollton Avenue on July 16, 1963. Each of the 800 series streetcars had two sixty-five horsepower Westinghouse type 306-CV4 motors, weighed 41,148 pounds, and the four-panel folding doors at each entranceway opened manually.

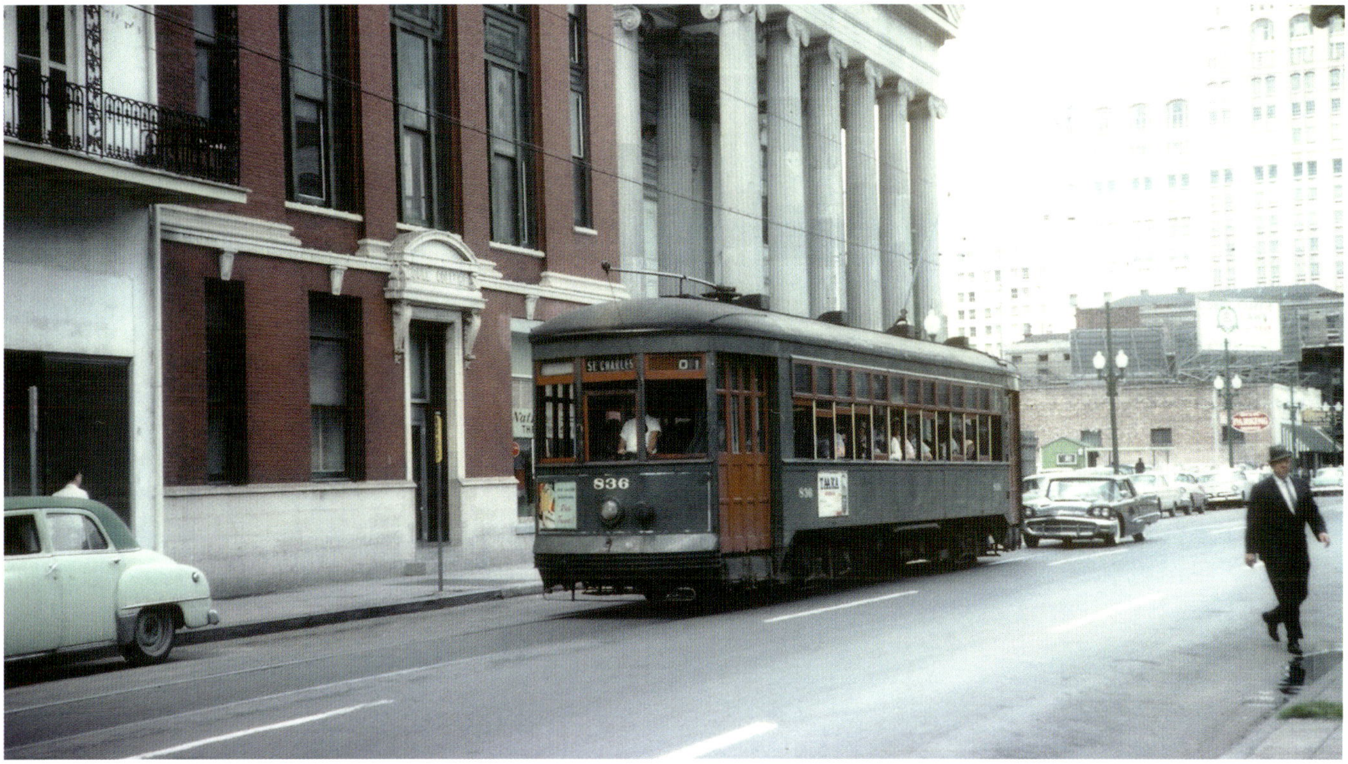

On July 16, 1963, New Orleans Public Service Inc. streetcar No. 836 is on St. Charles Avenue at Lafayette Street passing Gallier Hall with its six front (fluted Greek architectural style) columns named in honor of its architect James Gallier. Managed by the City of New Orleans, the building was dedicated on May 10, 1853 and served as city hall until the mid-1950s. Streetcar No. 836 has been preserved at the Connecticut Trolley Museum at East Windsor, Connecticut.

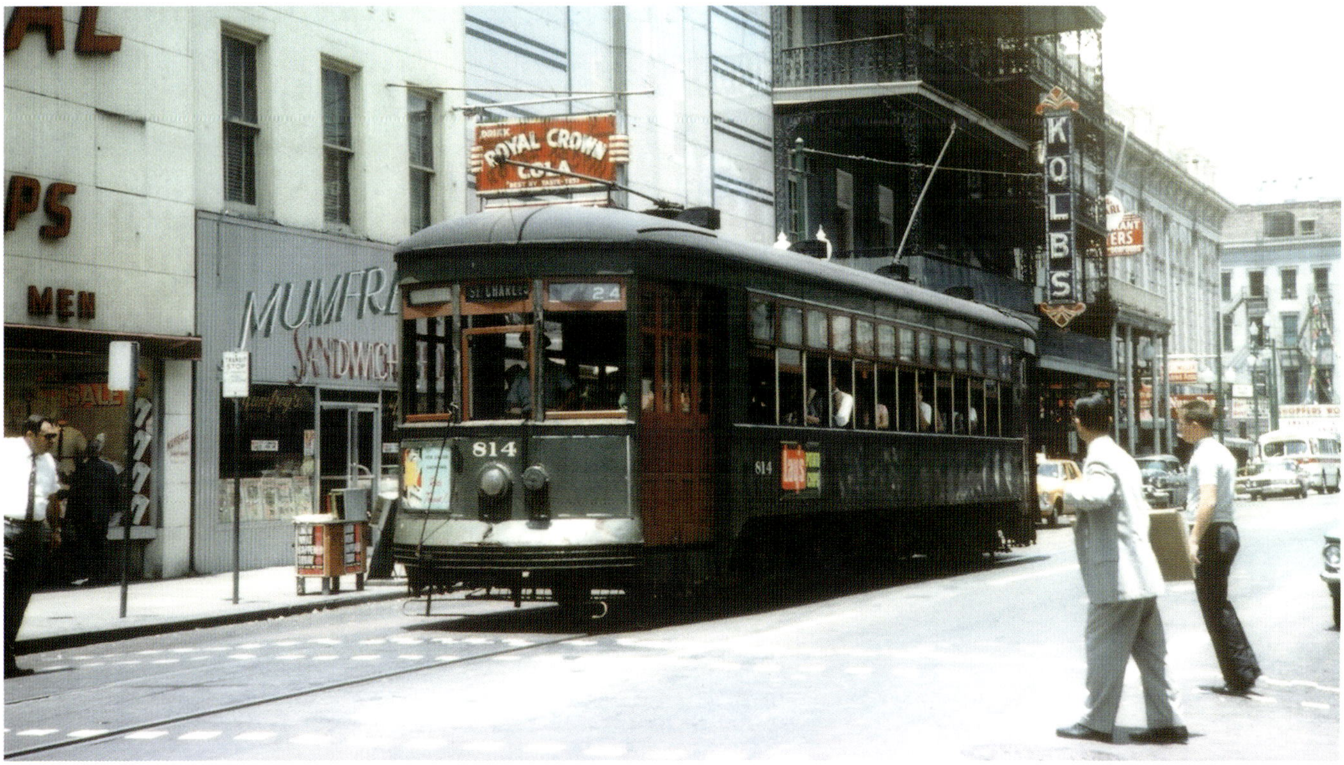

New Orleans Public Service Inc. streetcar No. 814 is approaching a passenger stop on St. Charles Avenue west of Canal Street on July 16, 1963. The number 24 (on the upper right hand window when facing the front the streetcar) indicated the order in which the streetcar left the streetcar barn that day. Hence streetcar No. 814 was the twenty-fourth streetcar to leave the streetcar barn that day.

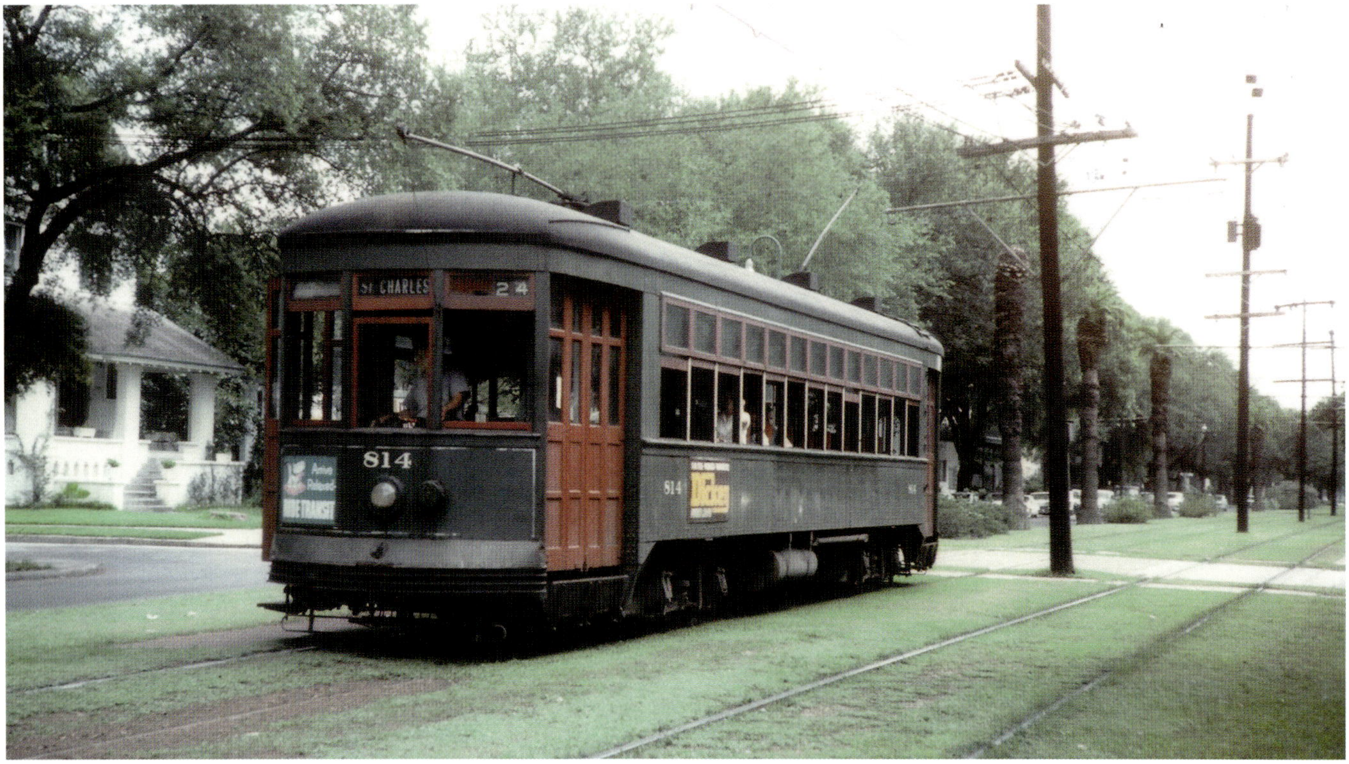

The wide grass-covered private right of way on South Carrollton Avenue provides traffic-free operation for New Orleans Public Service Inc. streetcar No. 814 on July 16, 1963. Operating in the median (neutral) strip in the center of St. Charles Avenue and South Carrollton Avenue, the St. Charles streetcar line is a delightful pleasure to ride in New Orleans.

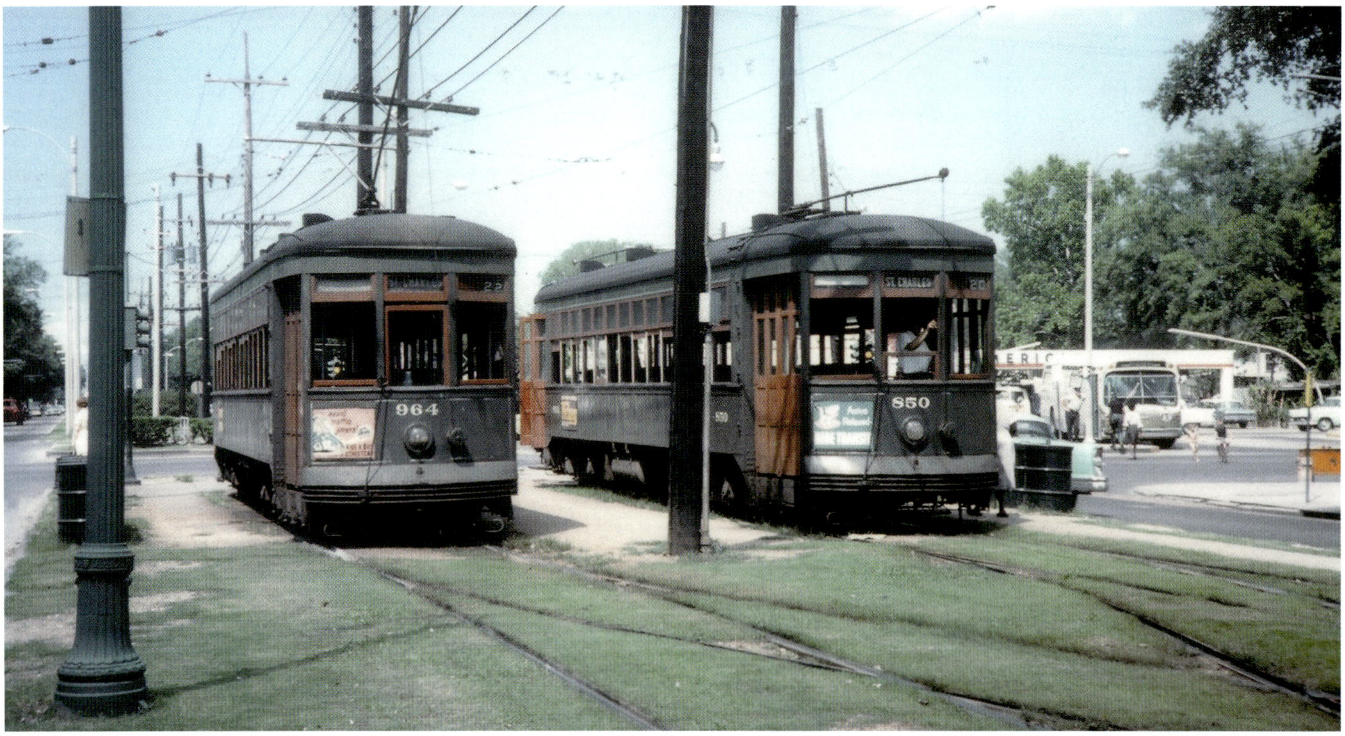

New Orleans Public Service Inc. streetcars Nos. 964 and 850 are at the terminus of the St. Charles line at South Carrollton Avenue and South Claiborne Avenue on July 16, 1963. The 800 and 900 series streetcars each had a steel underframe, steel side panels, wood and canvas roof, Crouse Hinds type ZP headlights, Brill type 76-E2 trucks, thirty-three inch diameter wheels, and five inch diameter axles. Streetcar No. 850 has been preserved at the Shore Line Trolley Museum in East Haven, Connecticut.

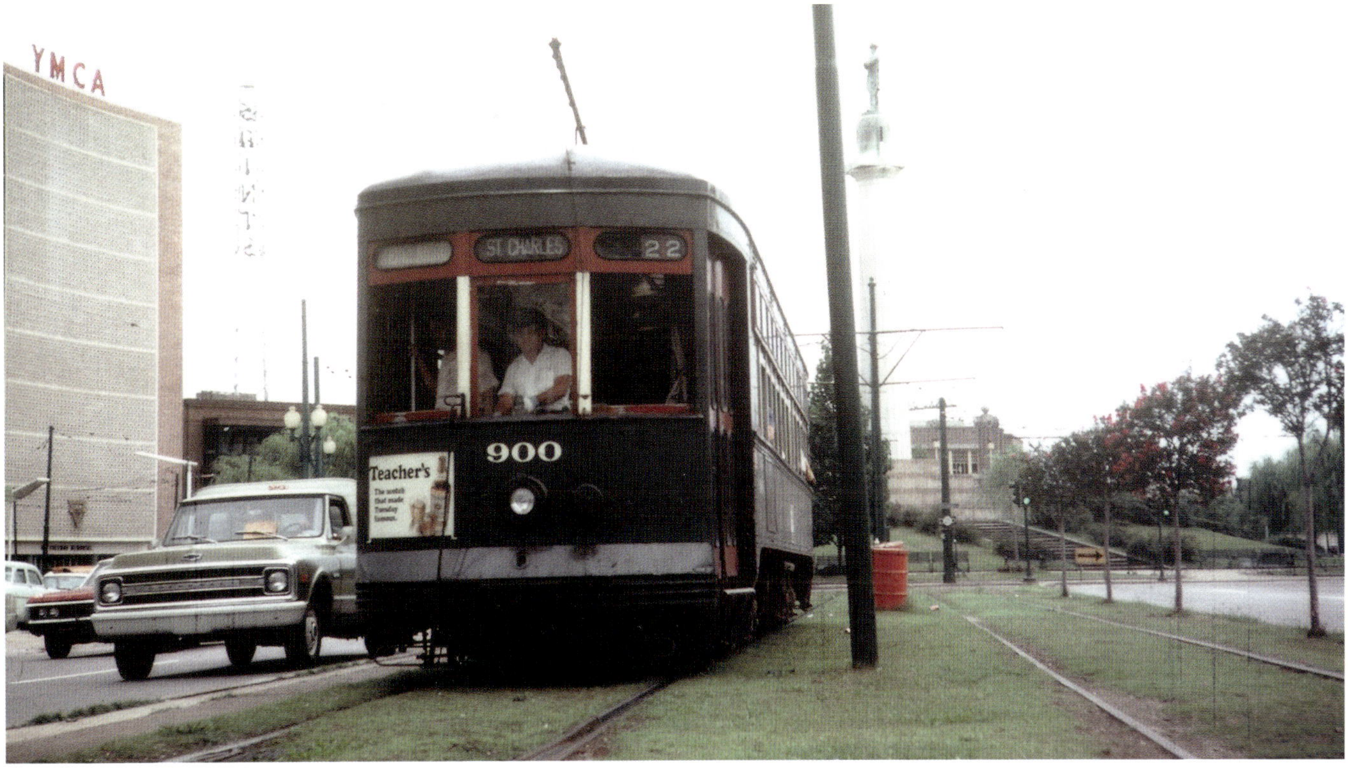

With the Lee Circle Monument in the background and the YMCA on the left, New Orleans Public Service Inc. streetcar No. 900 (originally weighing 42,036 pounds and powered by two General Electric type 263A motors) is on the reserved right of way in the center of Howard Avenue on June 18, 1971. When the Canal line was converted to bus operation on May 31, 1964, some of the 800 series streetcars were donated to museums and the rest were retired. Thirty-five of the best 900 series streetcars were retained for the St. Charles line.

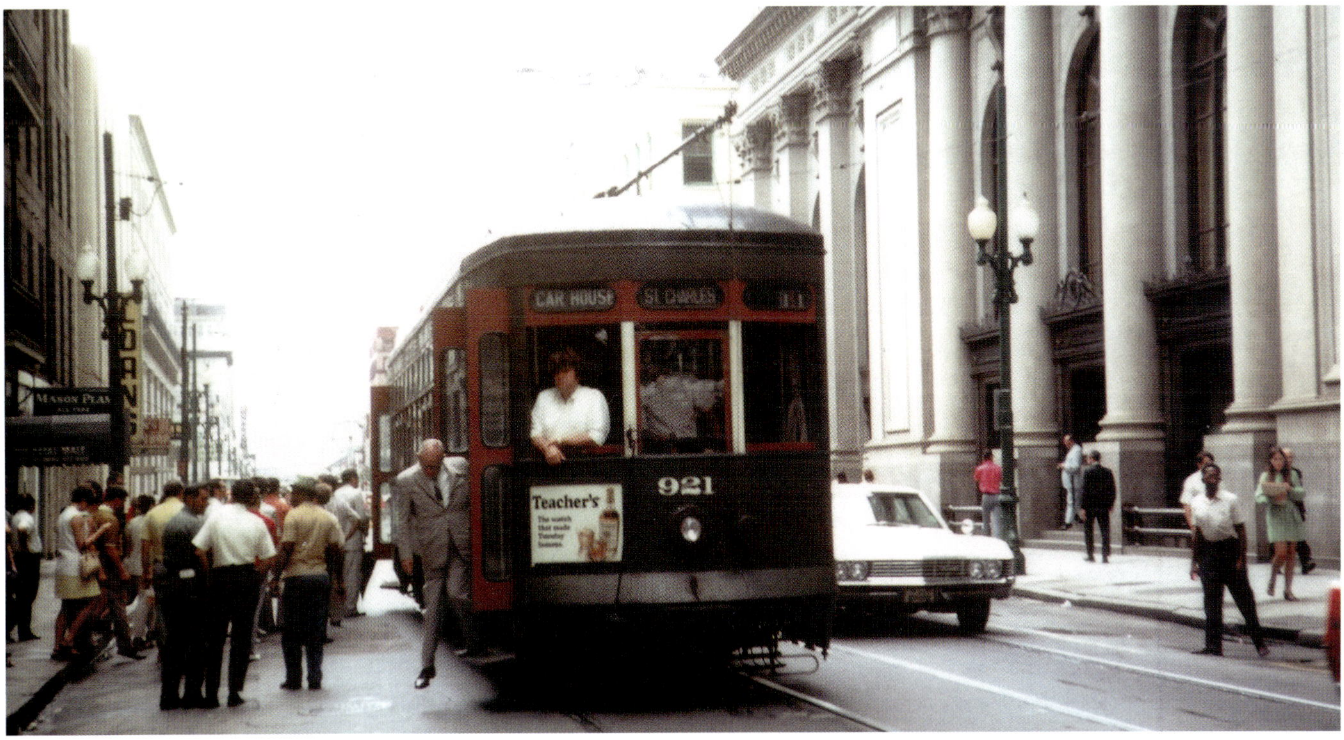

In the Central Business District on June 18, 1971, New Orleans Public Service Inc. streetcar No. 921 has arrived at a busy passenger stop on Carondelet Street at Gravier Street. On the right is the distinctive 23-story Hibernia National Bank building. When it was completed in 1921, this 355 foot high skyscraper was the tallest building in the state of Louisiana, but lost that title in 1932 to the state capitol.

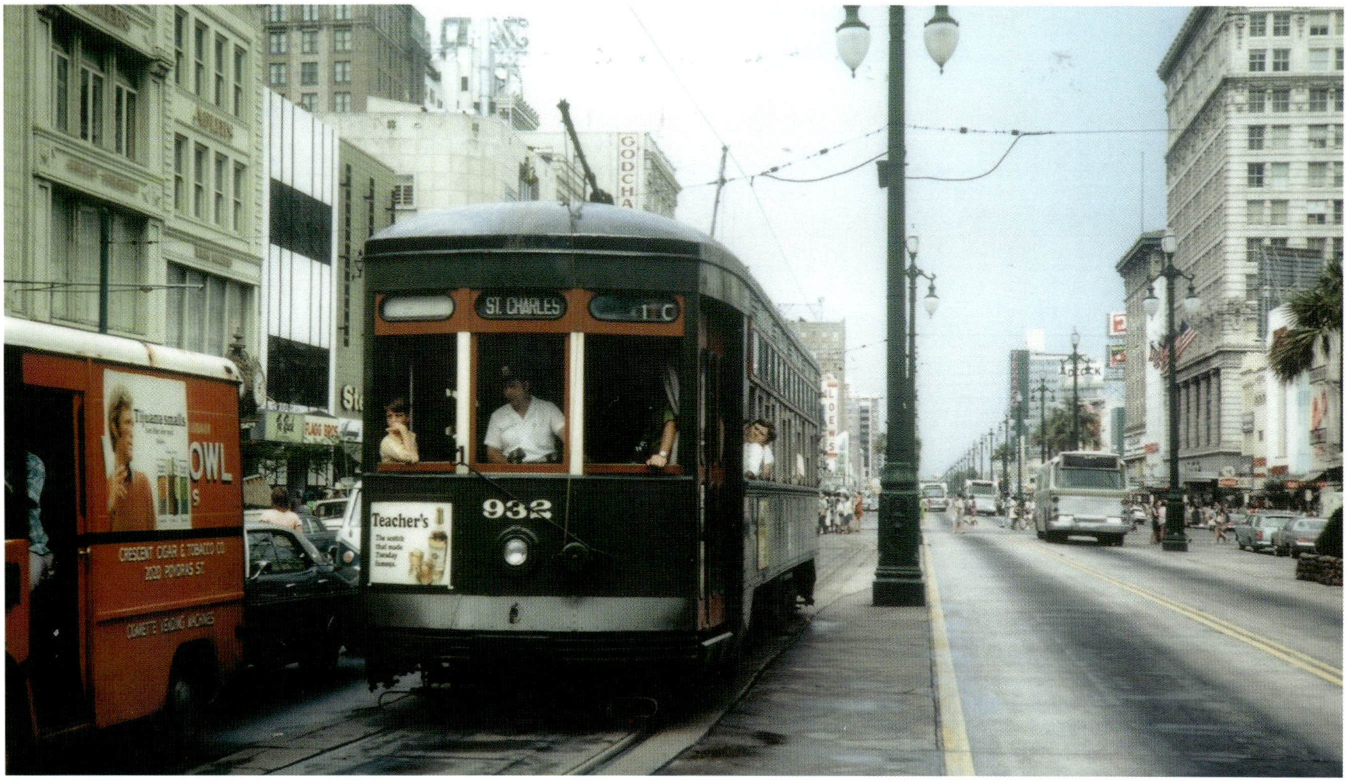

New Orleans Public Service Inc. streetcar No. 932 is on Canal Street, ready to turn onto St. Charles Avenue, on June 18, 1971. To the right of the streetcar is the former Canal streetcar line, which hosted buses on the reserved paved roadway. It was converted to bus operation on May 31, 1964. The St. Charles line is the oldest continuously operating street railway in the world.

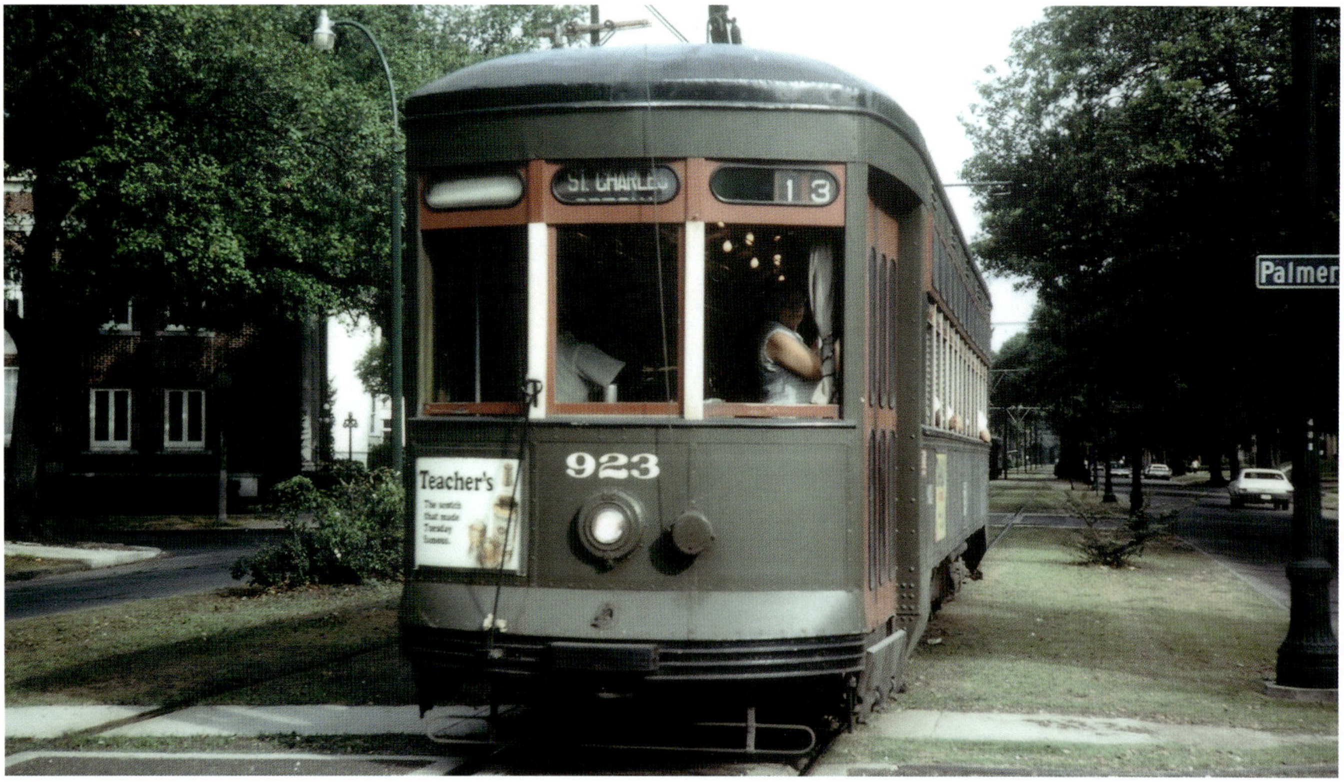

On June 19, 1971, New Orleans Public Service Inc. streetcar No. 923 is on the tree-lined reserved right of way of St. Charles Avenue at Palmer Avenue (about seven blocks west of Jefferson Avenue) in the Audubon neighborhood of New Orleans. St. Charles Avenue, with its graceful oak trees, wide private right of way (neutral ground), and vintage streetcar line, symbolizes New Orleans.

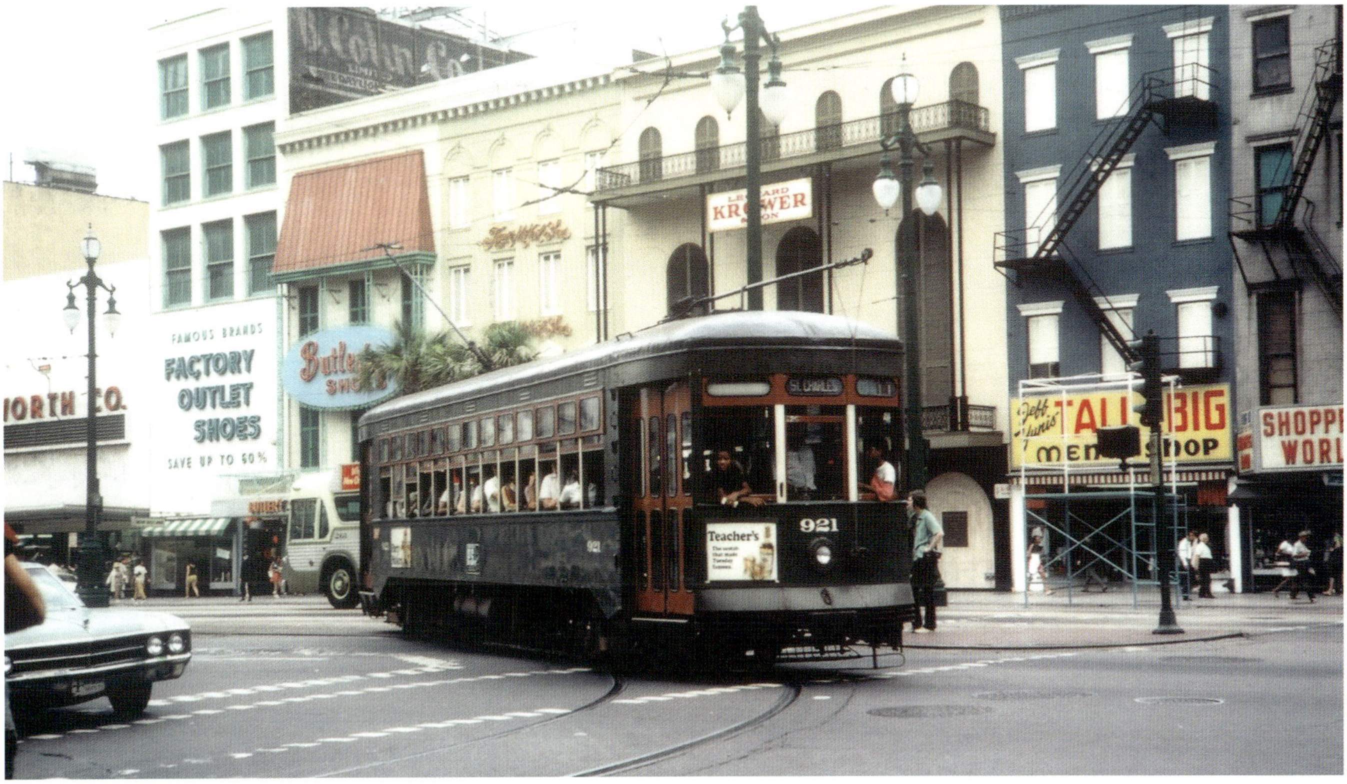

New Orleans Public Service Inc. streetcar No. 921 (originally weighing 42,036 pounds and powered by two General Electric type 263A motors) is turning from Canal Street onto St. Charles Avenue on June 18, 1971. With thirteen sets of windows that slide open, the 47.67 foot long 900 series streetcars seat fifty-two and have a maximum speed of twenty-eight miles per hour with an average speed of nine miles per hour.

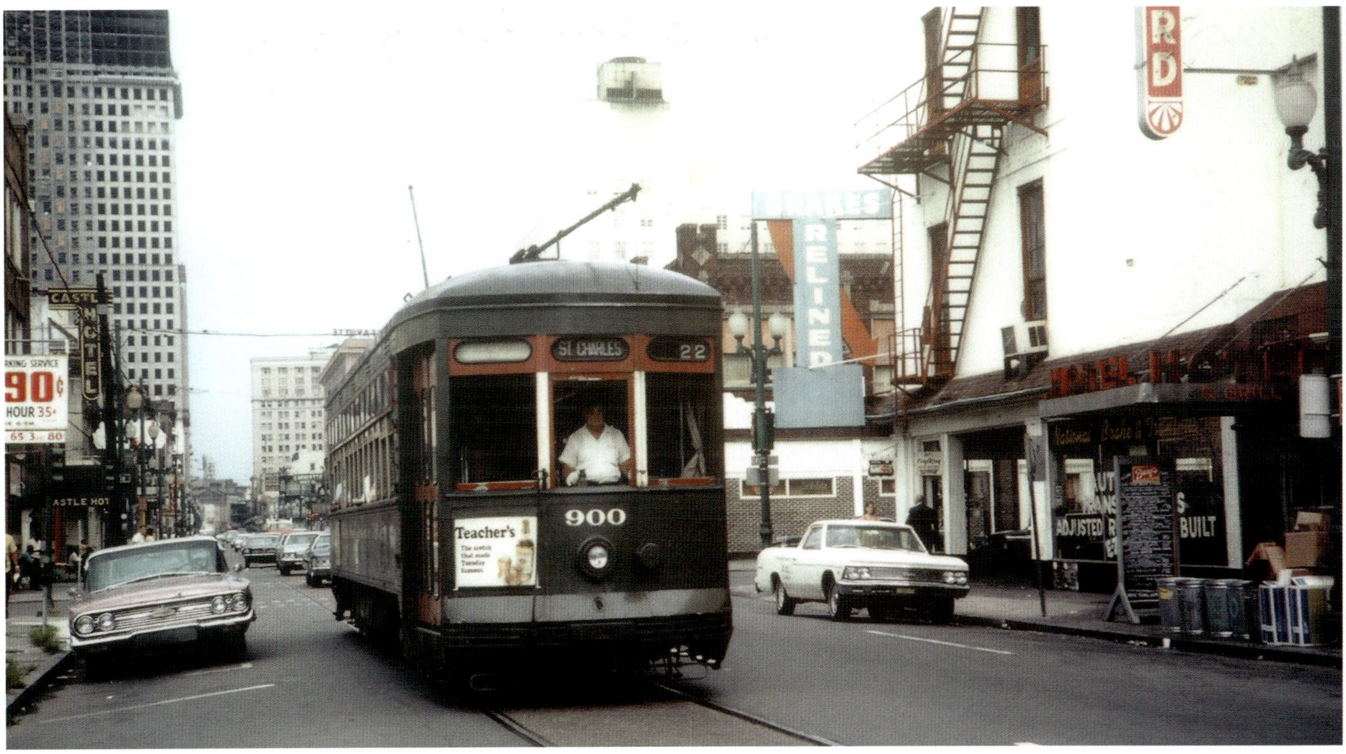

St. Charles streetcar No. 900 is passing through the Central Business District on June 18, 1971. Years later, on November 10, 2007, streetcar No. 900 led a line of streetcars in a ceremonial run celebrating the return of streetcar service on St. Charles Avenue, from Napoleon Avenue to the Lee Circle monument that had been shut down. This was because the high winds of Hurricane Katrina destroyed most of the St. Charles overhead power lines.

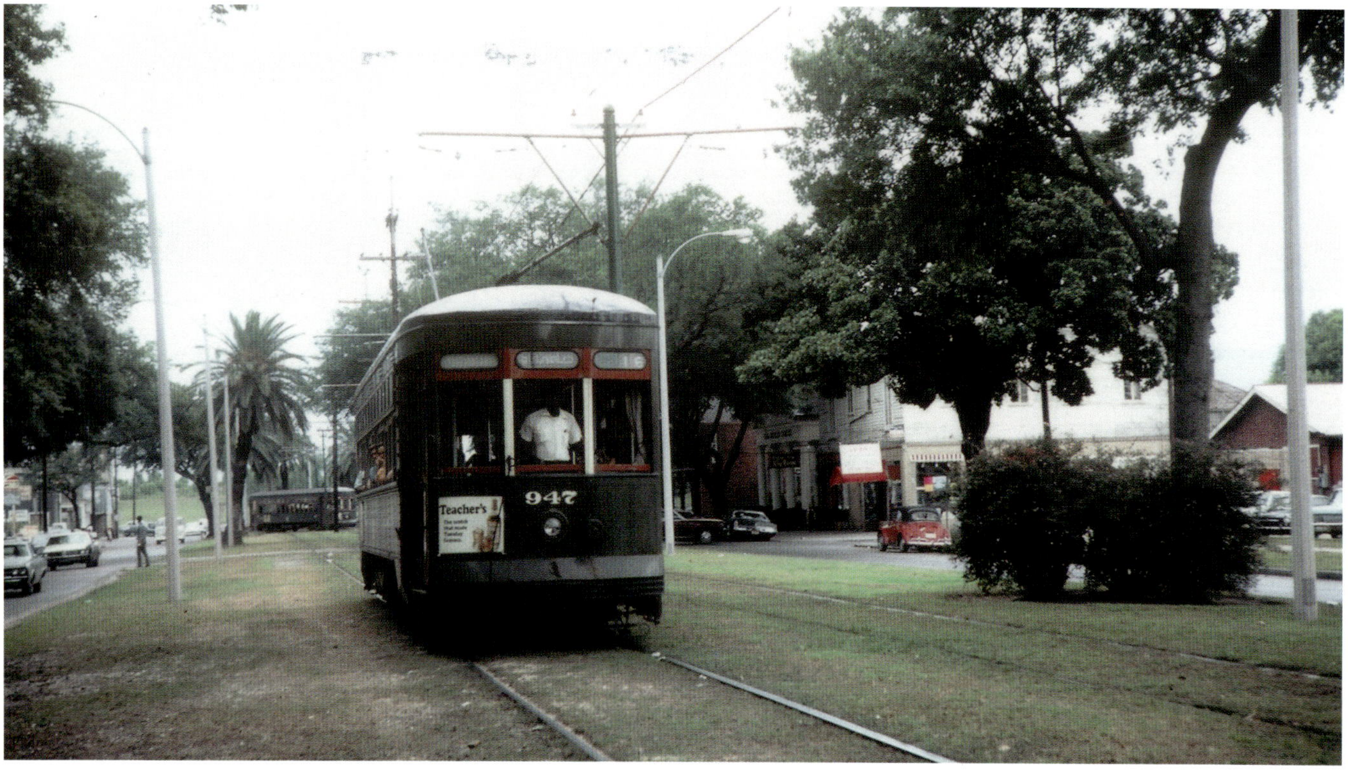

South Carrollton Avenue with the turn from St. Charles Avenue, about a block behind the streetcar (note the distant streetcar at that curve), finds New Orleans Public Service Inc. streetcar No. 947 (originally weighing 41,148 pounds and powered by two Westinghouse type 306-CV4 motors) moving along the wide private right of way on June 18, 1971.

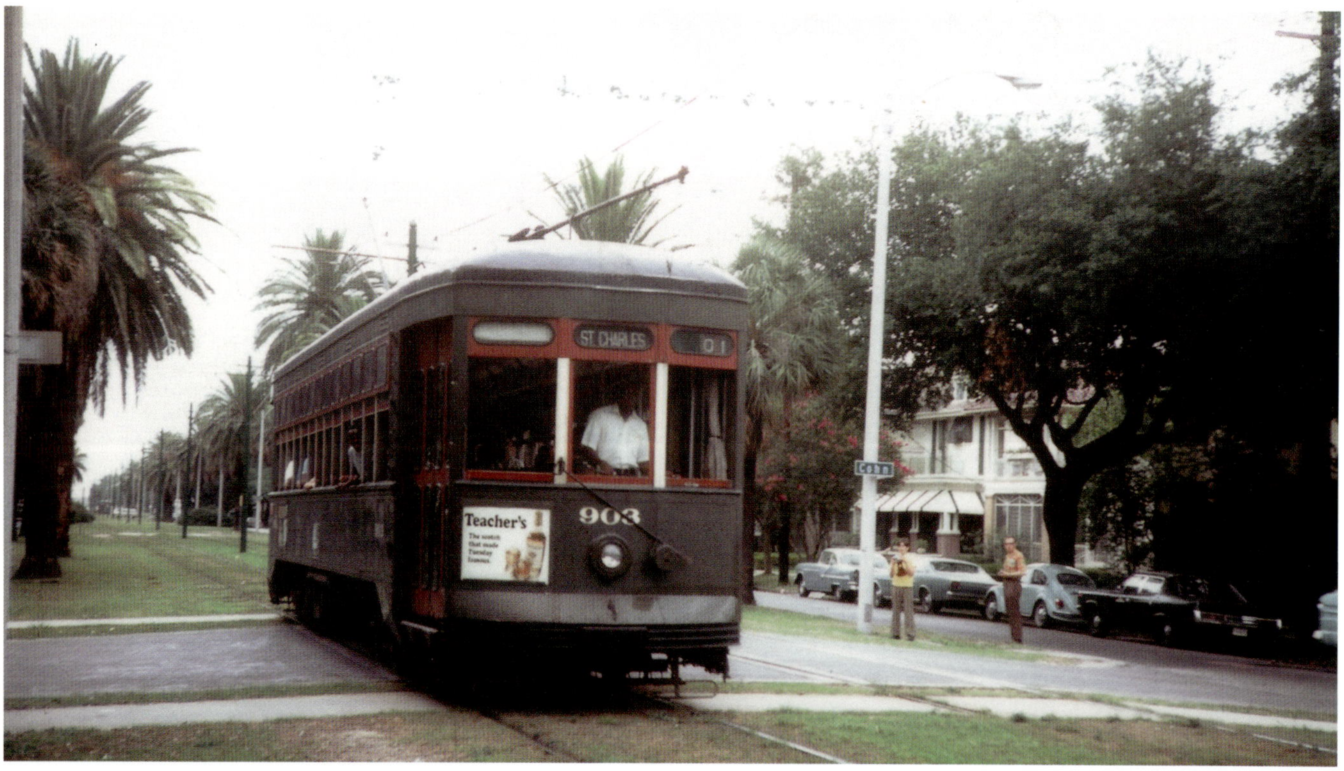

The wide grass-covered private right of way on South Carrollton Avenue is a delight to view as New Orleans Public Service Inc. streetcar No. 903 (originally weighing 42,036 pounds and powered by two General Electric type 263A motors) glides across Cohn Street on July 18, 1971. The St. Charles streetcar line is a great way to see the beauty of the residential areas along St. Charles Avenue and South Carrollton Avenue.

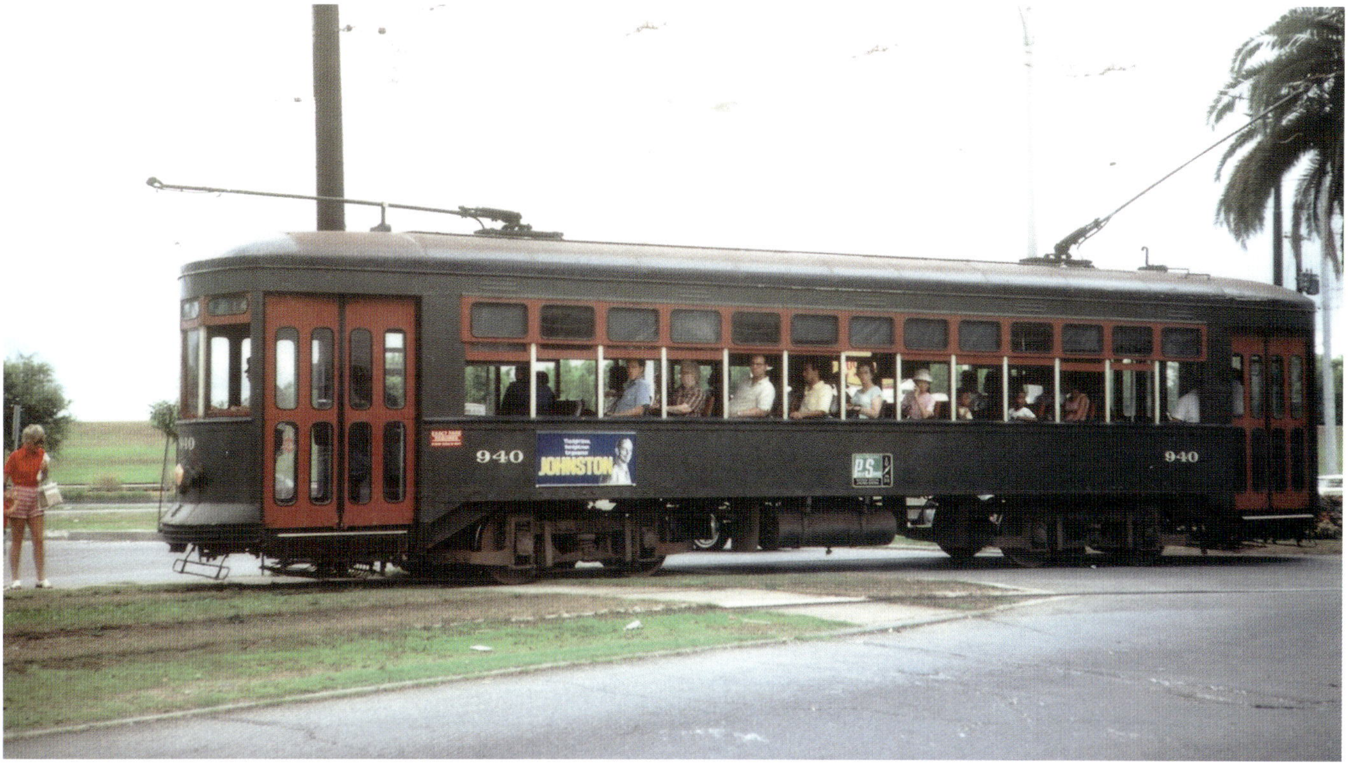

Rounding the curve from South Carrollton Avenue to St. Charles Avenue, New Orleans Public Service Inc. streetcar No. 940 is in the area known as Riverbend where St. Charles Avenue meets South Carrollton Avenue, on July 18, 1971. The streetcars were designed for the motorman to operate the streetcar and the conductor to collect fares. With the installation of automatic fareboxes in June 4, 1972, the job of conductor was eliminated, and the streetcars became one-man operation.

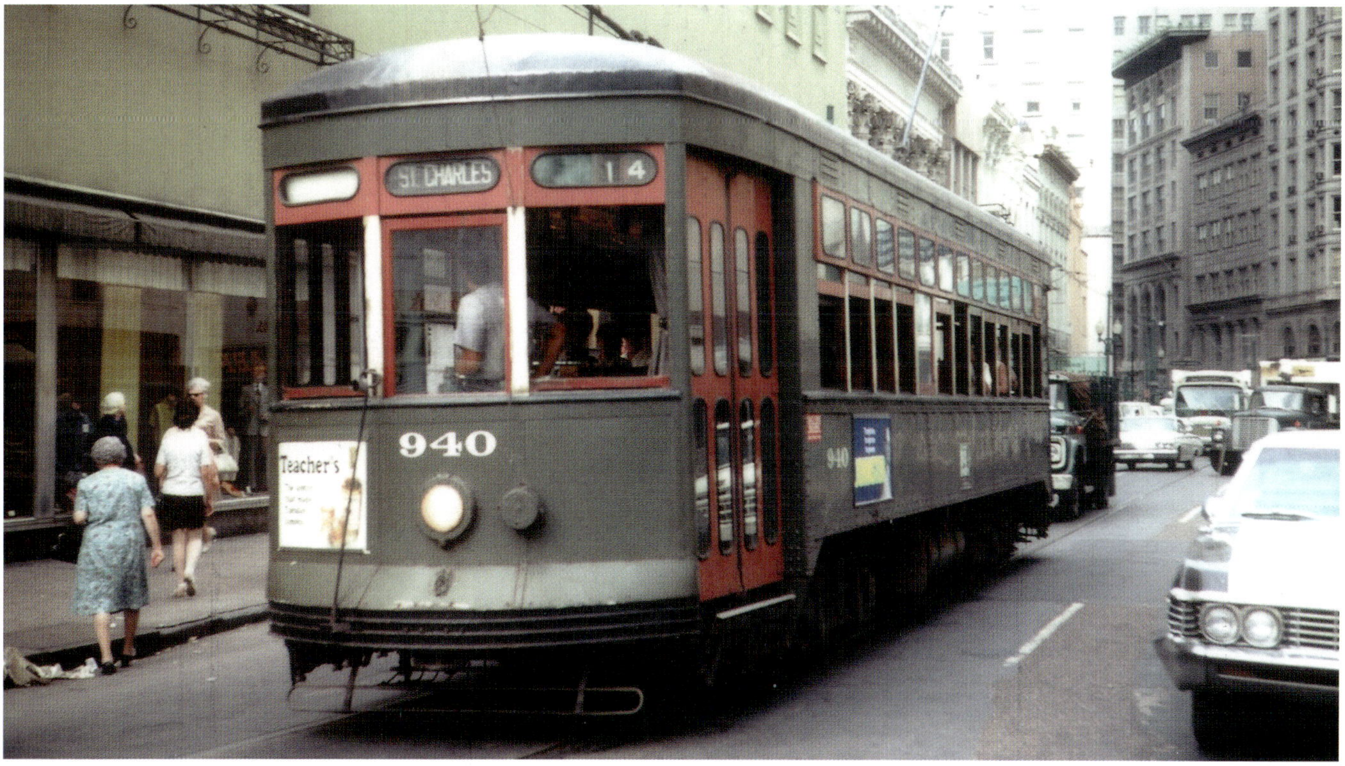

New Orleans Public Service Inc. streetcar No. 940 is on Carondelet Street at Canal Street on July 18, 1971 in the heart of the Central Business District. Carondelet Street was named for the Spanish colonial governor Francisco Luis Hector de Carondelet; the section of the street near Canal Street was once the center of the cotton trade in New Orleans. After crossing Canal Street, it becomes Bourbon Street.

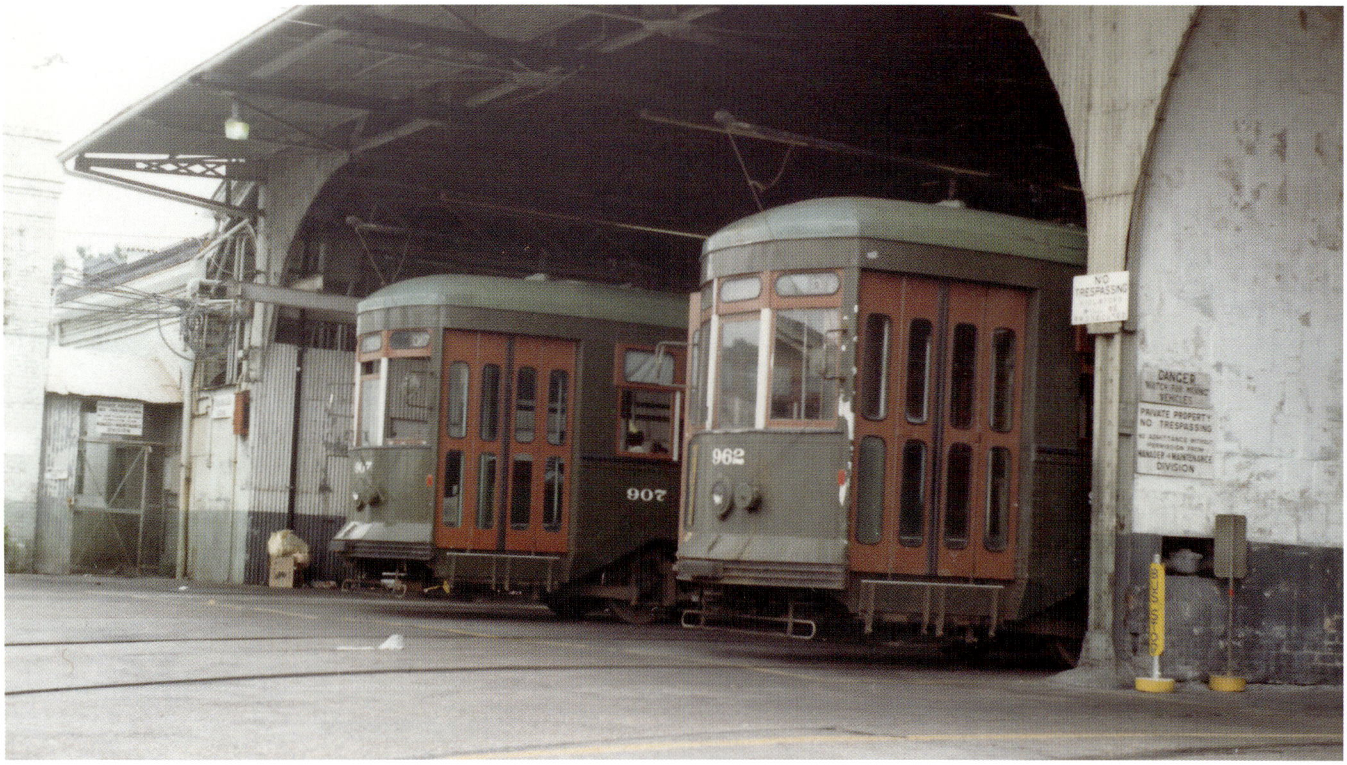

On July 28, 1985, at the Carrollton Station carbarn, New Orleans Regional Transit Authority (RTA) streetcars Nos. 907 and 962 (each originally weighing 42,036 pounds and powered by two General Electric type 263A motors) are ready for the next assignment. This carbarn was opened in 1893, closed on December 28, 1934 with streetcars transferred to the Canal Station carbarn, and reopened on March 1, 1943. The RTA took over New Orleans Public Service Inc. on July 1, 1983.

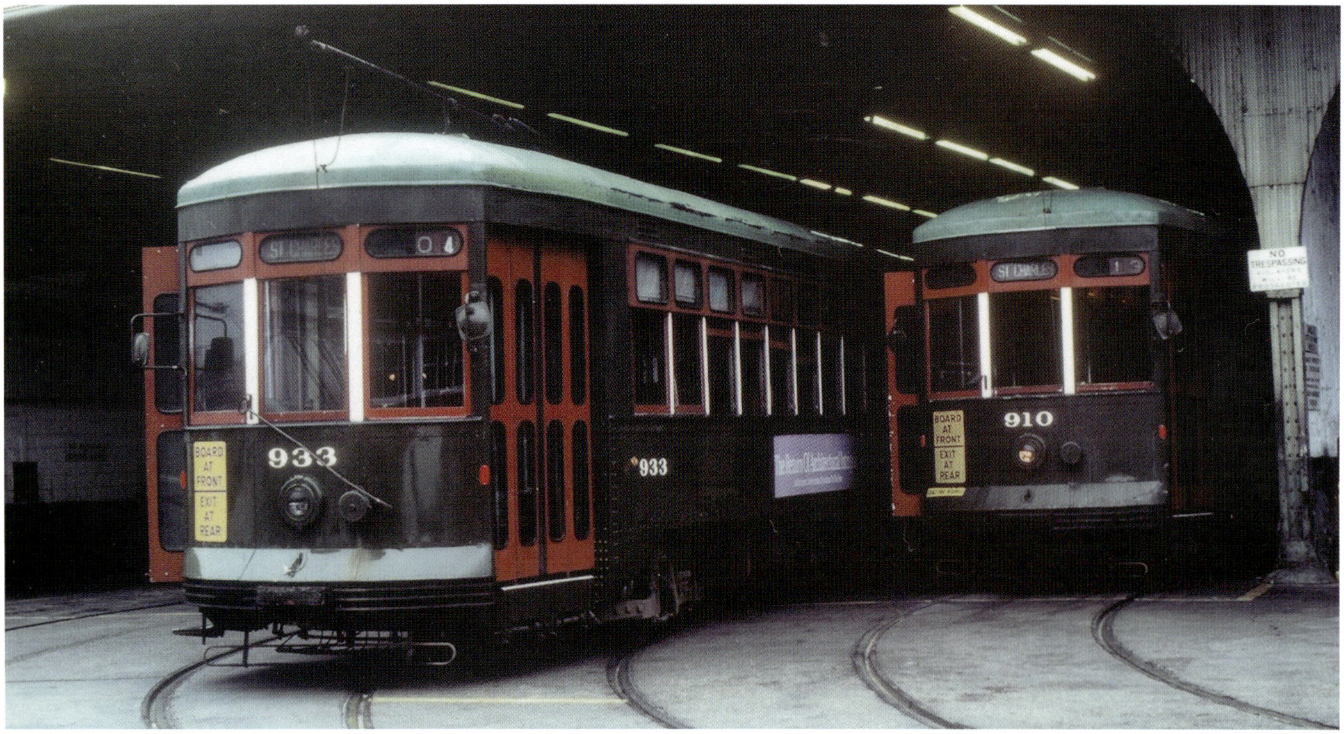

RTA streetcars No. 933 (originally weighing 41,148 pounds and powered by two Westinghouse type 306-CV4 motors) and No. 910 (originally weighing 42,036 pounds and powered by two General Electric type 263A motors) are at the Carrollton Station carbarn on August 2, 1985. To handle the constant start/stop operation workout these cars receive, they are carefully maintained at this facility. The skilled staff at the Carrollton Station shop have done everything from rewinding traction motor armatures to building entire new streetcars.

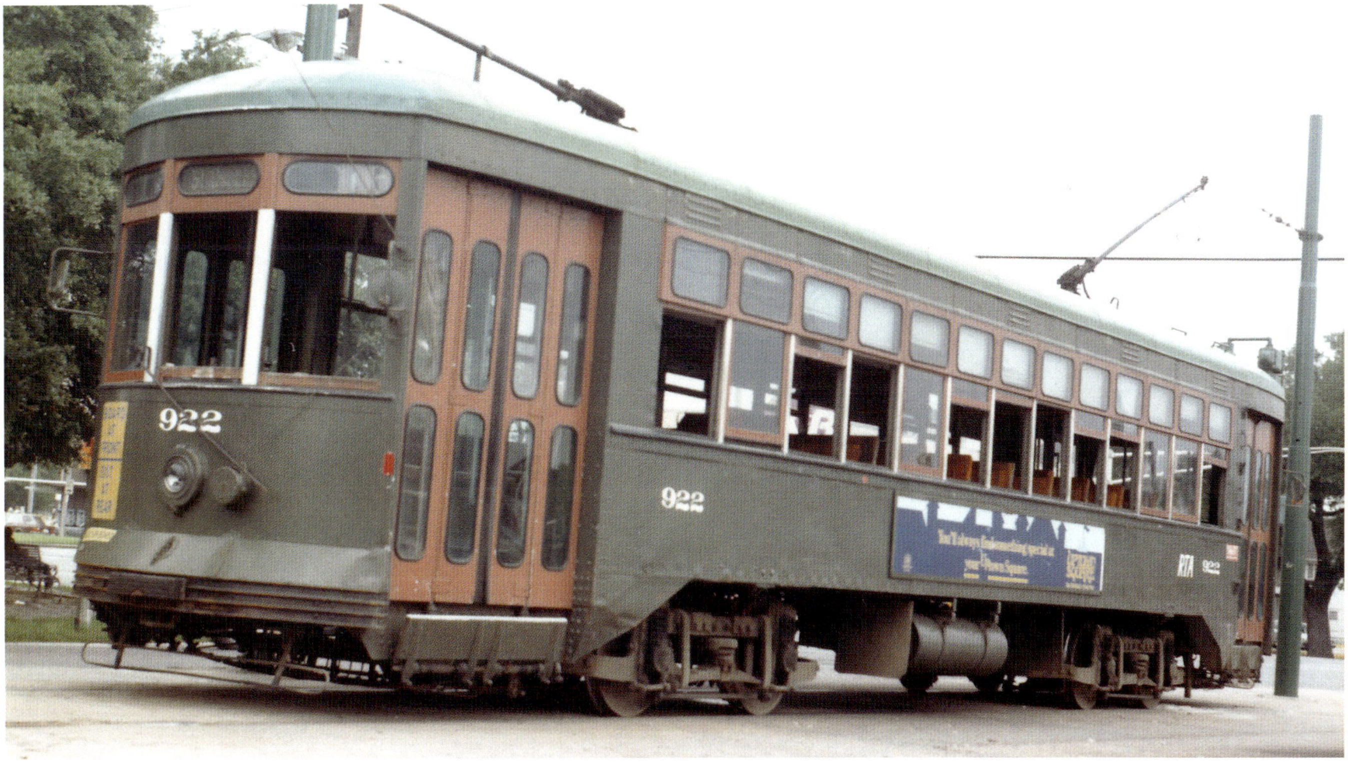

At the South Carrollton Avenue and South Claiborne Ave terminus of the St. Charles line, RTA streetcar No. 922 (originally weighing 42,036 pounds and powered by two General Electric type 263A motors) awaits departure time on July 28, 1985. Both of these streets are marked south, but neither street runs due south. While Carrollton Avenue is straight, Claiborne Avenue turns much like the Mississippi River.

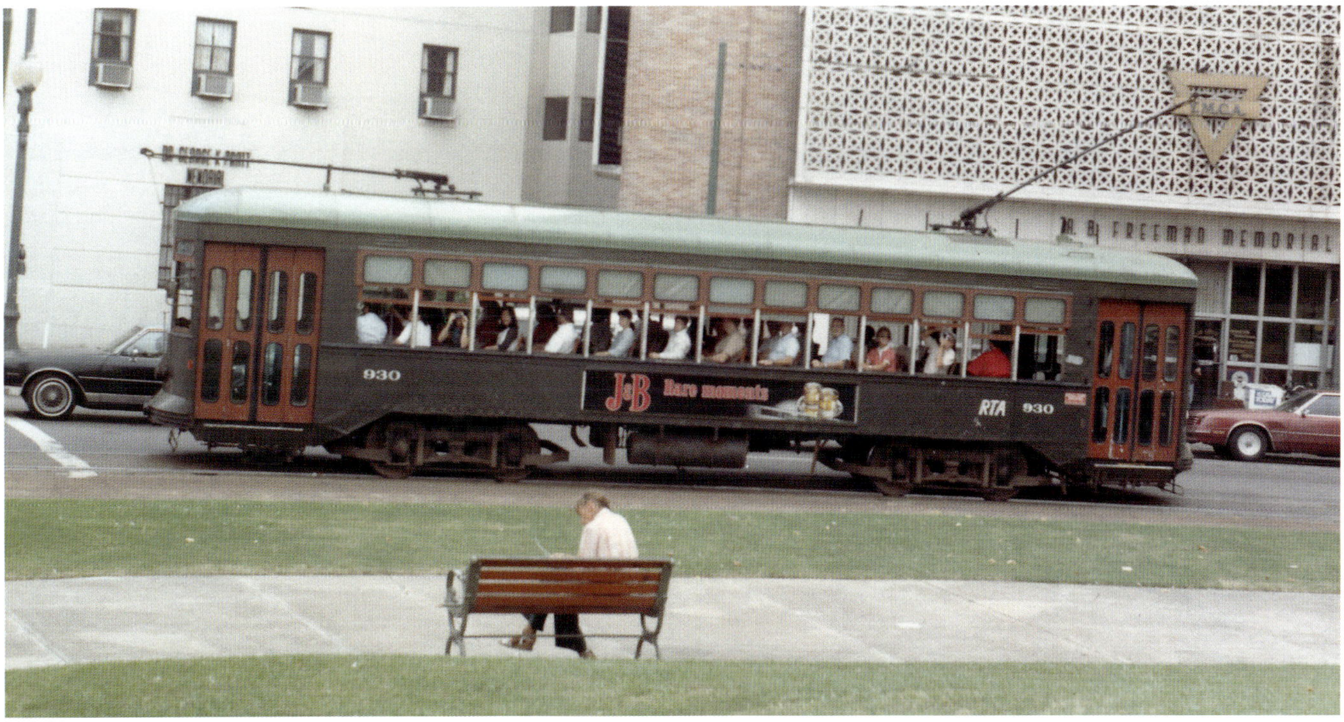

RTA streetcar No. 930 (originally weighing 41,148 pounds and powered by two Westinghouse type 306-CV4 motors) is going around the Lee Circle monument, a traffic circle with a monument to Confederate General Robert E. Lee, and the YMCA is on the right, August 2, 1985. A one way trip on the St. Charles line takes about forty to forty-five minutes depending on the time of day.

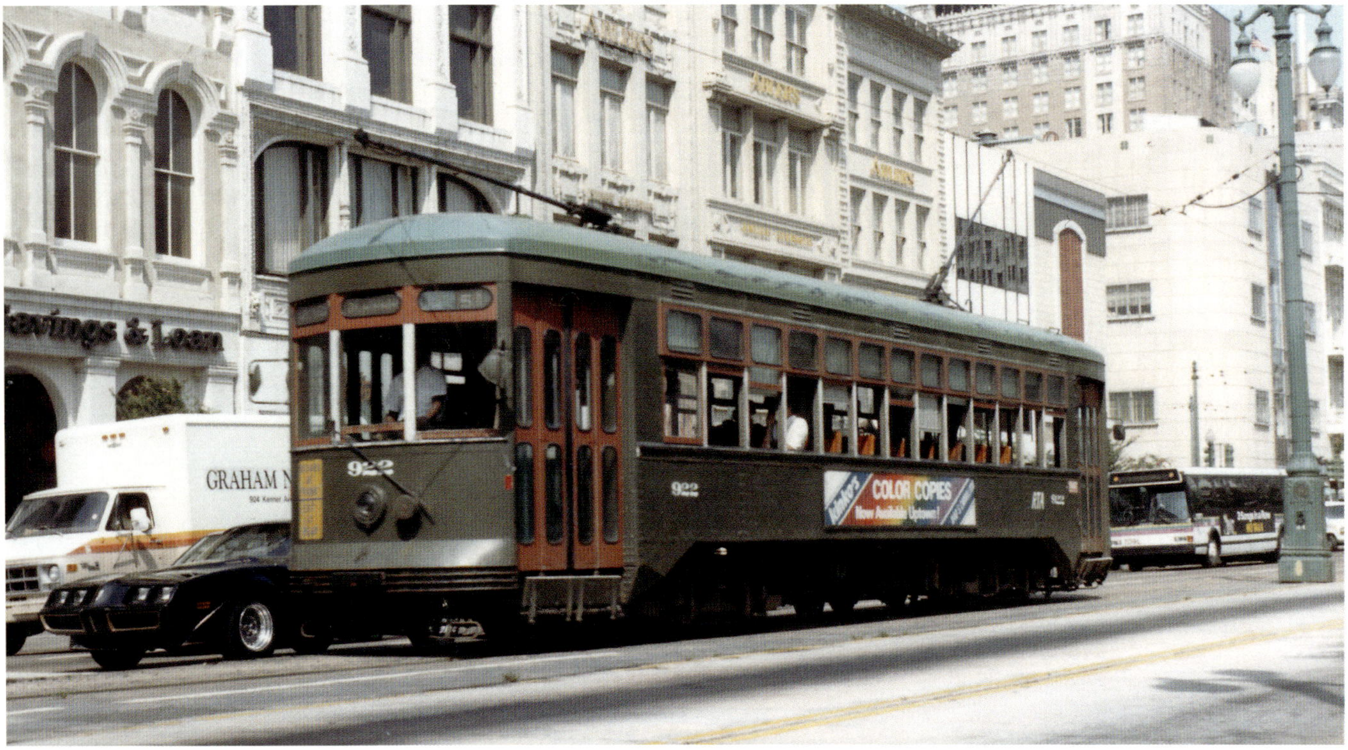

RTA streetcar No. 922 is on Canal Street between Carondelet Street and St. Charles Avenue on August 2, 1985, passing buildings that have ornamentation around the windows. The steel body, steel supports, and steel underframe of the 900 series streetcars, as designed by the Perley A. Thomas Car Company, have proven to be a durable design. Although Canal Street began to decline as a regional shopping center in the late 1960s, it is now undergoing a renewal.

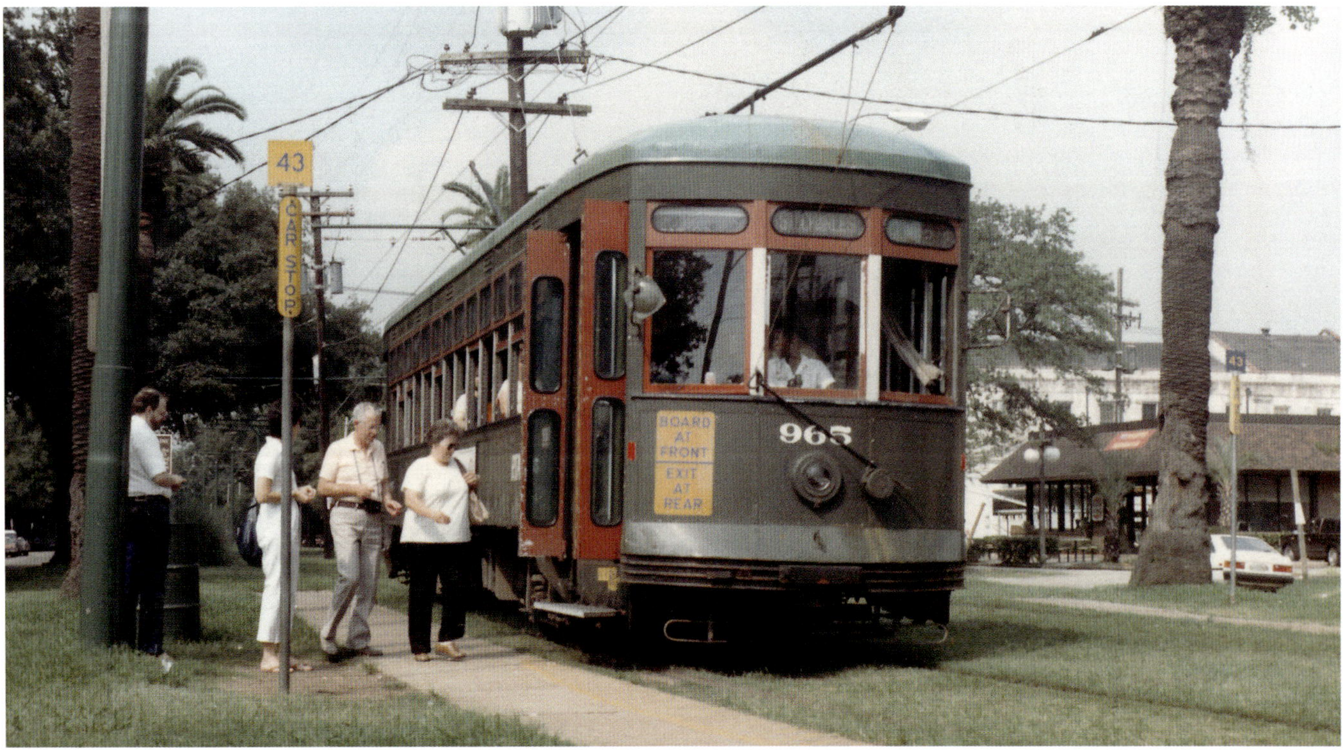

On the curve from South Carrollton Avenue to St. Charles Avenue on August 2, 1985, RTA streetcar No. 965 is picking up passengers. The operator handles the acceleration and braking of the streetcar with two hand controls. With the compressed air braking system, the brakes must be gradually pumped for a smooth stop and require a great distance for stopping. Pedestrians should never step out and motorists should never pull out in front of a moving streetcar.

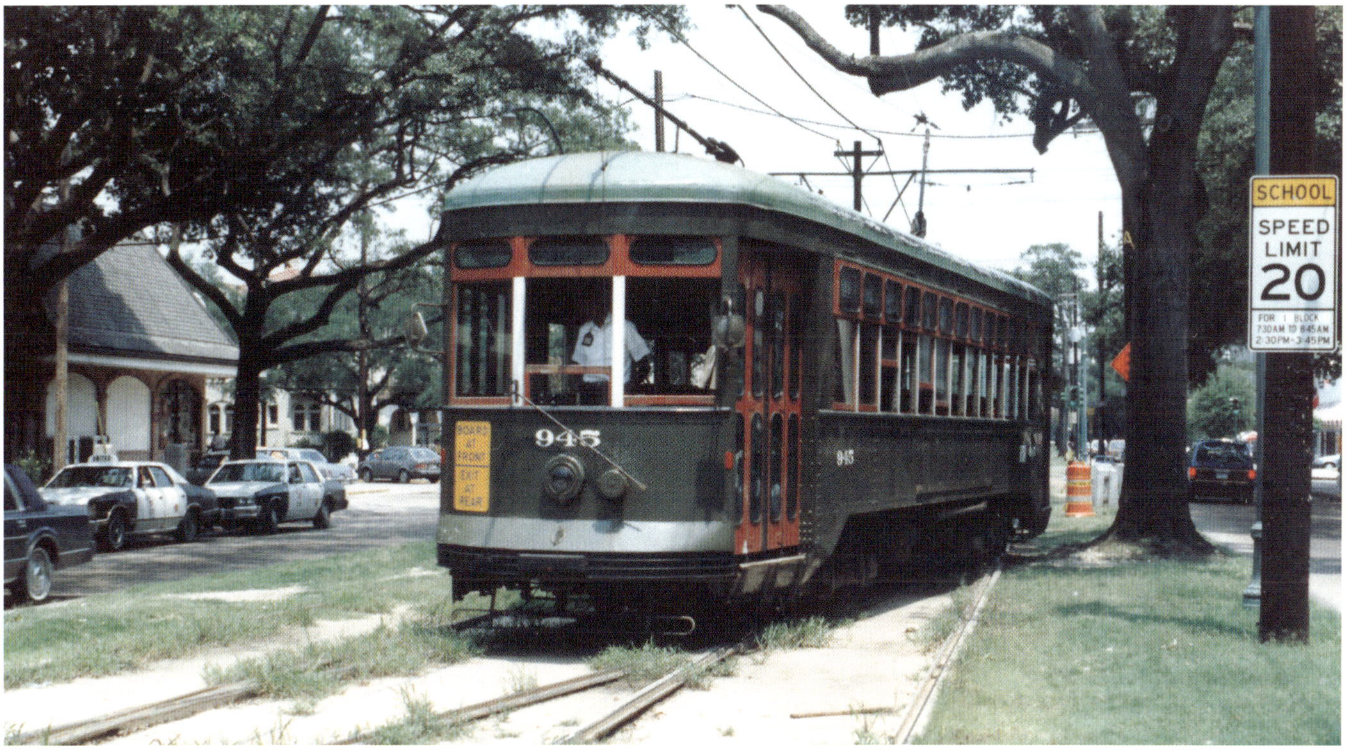

On August 2, 1985, RTA streetcar No. 945 (originally weighing 41,148 pounds and powered by two Westinghouse type 306-CV4 motors), on the private right of way in the center of St. Charles Avenue, is switching over at Cadiz Street in the Uptown neighborhood of New Orleans, because of a track reconstruction project. A bus shuttle operated beyond this point to the terminus on South Carrollton Avenue at South Claiborne Avenue.

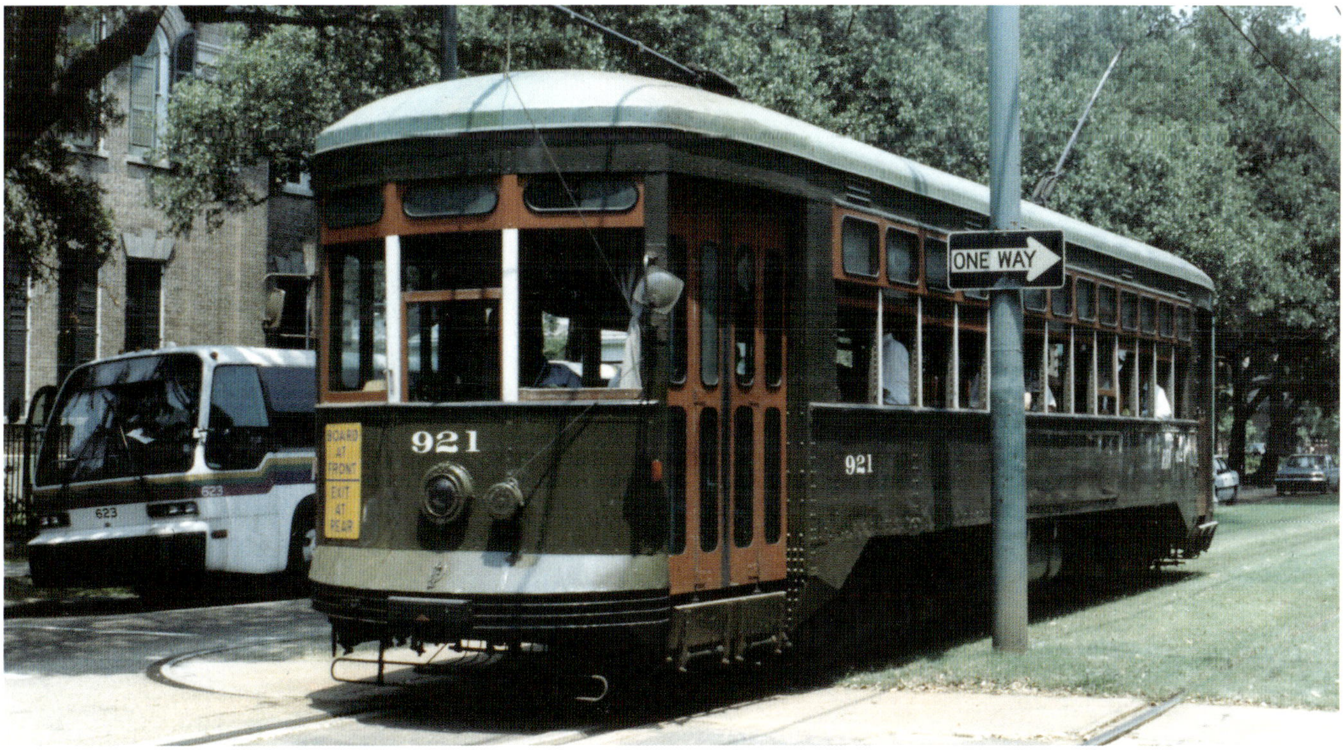

At St. Charles Avenue and Napoleon Avenue in the Uptown neighborhood of New Orleans, RTA bus No. 623 serves as a shuttle between South Carrollton Avenue and South Claiborne Avenue to this location, shown on August 2, 1985 during the track project. RTA streetcar No. 921 covered the rest of the trip to the Central Business District. From July 18, 1913 to December 27, 1934, the Napoleon Avenue line was one of the longest streetcar lines in New Orleans.

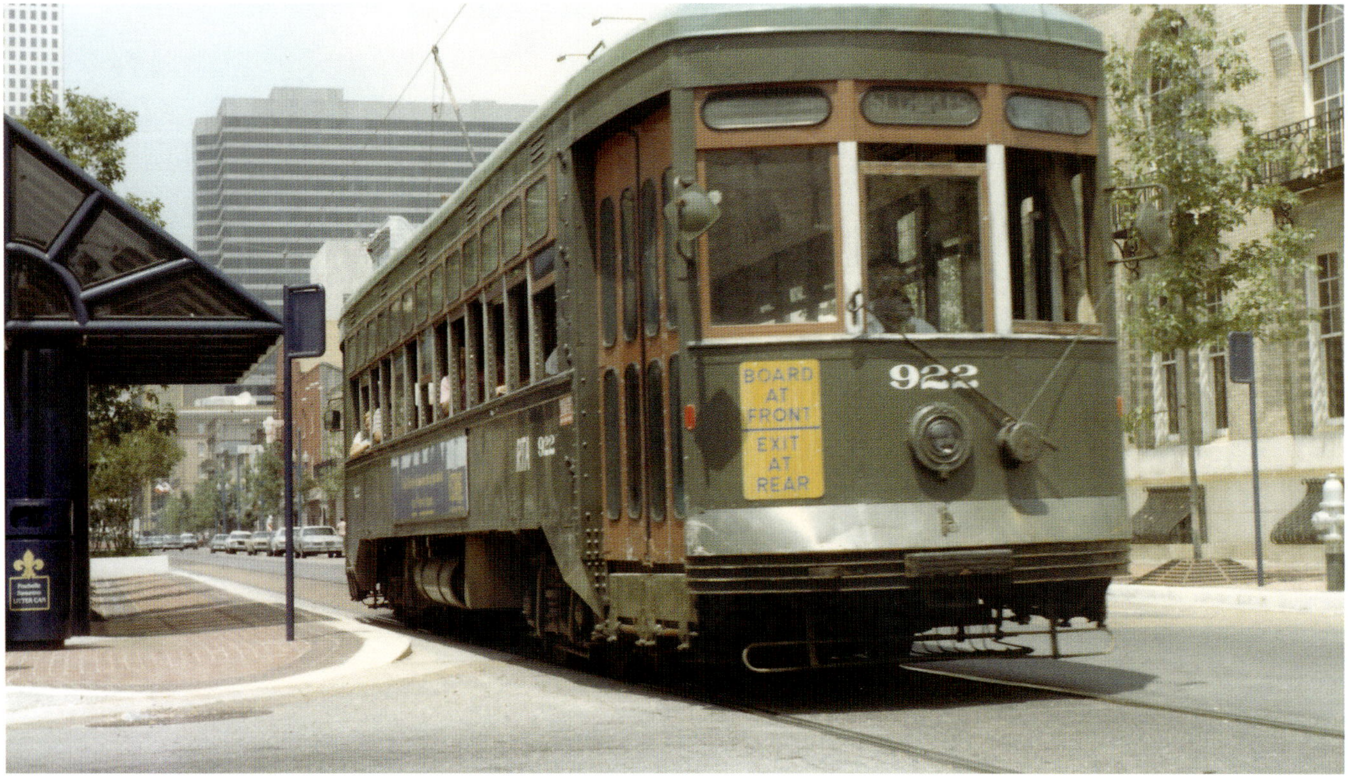

On August 1, 1985, RTA streetcar No. 922 is on St. Charles Avenue crossing St. Joseph Street in the Central Business District. Two Westinghouse type 306-CV4 motors were used on streetcars numbered 800 to 899, 912 to 917, and 923 to 947. Two General Electric type 263A motors were used on streetcars numbered 900 to 911, 918 to 922, and 948 to 972.

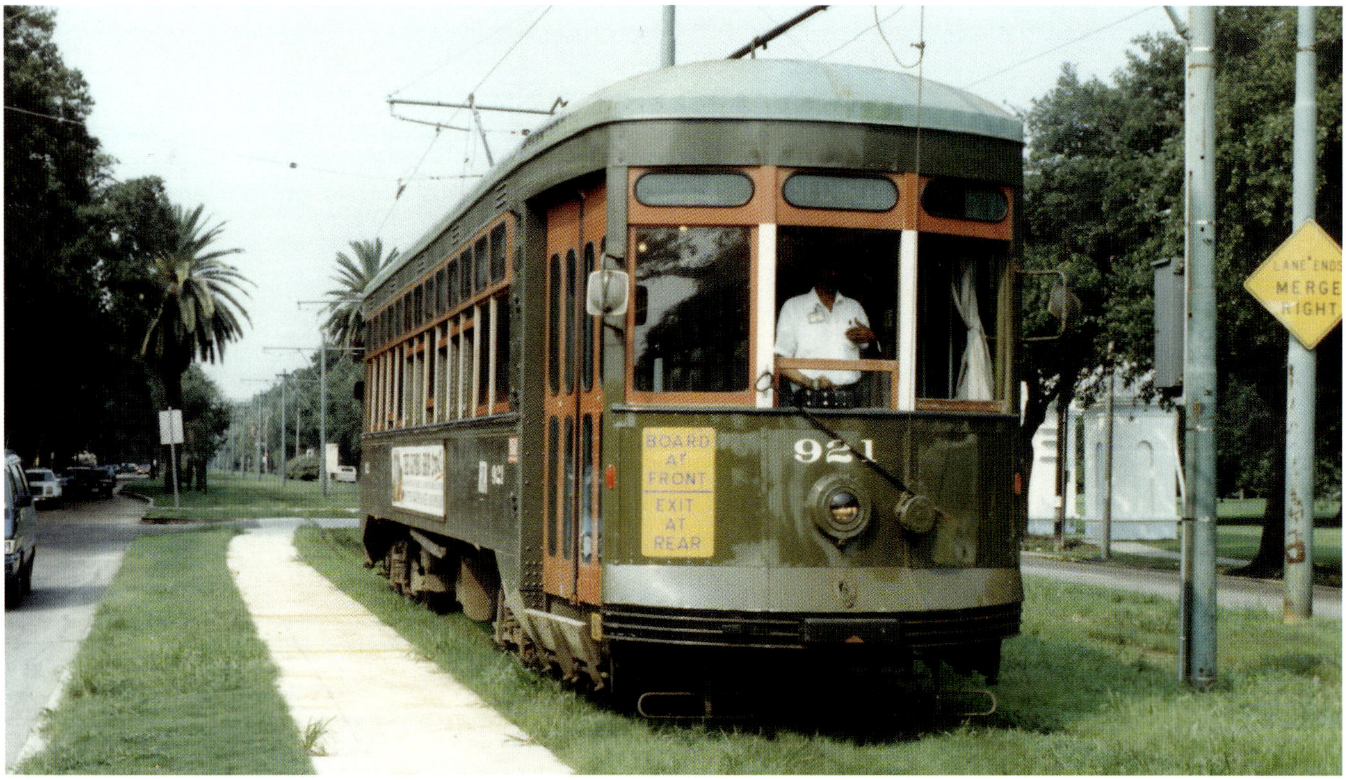

RTA streetcar No. 921 is at the terminus of the St. Charles line at South Carrolton Avenue and South Claiborne Avenue on July 29, 1989. This is the Carrollton neighborhood of New Orleans. Streetcars numbered 800 to 972 were originally built with No. 12 gauge steel side panels, steel underframe, wood and canvas roof, pine floor, and Hale and Kilburn type 300A wooden seats.

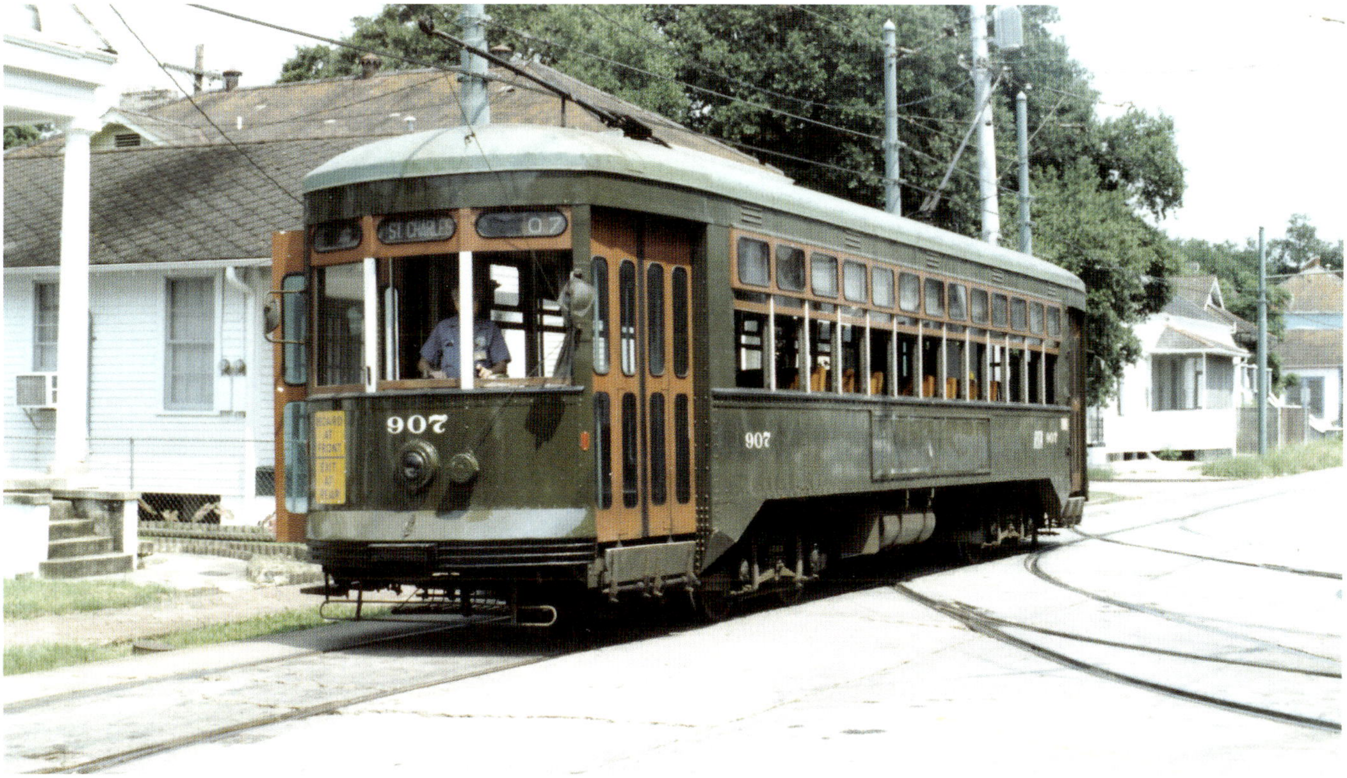

On July 27, 1989, RTA streetcar No. 907 is on Jeannette Street near South Carrollton Avenue preparing to enter the Carrolton Station carbarn. General Electric type CP-27 compressors were used on streetcars numbered 800 to 899, 918 to 922, and 948 to 972. Westinghouse type DH-16 compressors were used on streetcars numbered 900 to 917 and 923 to 947.

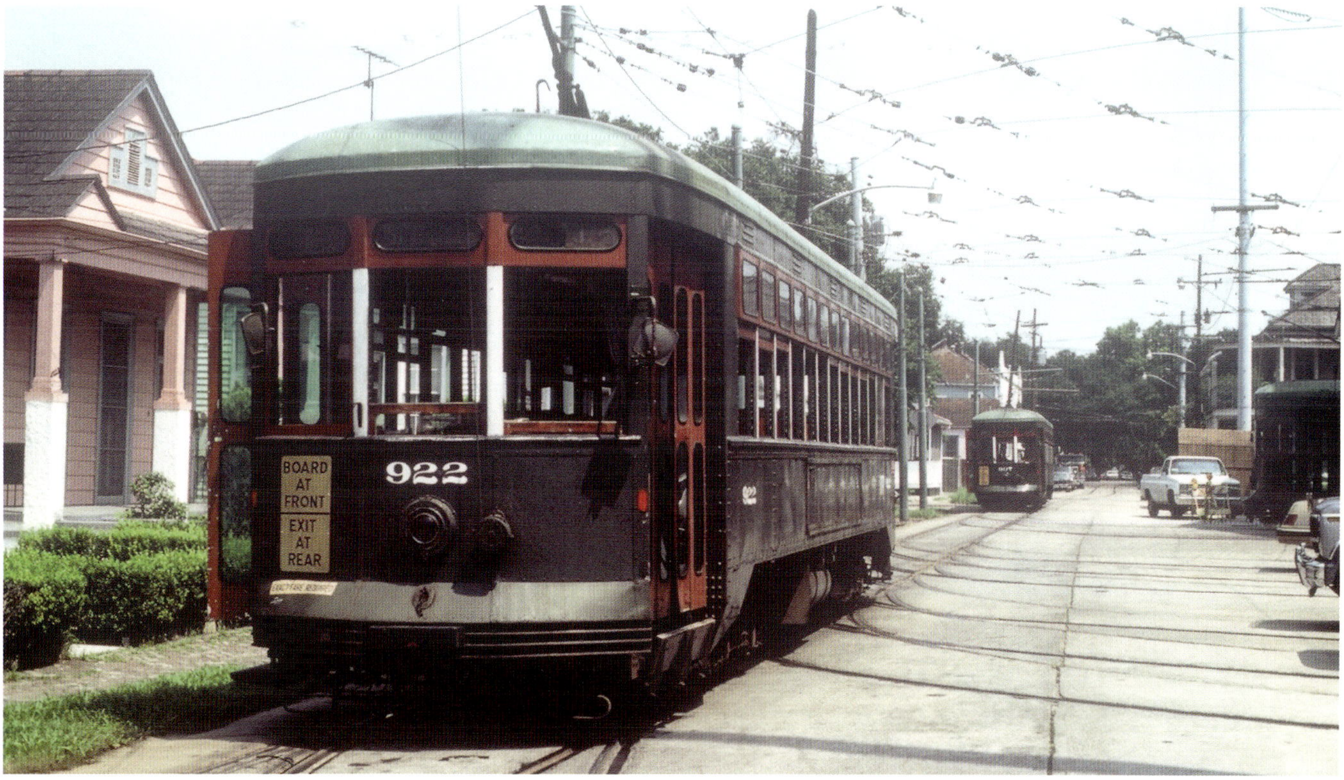

RTA streetcar No. 922 is on Jeannette Street, while streetcar No. 907 in the distance is ready to enter the Carrollton Station carbarn, on July 27, 1989. General Electric type S brake valves were used on streetcars numbered 800 to 899, 918 to 922, and 948 to 972. Westinghouse type PV-3 brake valves were used on streetcars numbered 900 to 917 and 923 to 947.

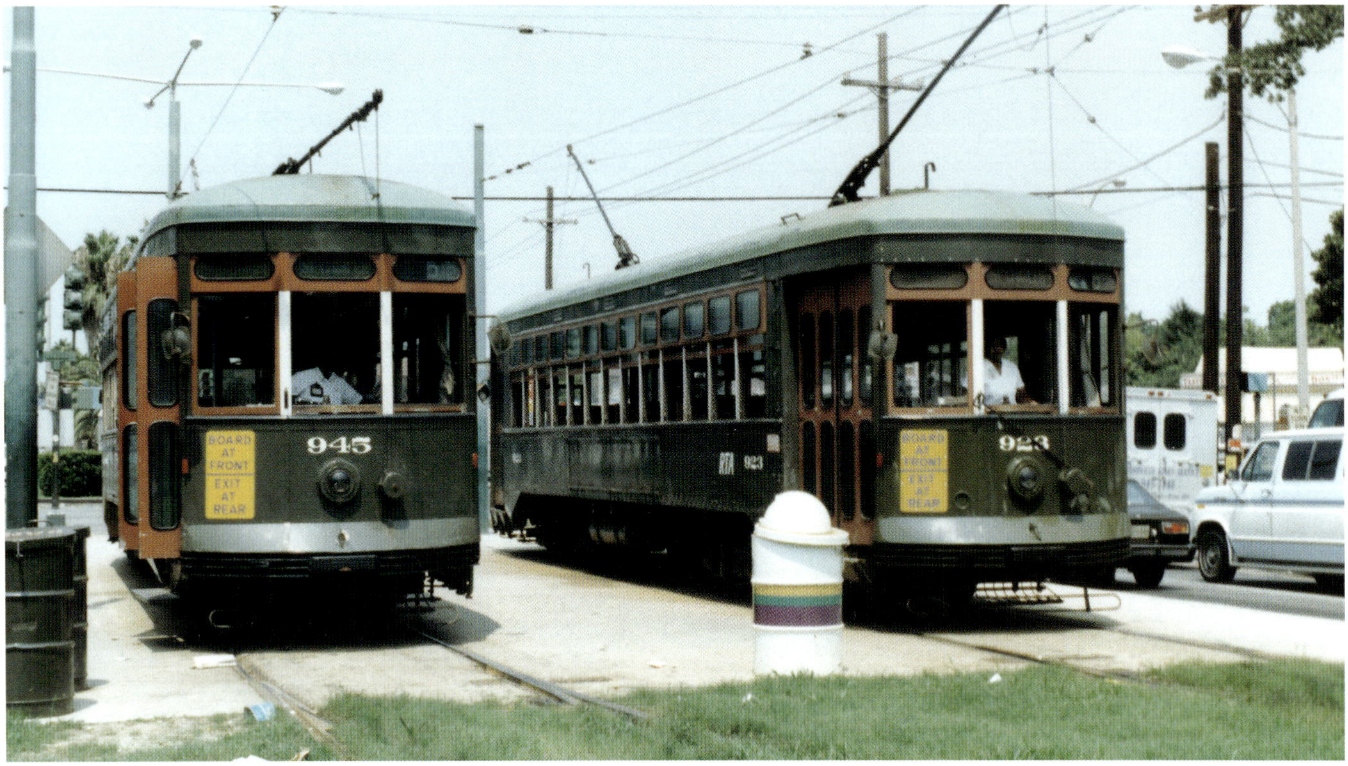

On July 27, 1989, RTA streetcars Nos. 945 and 923 are at South Carrollton Avenue and South Claiborne Avenue, which is the end of the St. Charles line. Since there are no turn-around loops in New Orleans, at the end of the line, the operator raises the front trolley pole and goes to the other end of the streetcar and lowers what was the rear pole. The rear pole conducts the 600 volts of DC current to the two motors of the streetcar.

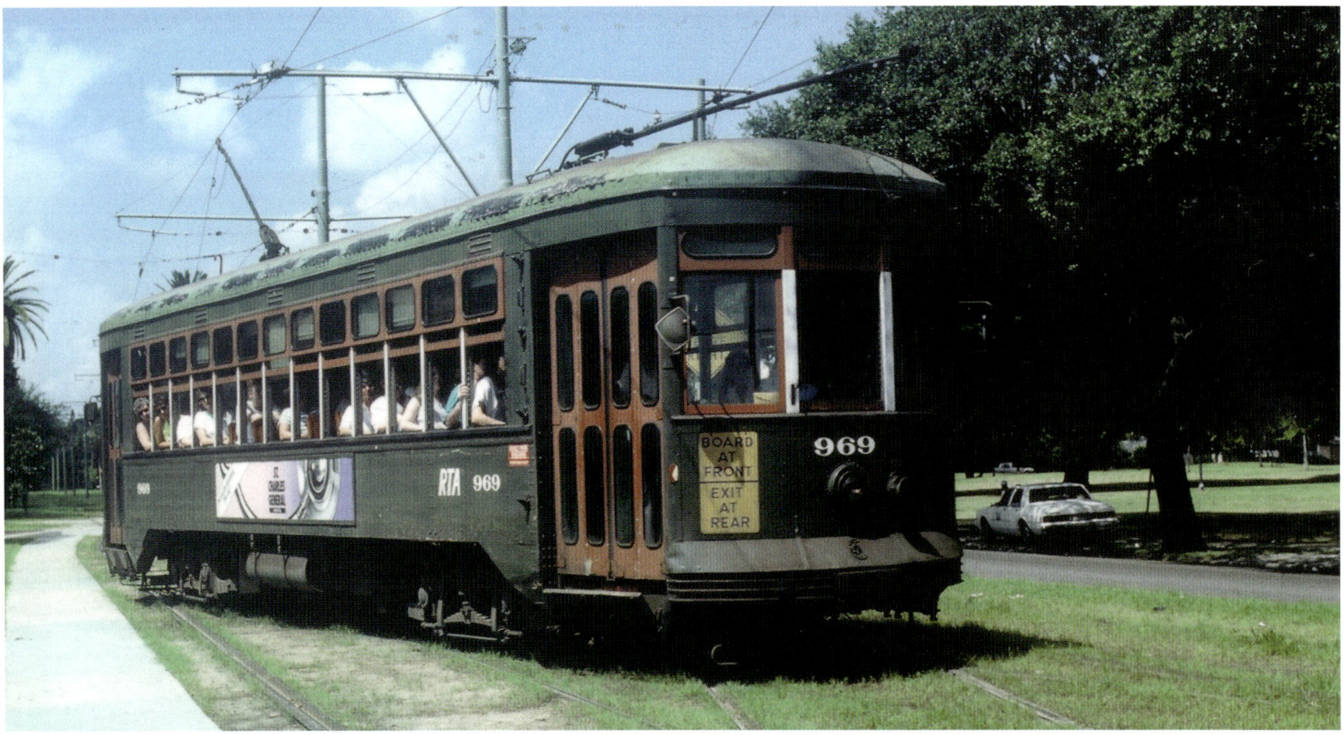

With a seated load, RTA streetcar No. 969 (originally weighing 42,036 pounds and powered by two General Electric type 263A motors) is coming into the South Carrollton Avenue and South Claiborne Avenue terminus of the St. Charles line on July 19, 1991.

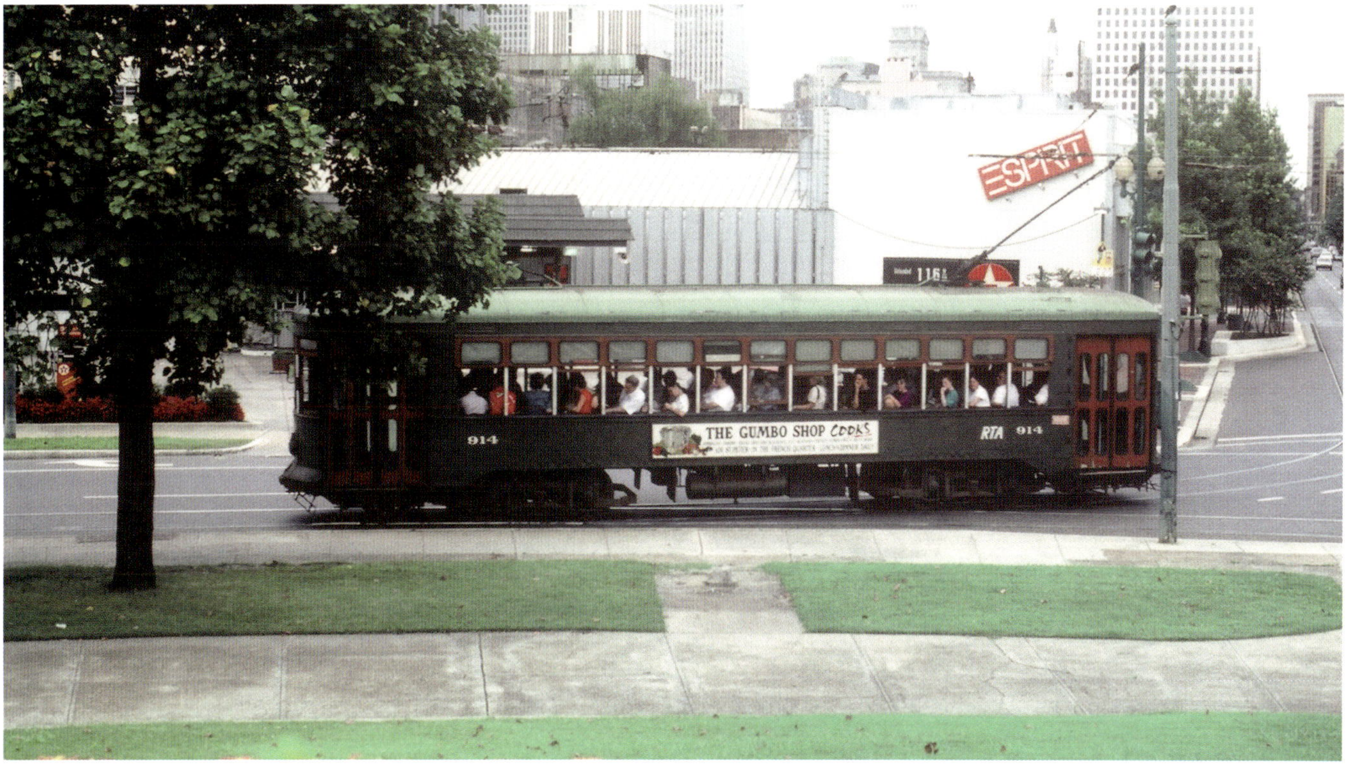

With the Central Business District in the background, RTA streetcar No. 914 (originally weighing 41,148 pounds and powered by two Westinghouse type 306-CV4 motors) is going around the Lee Circle Monument on July 19, 1991. The monument, located on St. Charles Avenue where it intersects Howard Avenue, acts as a gateway to the Lower Garden District, Garden District, and Uptown.

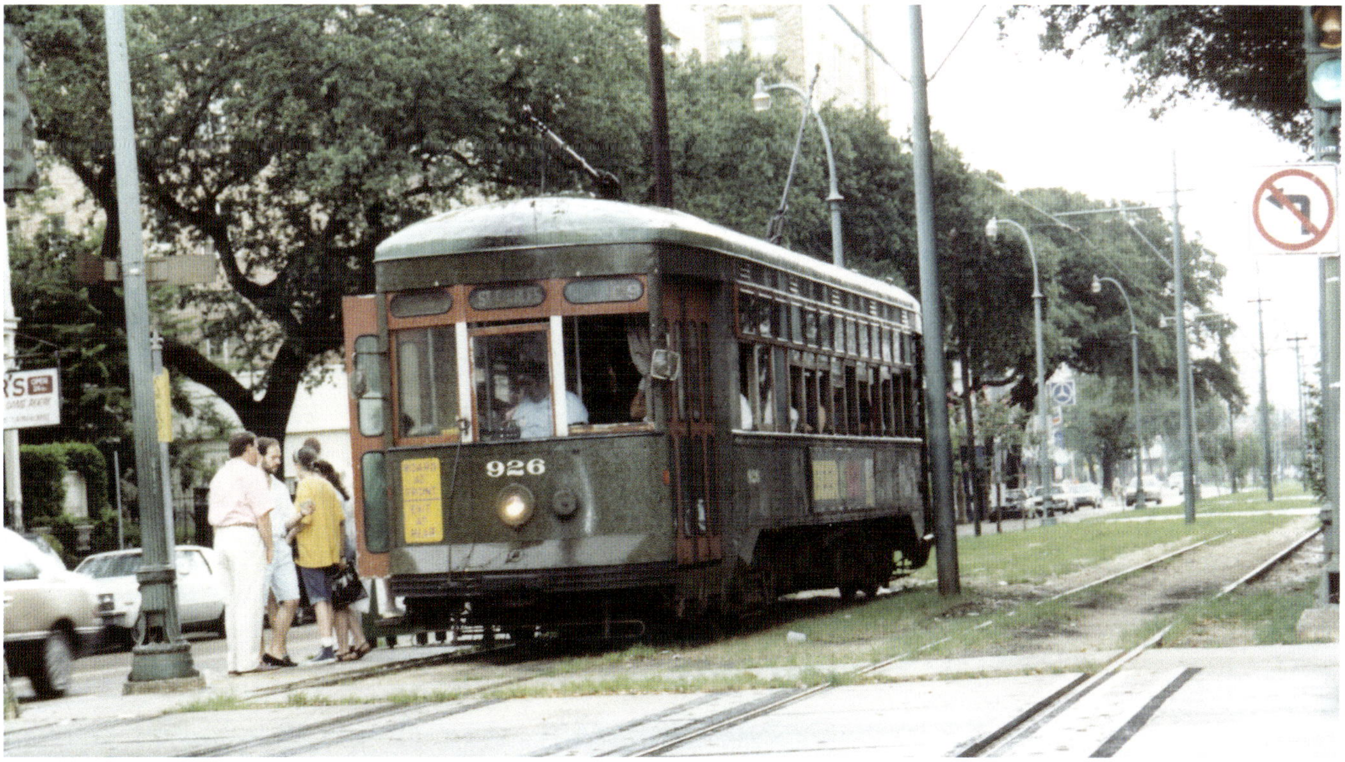

Passengers are getting off of RTA streetcar No. 926 on St. Charles Street at Jackson Avenue on July 21, 1991. This is the eastern boundary of the Garden District of New Orleans known for its magnificent mansions and gardens. The St. Charles Avenue Historic District, as designated in 1976 by the City of New Orleans Historic District Landmarks Commission, includes "all properties fronting on St. Charles Avenue between Jackson Avenue and Jena Street, with the exception of the properties that form the corner of Jackson and St. Charles Avenues."

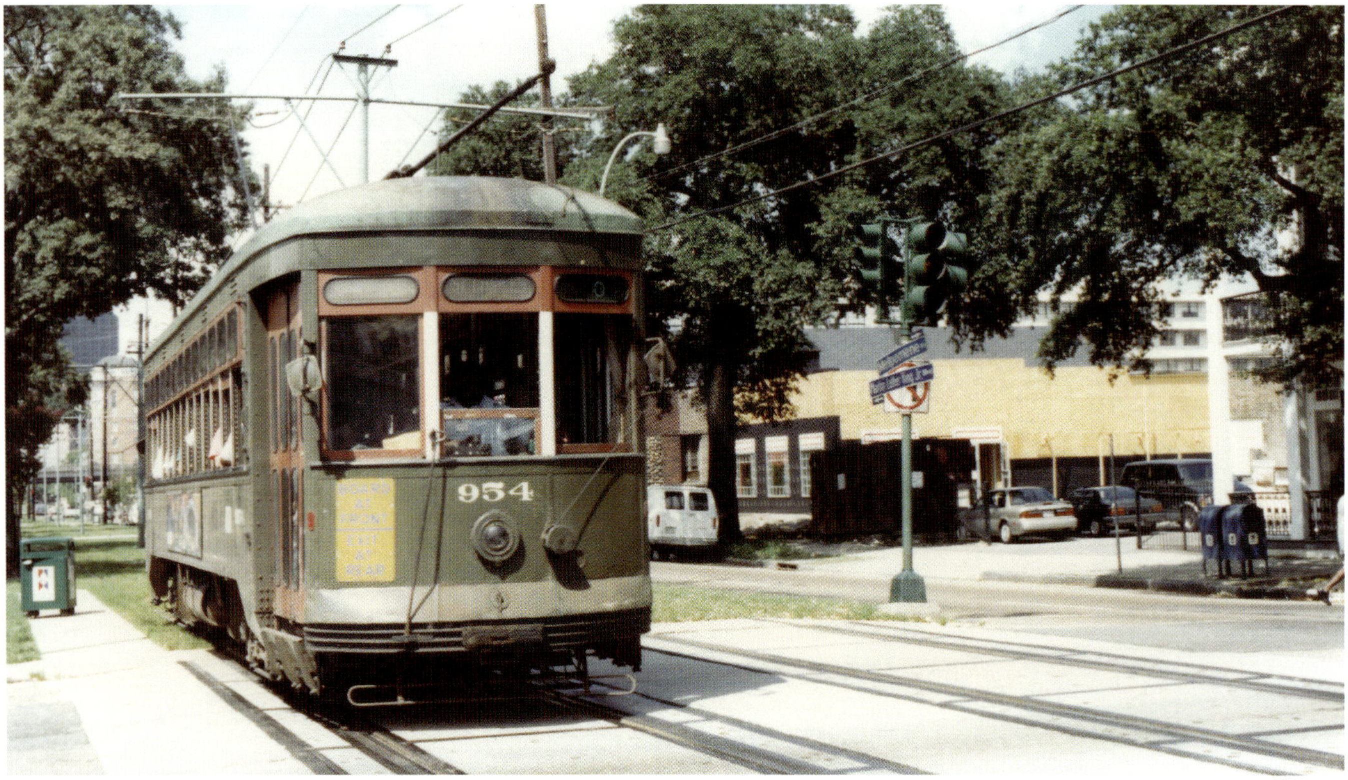

On July 22, 1991, RTA streetcar No. 954 (originally weighing 42,036 pounds and powered by two General Electric type 263A motors) is on St. Charles Avenue at Melpomene Street. This is in the Lower Garden District, about eight blocks east of Jackson Avenue. Passengers on the St. Charles streetcar line are treated to neighborhoods of architectural gems that convey the special charm and character of New Orleans.

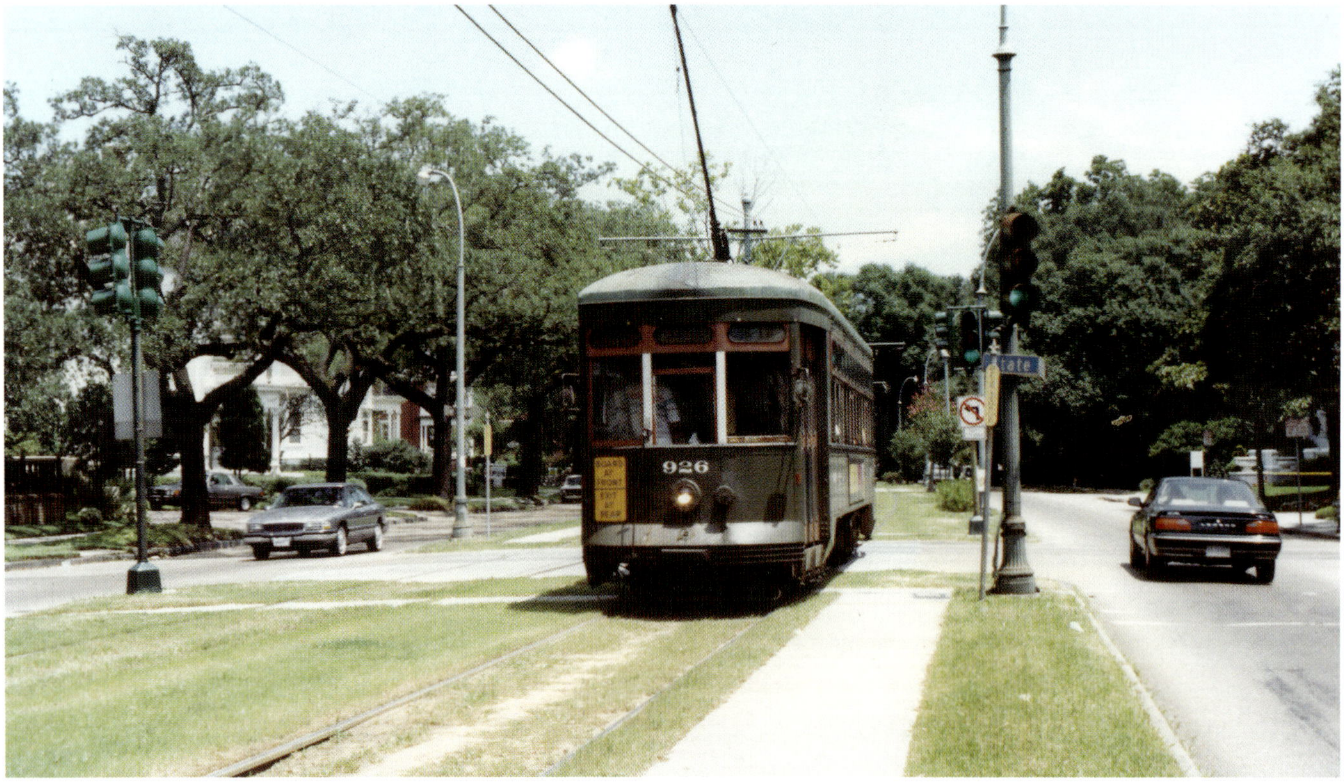

RTA streetcar No. 926 is on St. Charles Avenue crossing State Street (about six blocks west of Jefferson Avenue) in the Audubon neighborhood of New Orleans on July 22, 1991. The St. Charles streetcar line traverses a grassy median embellished by an abundance of trees, making it the prettiest streetcar line operated by a transit authority in the United States.

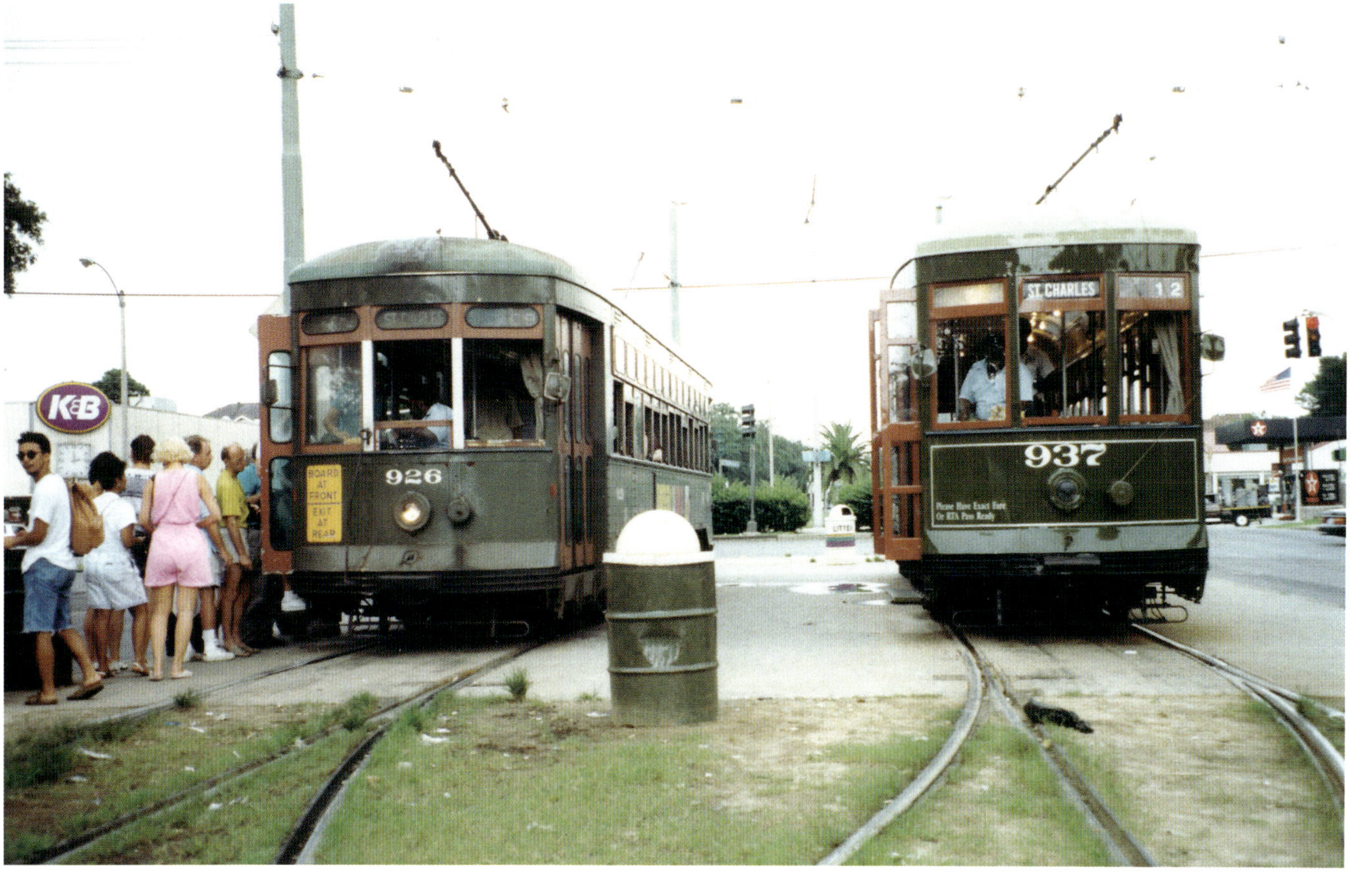

The busy South Carrollton Avenue and South Claiborne Avenue terminus of the St. Charles line, on July 21, 1991, finds RTA streetcars No. 926, boarding passengers, and No. 937, the first streetcar restored to original condition, with old style doors, silver stripes, and large car numbers. Armature and field coils were replaced, new brake shoes were installed, and the pine flooring was replaced with a plywood subfloor and oak tongue and groove top floor.

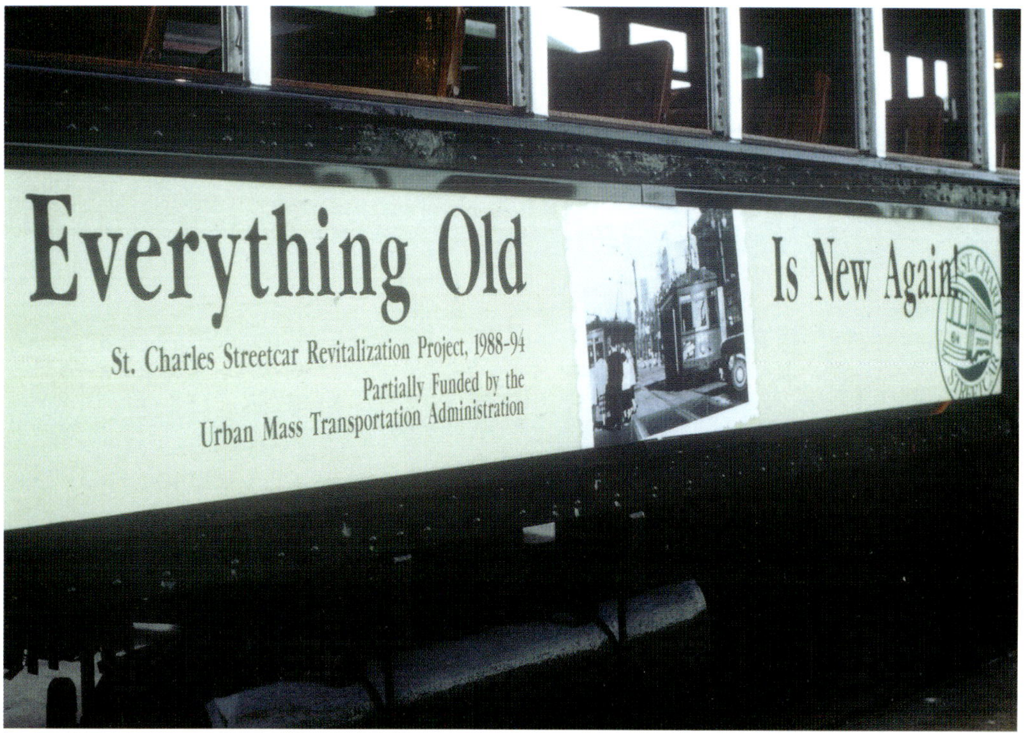

On July 20, 1991, RTA streetcar No. 937, at South Carrollton Avenue and South Claiborne Avenue, advertises on a side panel the St. Charles revitalization project, which restored it to its original condition. This was the first of thirty-five streetcars in a nine million dollar restoration project that was part of the larger forty-seven million dollar revitalization project, which included replacing 13.2 miles of track and the renovation of the Carrollton Station streetcar barn.

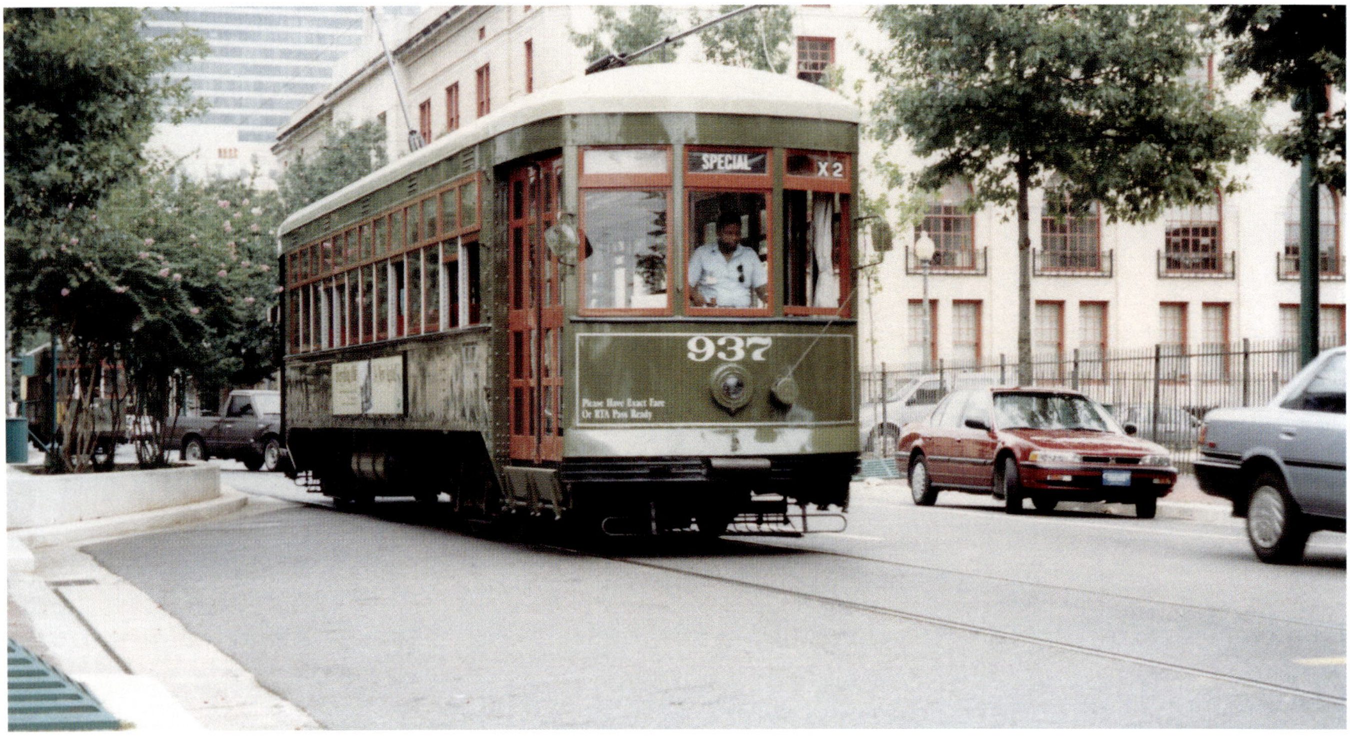

Operating a special run on St. Charles Street at St. Joseph Street on July 20, 1991, RTA streetcar No. 937 was the first streetcar to be restored to its original appearance. Since the St. Charles line was added to the United States National Register of Historic Places on August 4, 1973, federal law requires the 900 series streetcars built by Perley A. Thomas Car Company to be preserved as built, which makes riding the St. Charles streetcar line a ride through history.

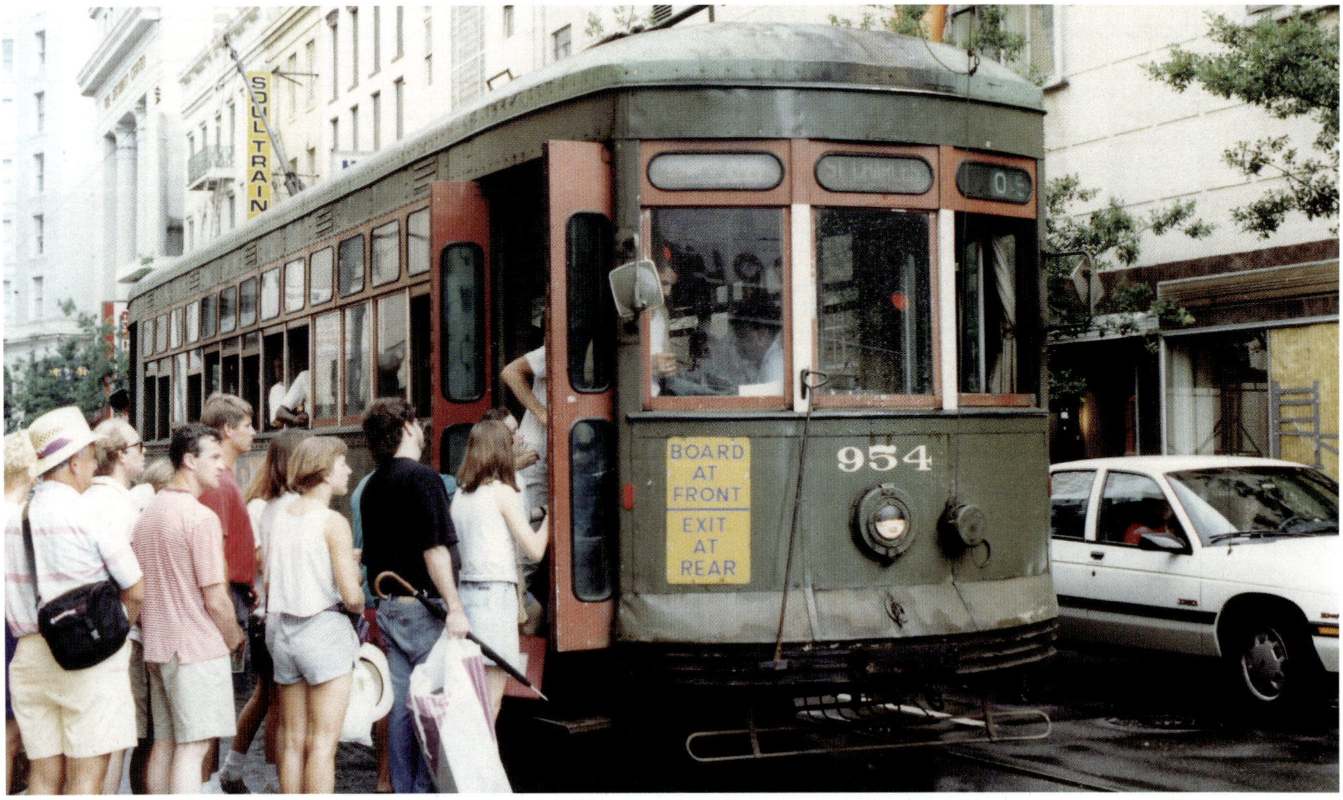

A large number of passengers are boarding RTA streetcar No. 954 at Carondelet Street and Canal Street on July 21, 1991. Doors were manually operated on streetcars numbered 800 to 899 and pneumatic operated on streetcars numbered 900 to 972. The St. Charles streetcar line is the most pleasant form of public transportation in the United States.

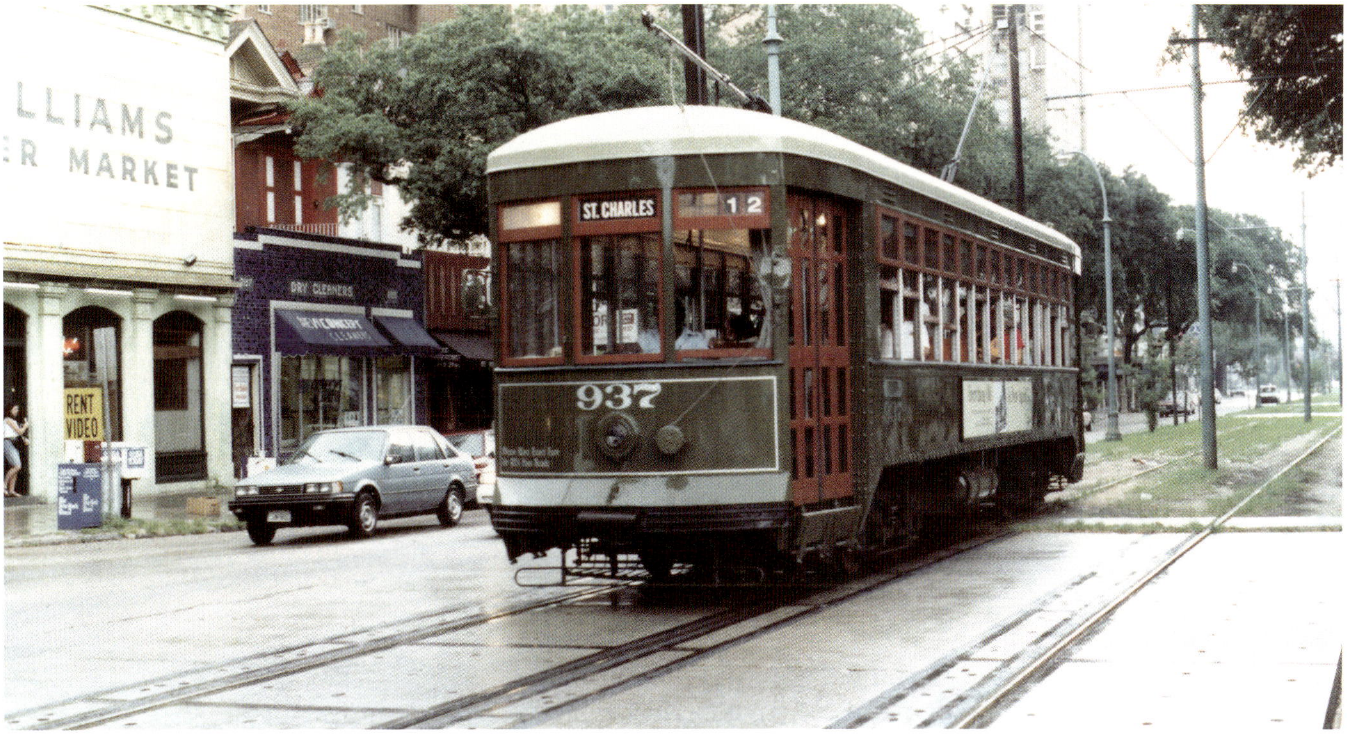

Refurbished RTA streetcar No. 937 (originally weighing 41,148 pounds and powered by two Westinghouse type 306-CV4 motors) is on St. Charles Avenue at Jackson Avenue on July 21, 1991. This streetcar was magnificently restored by the craftsman at the Carrollton Station shop. In 1991, the St. Charles streetcar line had an annual ridership of 7.2 million and twenty-two of the thirty-five streetcars were used during peak periods.

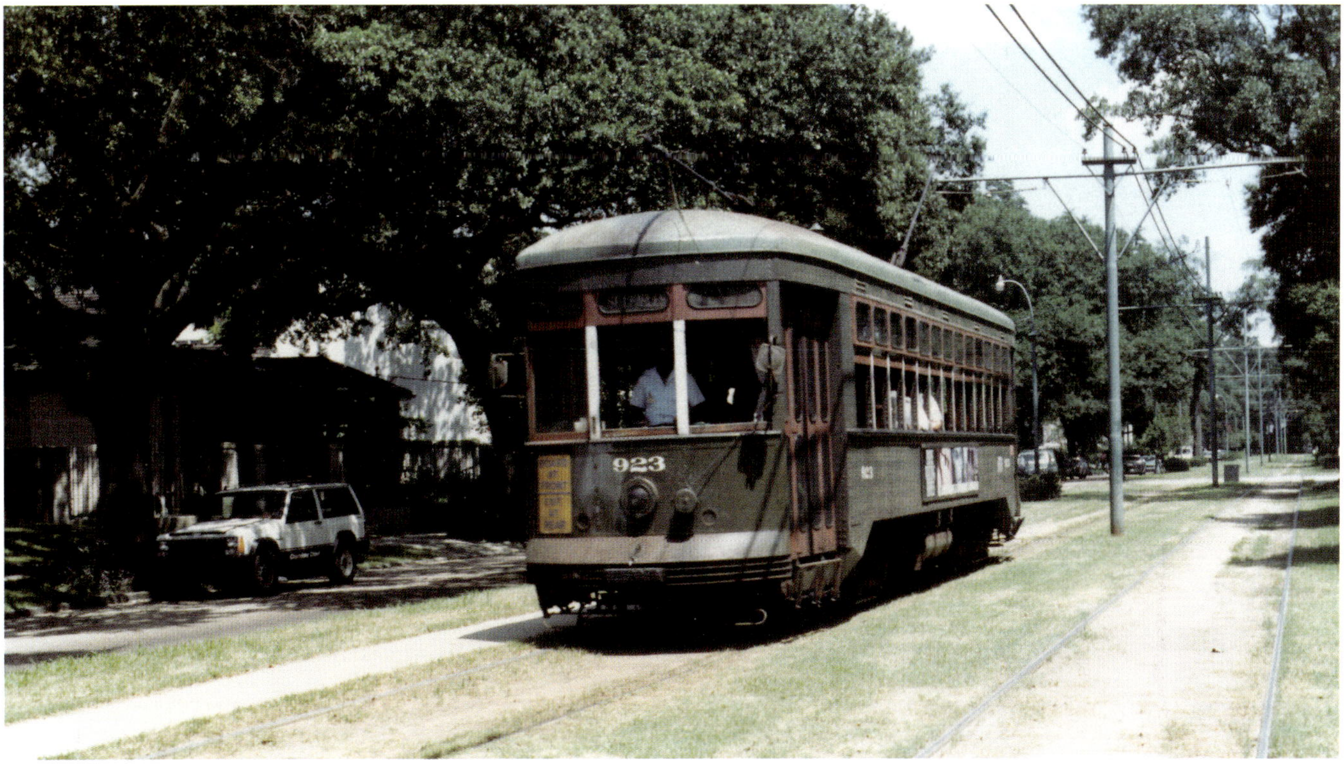

RTA streetcar No. 923 (originally weighing 41,148 pounds and powered by two Westinghouse type 306-CV4 motors) is on St. Charles Avenue at Philip Street (one block west of Jackson Avenue) in the Garden District of New Orleans on July 21, 1991. With the tree-lined streets and an amazing number of historic homes and variety of buildings, this is one of North America's most interesting streetcar lines.

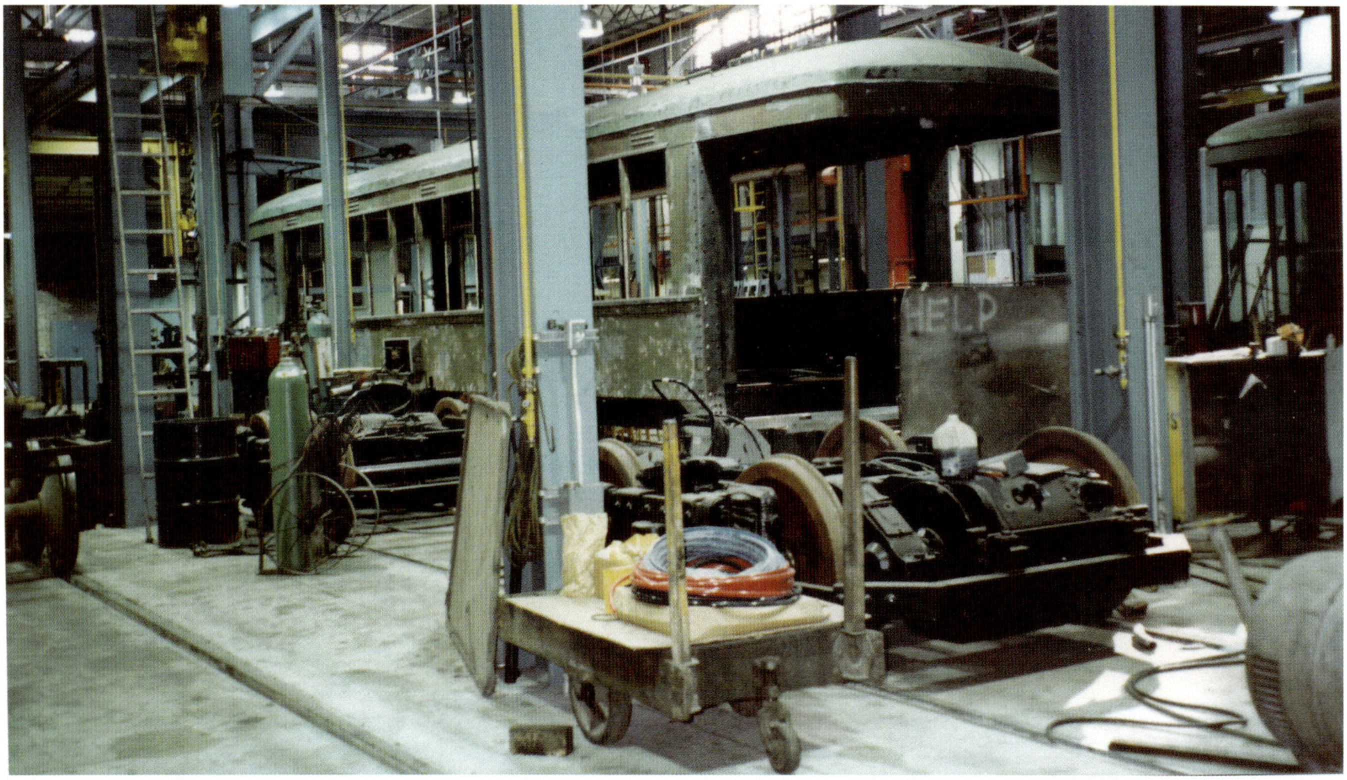

An interior view of the RTA Carrollton Station shop on July 19, 1991 shows a streetcar being rebuilt. The trucks and motors are near the streetcar. This facility, located on Willow Street, a block west of South Carrollton Avenue, is in the Leonidas or West Carrollton neighborhood of New Orleans. The skilled craftsmen at this facility have handled everything from maintenance to building brand new streetcars.

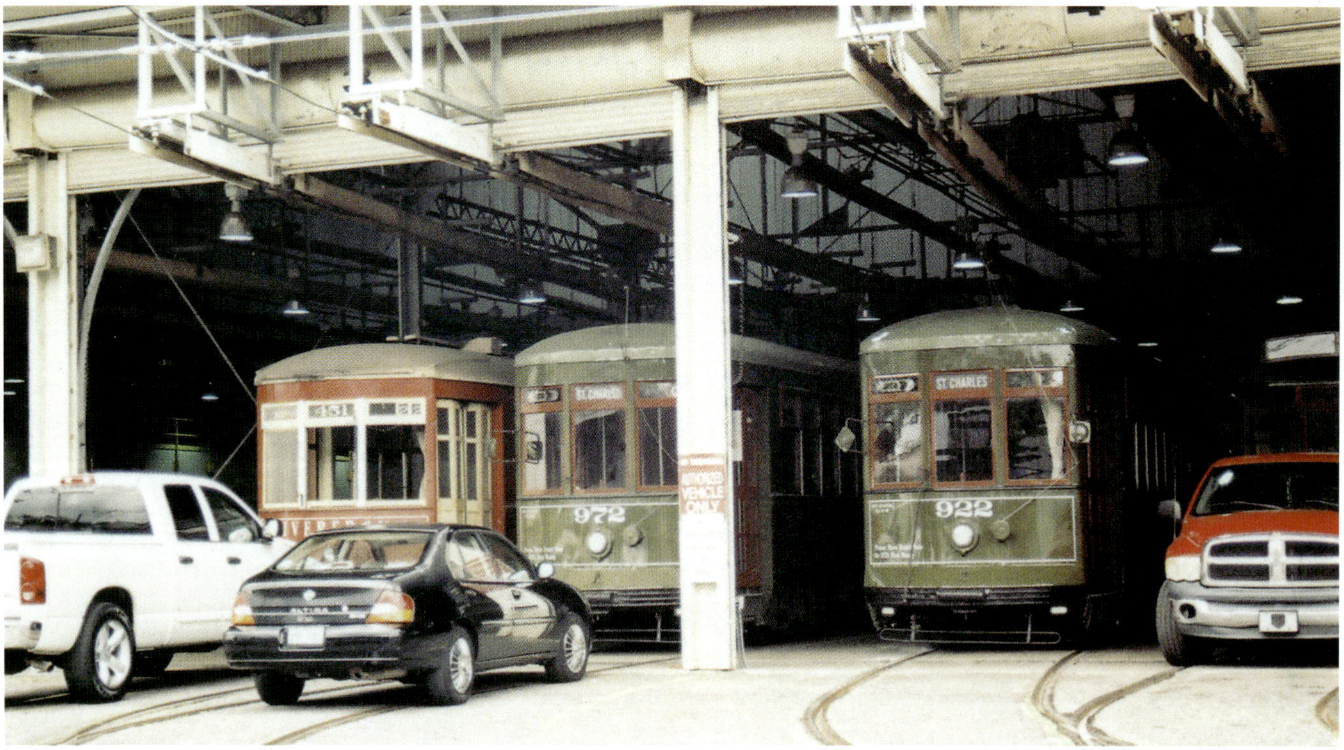

On April 22, 2013, RTA streetcars Nos. 451 (Riverfront originally New Orleans Public Service Inc. No. 919 returned from the Texas State Fairgrounds on September 19, 1985 and became No. 451), 972, and 922 are in view at the Willow Street side of the Carrollton Station carbarn. These three streetcars were built by Perley A. Thomas Car Company originally weighing 42,036 pounds and were powered by two General Electric type 263A motors.

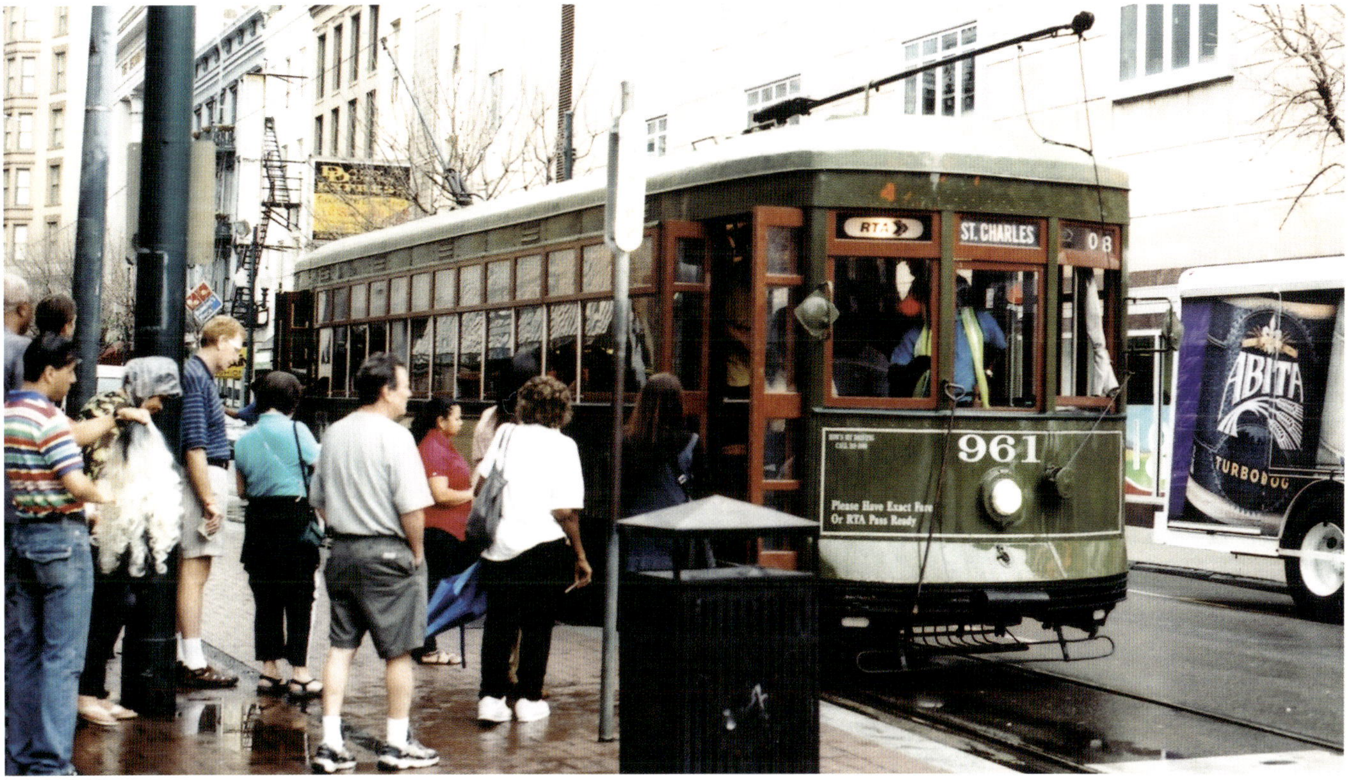

RTA streetcar No. 961 (originally weighing 42,036 pounds and powered by two General Electric type 263A motors) is on Carondelet Street at Canal Street, at this busy stop, on April 24, 2013. Because of the frequent cross streets, streetcar operators have to be vigilant about motorists turning across the tracks.

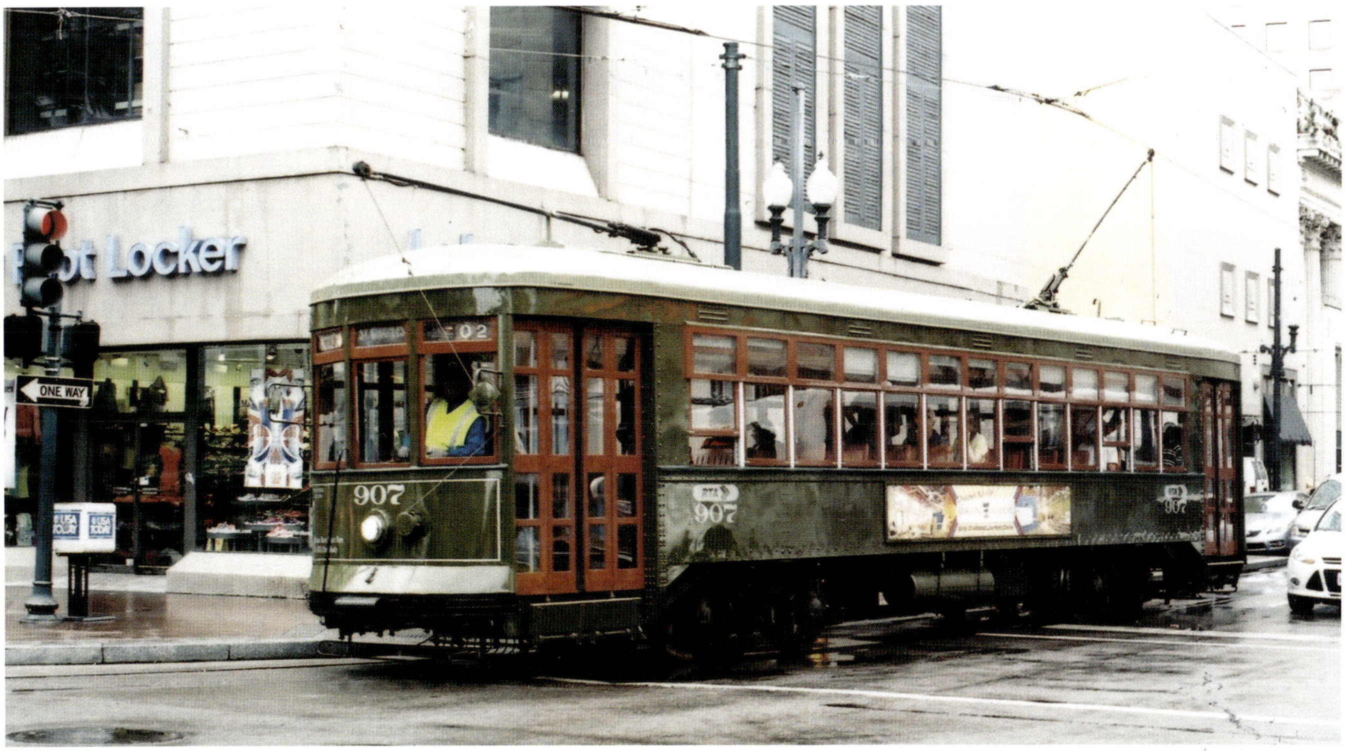

On a rainy April 24, 2013, RTA streetcar No. 907 is turning from Carondelet Street onto Canal Street. The St. Charles streetcar line is officially route 12, but that number is not displayed on the streetcar. However, when buses are used on the St. Charles line, the destination sign will show 12 St. Charles.

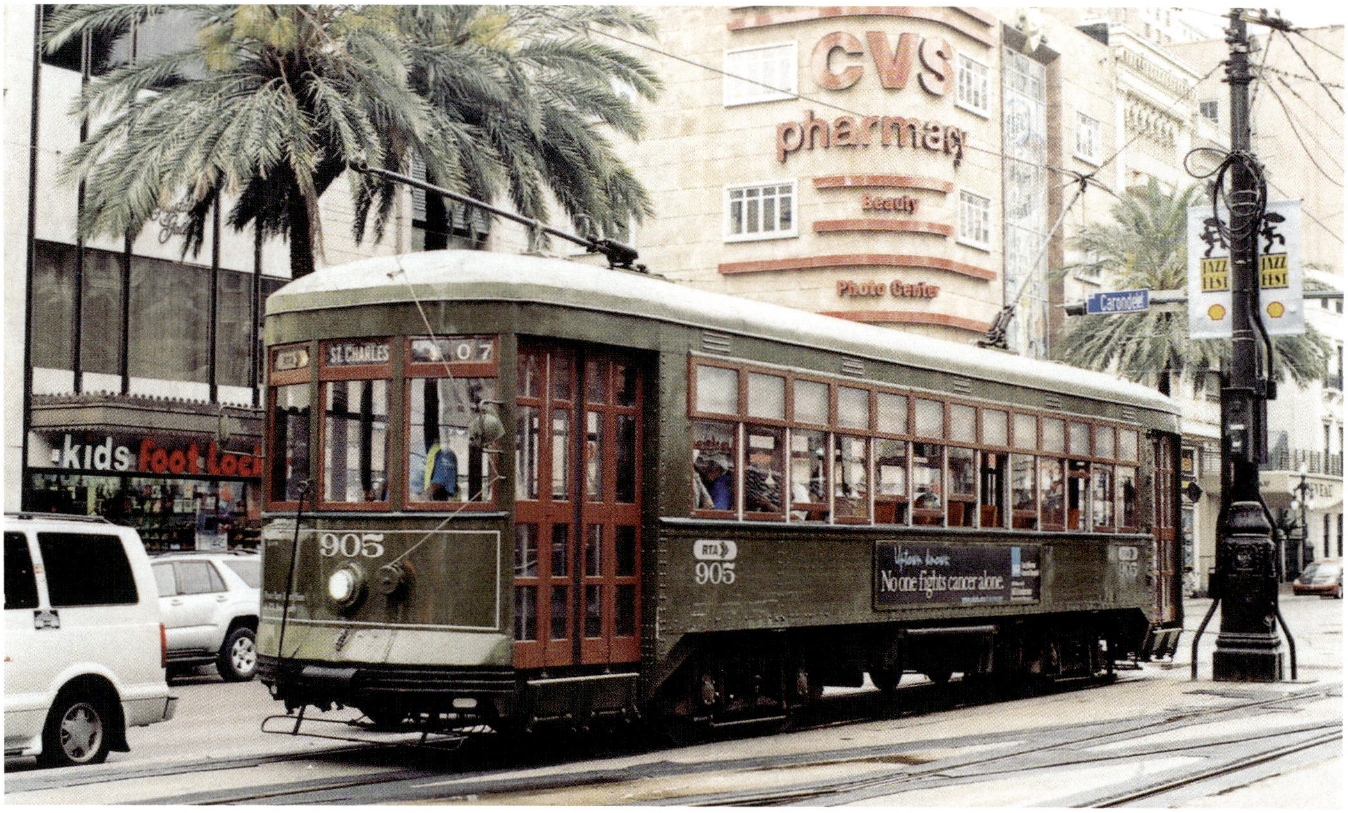

RTA streetcar No. 905 (originally weighing 42,036 pounds and powered by two General Electric type 263A motors) has completed the turn from Carondelet Street to Canal Street on April 24, 2013. The CVS Pharmacy was formerly the women's store Gus Mayer.

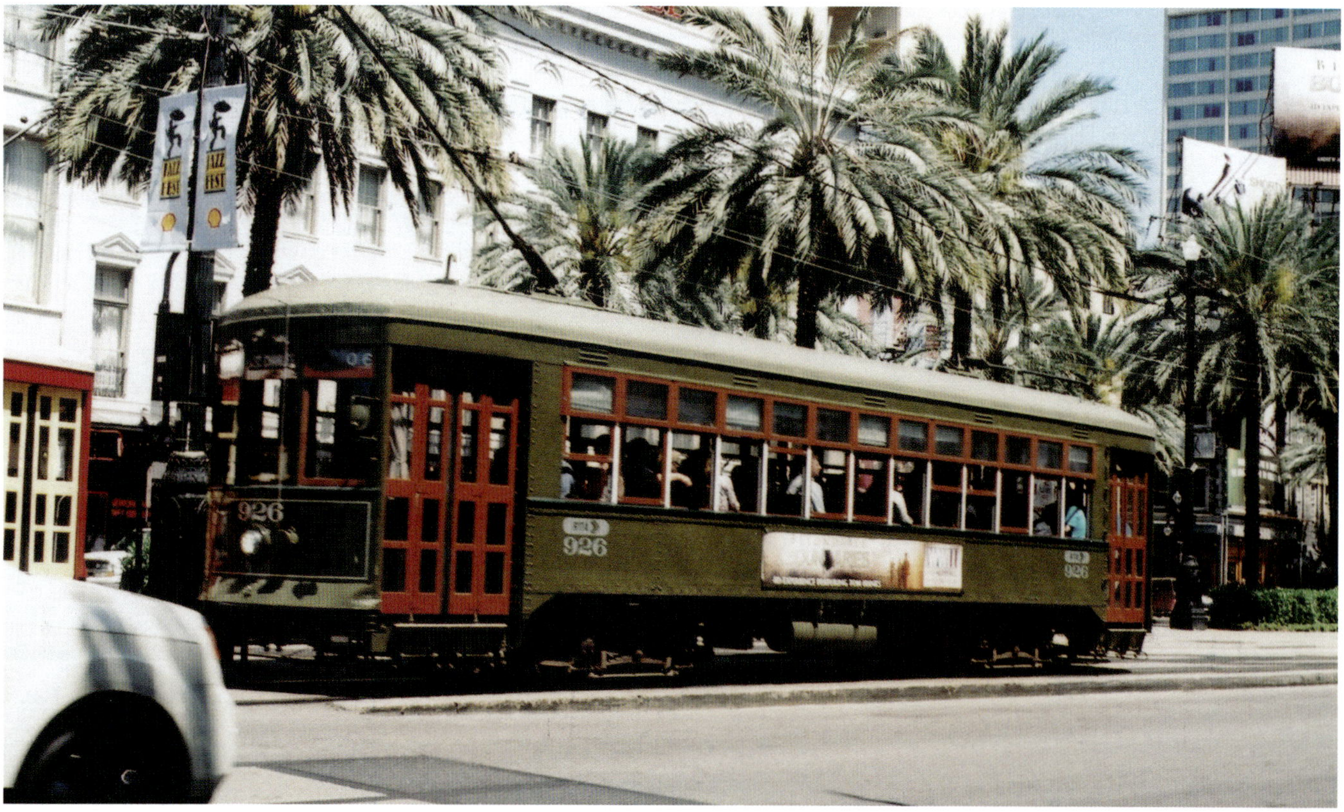

On Canal Street, RTA streetcar No. 926 (originally weighing 41,148 pounds and powered by two Westinghouse type 306-CV4 motors) on April 21, 2013 is on a separate track for one block where it then turns on St. Charles Avenue. The red streetcar on the left is a Canal streetcar.

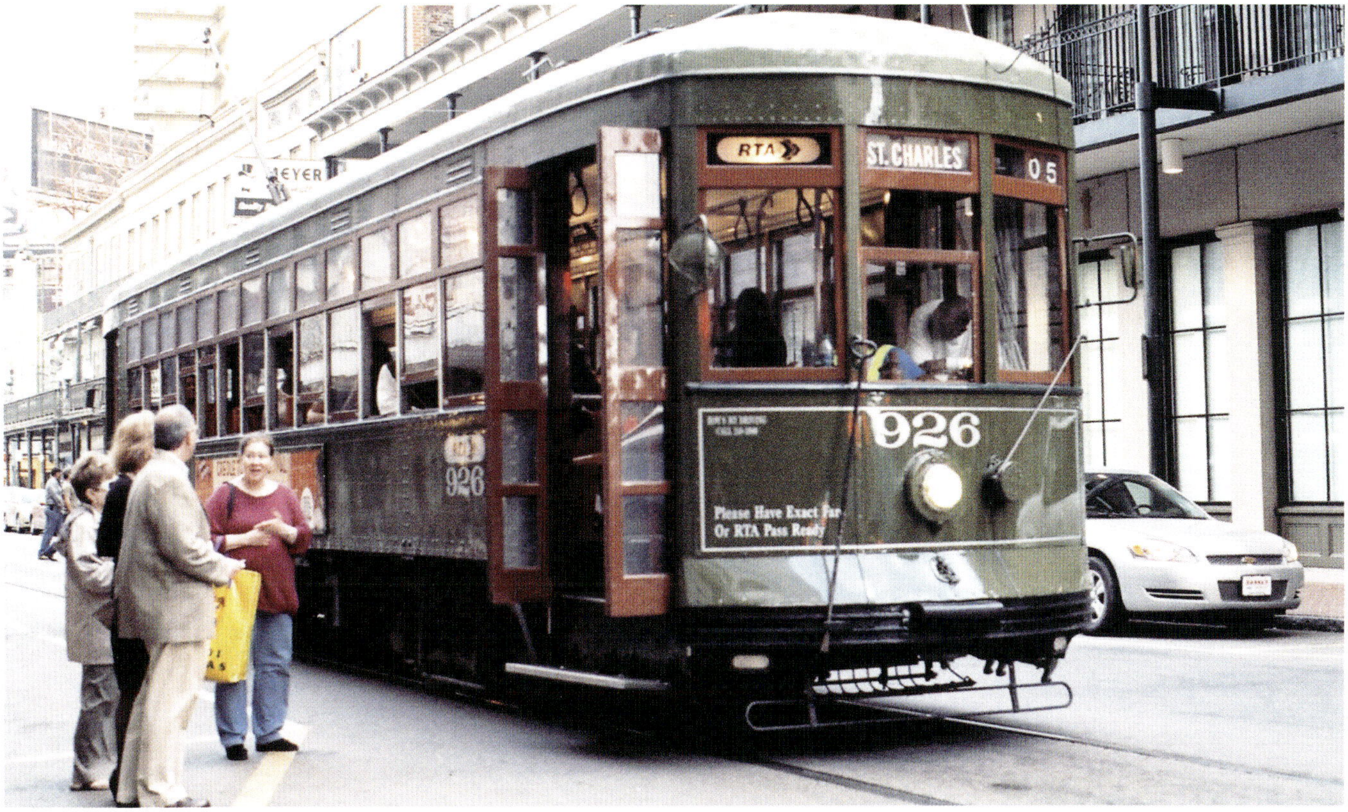

RTA streetcar No. 926 is on St. Charles Avenue at Common Street for a passenger stop on April 22, 2013. The St. Charles streetcar line provides a unique way to enjoy the city from the Central Business District via Lee Circle monument to its terminus in the Carrollton neighborhood.

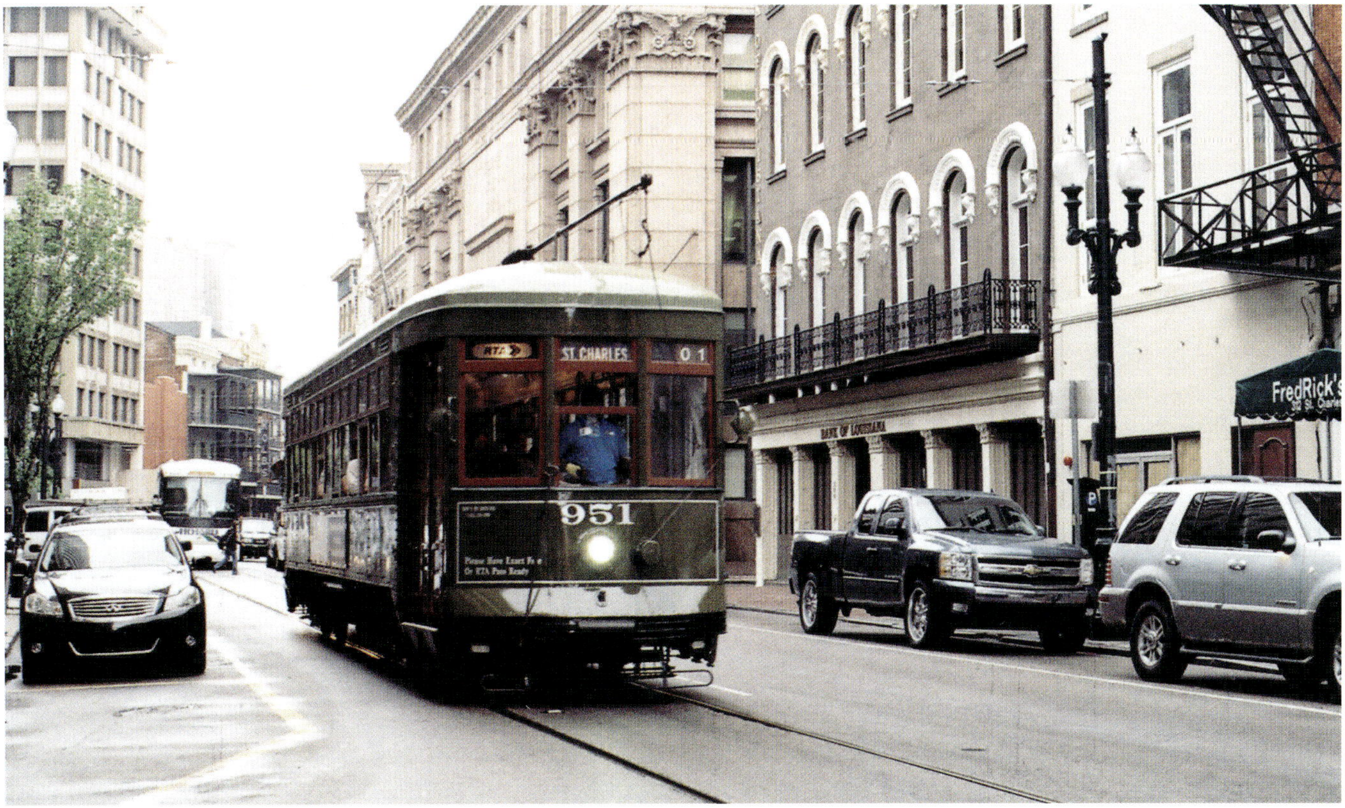

In the Central Business District, RTA streetcar No. 951 (originally weighing 42,036 pounds and powered by two General Electric type 263A motors) is on St. Charles Avenue at Union Street, on April 24, 2013.

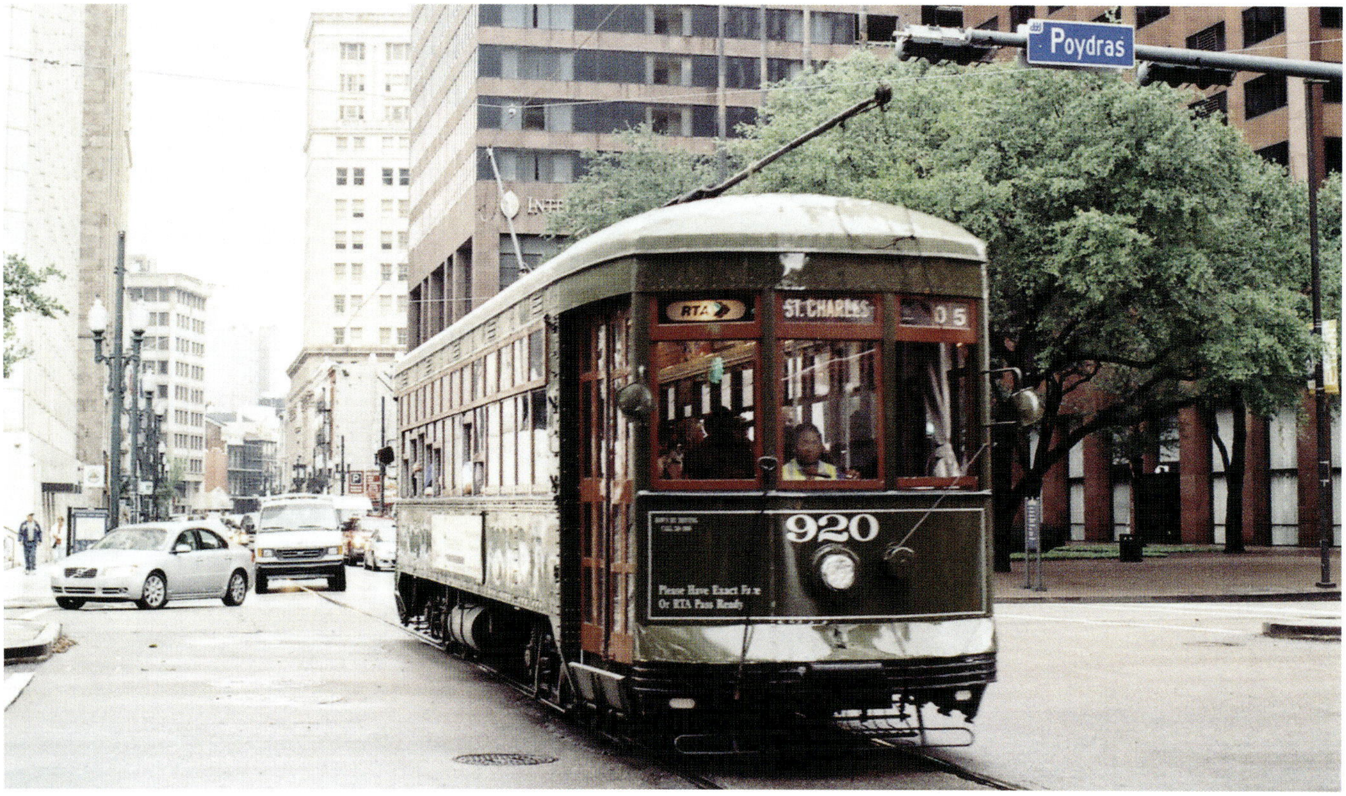

On an overcast April 24, 2013, RTA streetcar No. 920 (originally weighing 42,036 pounds and powered by two General Electric type 263A motors) is on St. Charles Avenue at Poydras Street. One Shell Square, a 51-story skyscraper that was completed in 1972, is on the left of the picture.

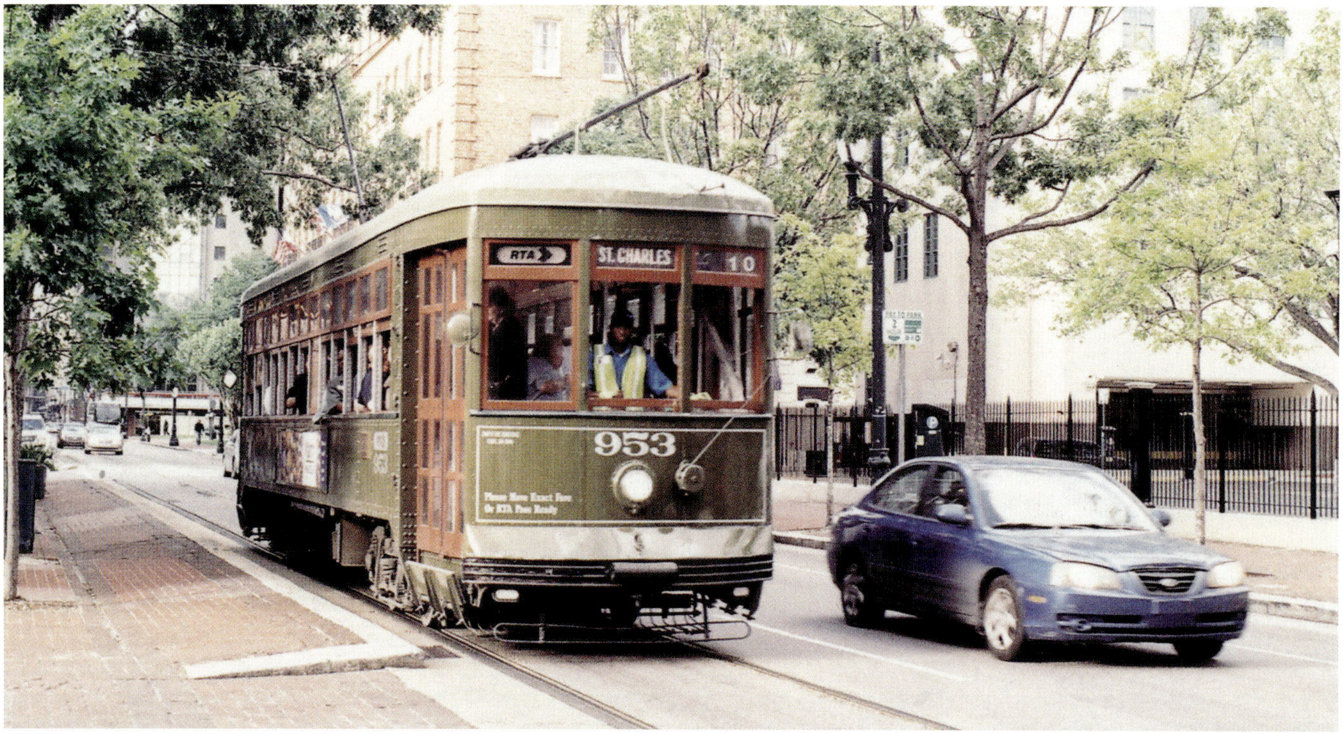

RTA streetcar No. 953 (originally weighing 42,036 pounds and powered by two General Electric type 263A motors) is on St. Charles Avenue at Girod Street on April 22, 2013. Streetcar No. 953 served as the model for commemorative stamp "St. Charles streetcar, New Orleans, La. 1923" issued by the U.S. Postal Service on October 8, 1983.

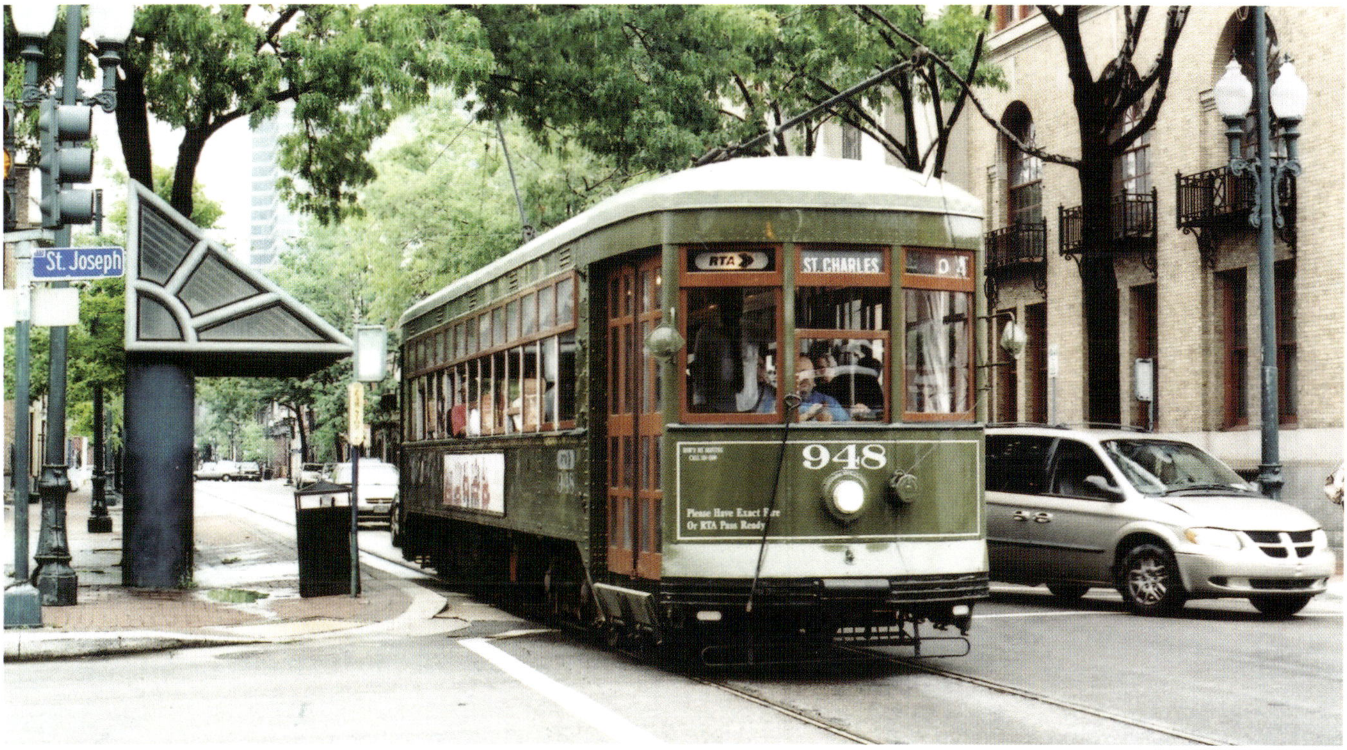

RTA streetcar No. 948 (originally weighing 42,036 pounds and powered by two General Electric type 263A motors) is on St. Charles Avenue crossing St. Joseph Street on April 24, 2013. In 2013, the 900 series streetcars built by Perley A. Thomas Car Company in 1923-24 have been in regular daily public transit service longer than most other streetcars in North America. Other systems that have even older streetcars in service include the San Francisco Municipal Railway in San Francisco, California and the McKinney Avenue Transit Authority in Dallas, Texas.

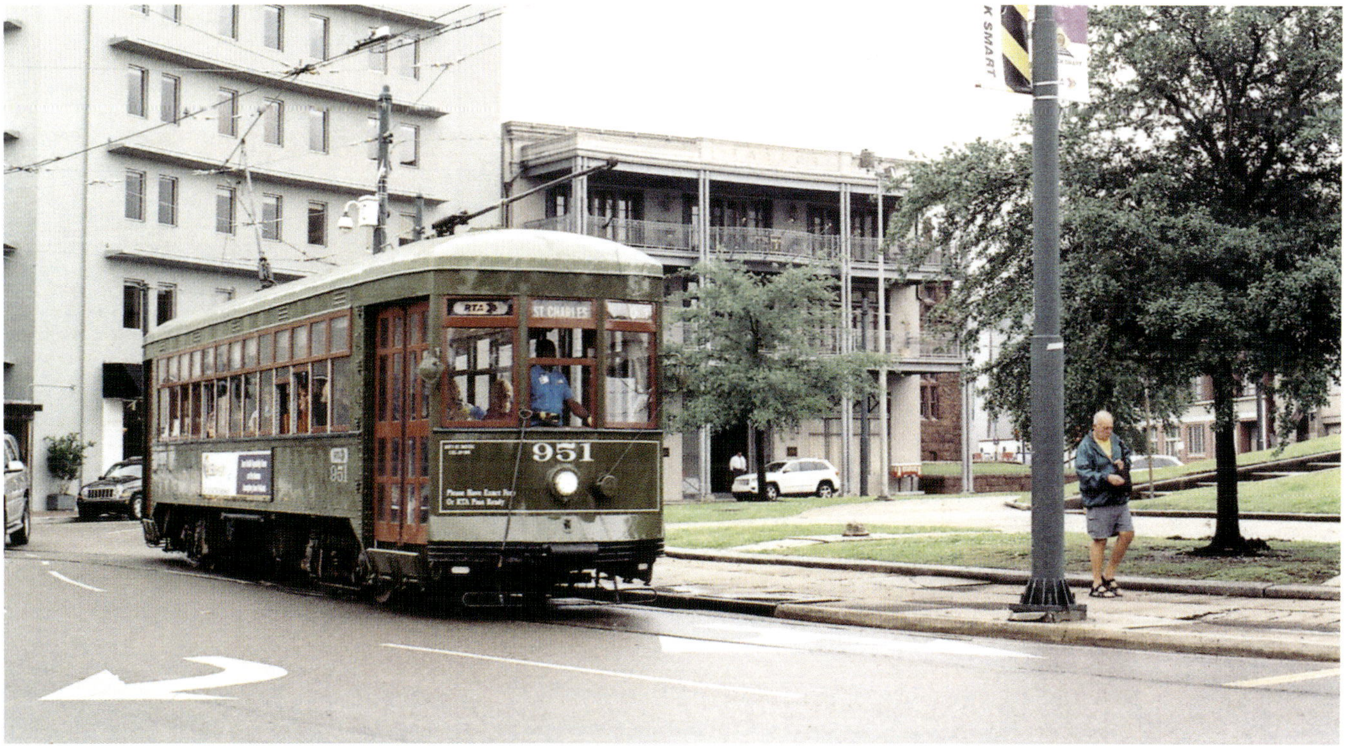

At the Lee Circle Monument, RTA streetcar No. 951 is in the turn and will shortly switch off to Howard Avenue and Carondelet Street to Canal Street, on April 24, 2013. Lee Circle was created in 1807 by Architect Barthelemy Lafon and was called Tivoli Circle. Rising high over the traffic circle is the magnificent statue of Robert E. Lee, the Confederate War General.

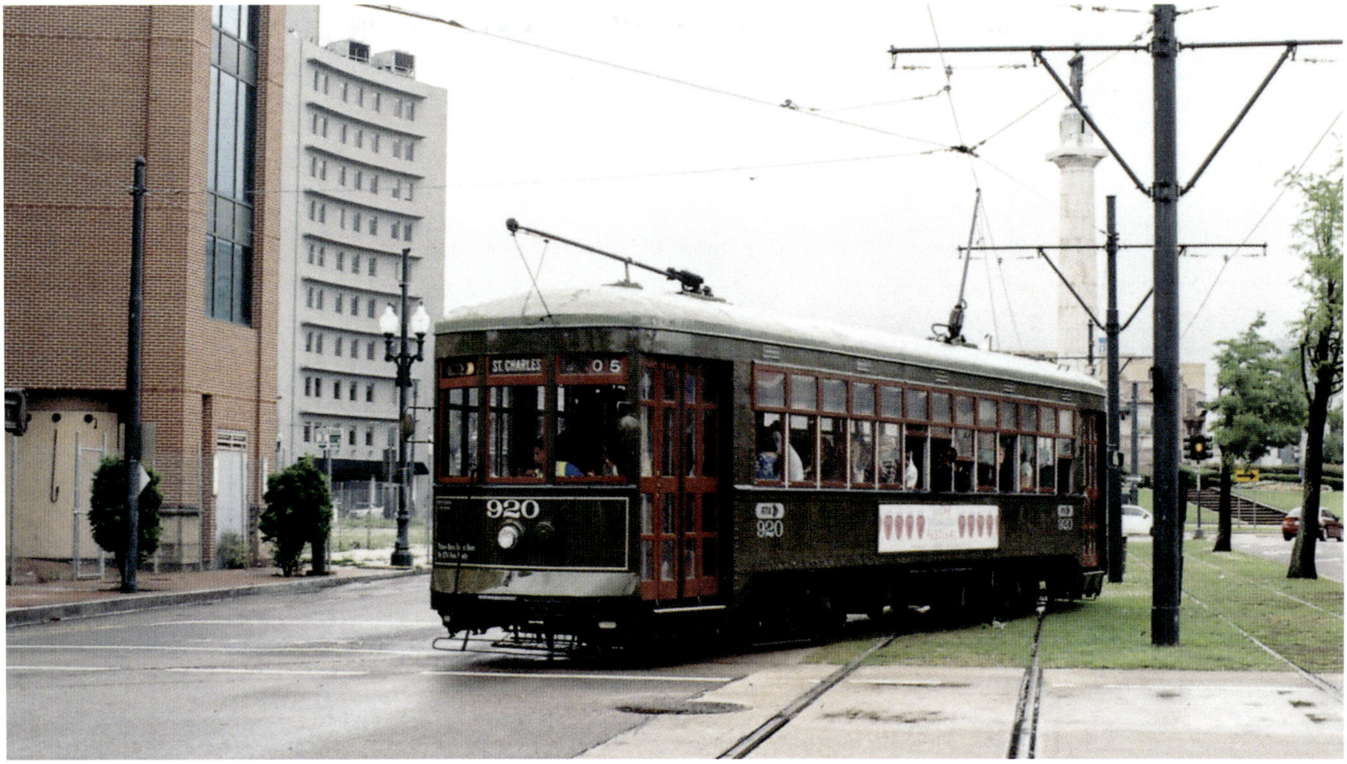

With the Lee Circle Monument in the background on April 24, 2013, RTA streetcar No. 920 is turning from the Howard Avenue center-of-the-road private right of way onto Carondelet Street. The monument honoring Confederate General Robert E. Lee, inaugurated in 1884, has a twelve foot statue of General Lee standing towards the north (sculpted by Alexander Doyle) on top of a sixty foot tall Doric column, which is set on a rectangular base at the center of the traffic circle.

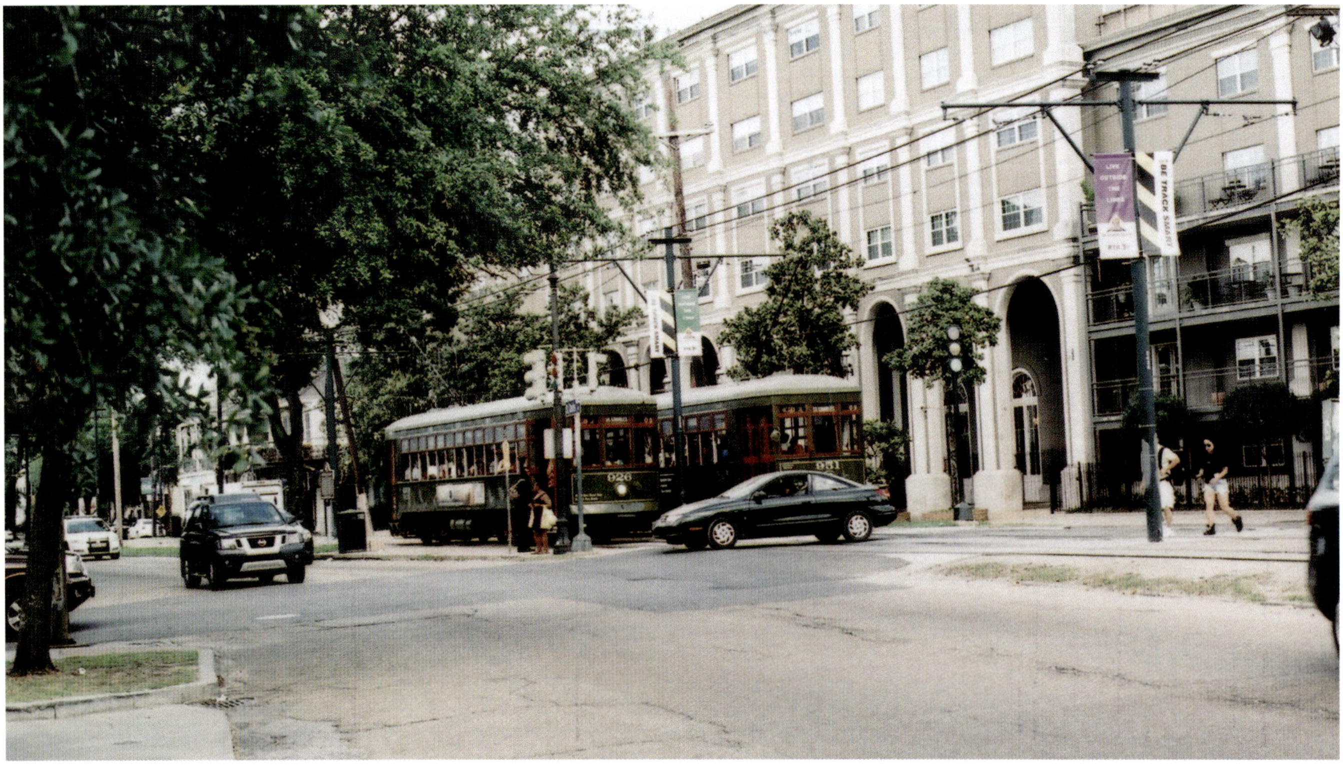

On St. Charles Avenue, four blocks east of Jackson Avenue is Felicity Street in the Lower Garden District where RTA streetcar No. 926 is passing No. 951 on April 22, 2013. These streetcars feature beautiful wooden seats. Although there is no air conditioning, with the windows open a pleasant breeze enters the streetcar when it is moving.

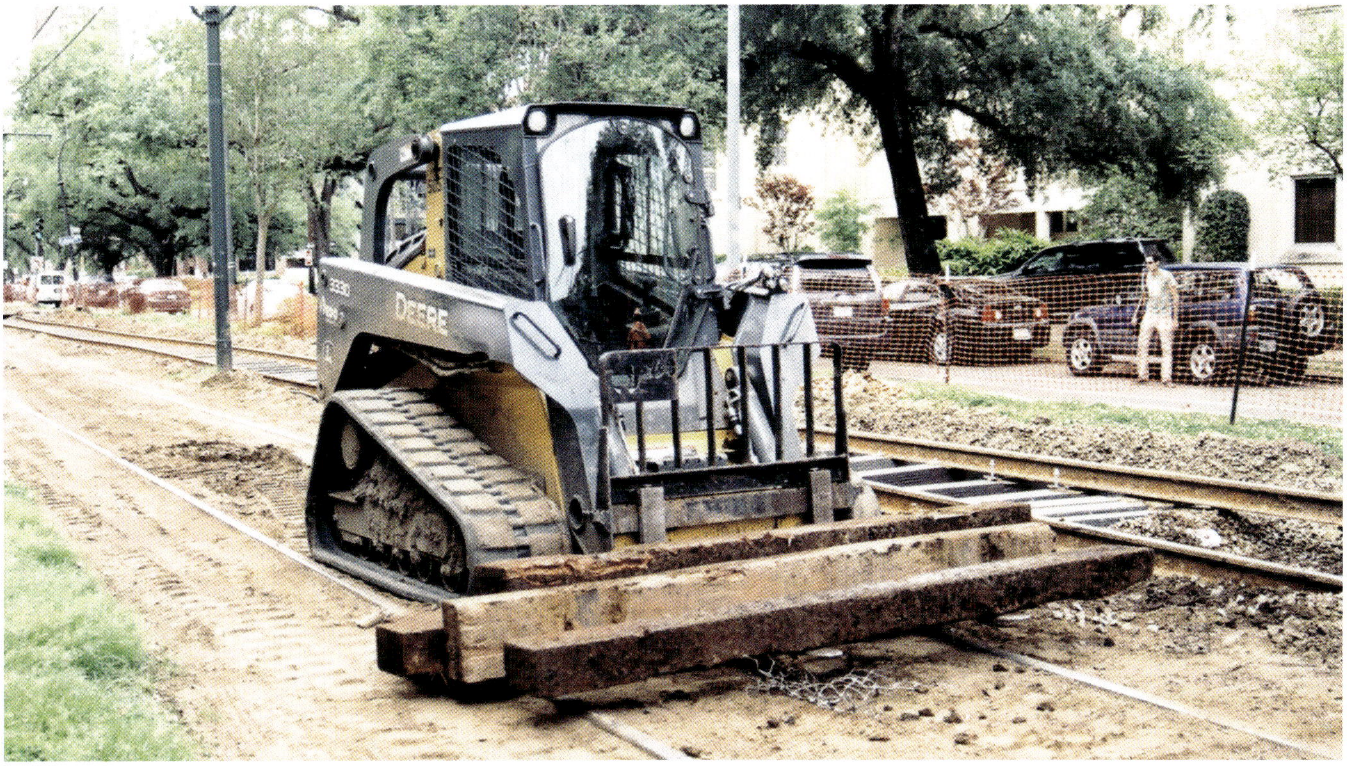

A major tie replacement project is under way on St. Charles Avenue at Palmer Avenue on April 22, 2013. This necessitated replacement of streetcars with buses, from Jefferson Avenue to the end of the line at South Carrollton Avenue and South Claiborne Avenue.

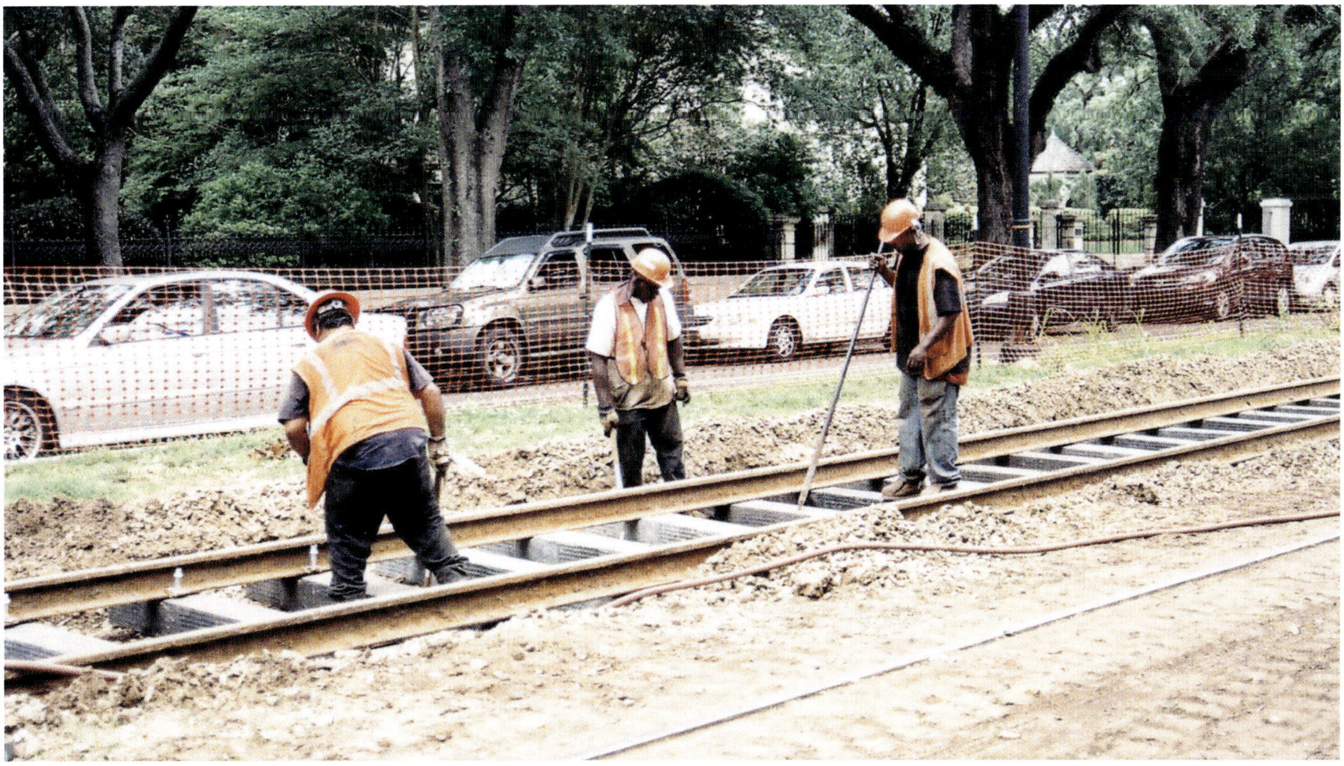

With new ties in place, the track crew is securing the rail to the ties on St. Charles Avenue at Palmer Avenue on April 22, 2013. Ties were last replaced during 1988 but have deteriorated due to termite infestation and rot resulting from the hot, humid climate in New Orleans.

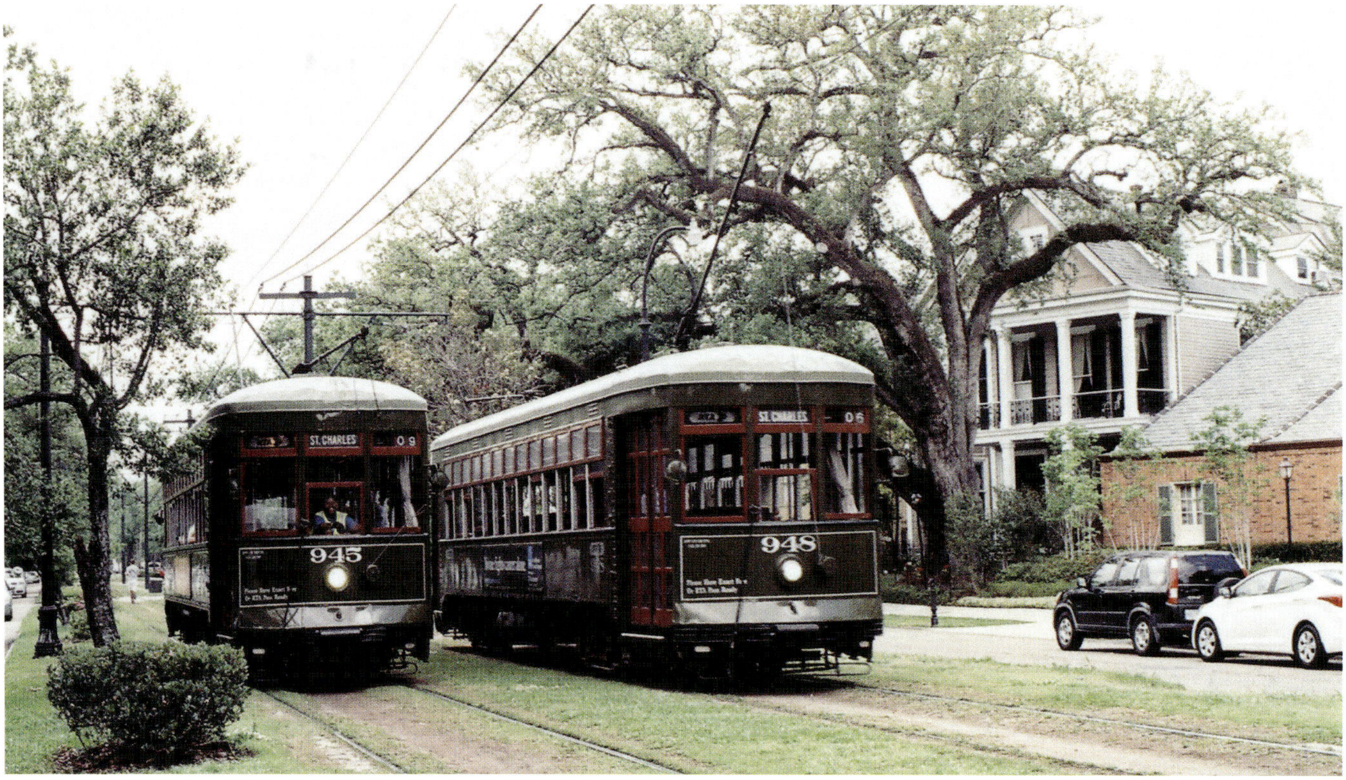

Because of the tie replacement project, the temporary terminus of the St. Charles Avenue streetcars is at Jefferson Avenue where RTA streetcars Nos. 945 and 948 await the departure time, on April 22, 2013. These ninety year old vintage streetcars in 2013 look brand new.

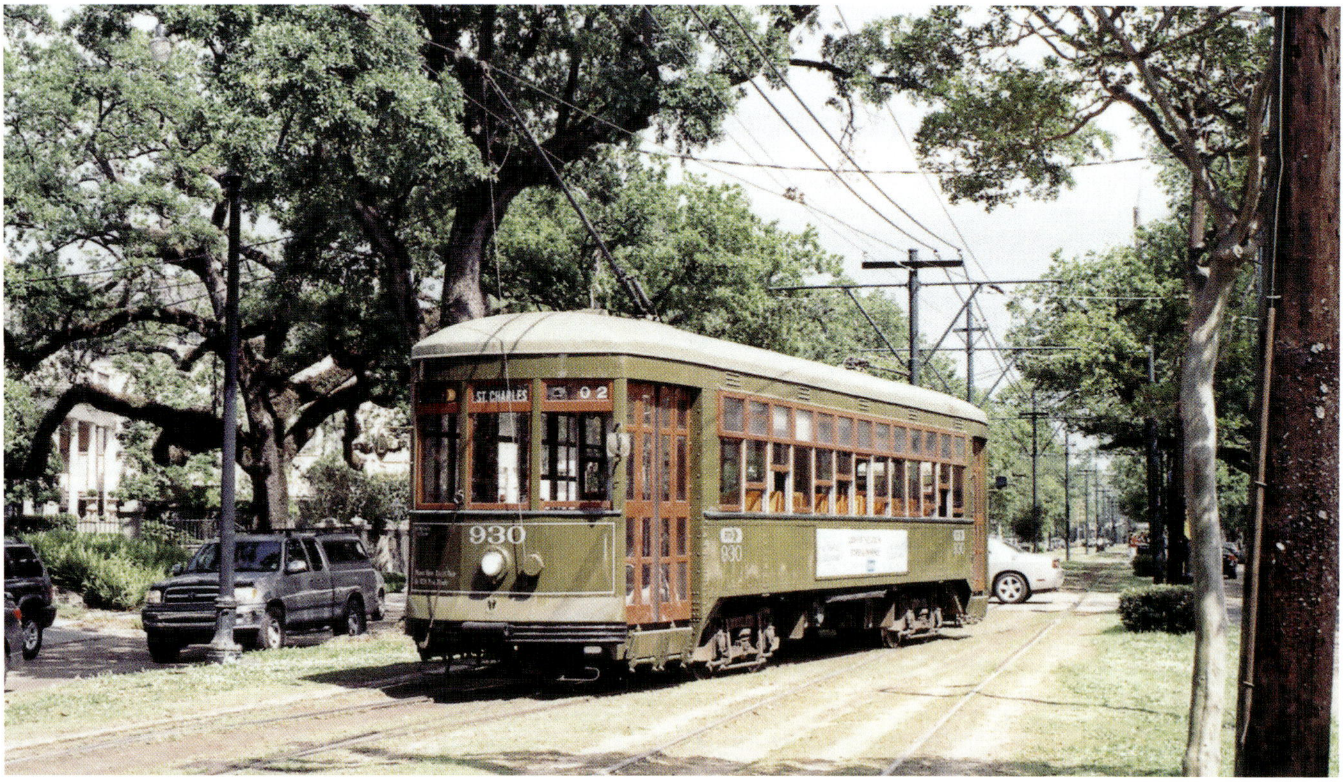

On St. Charles Avenue near Jefferson Avenue, RTA streetcar No. 930 is crossing over for the trip to Canal Street on April 22, 2013. Hurricane Katrina hit New Orleans on August 29, 2005 flooding most of the city and damaging thirty streetcars. On December 12, 2005, streetcar No. 930, towed from the Carrollton Station shop, made the first test runs on Canal Street and made the first public run over a portion of the Canal and Riverfront streetcar lines on December 18, 2005.

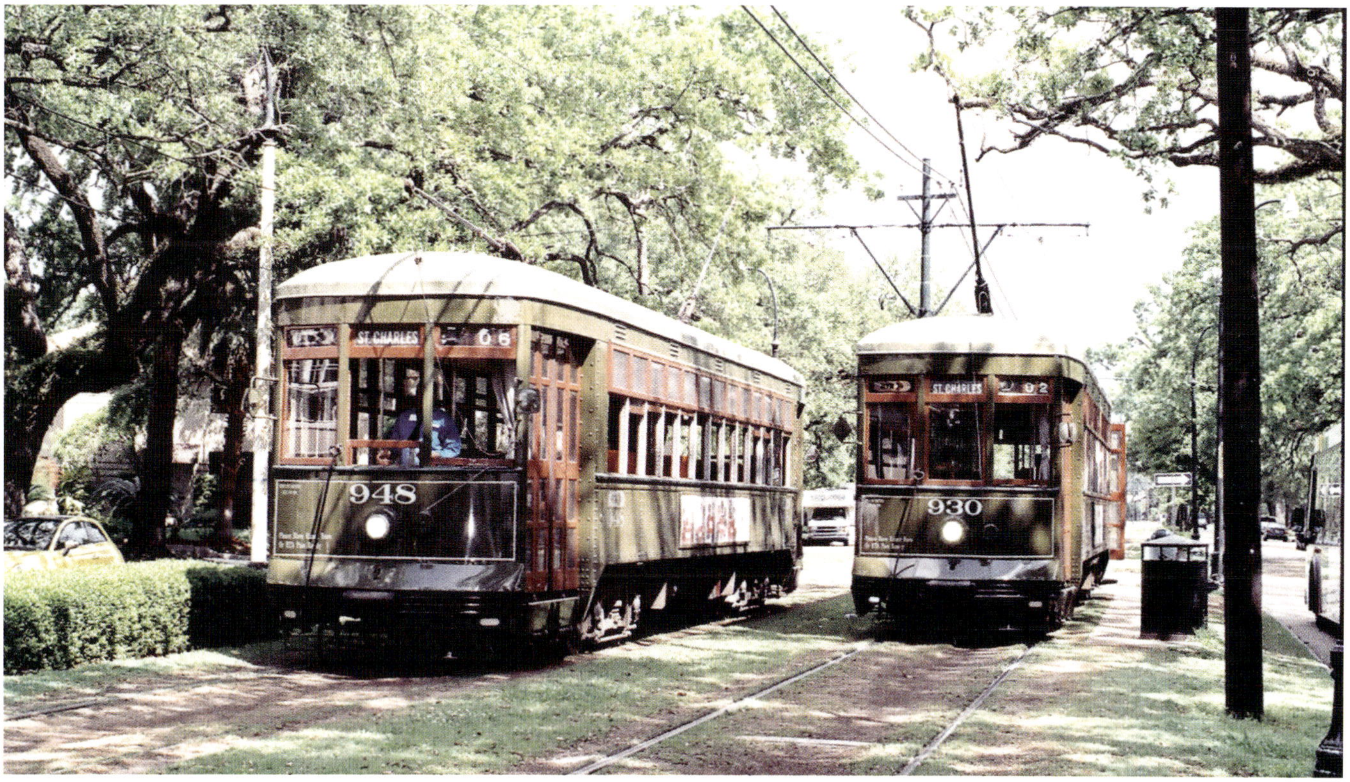

RTA streetcars Nos. 948 and 930 are on St. Charles Avenue near Jefferson Avenue on April 22, 2013 at the temporary terminus of the line, because of extensive replacement of ties.

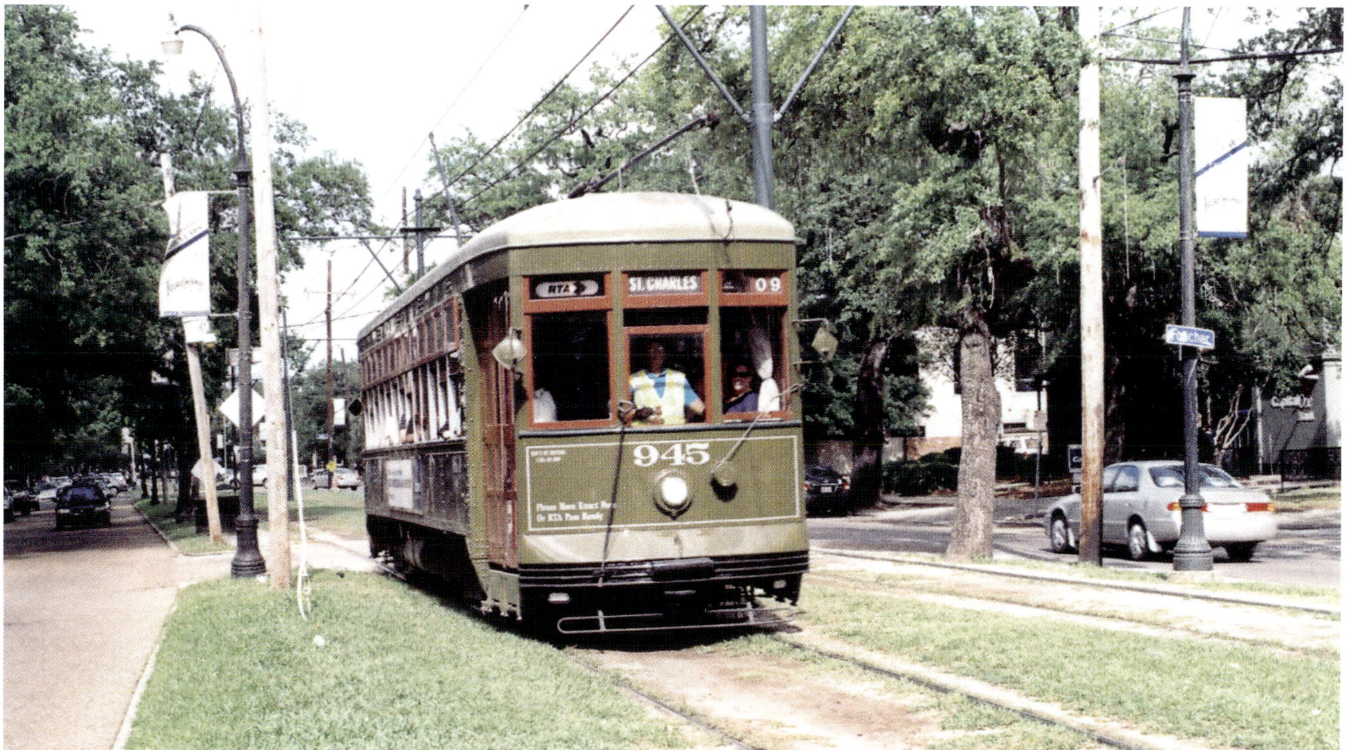

RTA streetcar No. 945 is on the reserved, grass-covered right of way in the center of St. Charles Avenue at Foucher Street (about three blocks west of Louisiana Avenue) on April 22, 2013. This is in the Milan neighborhood of New Orleans.

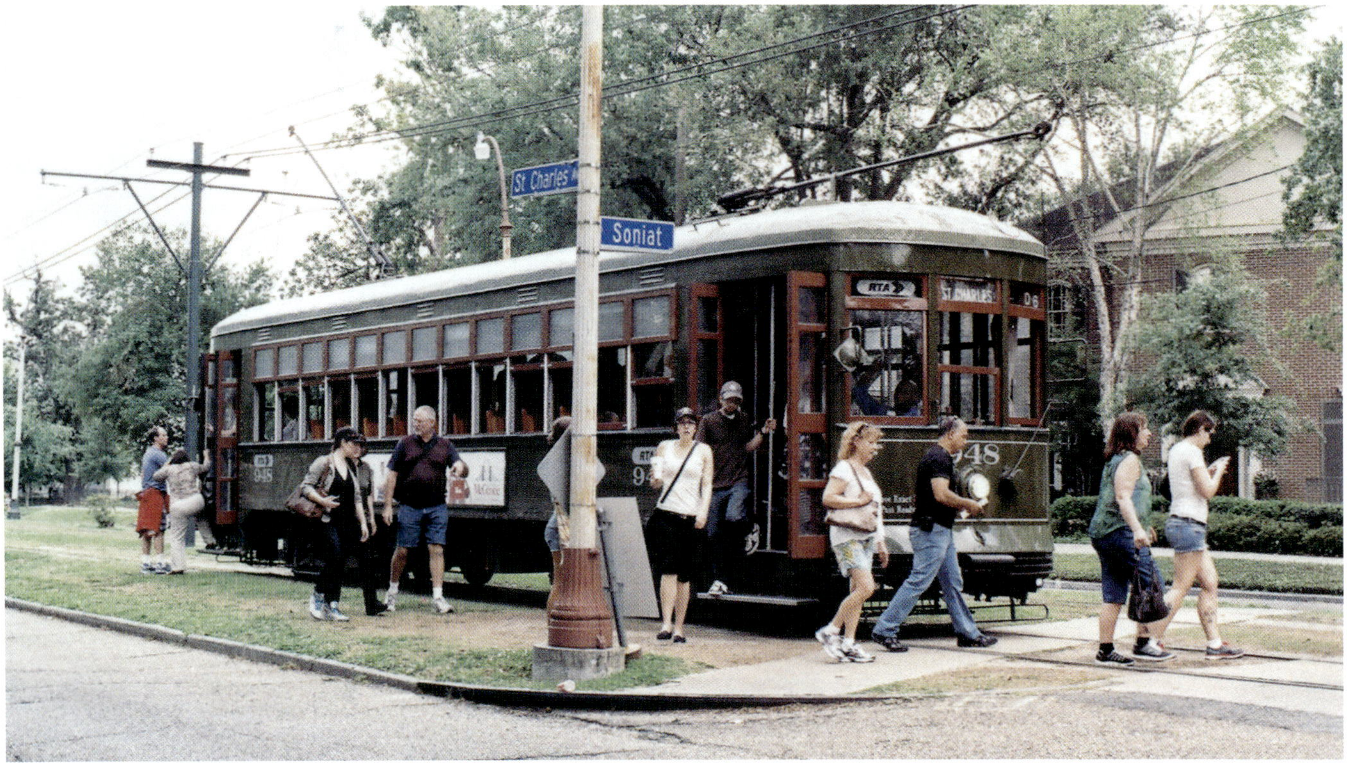

RTA streetcar No. 948 is at St. Charles Avenue at Soniat Street (about four blocks east of Jefferson Avenue) on April 22, 2013 in the Uptown neighborhood of New Orleans. The St. Charles streetcar line is a charming way to travel from the Central Business District to the Uptown neighborhood of New Orleans.

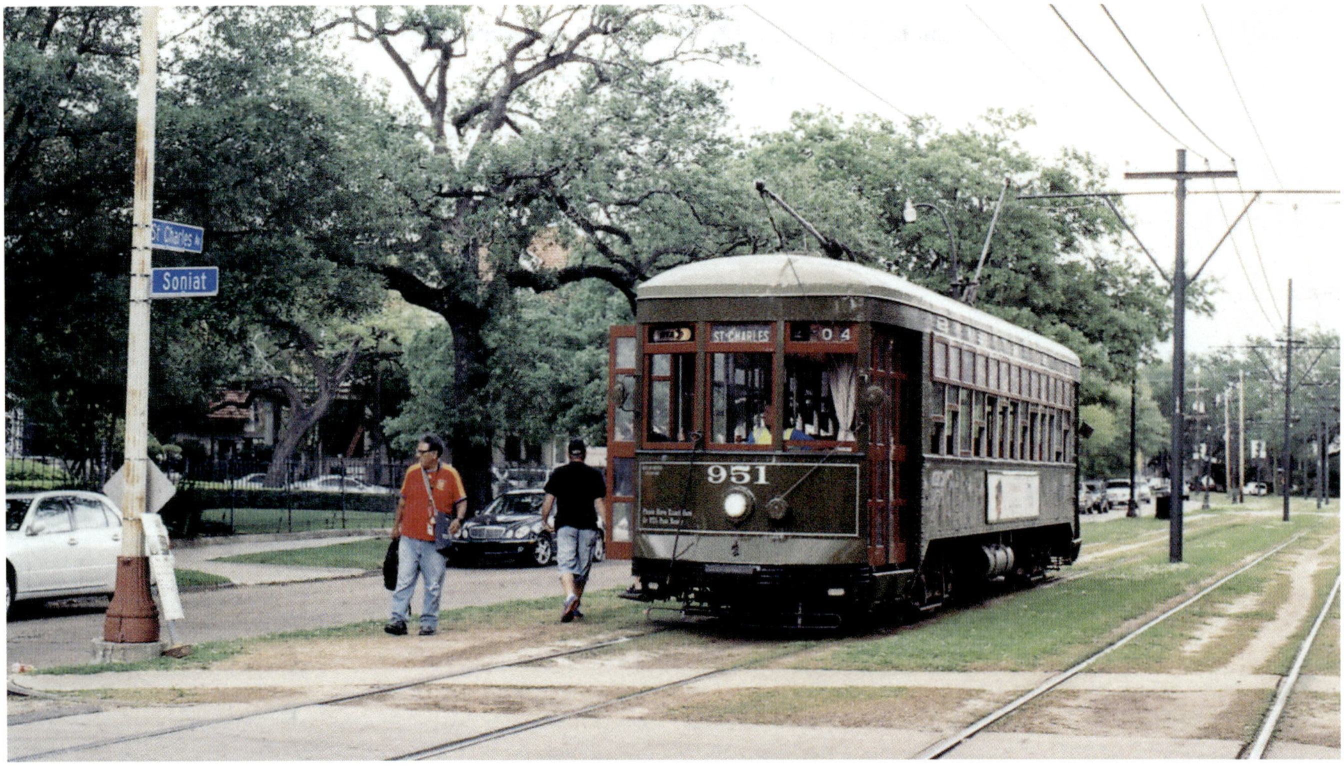

On April 22, 2013, RTA streetcar No. 951 is on St. Charles Avenue for a passenger stop at Soniat Street. This is the most picturesque urban streetcar line in North America.

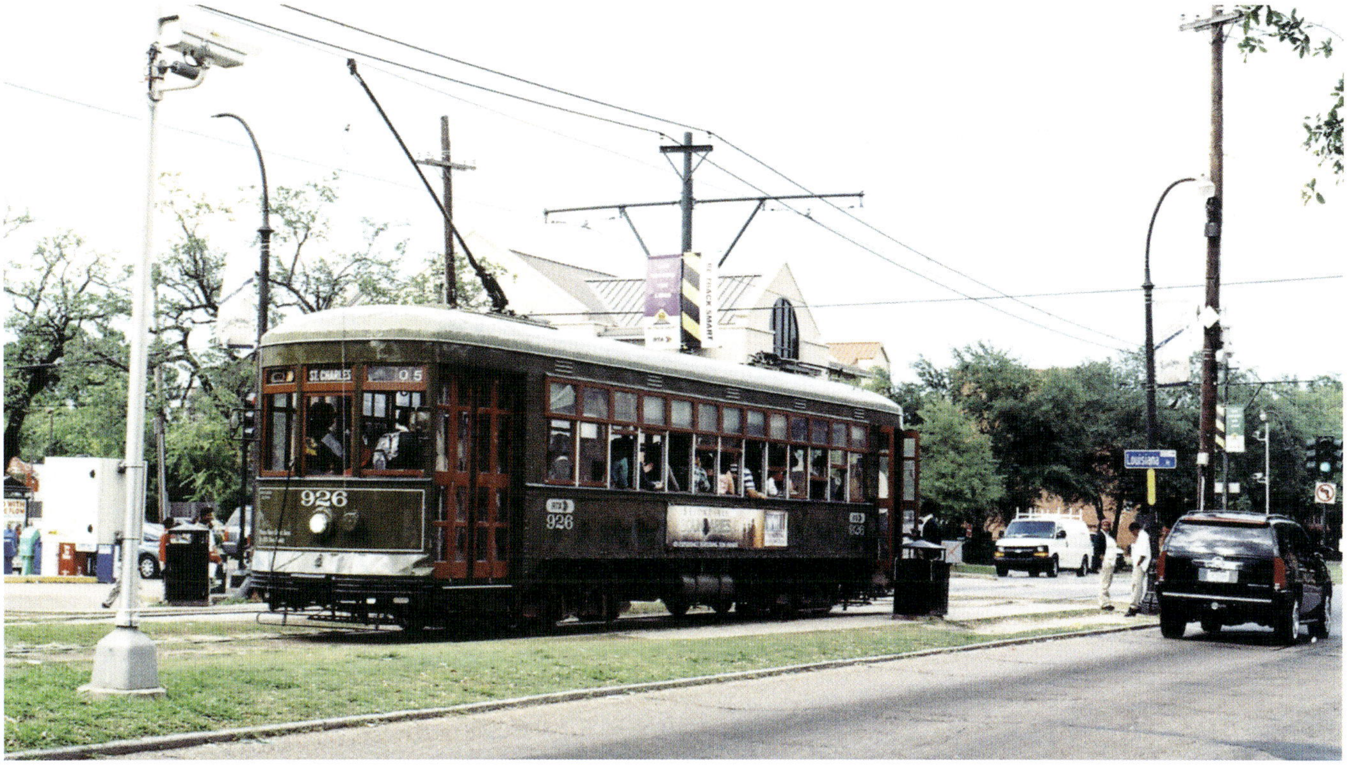

On April 22, 2013, RTA streetcar No. 926 is on St. Charles Avenue at Louisiana Avenue. North of St. Charles Avenue, Louisiana Avenue is in the Milan neighborhood of New Orleans. South of St. Charles Avenue, Louisiana Avenue is in the Touro neighborhood of New Orleans. The Louisiana line operated as a streetcar line on Louisiana Avenue from August 27, 1913 until it was converted to bus operation on December 27, 1934.

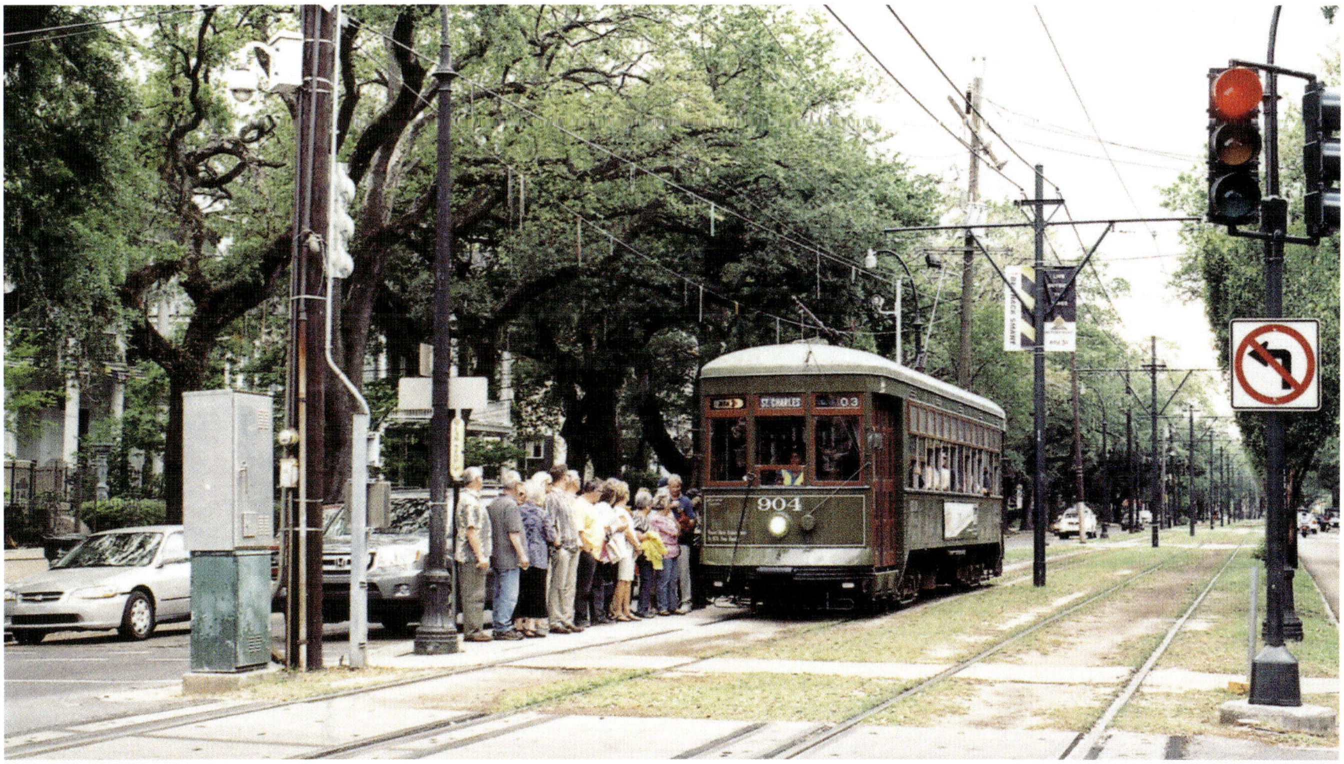

A group of passengers are boarding RTA streetcar No. 904 (originally weighing 42,036 pounds and powered by two General Electric type 263A motors) on St. Charles Avenue near Harmony Street (about three blocks east of Louisiana Avenue), on April 22, 2013. This is in the Garden District, which attracts tourists.

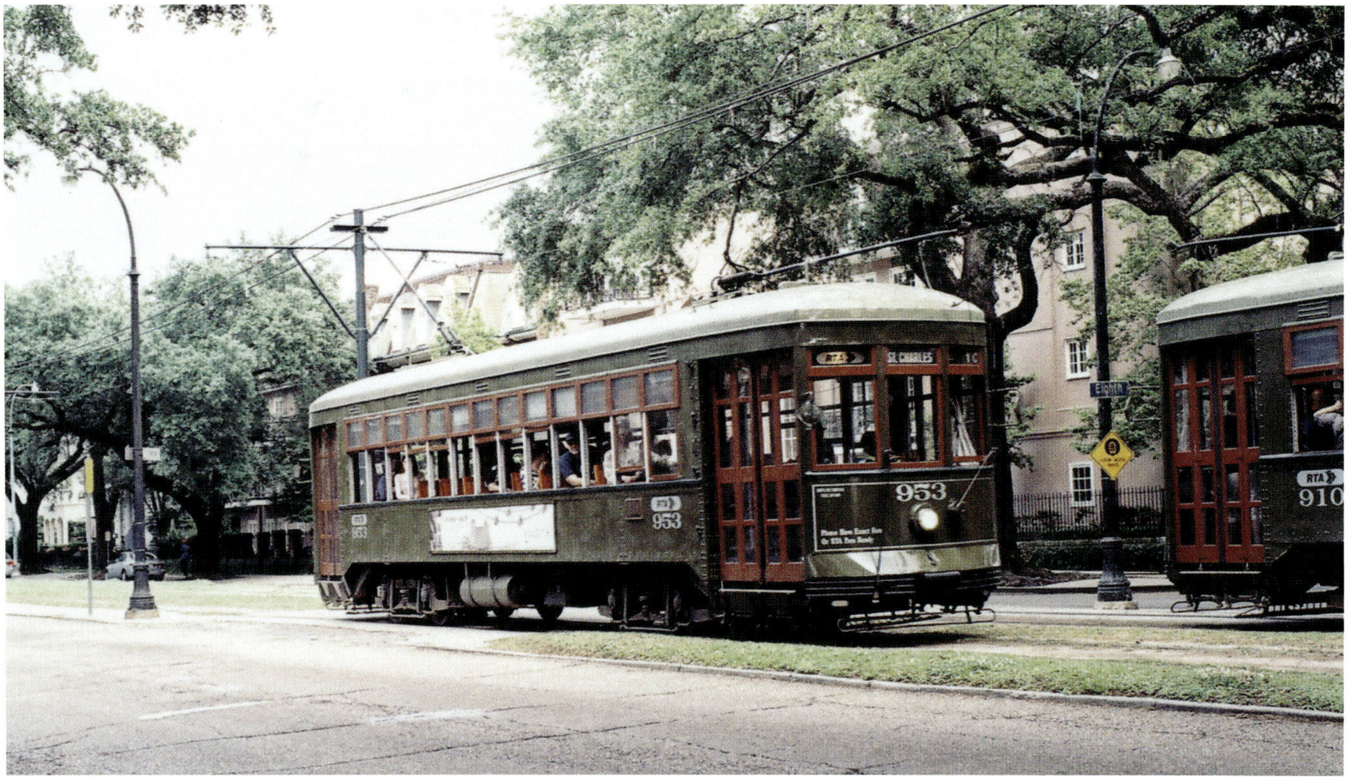

On St. Charles Avenue at Eighth Street, RTA streetcar No. 953 is about to pass No. 910 in the Garden District of New Orleans on April 22, 2013. These streetcars have been completely rebuilt and have had numerous upgrades made over the years, but in their last major restoration, completed in 1992, careful attention was made to restore them in accordance with the original design.

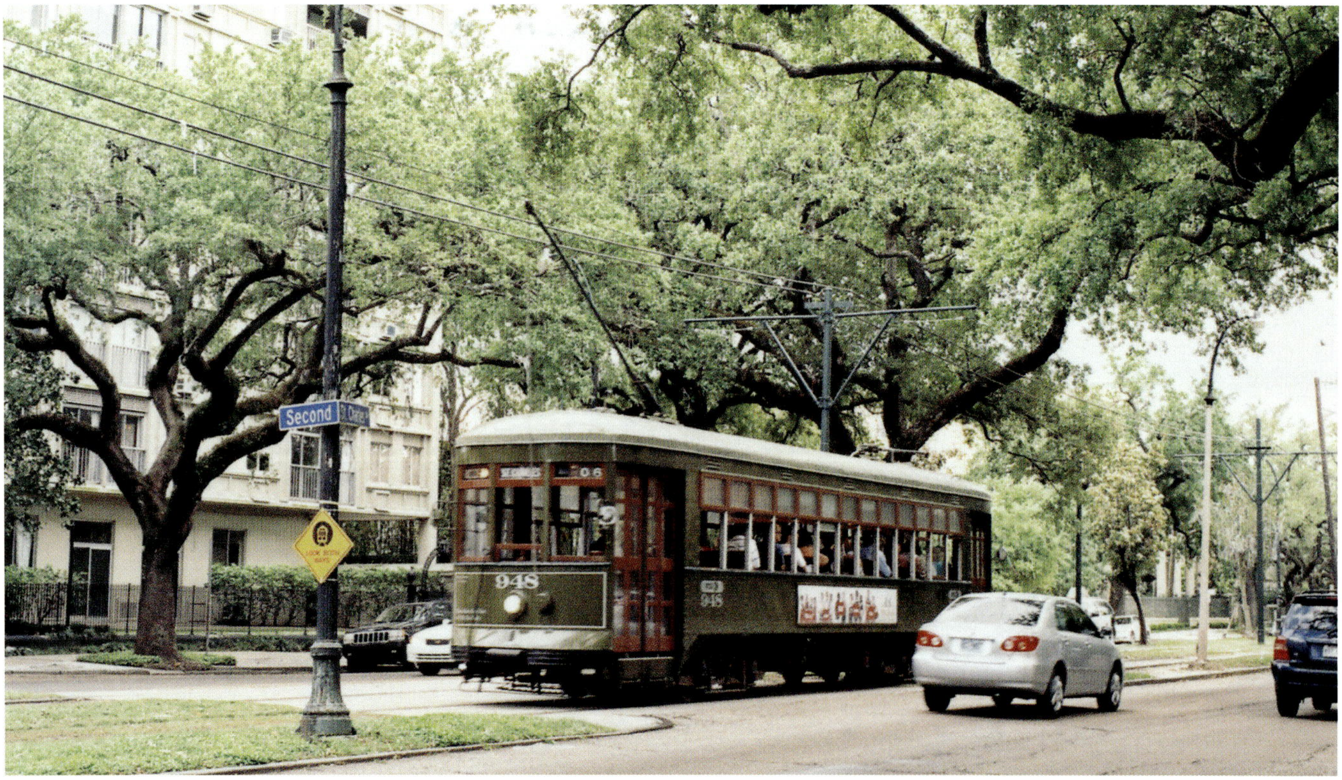

Flanked by magnificent trees on both sides of St. Charles Avenue on April 22, 2013, RTA streetcar No. 948 has crossed Second Street on St. Charles Avenue in the Garden District of New Orleans. The St. Charles streetcar line, cherished by New Orleans residents, traverses an area of beautiful homes, public institutions, and an amazing assortment of trees, making it the most delightful streetcar ride in North America.

Chapter 3

Riverfront Streetcar Line

On August 14, 1988, the RTA opened the new 1.5 mile Riverfront streetcar line, using an existing New Orleans Public Belt Railroad track that was no longer needed along the bank of the Mississippi River from Julia Street in the Warehouse District to Esplanade Avenue in the French Quarter. This single track line had a passing siding located between Conti and St. Louis Streets. The line was 4 foot 8.5 inch standard gauge, while the St. Charles track was a 5 foot 2.5 inch broad track gauge. Initially, Riverfront cars were operated with a two person crew: an RTA operator and a uniformed tour guide who handled fare collection and assisted passengers.

For this new line, a special group named "Bring Our Streetcars Home" had been organized to locate and acquire streetcars that been disposed of when the Canal line was discontinued in 1964. Four streetcars originally built by Perley A. Thomas Car Company (Nos. 919, 924, 952, and 957) were located and acquired. Car No. 924, from Atlanta, was the first car refurbished mechanically, electrically, painted red, and renumbered 450 for the Riverfront line. It was tested on the St. Charles line, and then its trucks were changed from the 5 foot 2.5 inch wide gauge of the St. Charles line to the 4 foot 8.5 inch standard gauge of the Riverfront line. Car No. 919, from the Texas State Fairgrounds arrived on September 19, 1985, was next and became No. 451. After a two month shutdown, the Riverfront line was reopened on August 31, 1990 featuring a double track and a nearly half-mile extension to the Convention Center.

Three handicapped accessible class W-2 streetcars from the Melbourne and Metropolitan Tramways Board of Melbourne, Australia were acquired. Melbourne car No. 626 became No. 452, Melbourne car No. 478 became No. 454, and Melbourne car 331 became No. 455. The number 453 was skipped, because there was still a vintage Brill semi-convertible car No. 453 in existence. Car No. 952, acquired from Chattanooga, Tennessee, arrived in March 1990 and became No. 456. Car No. 957 was acquired from the McKinney Avenue Transit Authority in Dallas, Texas in March 1986.

When a wheelchair door was cut into the side of car No. 957 for wheelchair accessibility, and it became car No. 457, preservationists reacted with horror over that modification. Consequently, the RTA decided to build new car bodies rather than to continue modifying any of the earlier cars. Nine Presidents' Conference Committee (PCC) streetcars were purchased from the Southeastern Pennsylvania Transportation Authority (SEPTA) in Philadelphia to provide the motors, controls, and trucks for the new cars. Eventually six new cars (one person operated) numbered 458 to 463 were built patterned after the Perley A. Thomas Car Company cars used on the St. Charles line, with modern propulsion equipment including new trucks and controls from CKD (Ceskomoravska Kolben-Danek) Tatra, a company producing streetcars in the Czech Republic. The SEPTA cars and equipment were sold or scrapped.

On September 7, 1997, the Riverfront line was closed, and the track gauge was changed from the 4 foot 8.5 inch standard gauge to the 5 foot 2.5 inch broad gauge of the St. Charles line. The three former Melbourne streetcars Nos. 626, 478, and 331 which became RTA Nos. 452, 454, and 455, were sold to Memphis Area Transportation Authority (MATA), and were rebuilt by the Gomaco Trolley Company before placement in service in Memphis, Tennessee. Cars Nos. 450, 451, and 456 were retired. Parts from cars numbered 450 and 451 were used in building the new cars. Car No. 456, restored to its original look, received its original number 952 and went to the San Francisco Municipal Railway on a long term lease.

On December 7, 1997, the Riverfront line reopened with wide gauge track and the new cars numbered 457 to 463, built at the Carrollton Station shop in New Orleans. When the Canal line reopened on April 18, 2004, the seven Riverfront streetcars were kept at the Service, Inspection, and Storage facility at the Canal Station carbarn behind the A. Philip Randolph building. Major repairs were done at the Carrollton Station shop. Some Canal line trips operated over a portion of the Riverfront line from Canal Street to the terminal at Esplanade Avenue, which has been renamed "French Market." When Hurricane Katrina hit New Orleans on August 29, 2005, the twenty-four Canal cars and six of the seven Riverfront cars were flooded, destroying their motors and controls. Car No. 461, which was at the Carrollton Station shop for repainting, and the thirty-five St. Charles cars escaped damage from the storm. By March 15, 2010, cars numbered 457 to 463 were back in service.

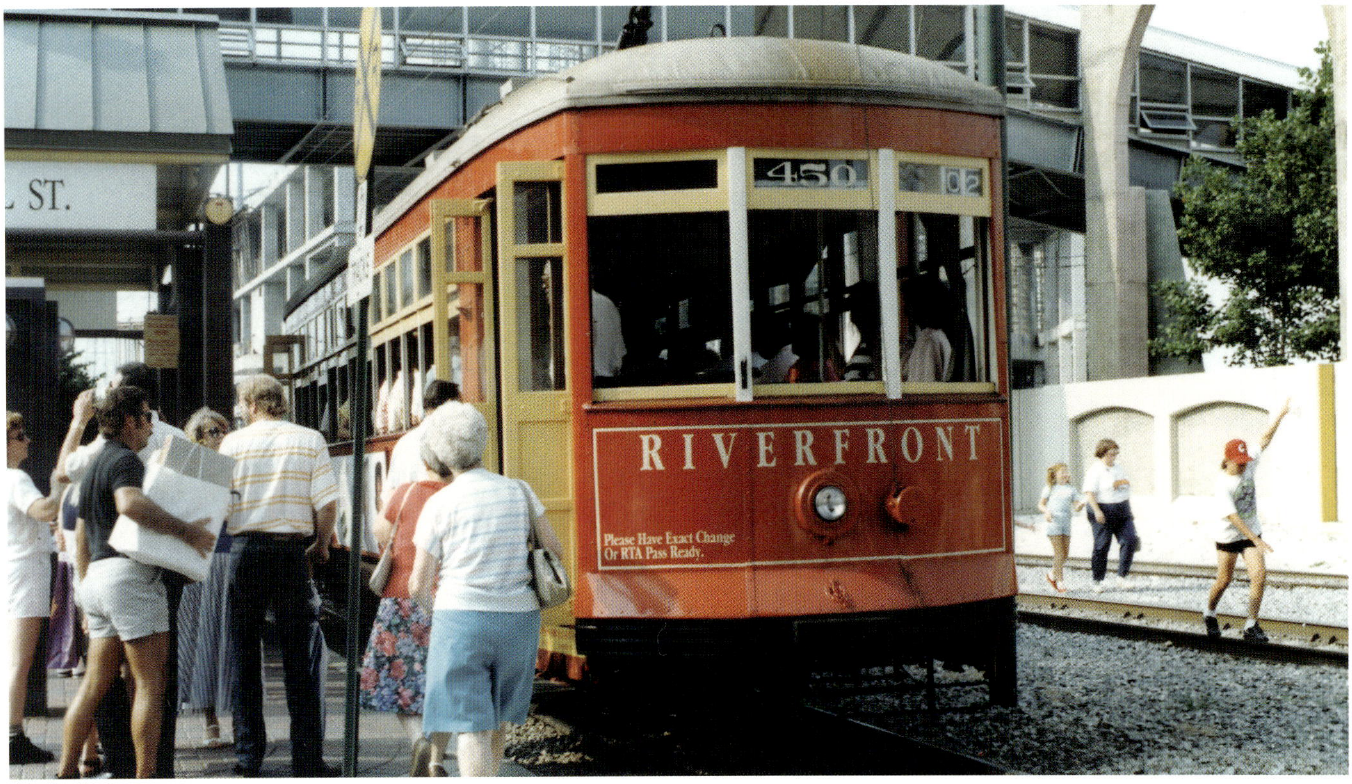

Passengers are boarding RTA streetcar No. 450 at Canal Street on the Riverfront line on July 27, 1989. This streetcar, originally New Orleans Public Service Inc. car No. 924, was obtained from Atlanta and was the first to be restored and renumbered 450. The Riverfront line linked together the Riverwalk Marketplace, the Canal Street commercial area, and the French Quarter.

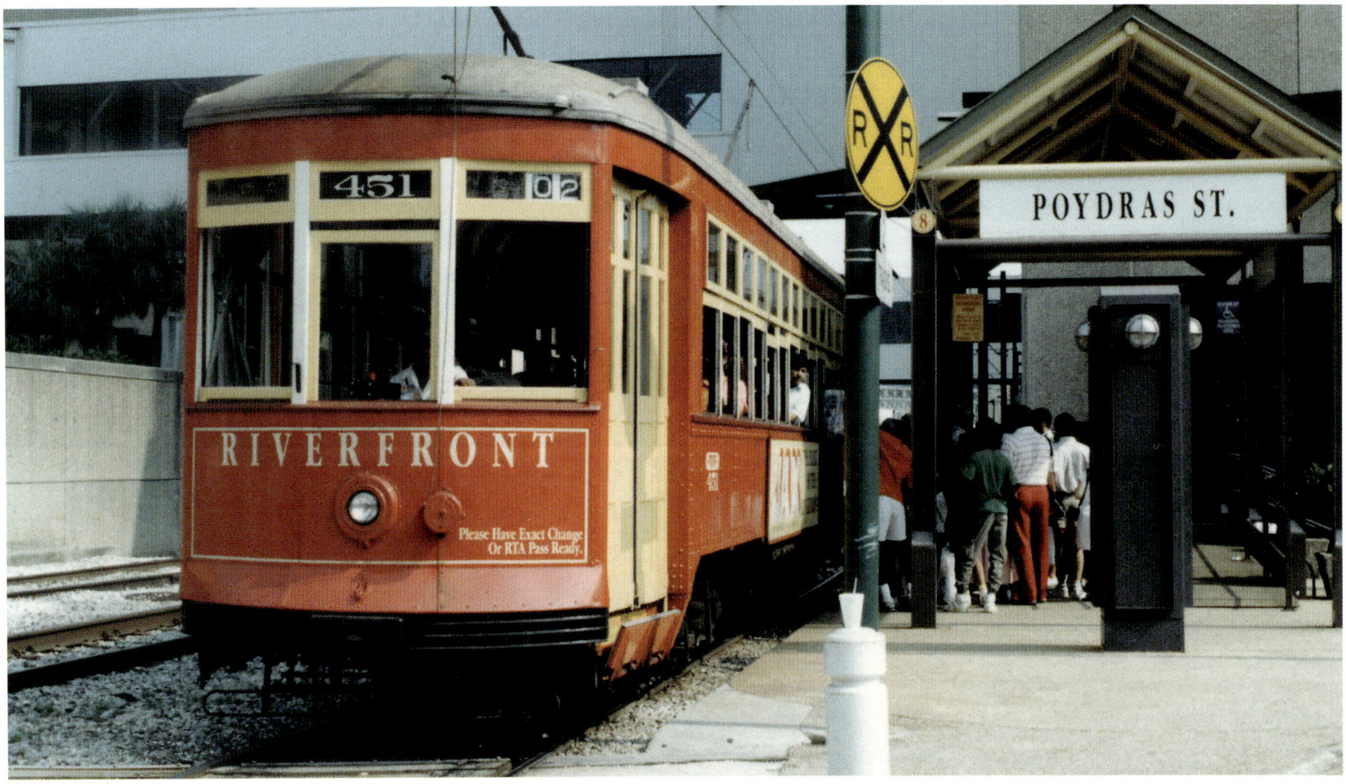

RTA streetcar No. 451 is boarding passengers at Poydras Street on the Riverfront line on July 27, 1989. New Orleans Public Service Inc. streetcar No. 919, from the Texas State Fairgrounds became No. 451. The skilled craftsmen at the Carrolton shop handled the streetcar restoration.

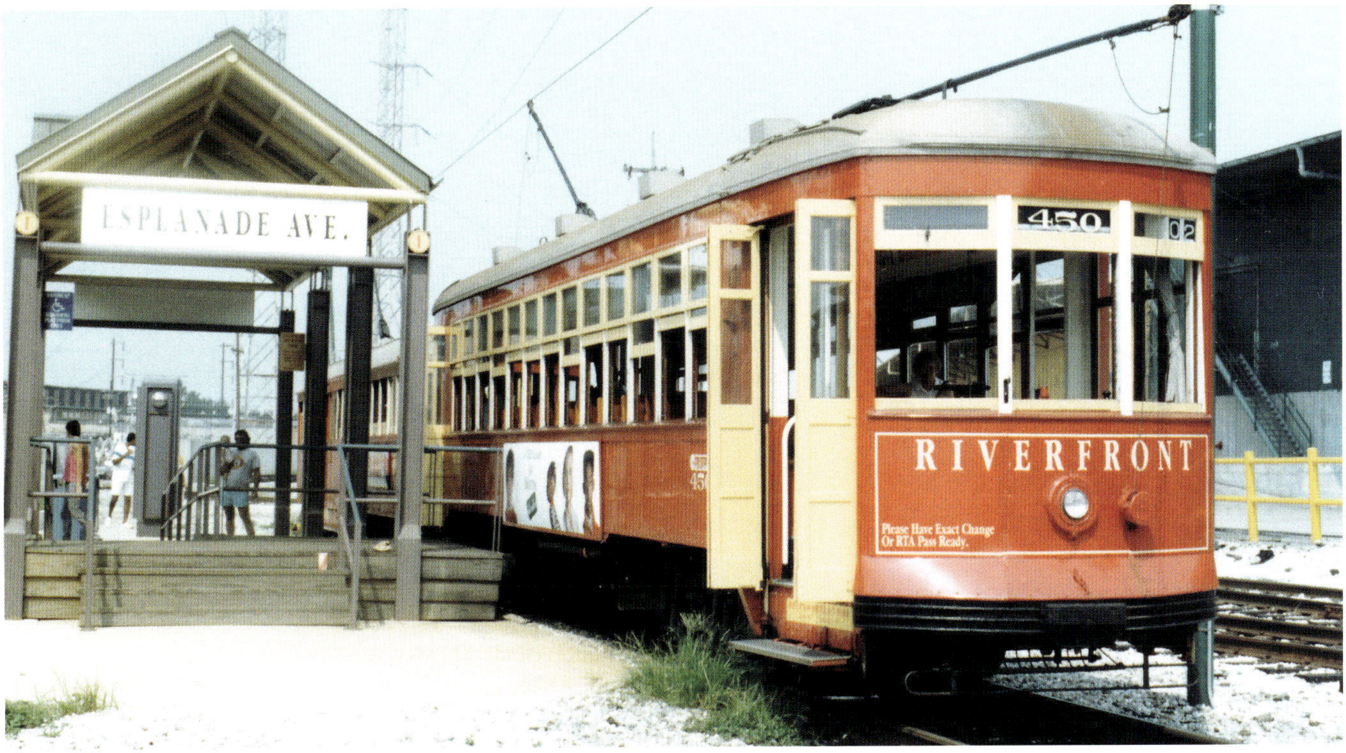

At Esplanade Avenue – the eastern terminus of the Riverfront line – RTA streetcar No. 450 is waiting for departure time, with a former Melbourne, Australia streetcar in the rear, on July 27, 1989. This was built as a single track line with a passing siding located between Conti and St. Louis Streets. Esplanade Avenue runs northwest from the Mississippi River to City Park, and was a nineteenth century trade route from the Mississippi River to the stream that went to Lake Pontchartrain.

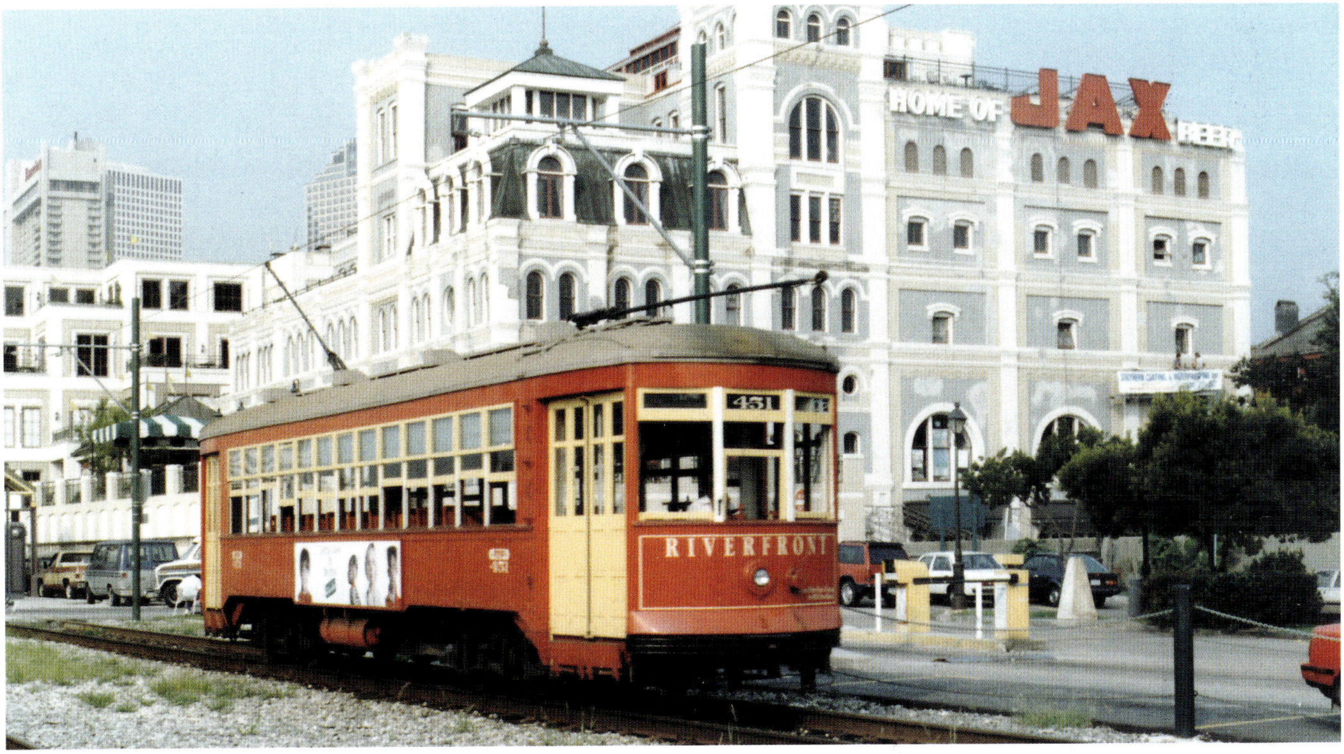

Passing the Jackson Brewery (seen behind the streetcar) and St. Peter Street in the French Quarter, RTA streetcar No. 451 is eastbound on the Riverfront line on July 27, 1989. The Jackson Brewery, designed by German born architect Dietrich Einsiedel in 1891 for the brewing and bottling of Jax Beer, was the largest independent southern brewery and the tenth largest single-plant brewery in the United States. It closed in 1974 and was remodeled into retail shops.

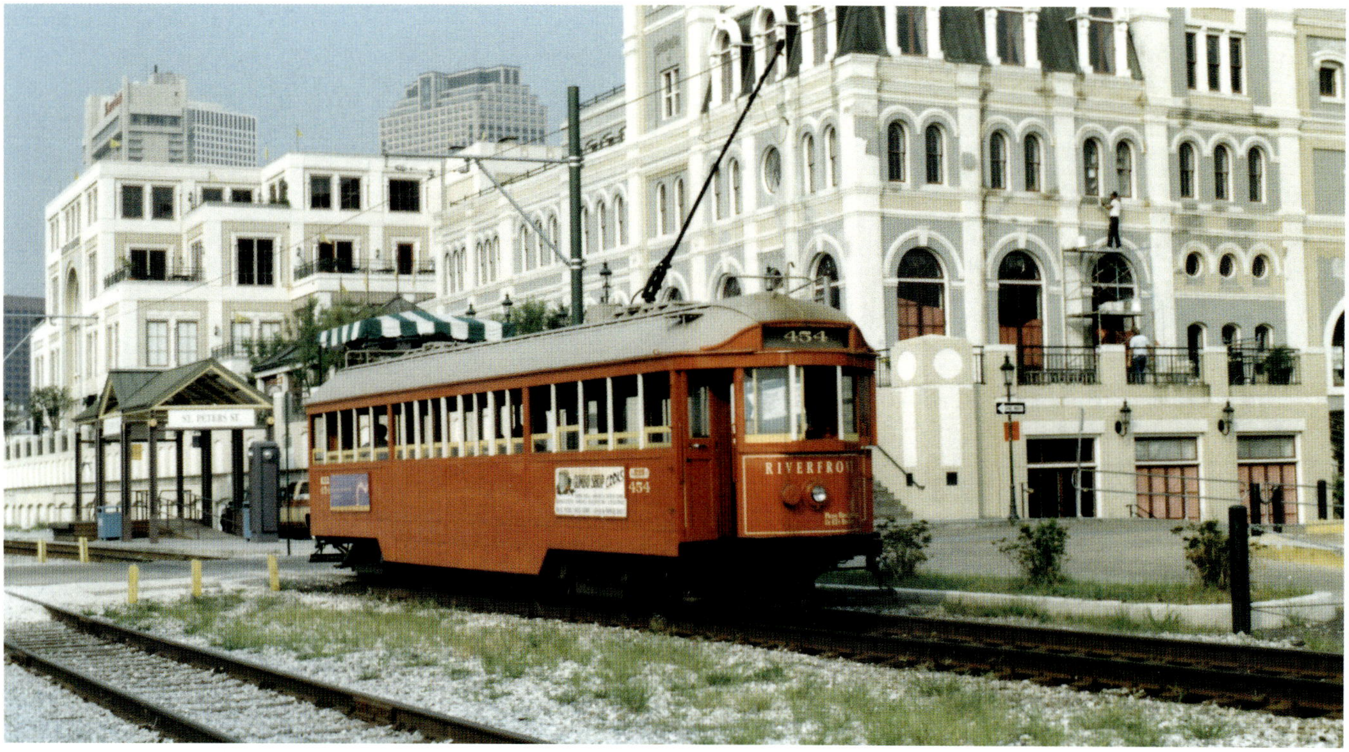

RTA streetcar No. 454 (formerly Melbourne and Metropolitan Tramways Board of Melbourne, Australia W-2 class car No. 478) is westbound near the St. Peter Street station on the Riverfront line, on July 27, 1989. From 1923 to 1956, the Preston shops of the Melbourne and Metropolitan Tramways Board built a majority of the 752 streetcars of various W classes. In 2013, about 38 W class streetcars operate in Melbourne, and many have been preserved in other countries.

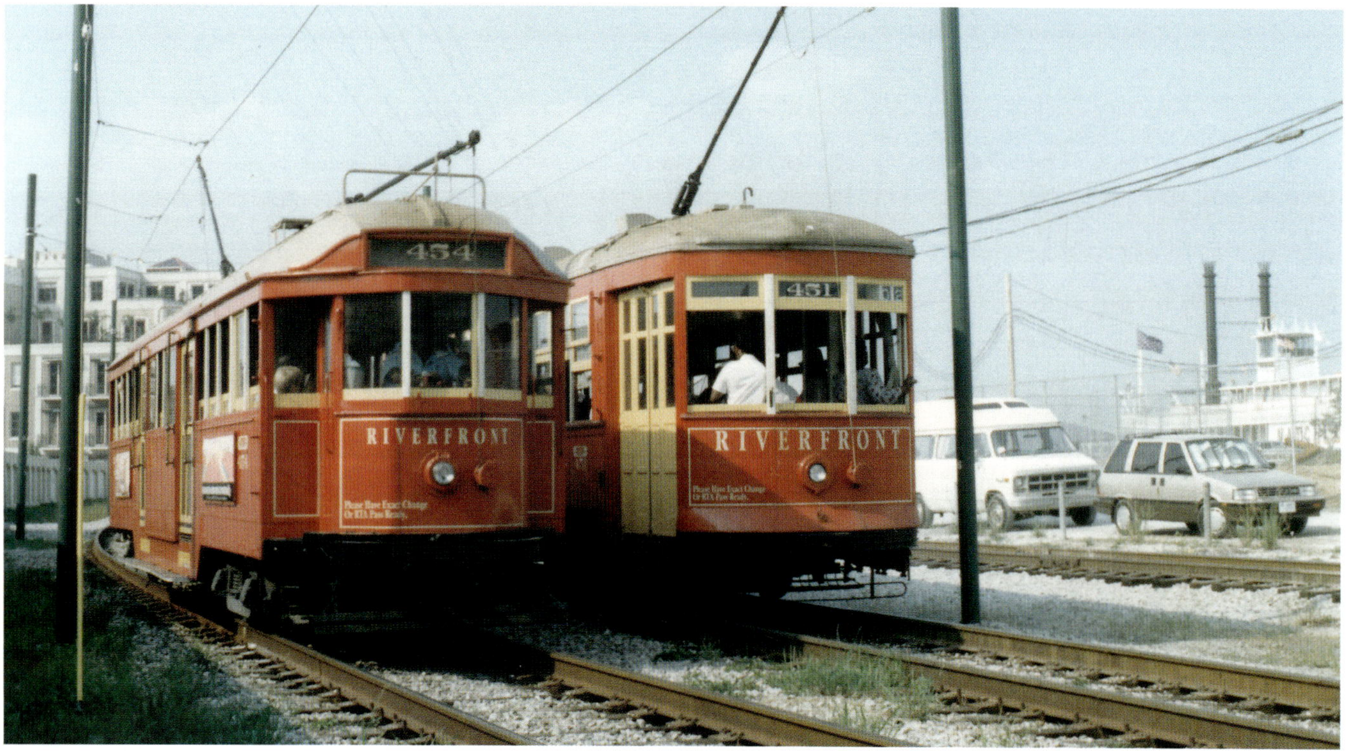

With a boat on the Mississippi River on the right side of the picture, shown on July 27, 1989, RTA streetcar No. 454 is passing No. 451 via the siding located between Conti and St. Louis Streets on the Riverfront line. The Riverfront line runs along the southern edge of the French Quarter, and a one way trip takes about fifteen minutes.

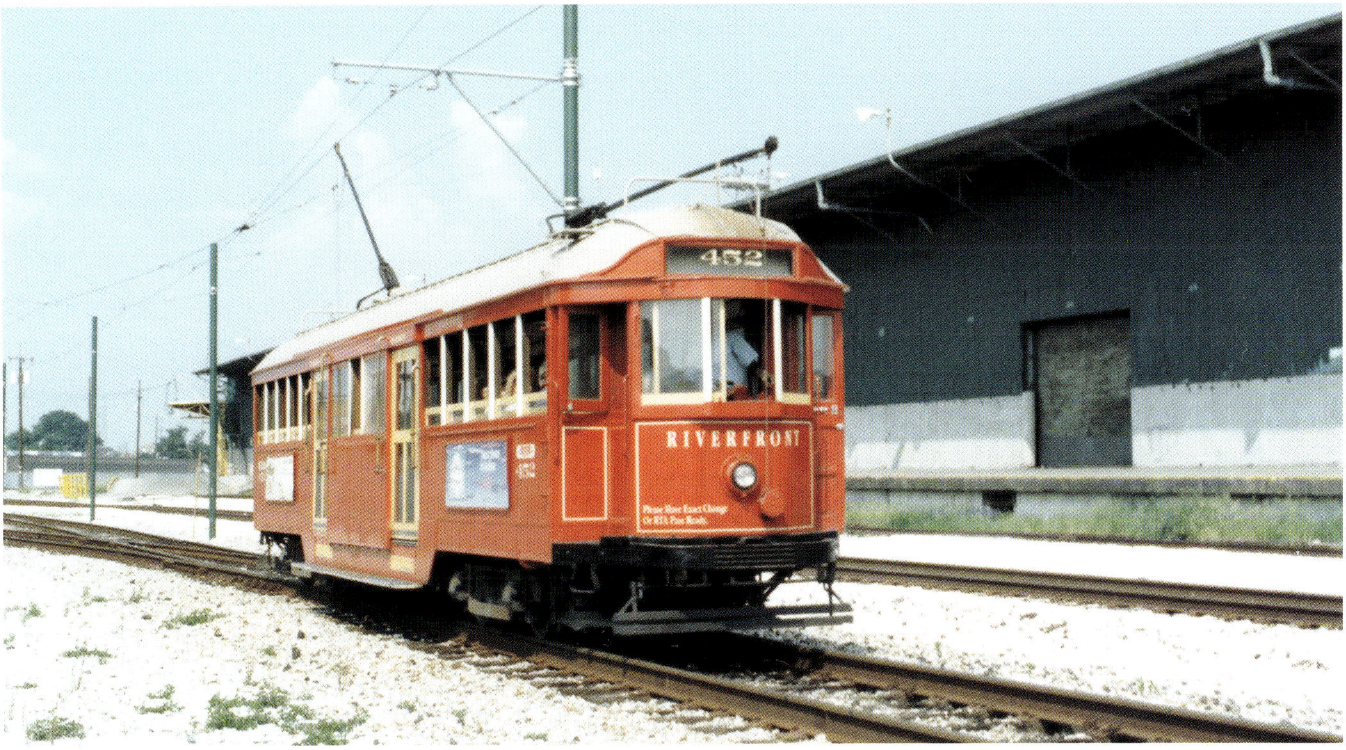

On July 27, 1989, west of the Esplanade Avenue station, RTA streetcar 452 (formerly Melbourne and Metropolitan Tramways Board, of Melbourne, Australia W-2 class car No. 626) is westbound on the Riverfront line. Of the 752 W class Melbourne, Australia streetcars, 406 were class W-2, built in the 1920s, with wooden seats. These formed the backbone of the Melbourne and Metropolitan Tramways Board fleet, with 326 streetcars of the W-2 class still in service on July 1, 1977.

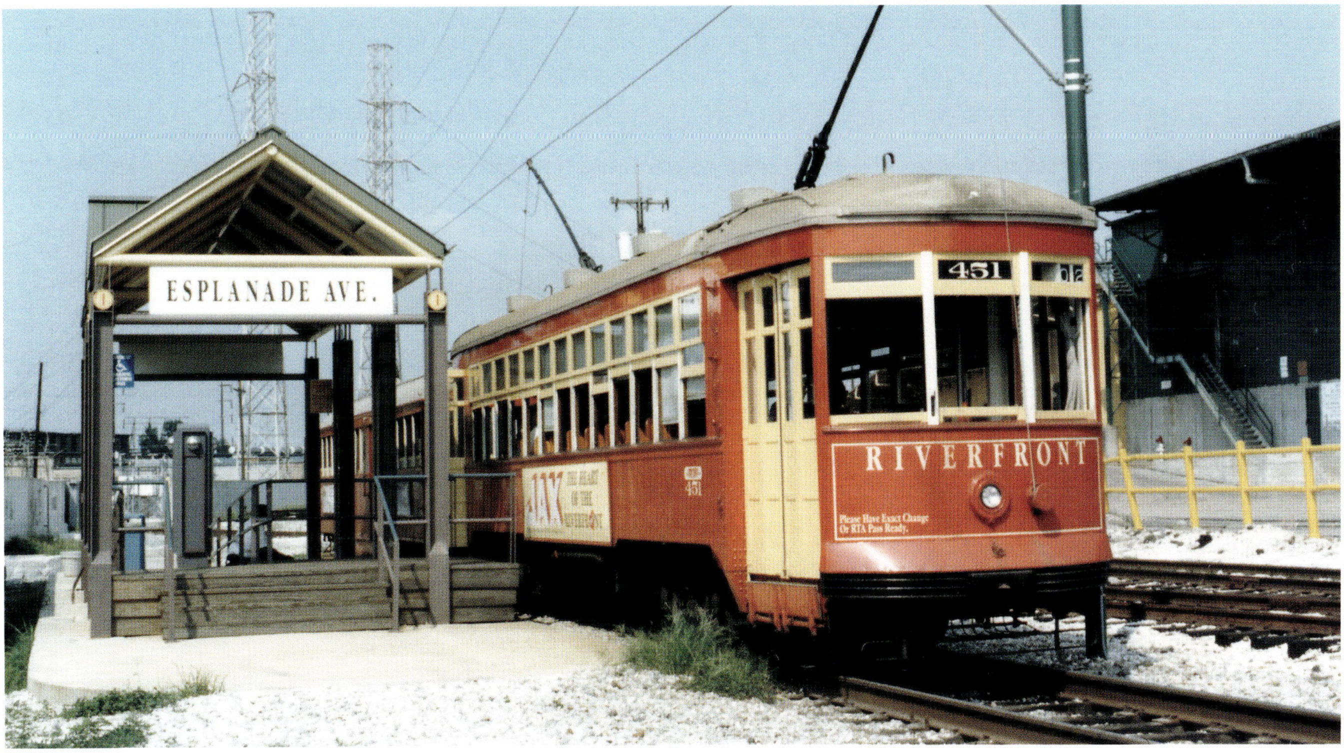

RTA streetcar No. 451 is at the Esplanade Avenue station, with the back pole up; the front pole will shortly be pulled down for the next westbound run on the Riverfront line, on July 27. 1989. At this end of the line is the French Market, the oldest public market in the United States. The Riverfront line passes by Woldenberg Park (named after Malcolm Woldenberg who helped fund it), the Aquarium of the Americas, and the Riverwalk Marketplace.

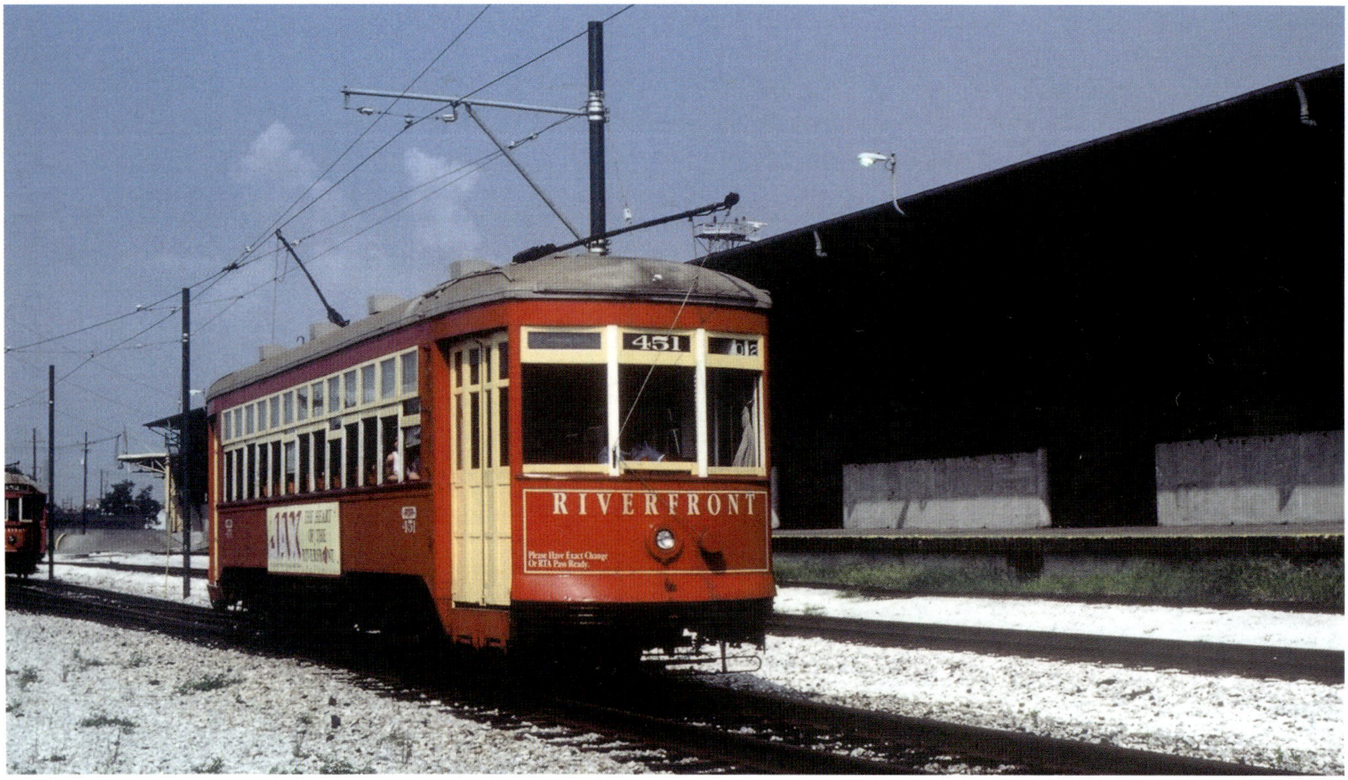

On July 27, 1989, RTA streetcar No. 451 is west of Esplanade Avenue station for a westbound run on the Riverfront line, followed by streetcar No. 452. To the right of the streetcar is the active freight line of the New Orleans Public Belt Railroad, which parallels the entire length of the Riverfront line.

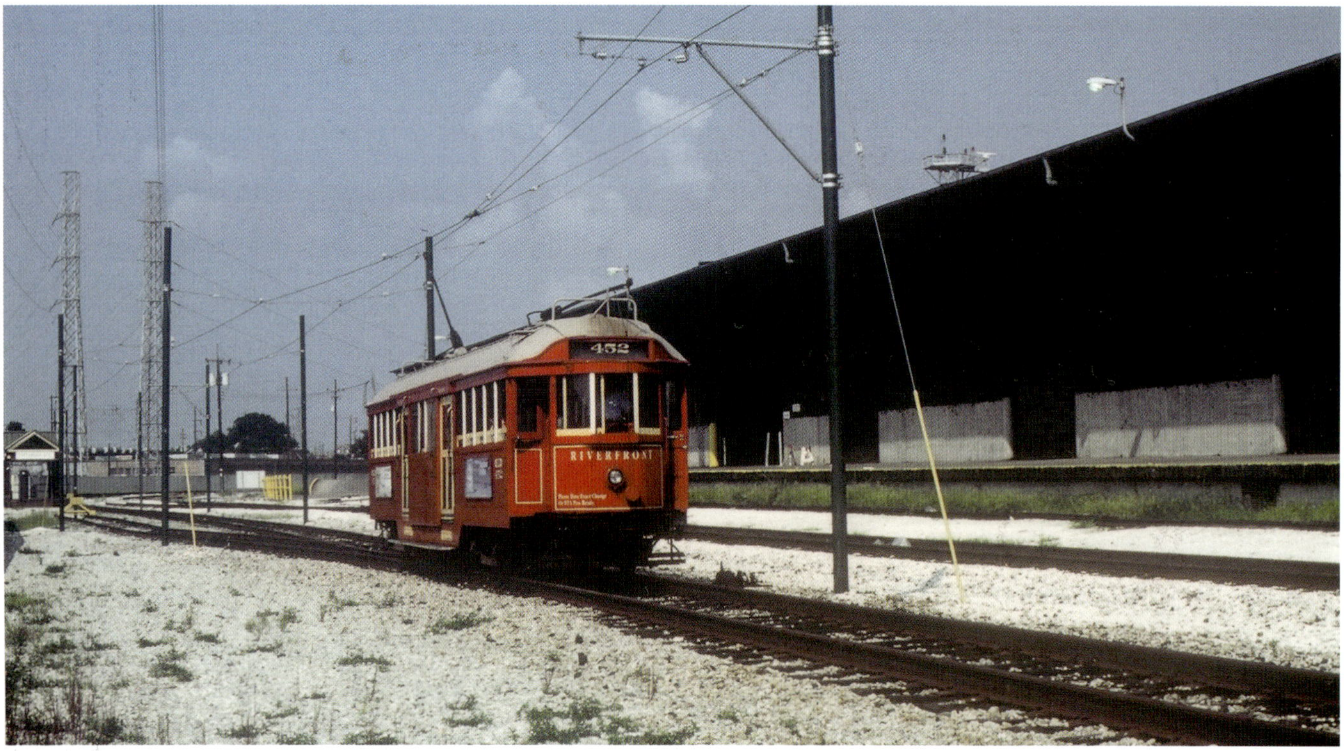

RTA streetcar No. 452 is westbound on the Riverfront line just west of Esplanade Avenue station on July 27, 1889. The Riverfront line became a convenient form of transportation for people attending conventions or arriving from cruise ships to visit the French Quarter and Jackson Square. Tourism has become important to the economy of New Orleans.

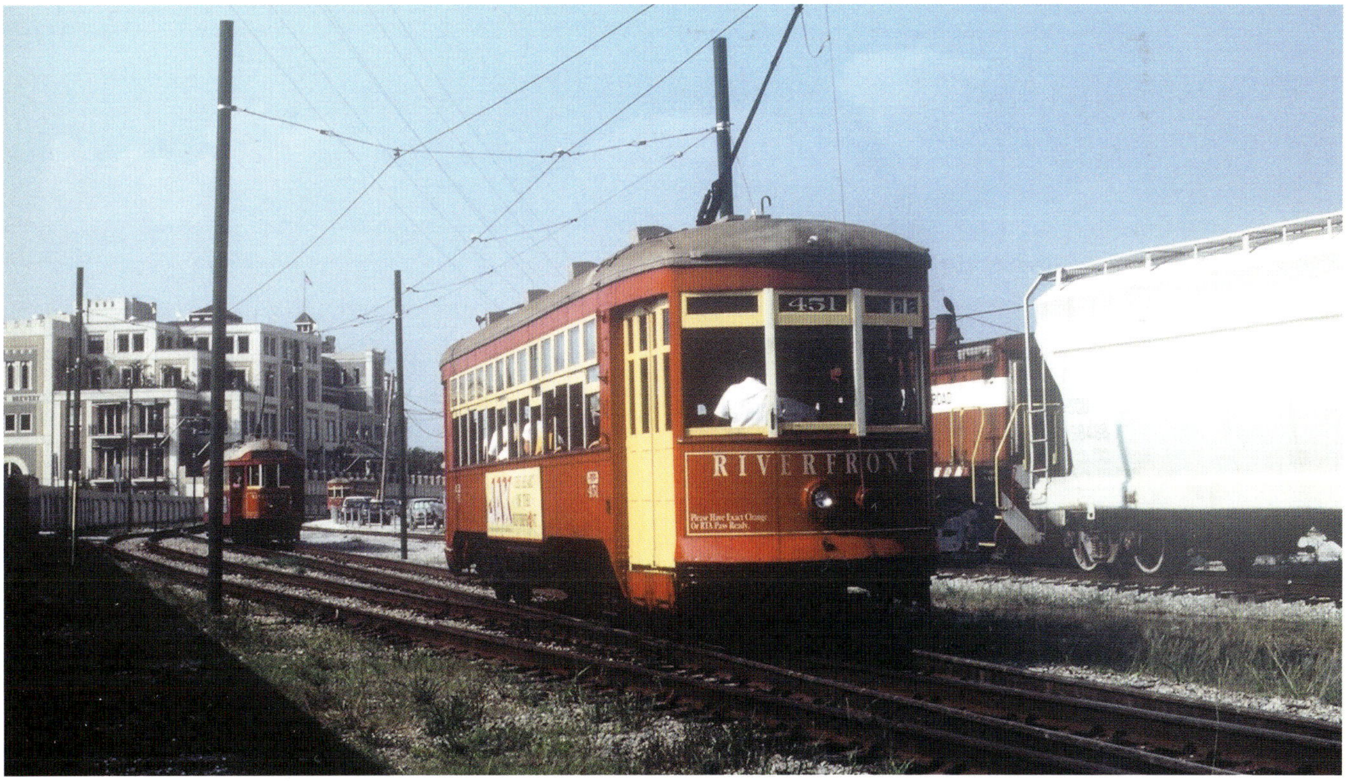

Entering the passing siding on the Riverfront line, RTA streetcar No. 451 is parallel to a New Orleans Public Belt Railroad freight train, on July 23, 1989. The multi-level Jackson Brewery Marketplace is in the distance on the left side of the picture.

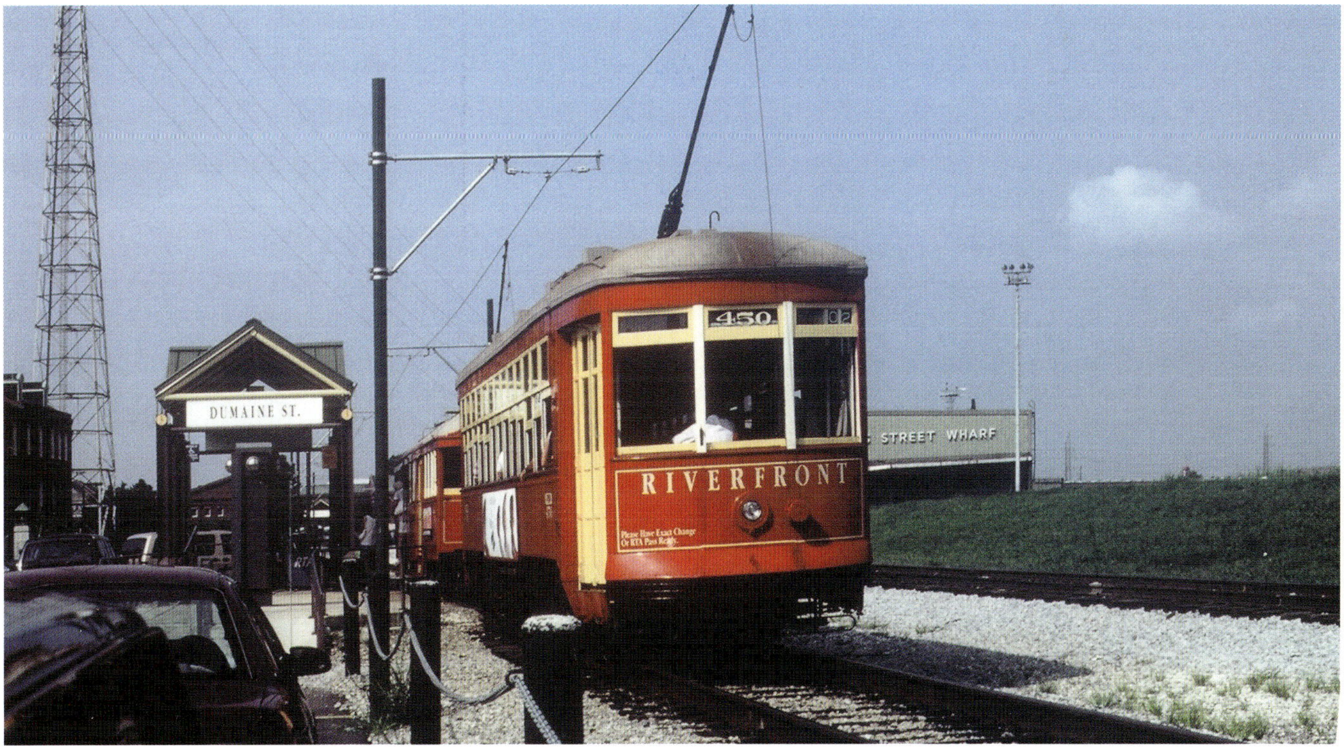

On July 27, 1989, RTA streetcar No. 450 is behind a former Melbourne, Australia streetcar at Dumaine Street on the Riverfront line. The Riverfront line was built as a single track line with one passing siding in the middle of the line. With four streetcars scheduled on the line, it was sometimes necessary for a streetcar to get into the siding and allow two streetcars going in the opposite direction to pass, which meant longer waiting times for passengers.

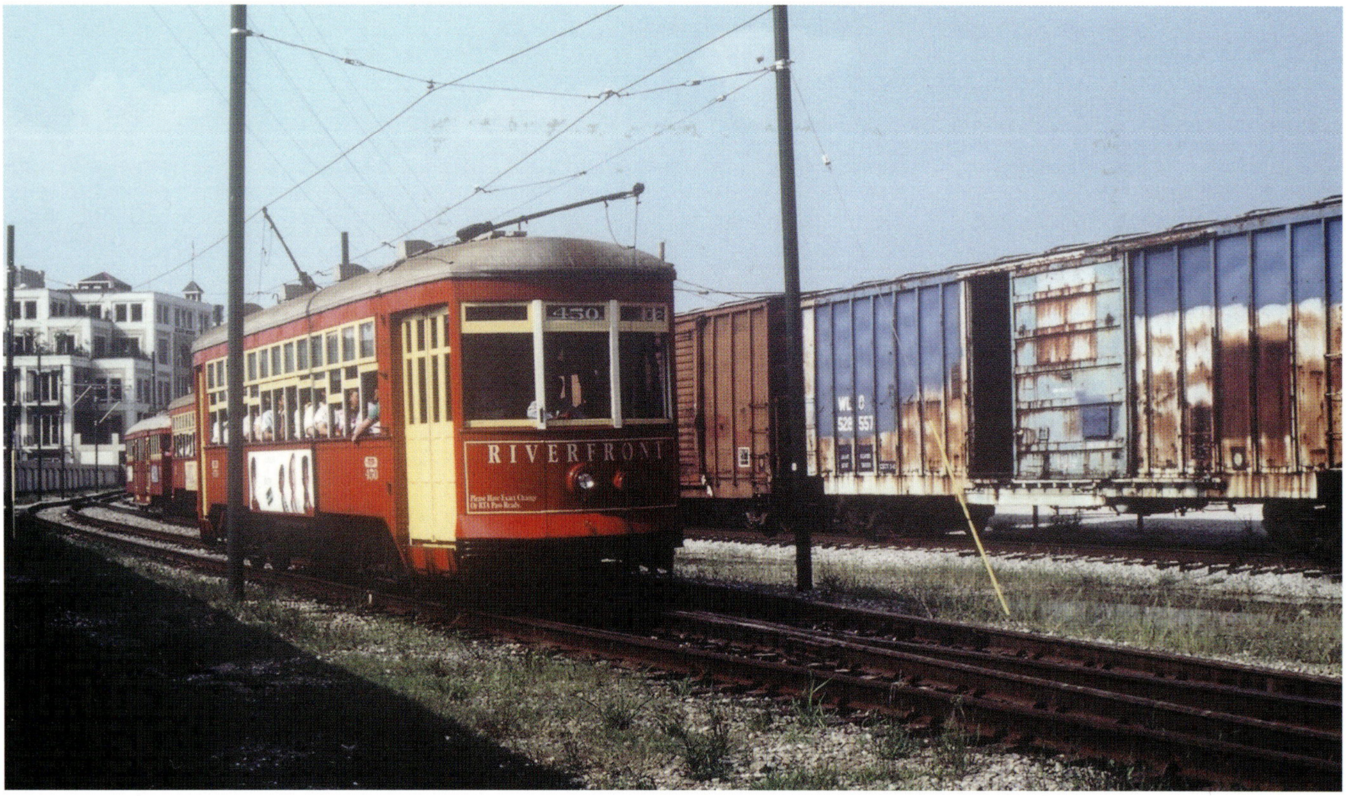

With a New Orleans Public Belt Railroad freight train passing by, RTA streetcar No. 450 is westbound on the siding passing two streetcars on the Riverfront line on July 27, 1989. The multi-level Jackson Brewery Marketplace is in the distance on the left.

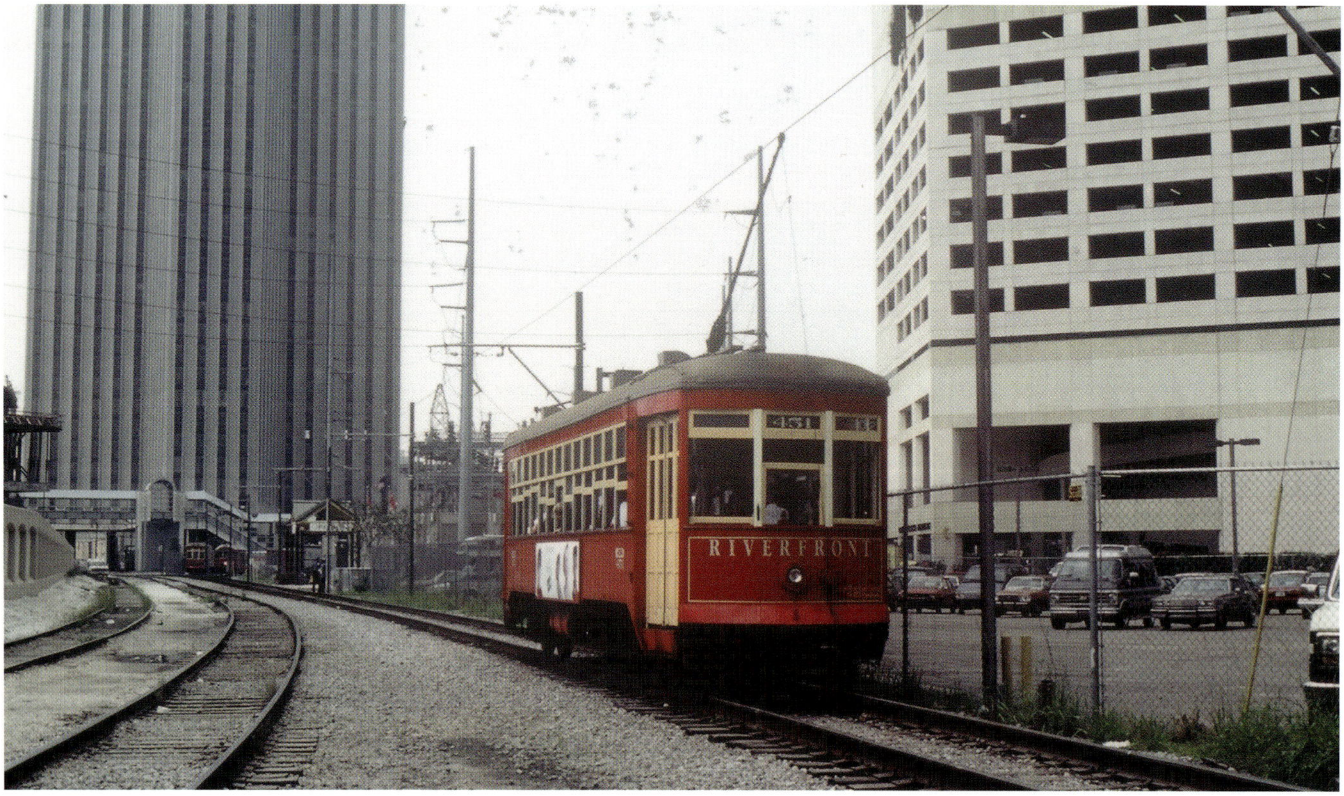

RTA streetcar No. 451 is westbound on the Riverfront line on July 27, 1989 with the 33-story New Orleans World Trade Center skyscraper on the left of the picture. The Riverfront streetcar is a great time saver for exploring the New Orleans riverfront.

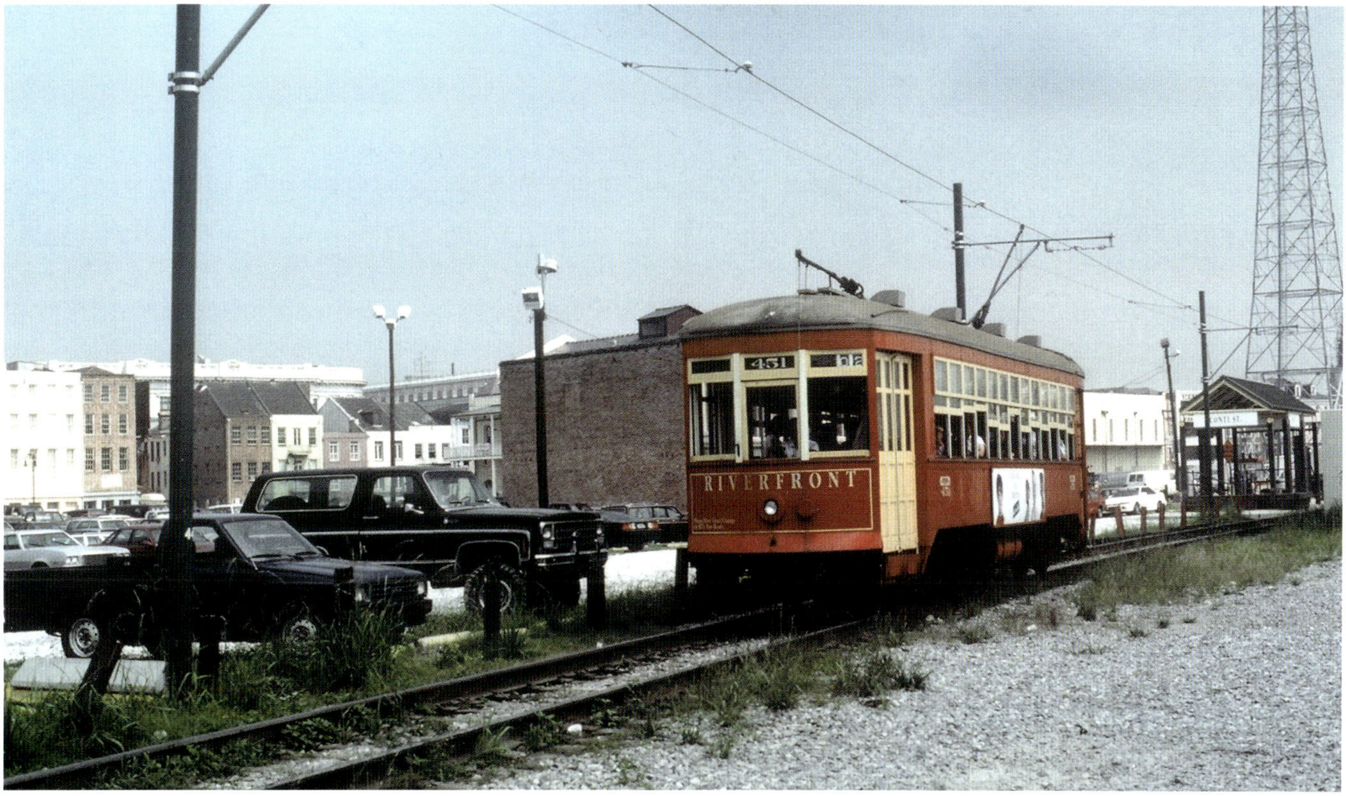

West of Conti Street station on the Riverfront line, RTA streetcar No. 451 is westbound on July 27, 1989. This line has become popular with residents and tourists.

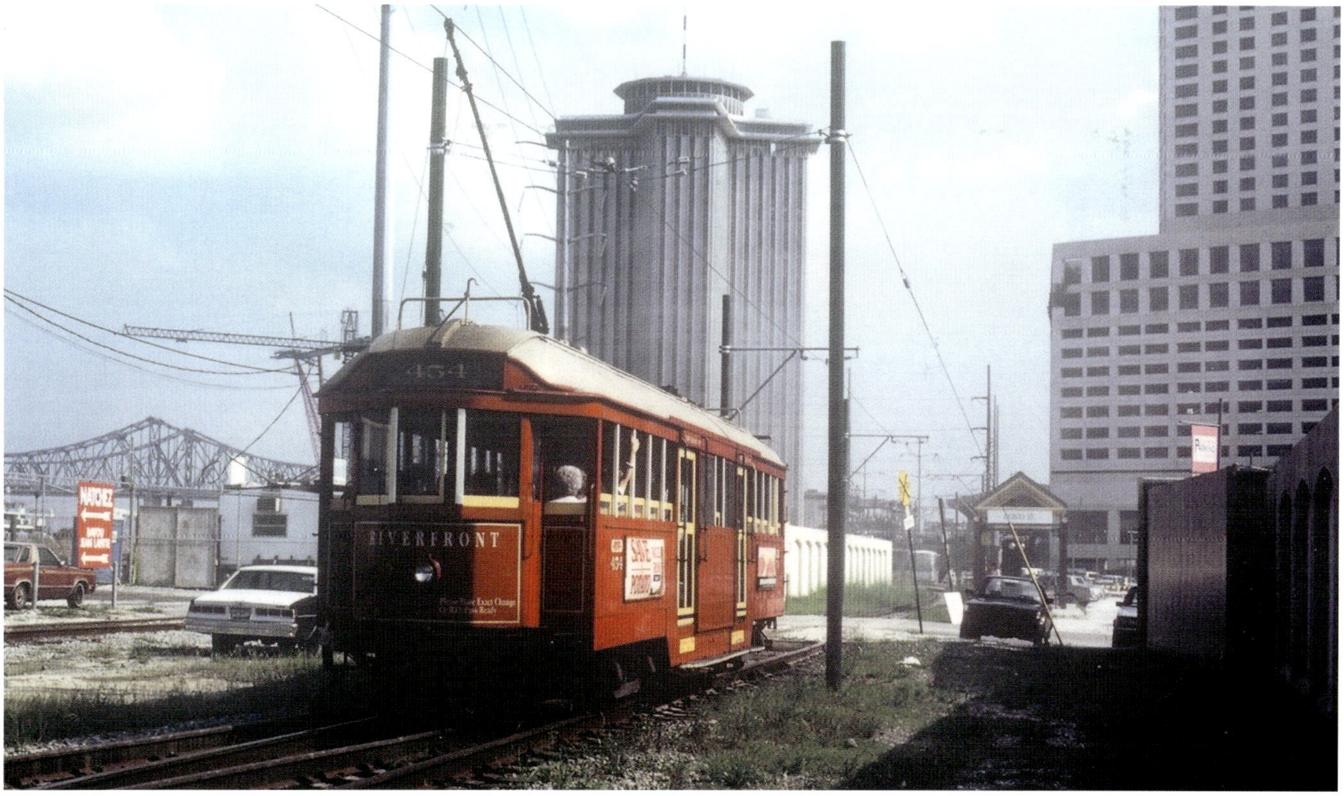

East of the Conti Street station, RTA streetcar No. 454 (formerly Melbourne and Metropolitan Tramways Board of Melbourne, Australia W-2 class car No. 478) is westbound on the Riverfront line, on July 27, 1989. The bridges over the Mississippi River are on the left side of the picture.

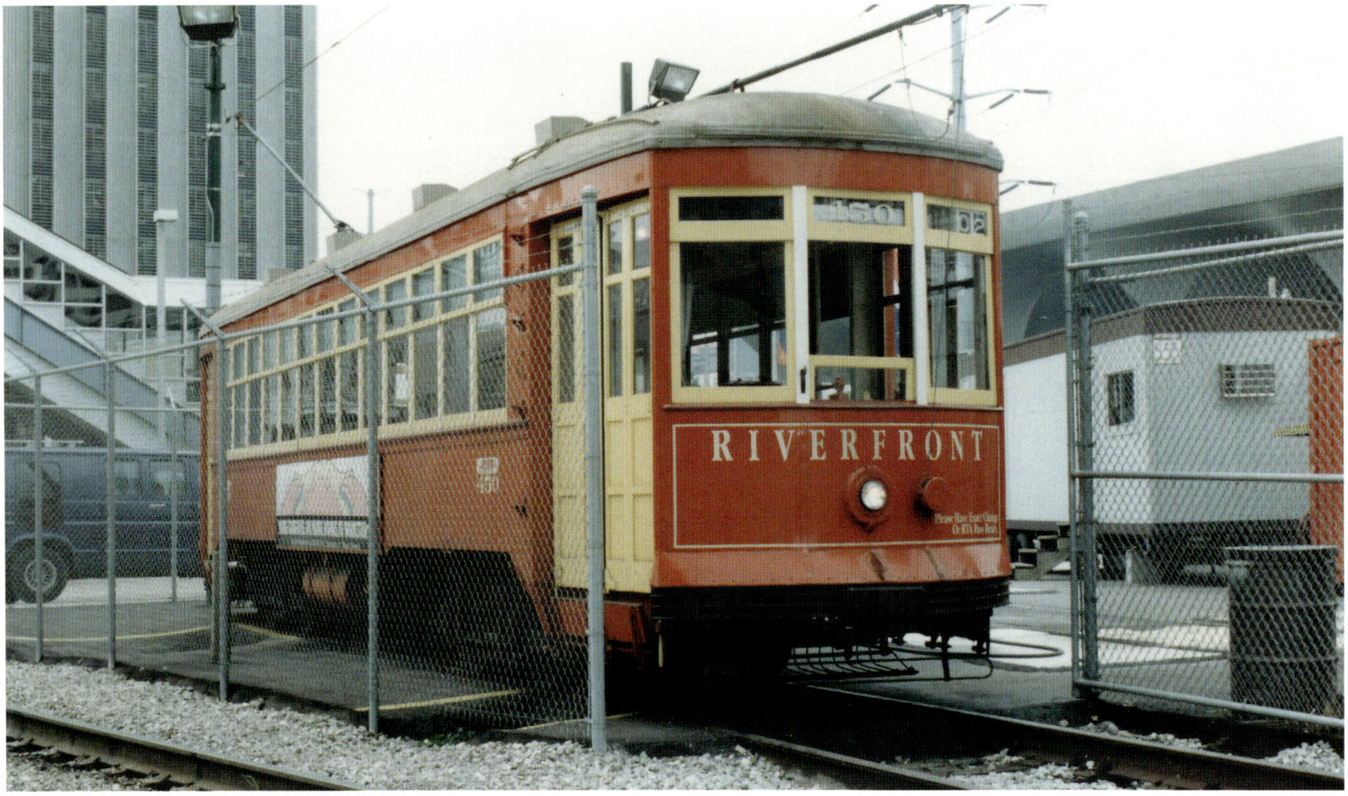

RTA streetcar No. 450 is stored in a fenced in yard on the Riverfront line on July 29, 1989. Originally the Riverfront line was isolated but with the completion of a six block long section on Canal Street in 1999, the Riverfront line was connected with the St. Charles line.

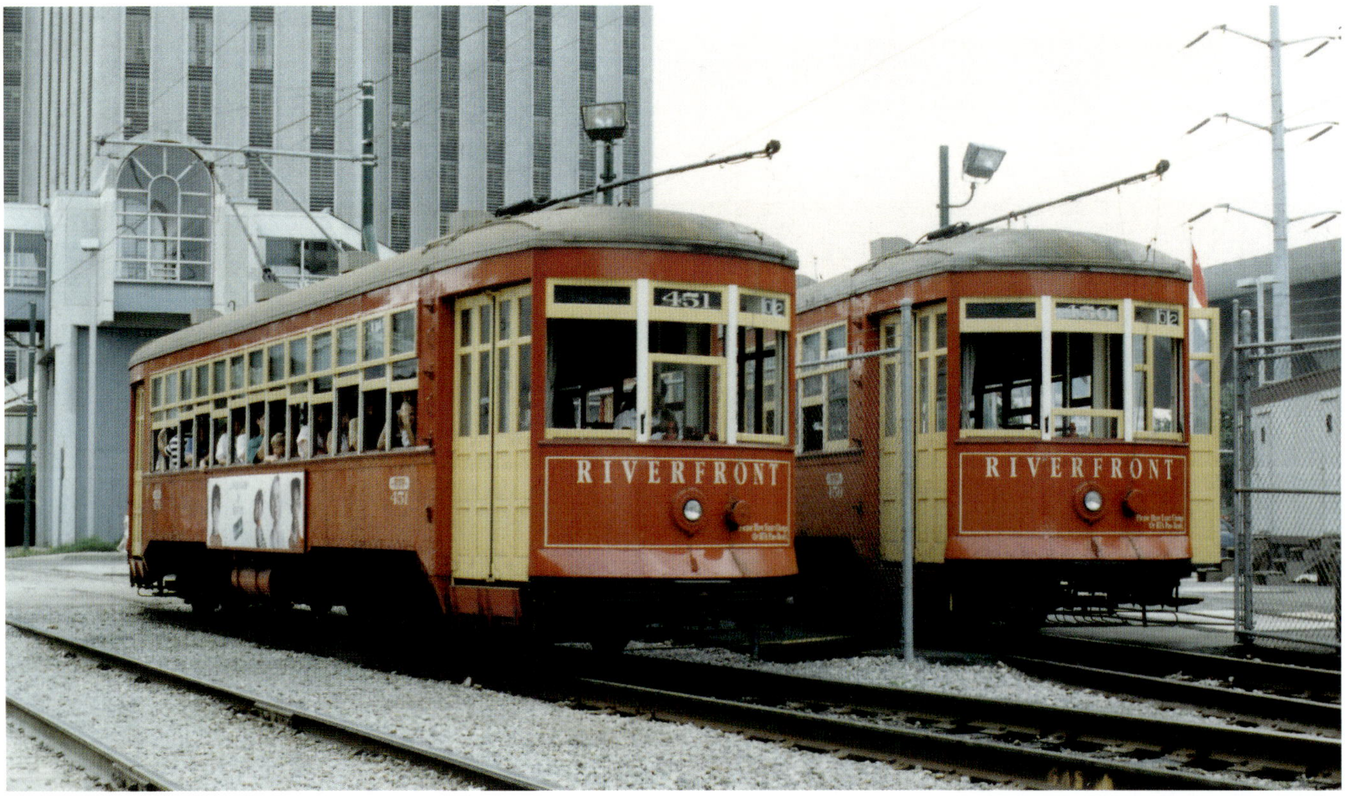

On the single track Riverfront line, RTA streetcar No. 451 is passing by car No. 450 in the outdoor car storage yard on July 29, 1989 at Canal Street. The outdoor storage area exposed the streetcars to the elements. Since 2004, these streetcars are stored at the Canal Station carbarn.

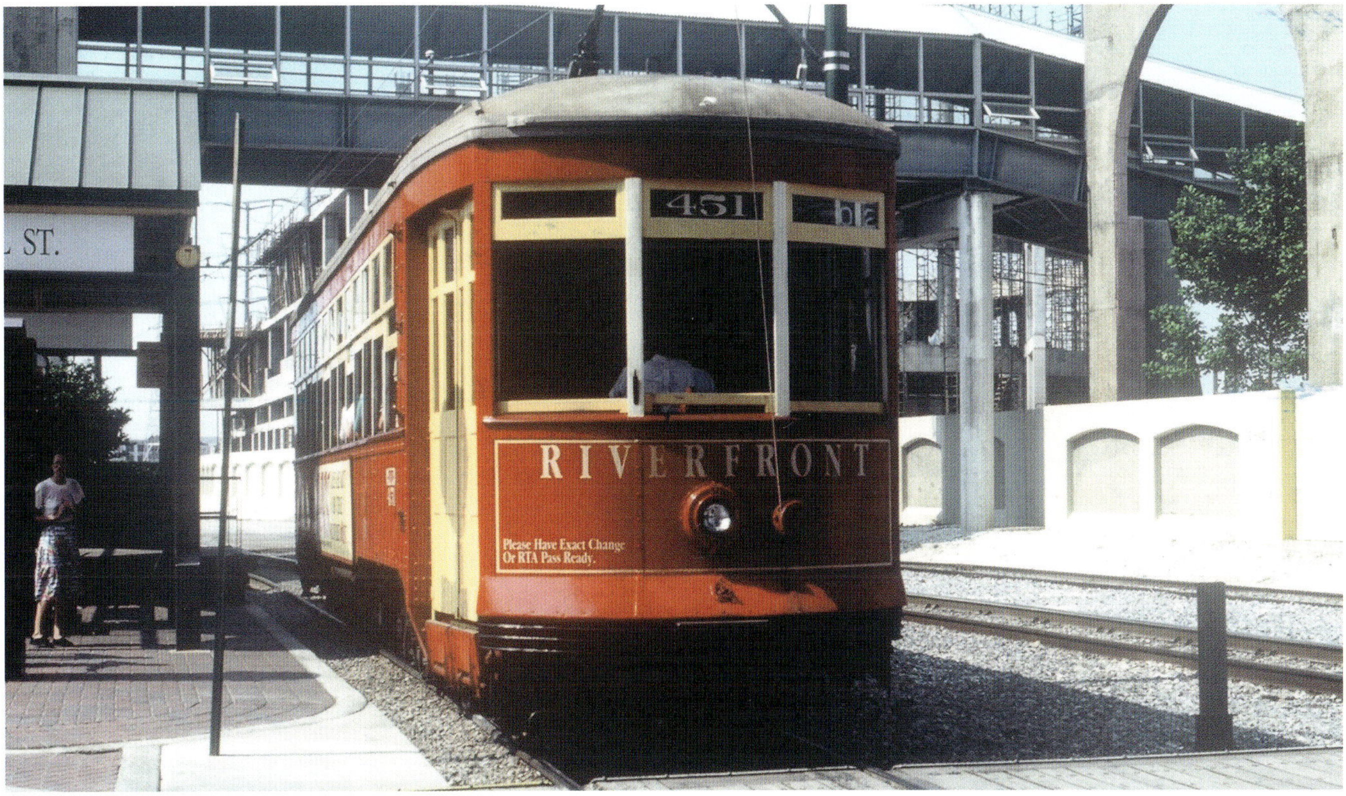

On July 27, 1989, RTA streetcar No. 451 is at the Canal Street station of the Riverfront line. This station serves the Canal Street-Algiers Ferry, plus a variety of retail shops, restaurants, and hotels along Canal Street.

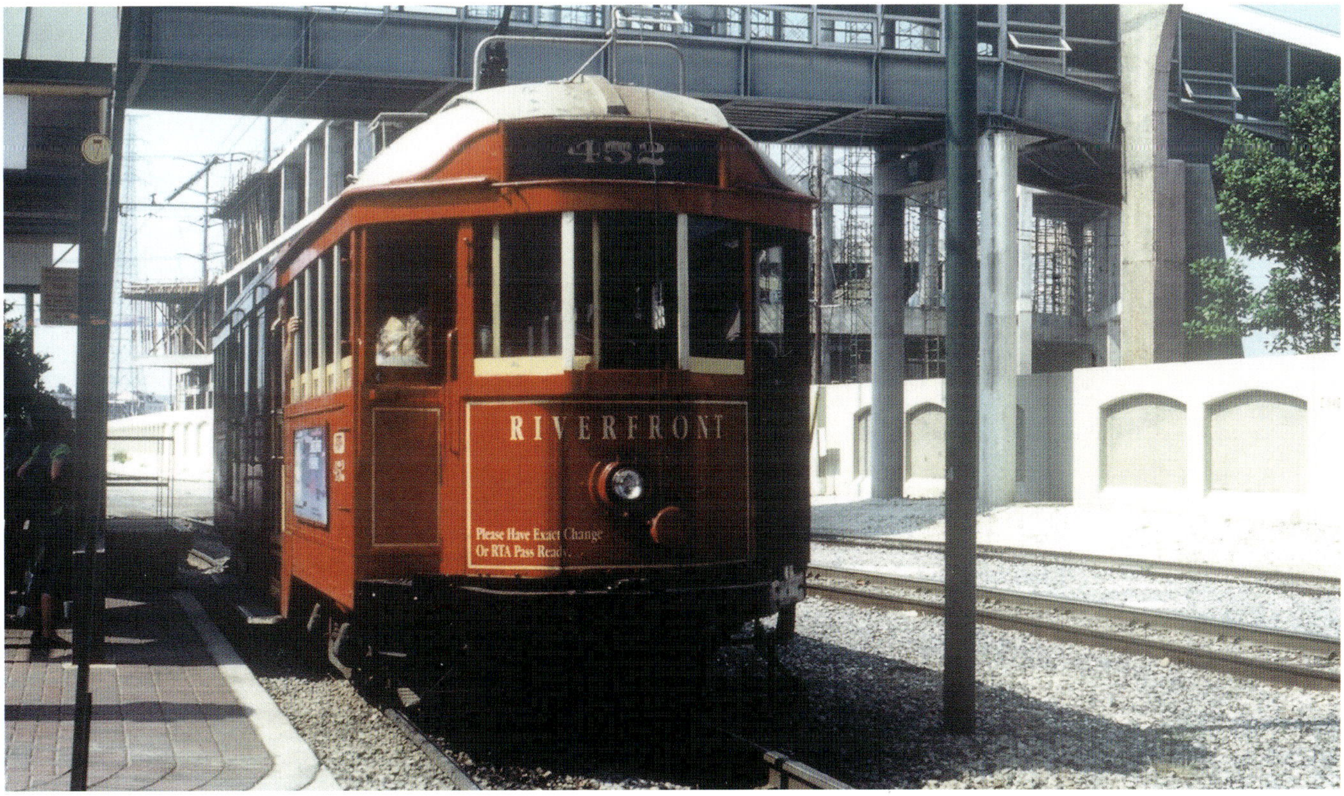

The Canal Street station on the Riverfront line is the scene for RTA streetcar No. 452 (formerly Melbourne and Metropolitan Tramways Board of Melbourne, Australia W-2 class car No. 626) on July 27, 1989. The foot of Canal Street has become a dynamic business section of New Orleans.

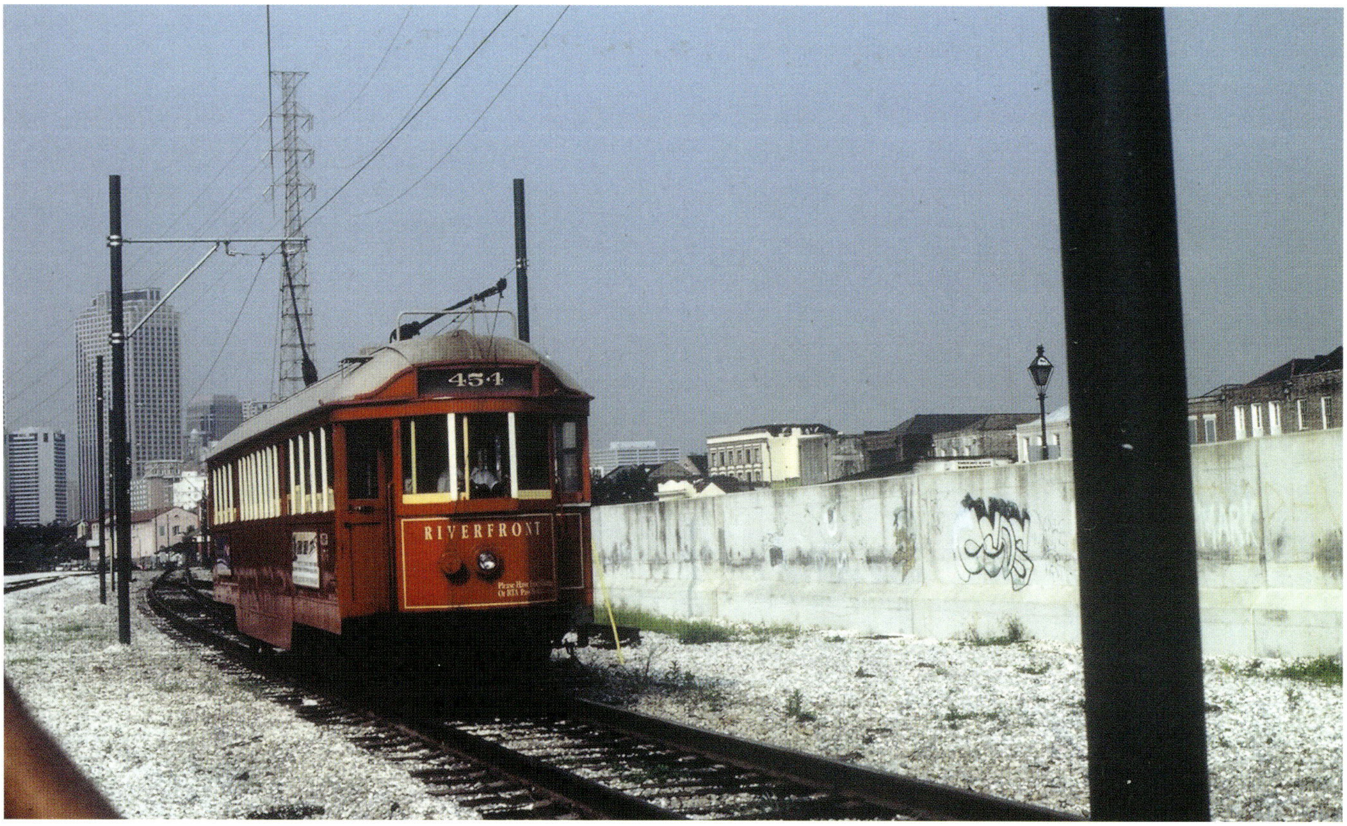

RTA streetcar No. 454 is operating alongside the concrete levee on the Riverfront line on July 27, 1989, with the Central Business District skyscrapers in the distance.

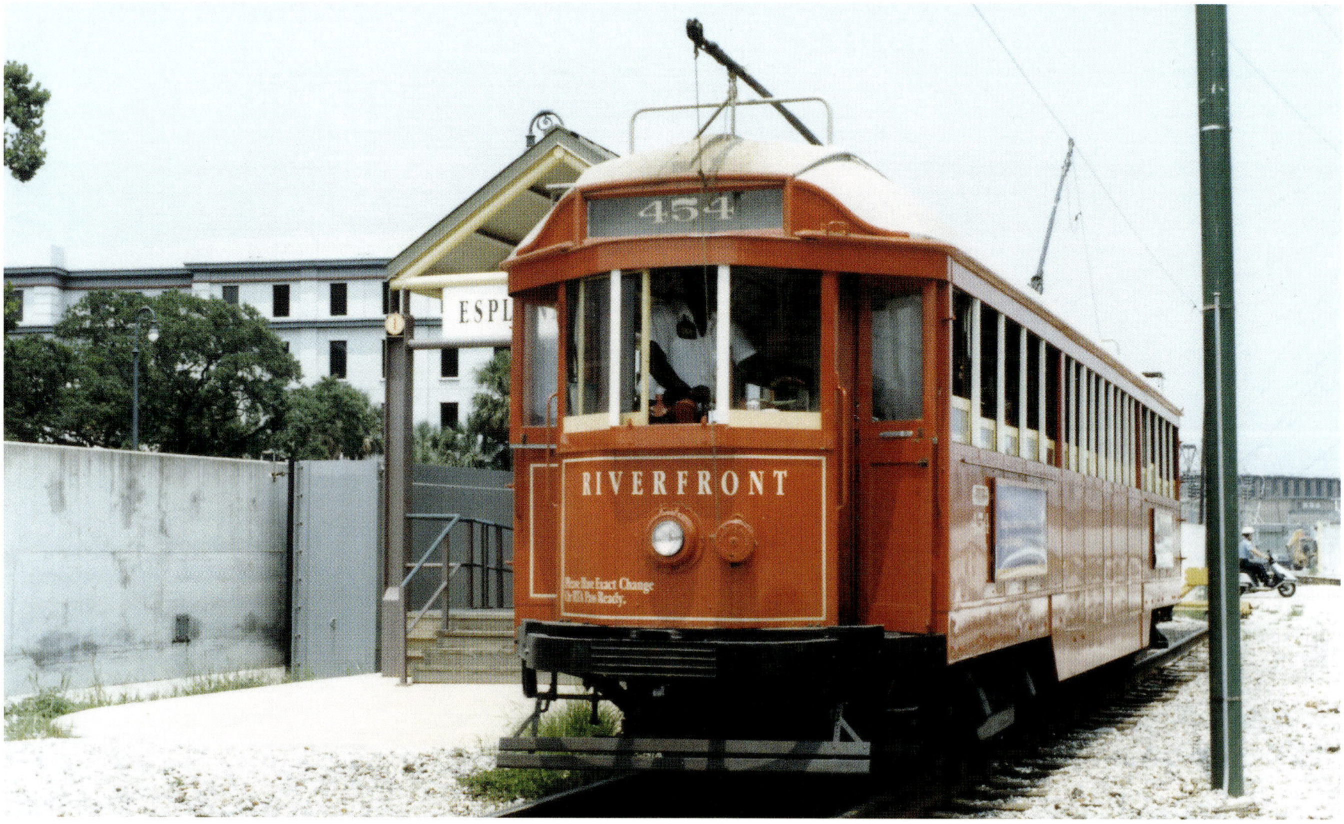

At Esplanade Avenue, the eastern end of the Riverfront line, RTA streetcar No. 454 is awaiting departure time on July 29, 1989.

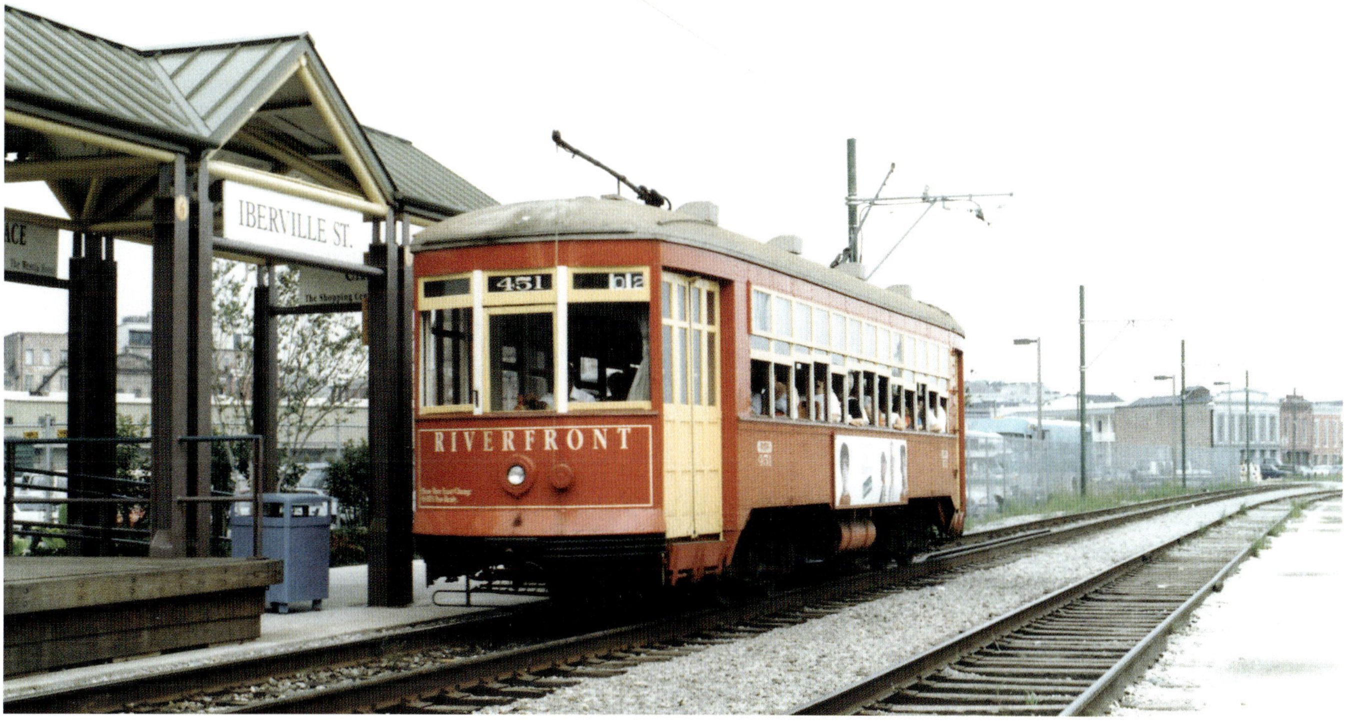

Above: RTA streetcar No. 451 is at the Riverfront line Iberville Street station on July 29, 1989.

Right: Along the Riverfront line, RTA streetcar No. 450 shows a reflection in a temporary pond after a rain, on July 27, 1989. A former Melbourne, Australia streetcar is ahead of this streetcar.

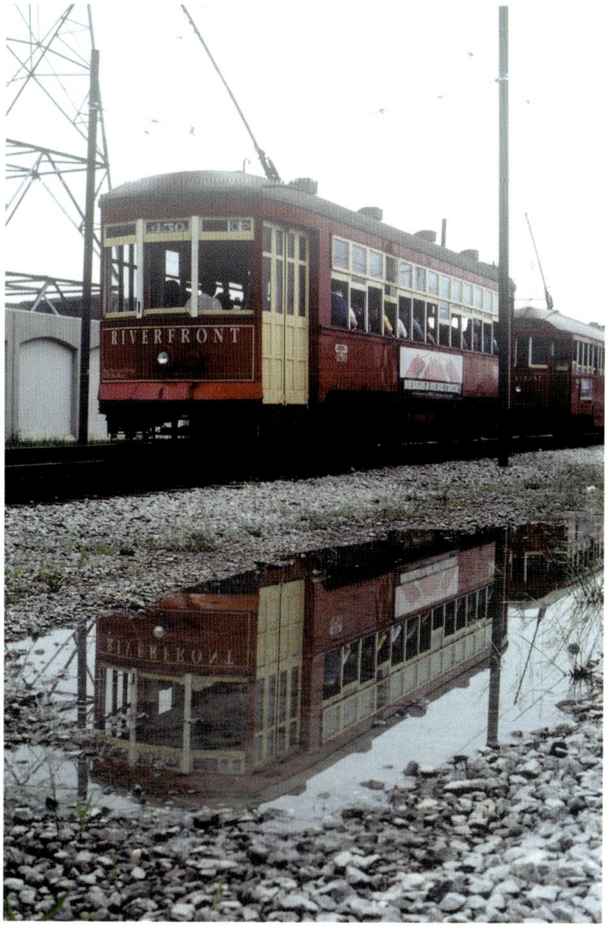

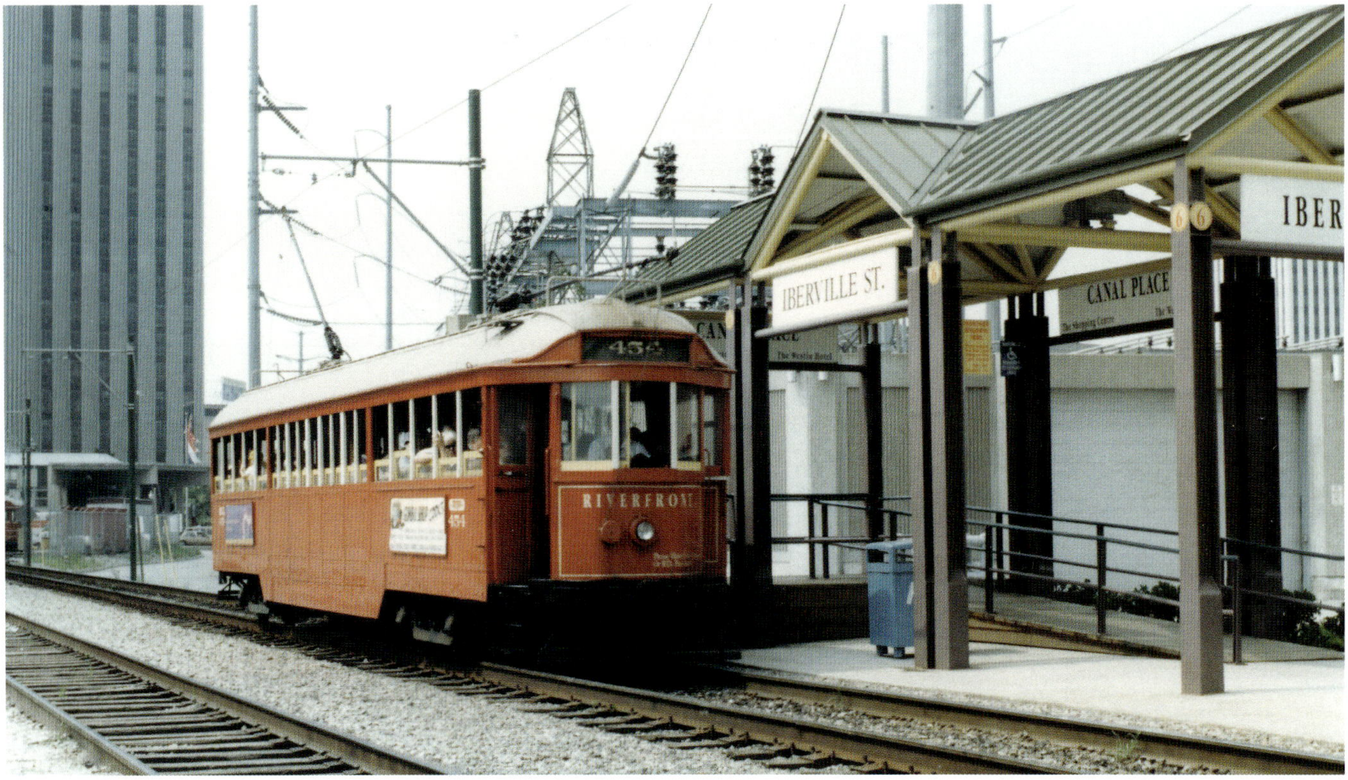

Here is a look at RTA streetcar No. 454 arriving at Iberville Street station on the Riverfront line for a passenger stop one block from Canal Street on July 29, 1989.

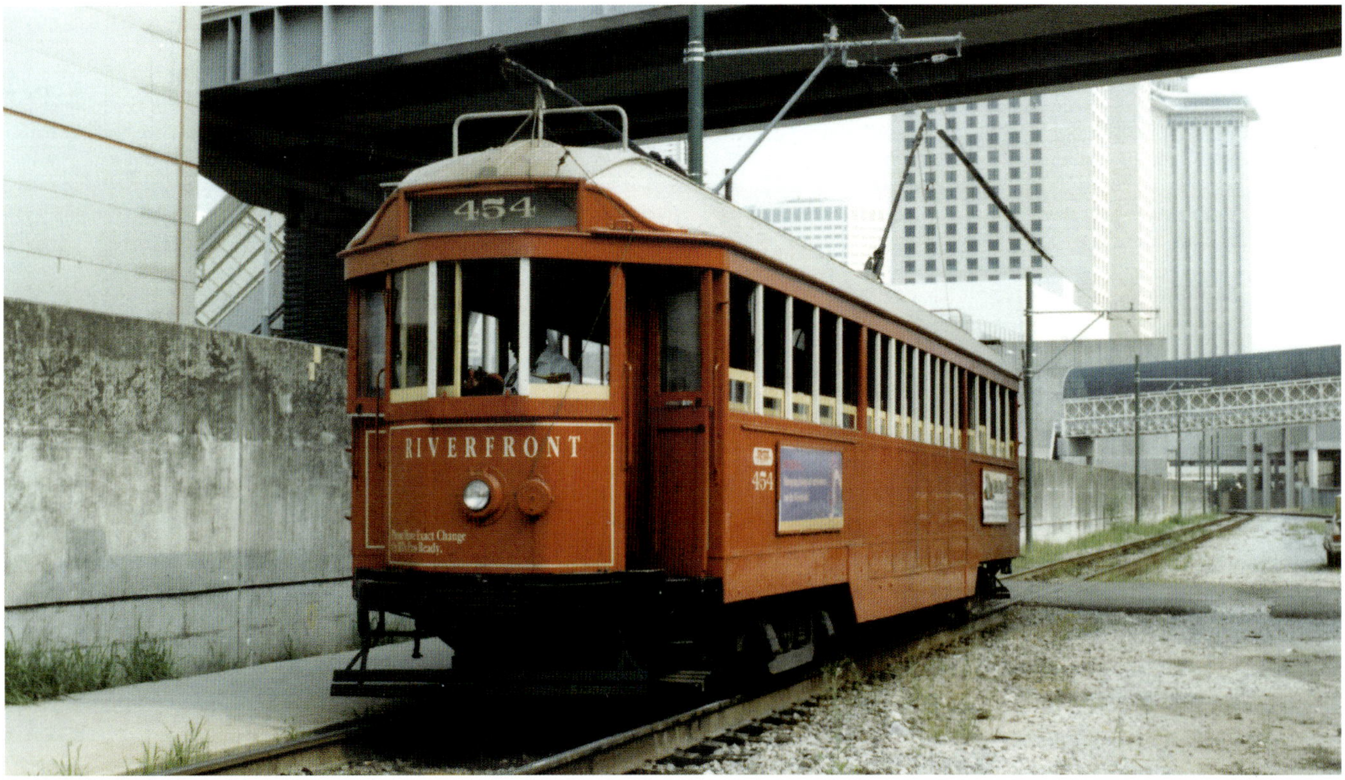

RTA streetcar No. 454 is at Julia Street on the Riverfront line on July 29, 1989.

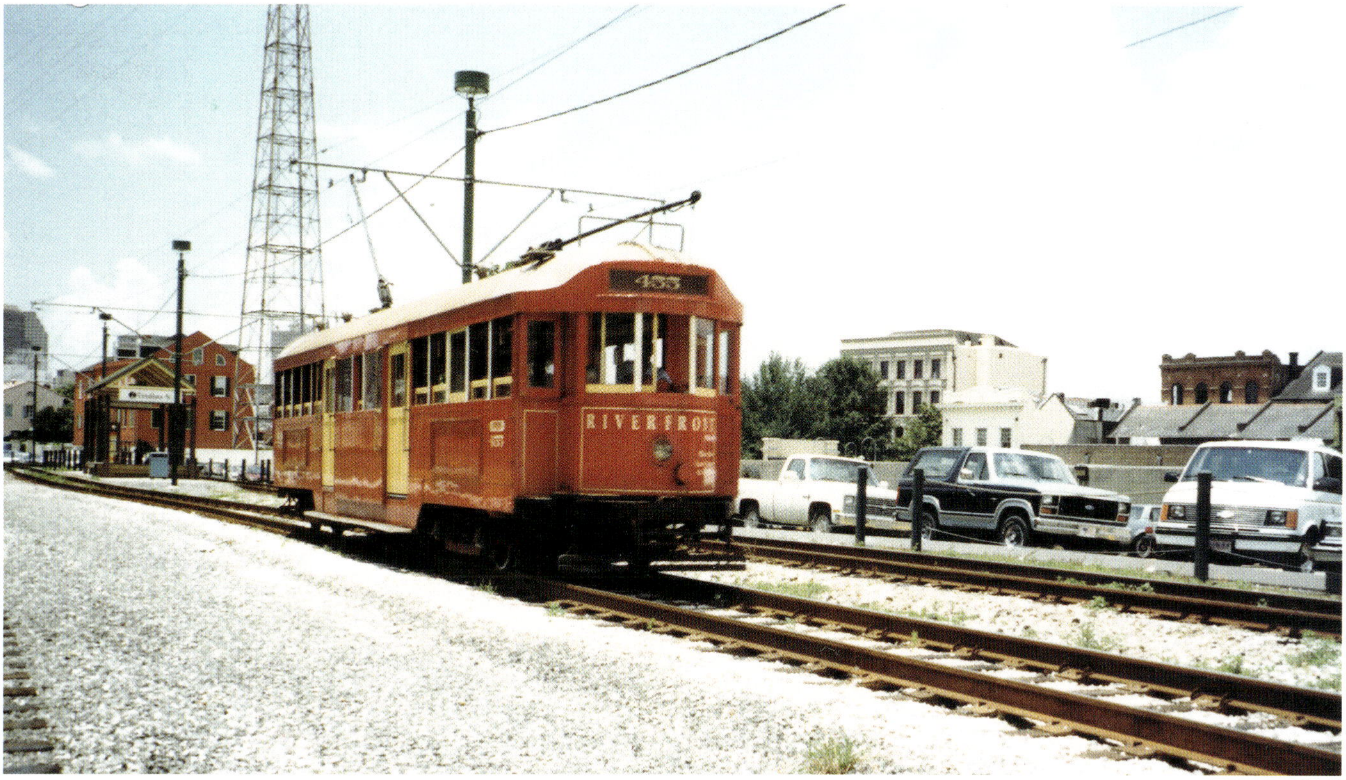

East of Ursulines Avenue station on July 19, 1991, RTA streetcar No. 455 (formerly Melbourne and Metropolitan Tramways Board of Melbourne, Australia W-2 class car No. 331) is eastbound on the Riverfront line. Following a two month shutdown, on August 31, 1990 the Riverfront line was reopened with a nearly half-mile extension to the Convention Center, and was double tracked.

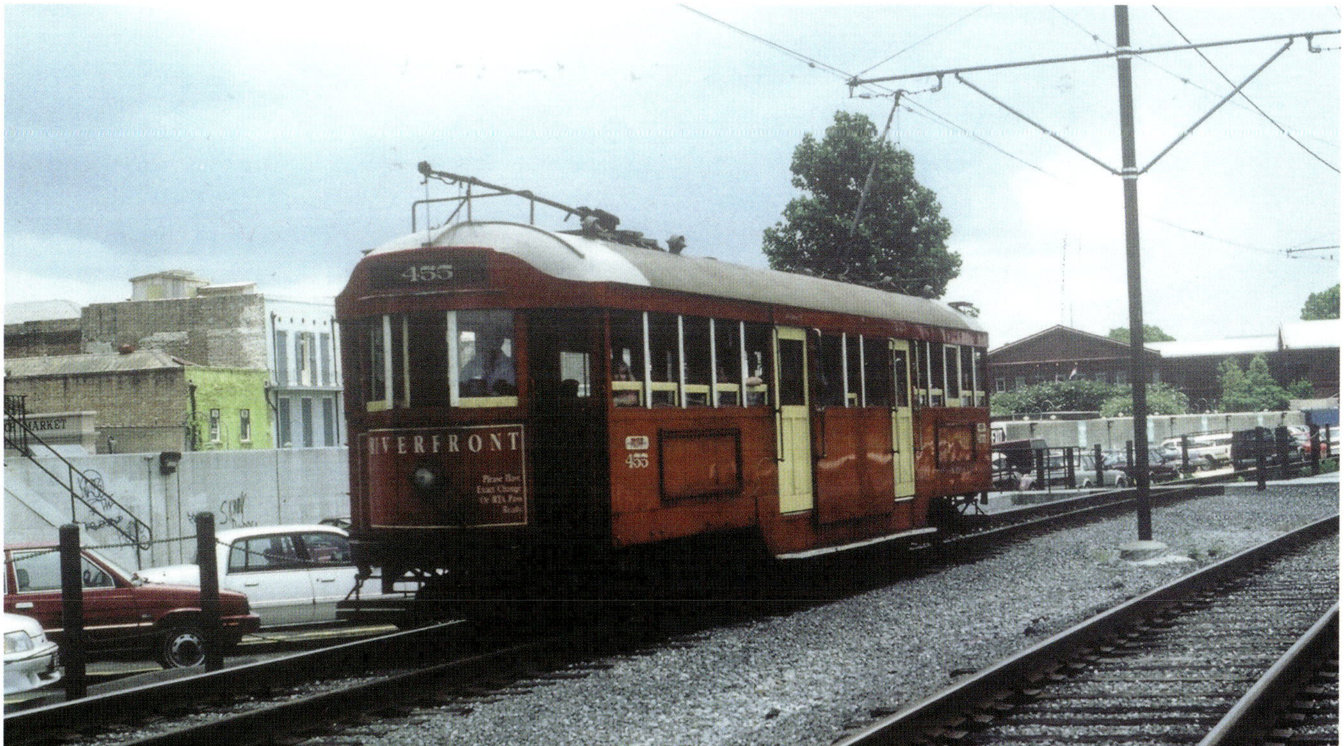

On July 19, 1991, RTA streetcar No. 455 (formerly Melbourne and Metropolitan Tramways Board of Melbourne, Australia W-2 class car No. 331) is on the Riverfront line. The W-2 class streetcars, highly popular in museum operation throughout Australia and the United States, are forty-eight feet long with a capacity of fifty-two seated passengers and ninety-eight standing, or a total capacity of 150 passengers.

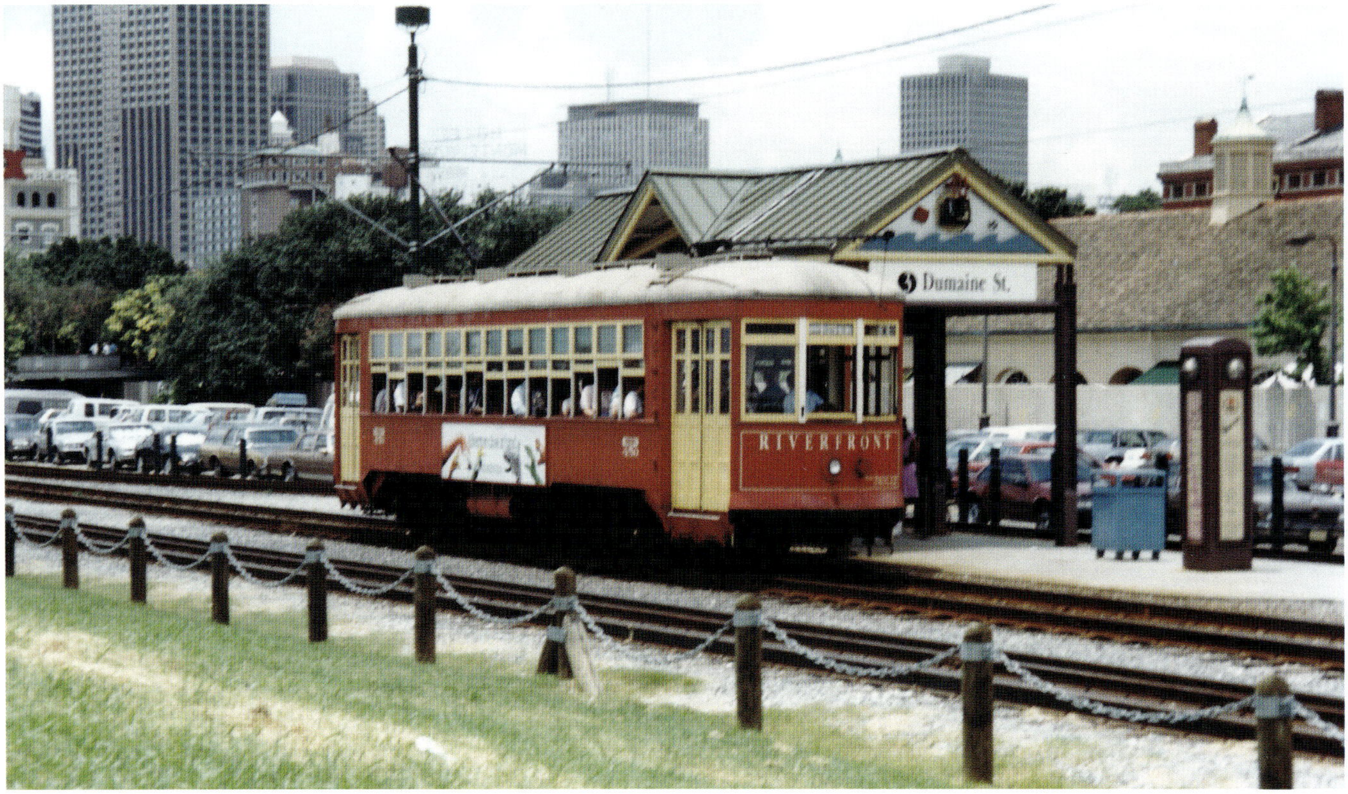

Dumaine Street station is the location of RTA streetcar No. 450, pictured travelling eastbound on the Riverfront line on July 19, 1991, with the Central Business District skyline in the background.

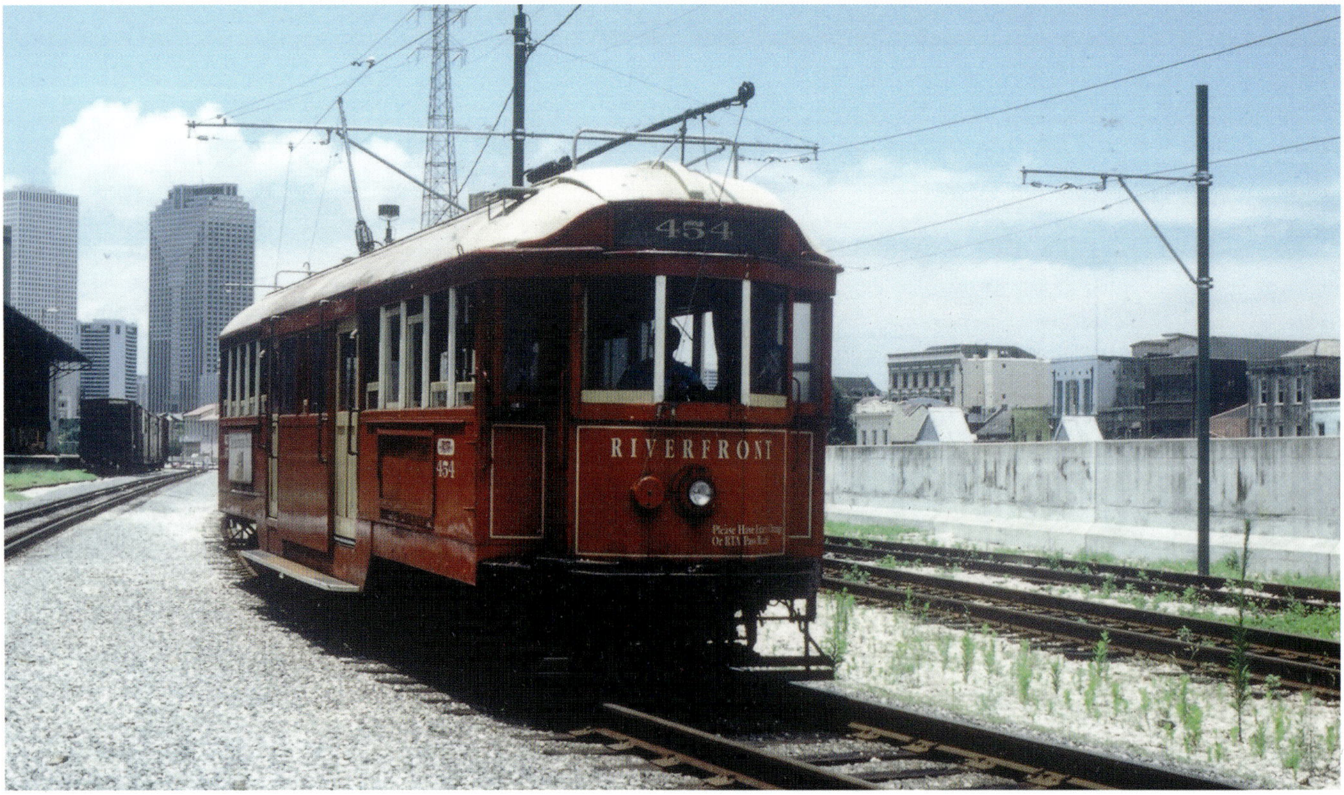

RTA streetcar No. 454 is on the Riverfront line on July 20, 1991, with the Canal Street skyline in the distance. The New Orleans Public Belt Railroad track is on the left.

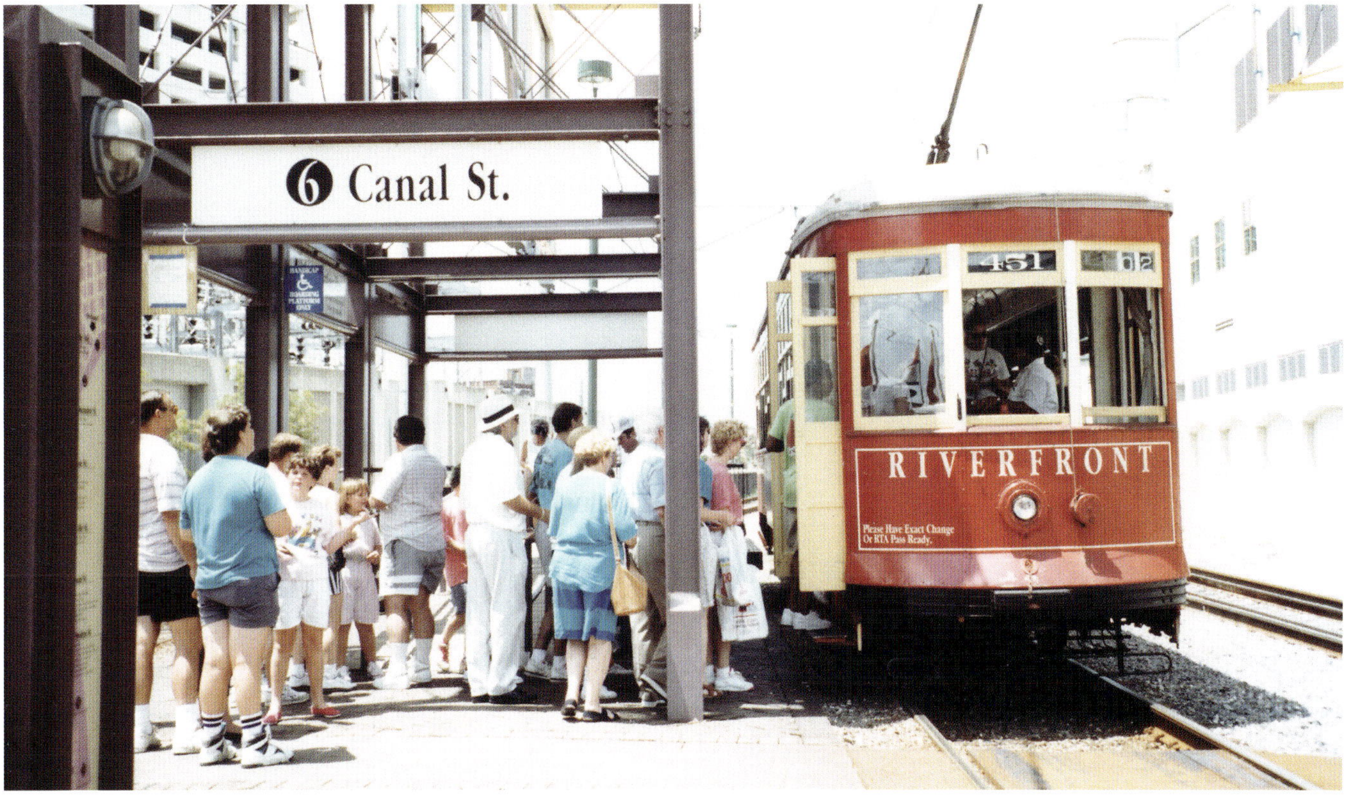

On a warm July 19, 1991, a nice group of passengers are boarding RTA streetcar No. 451 at the Canal Street station for an eastbound trip to Esplanade Avenue on the Riverfront line.

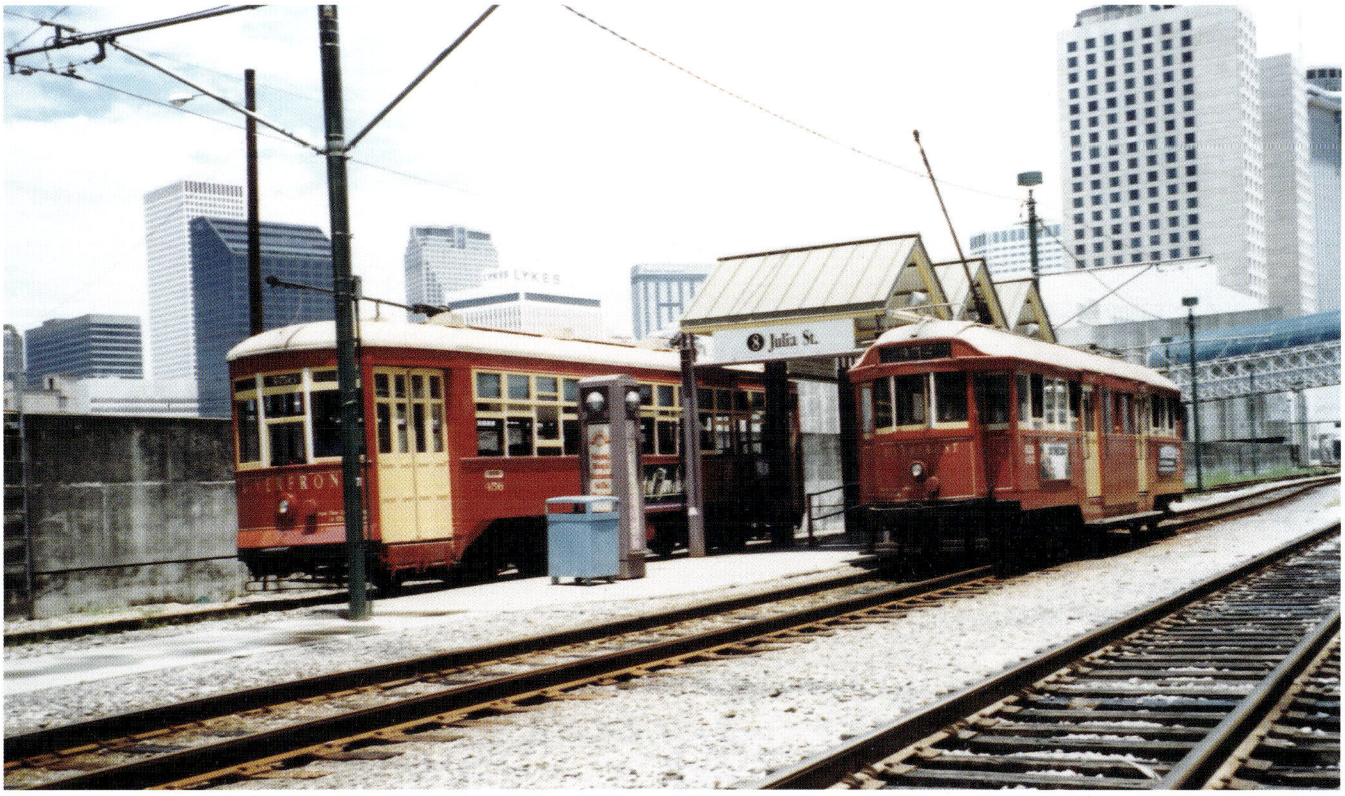

Julia Street station on the Riverfront line is the location for RTA streetcars No. 456 (originally No. 952, purchased from the Tennessee Valley Railway Museum in Chattanooga, Tennessee) and 452 (formerly Melbourne and Metropolitan Tramways Board of Melbourne, Australia W-2 class car No. 626), shown on July 19, 1991. The Ernest N. Morial Convention Center is near this station.

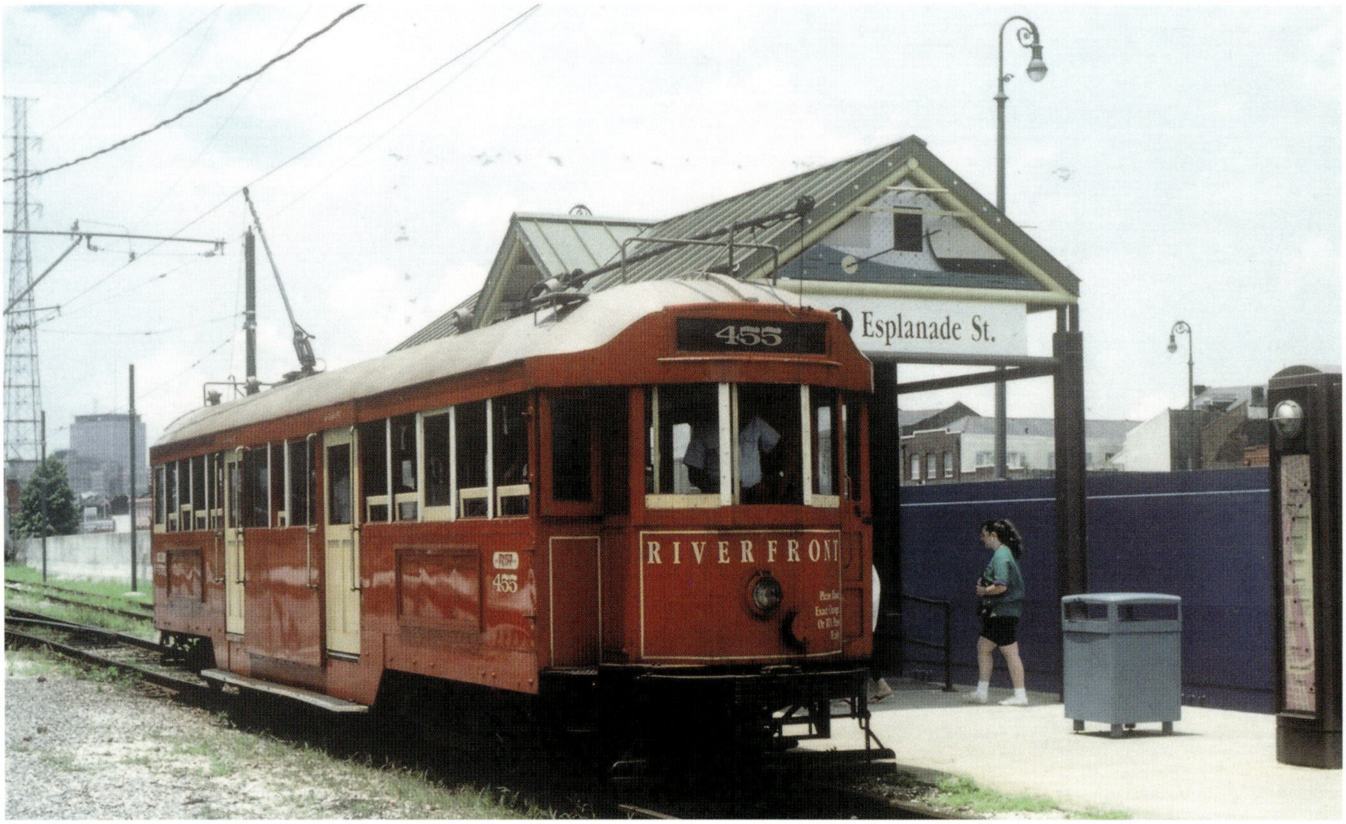

On July 19, 1991, RTA streetcar No. 455 is at Esplanade Avenue station on the Riverfront line.

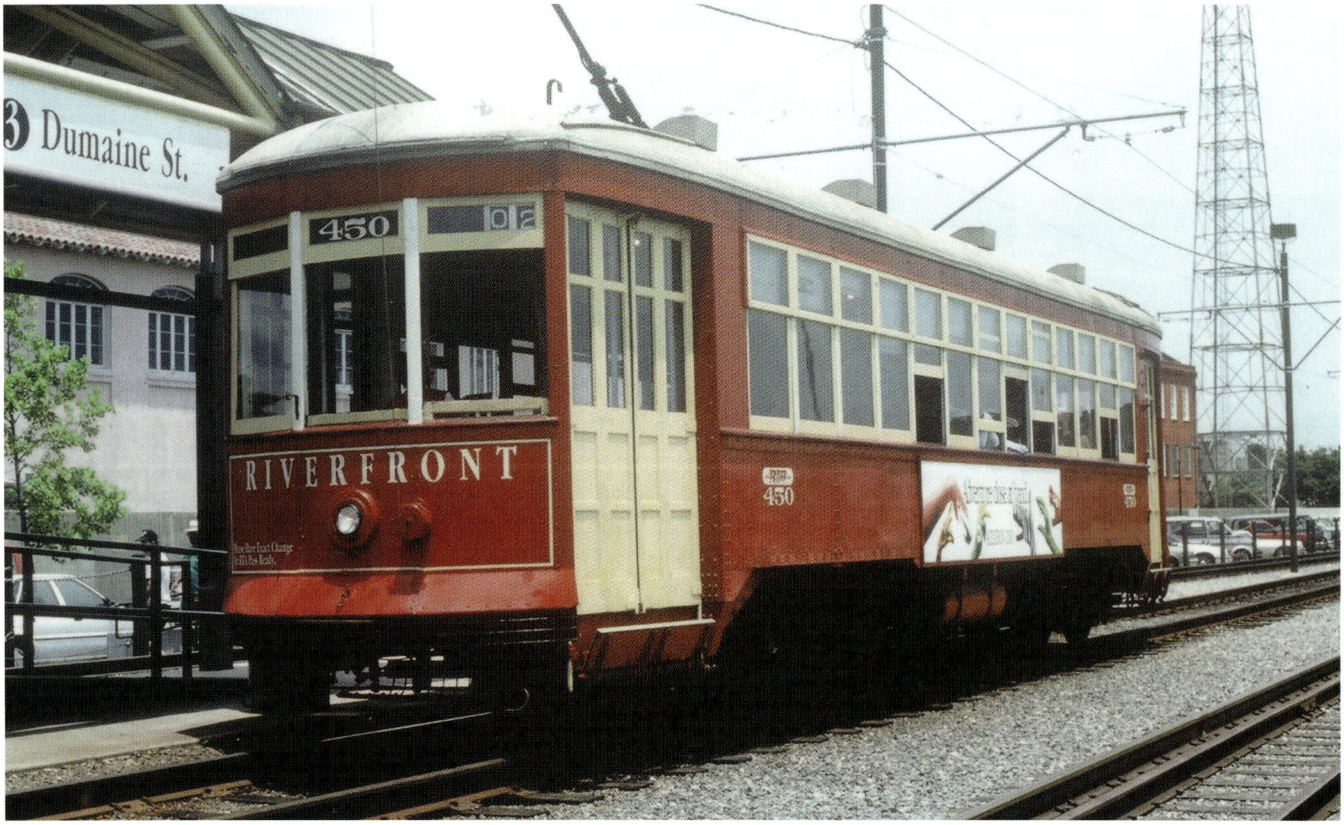

RTA streetcar No. 450 is at Dumaine Street station on the Riverfront line on July 19, 1991.

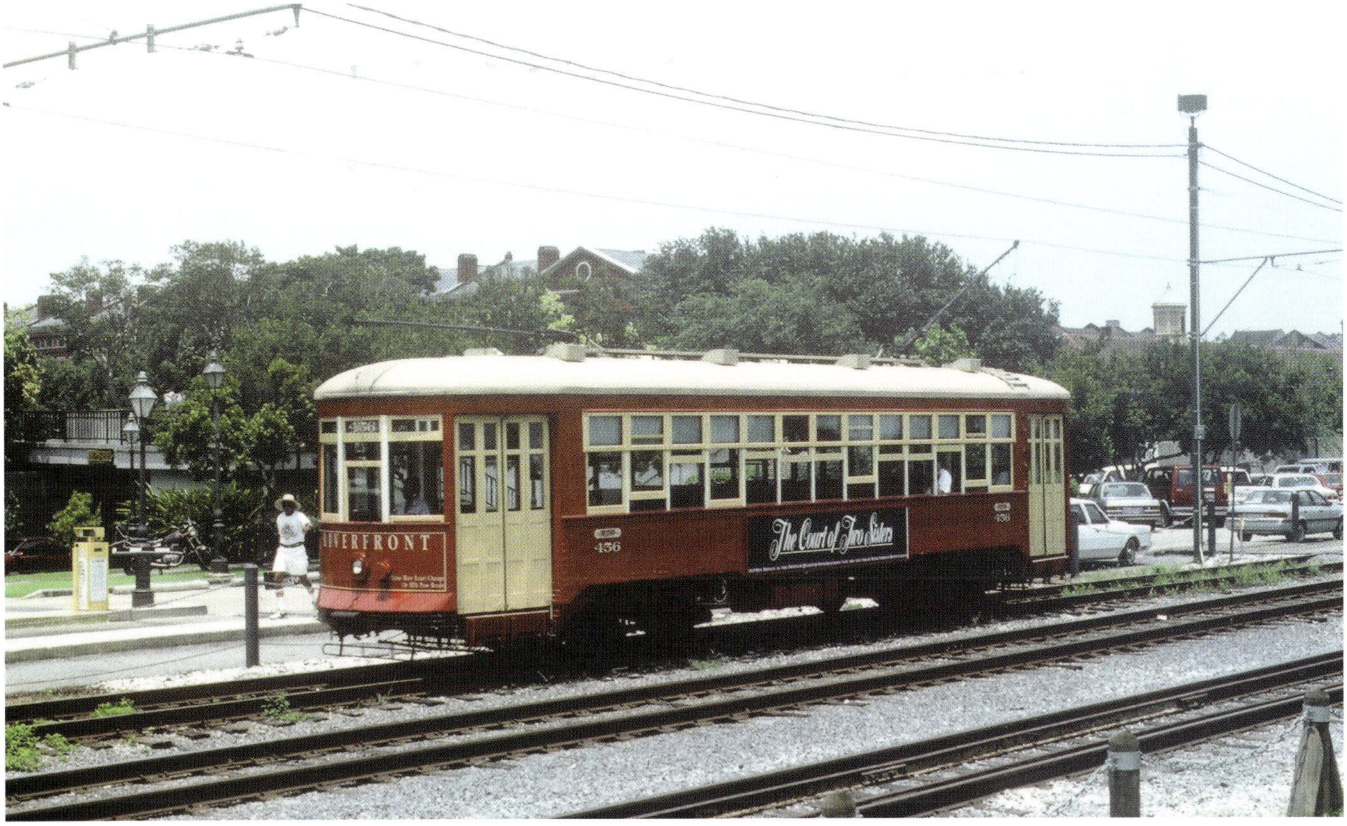

On July 19, 1991, RTA streetcar No. 456 is westbound on the Riverfront line.

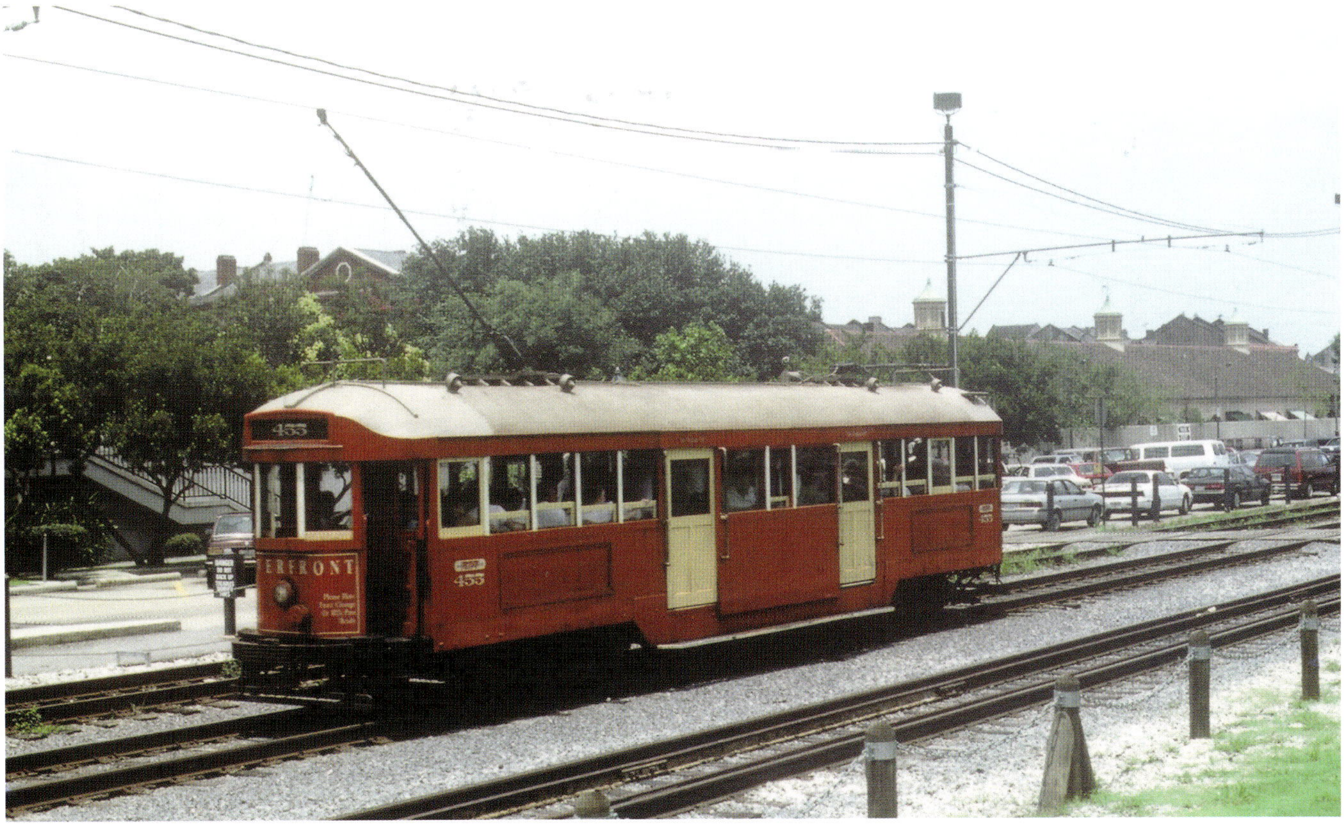

Eastbound RTA streetcar No. 455 (formerly Melbourne and Metropolitan Tramways Board of Melbourne, Australia W-2 class car No. 331) is on the Riverfront line on July 19, 1991.

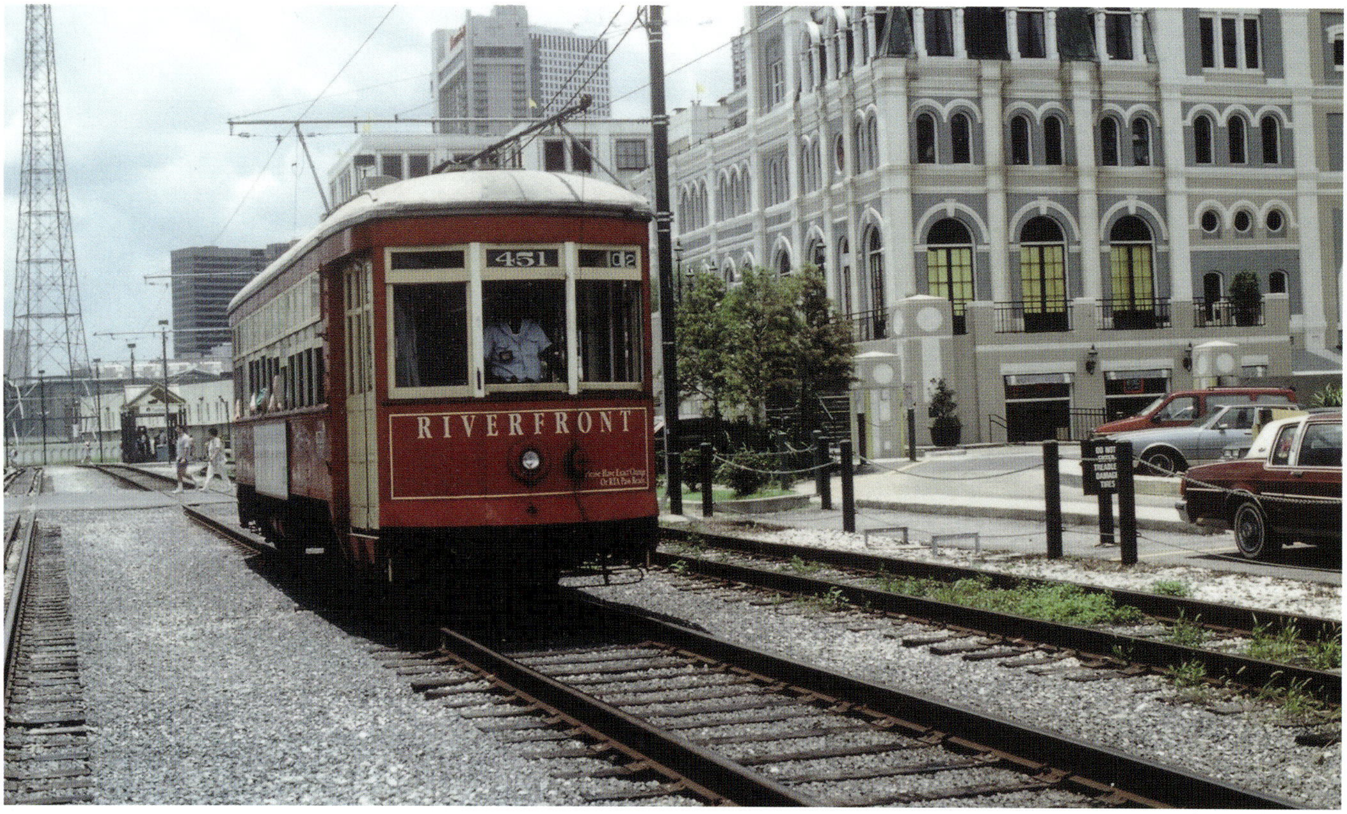

East of the Riverfront line Toulouse Street station, RTA streetcar No. 451 is eastbound for Esplanade Avenue on July 19, 1991, passing the multi-level Jackson Brewery Marketplace.

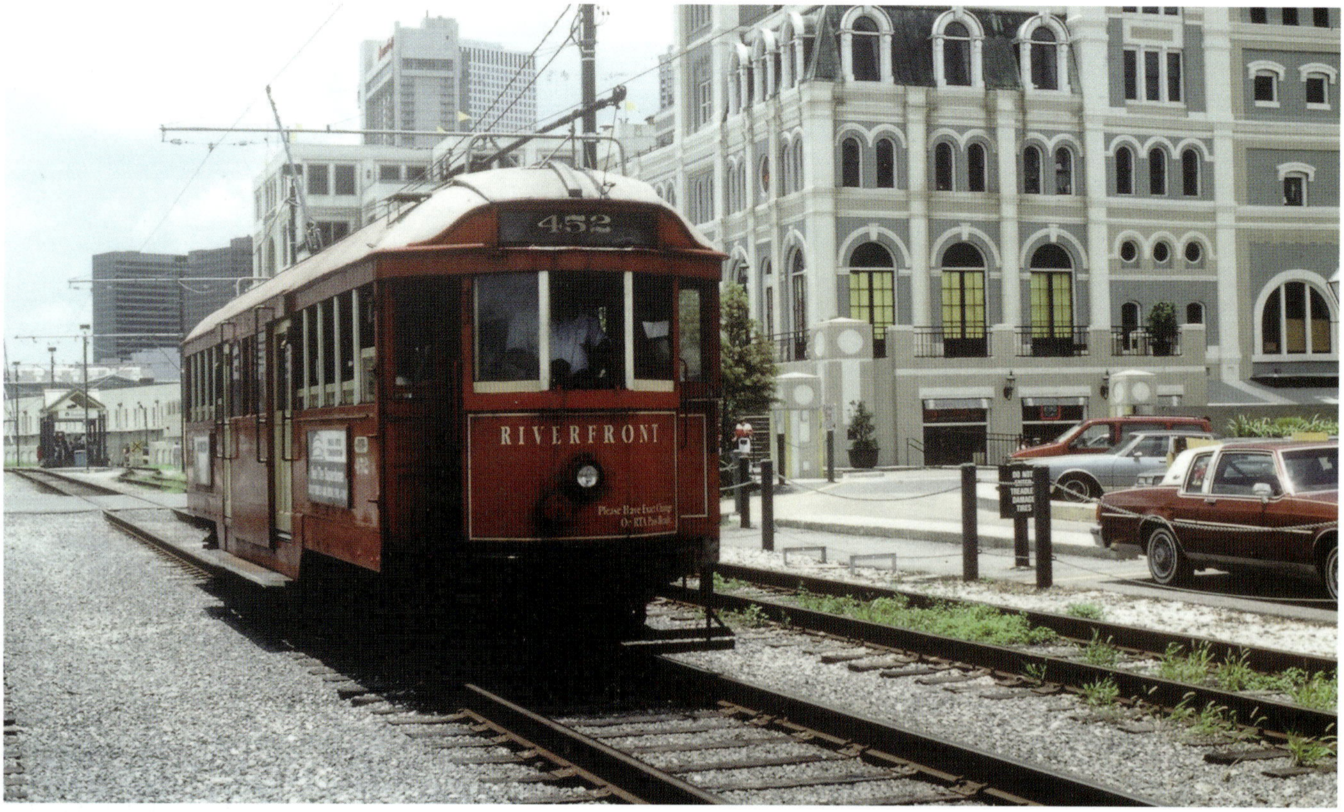

RTA streetcar No. 452 is east of Toulouse Street station, making its way eastbound on the Riverfront line on July 19, 1991, near the multi-level Jackson Brewery Marketplace.

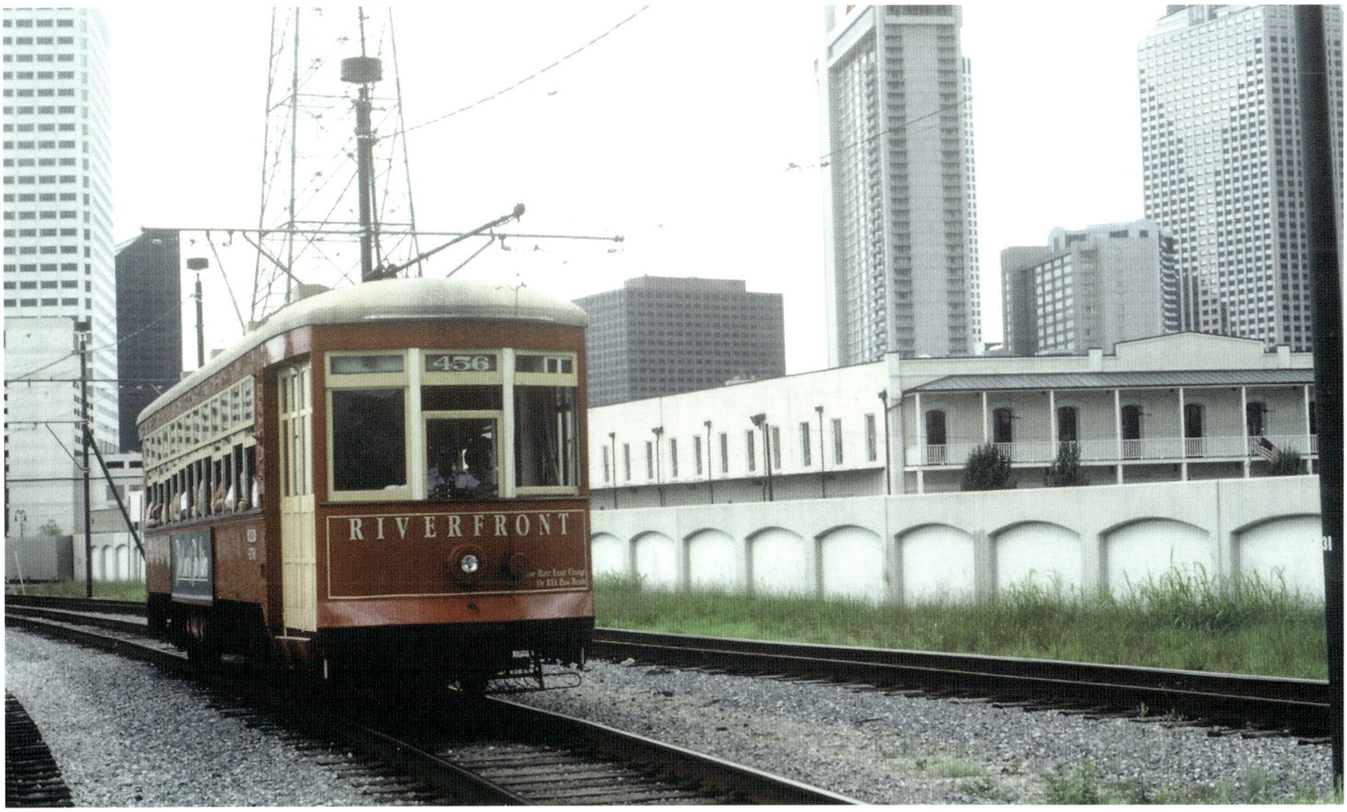

On July 19, 1991, eastbound RTA streetcar No. 456 is heading for the Esplanade Avenue station on the Riverfront line. The Old United States Mint is near this station.

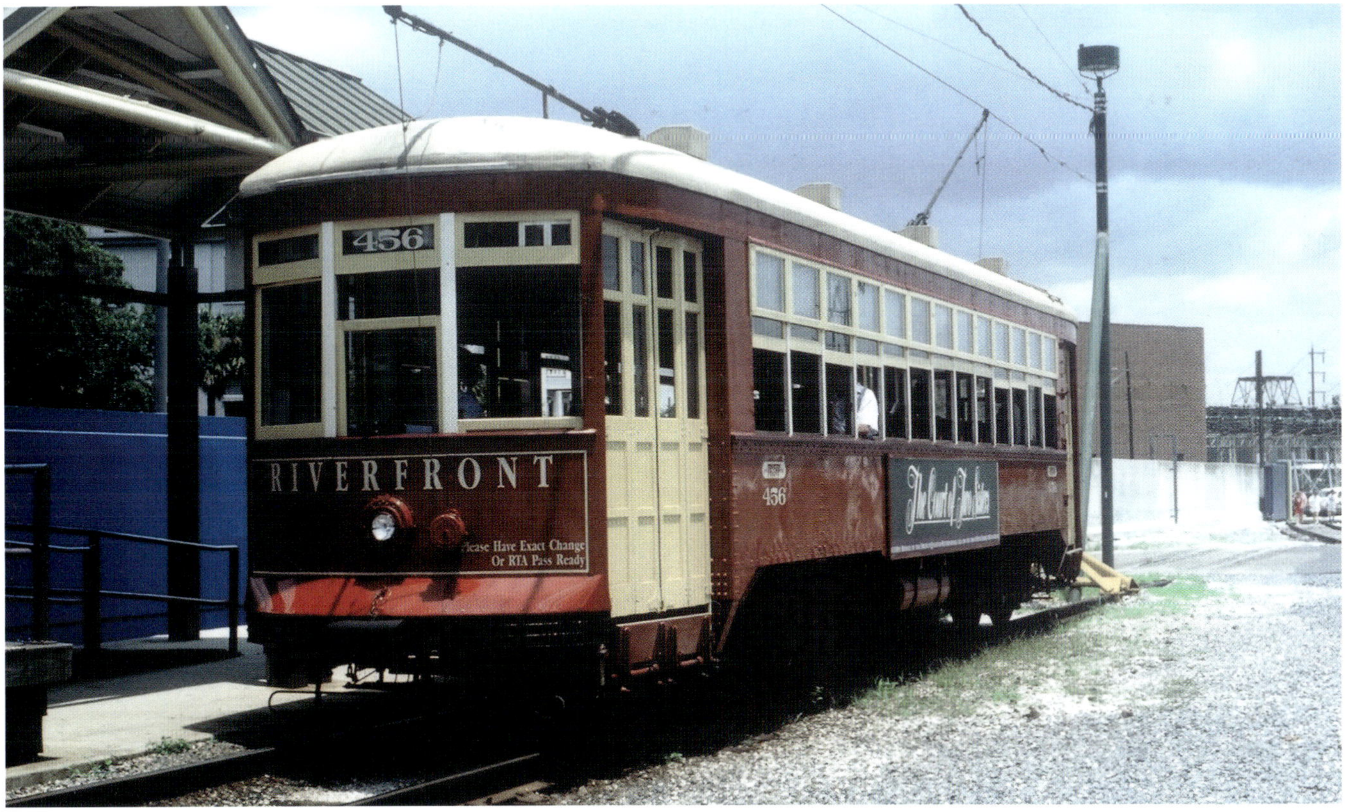

At the Esplanade Avenue station on July 19, 1991, RTA streetcar No. 456 is awaiting the departure time for the next westbound trip on the Riverfront line.

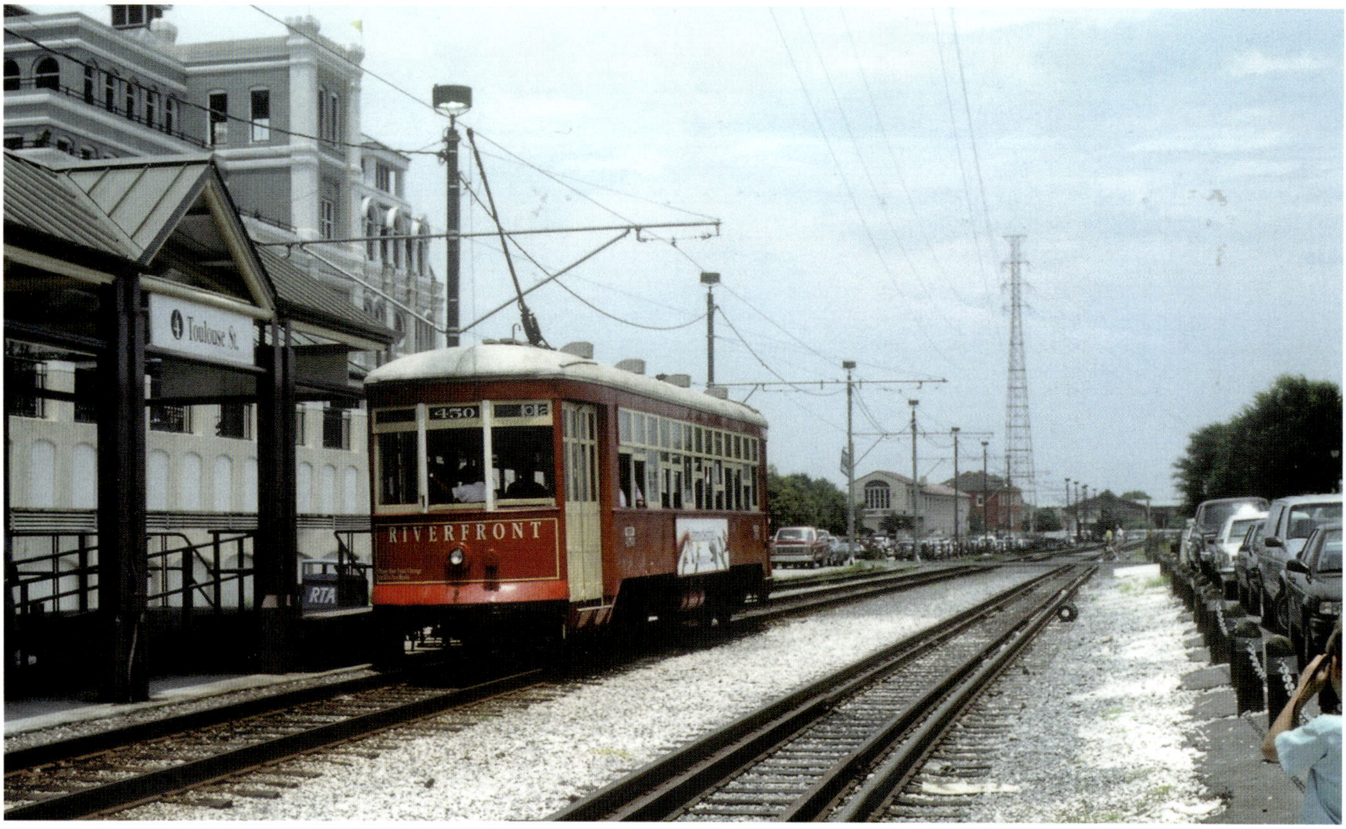

Eastbound RTA streetcar No. 450 is leaving the Toulouse Street station on the Riverfront line on July 20, 1991, with the multi-level Jackson Brewery Marketplace on the left.

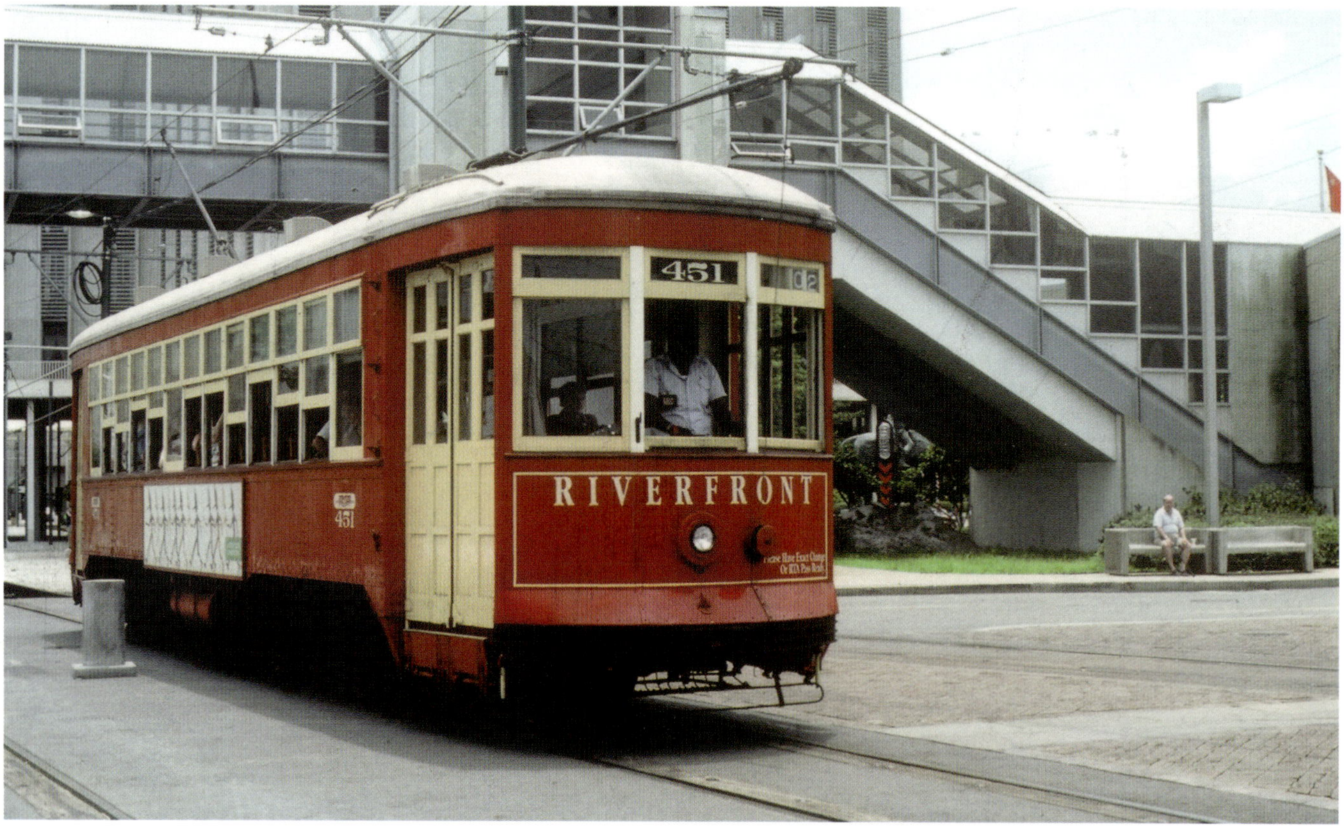

RTA streetcar No. 451 is approaching the Canal Street station heading east to Esplanade Avenue, on the Riverfront line on July 20, 1991.

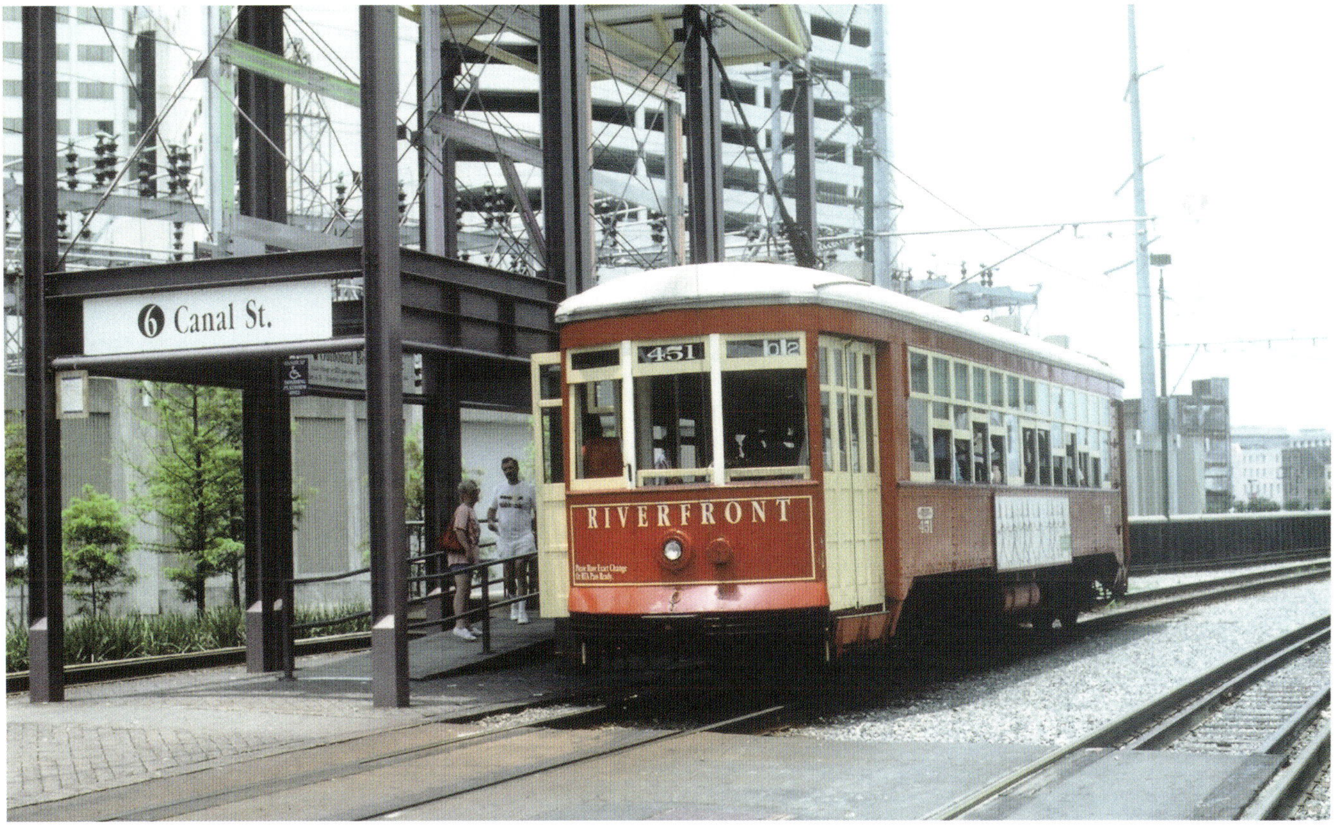

Canal Street station on the Riverfront line is the location for RTA streetcar No. 451, on July 20, 1991. This station is close to the Aquarium of the Americas and the Canal Street Ferry.

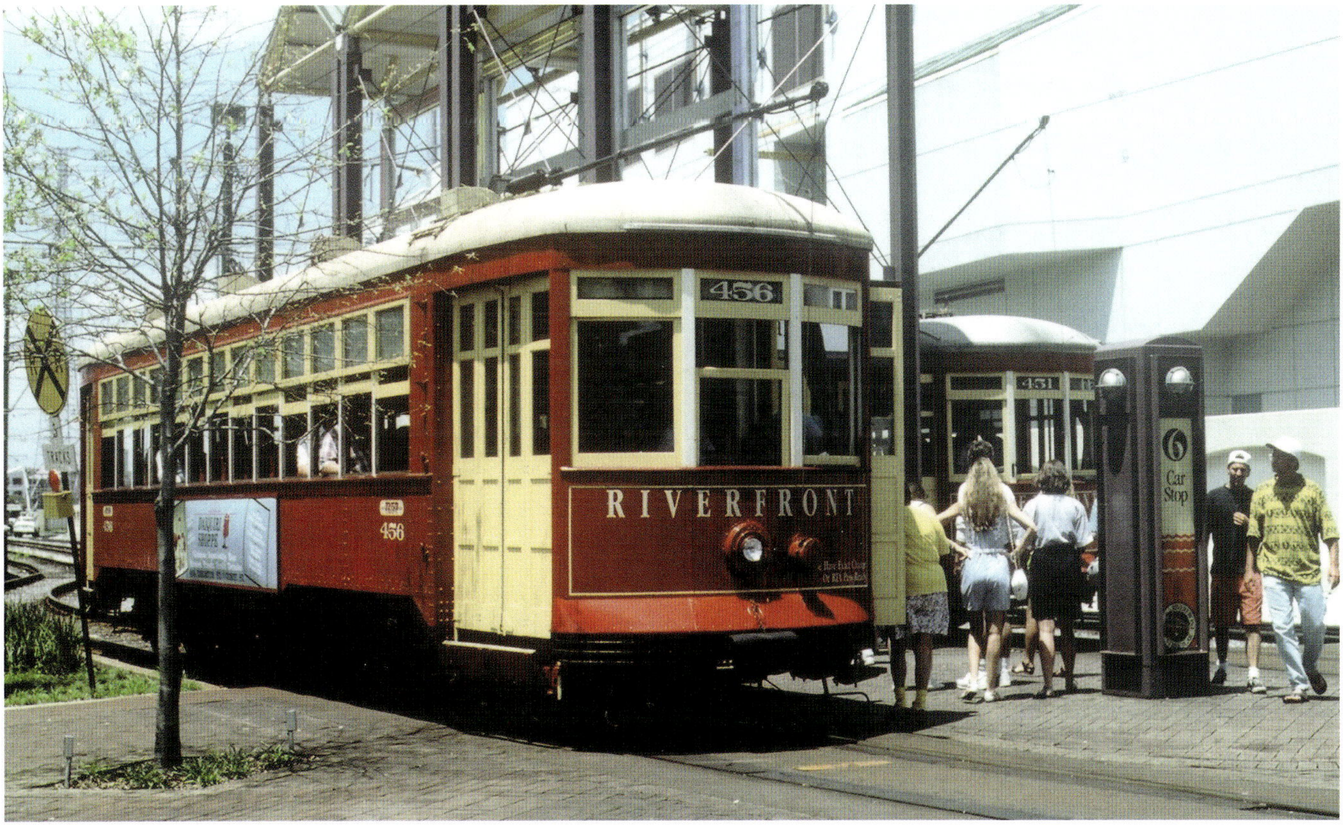

Westbound RTA streetcar No. 456 meets eastbound streetcar No. 451 at the Canal Street station on the Riverfront line on July 20, 1991.

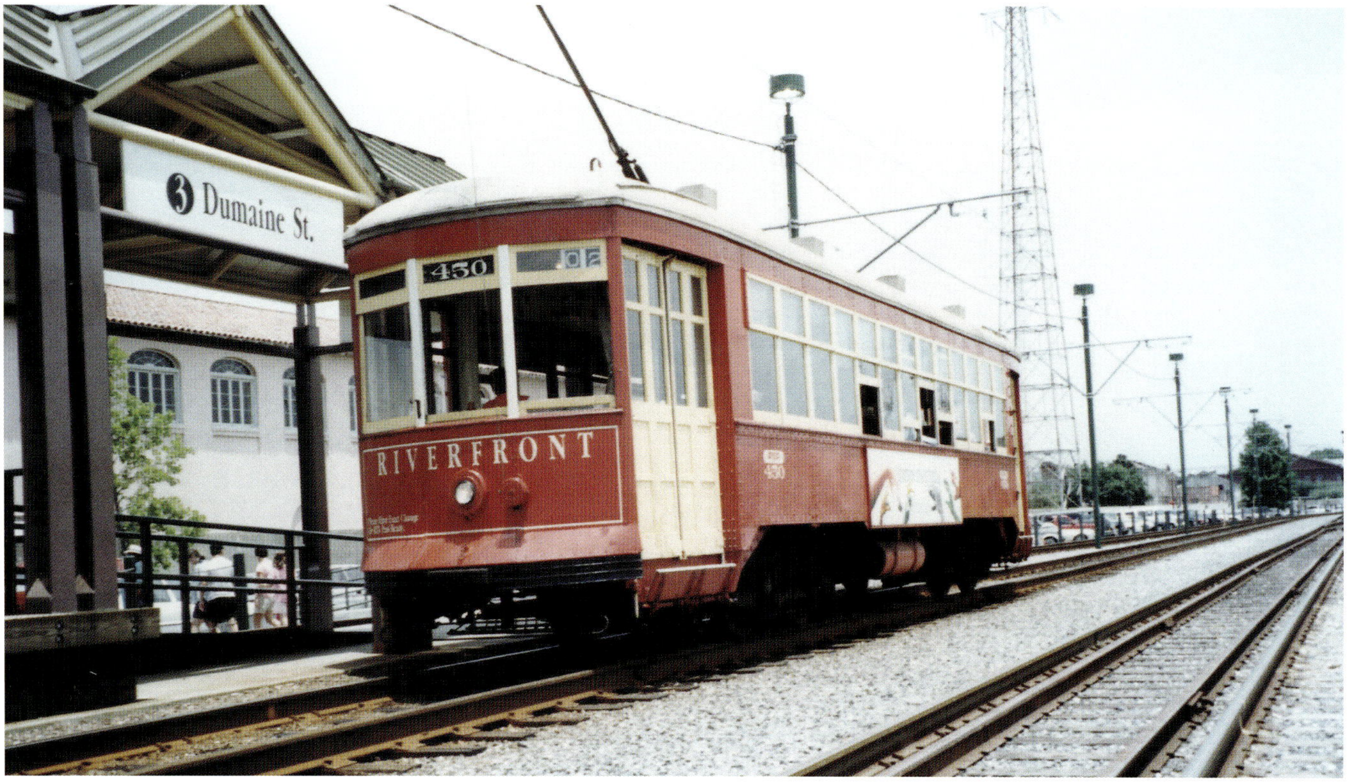

Eastbound RTA streetcar No. 450 is at the Dumaine Street station on the Riverfront line, on July 21, 1991. The New Orleans Public Belt Railroad track is on the right.

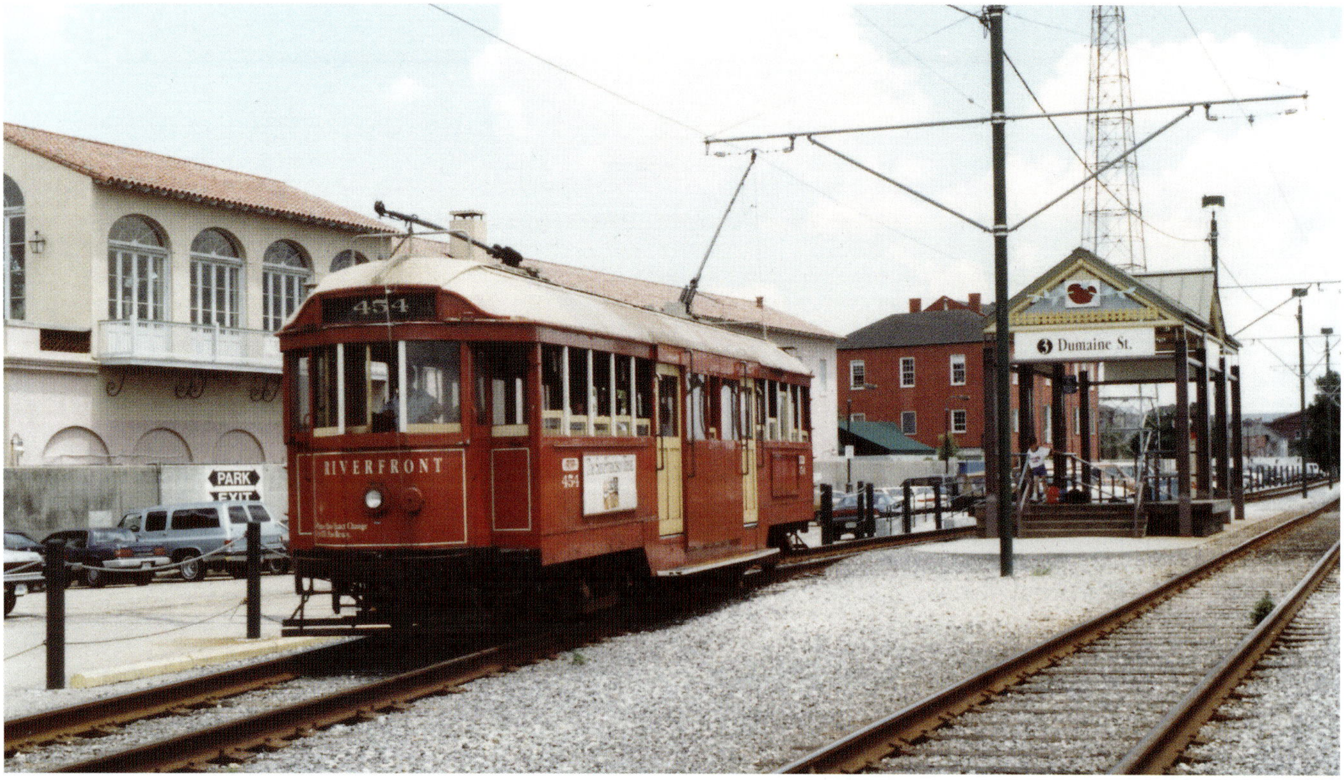

On July 21, 1991, RTA streetcar No. 454 has left the Dumaine Street station for a westbound trip on the Riverfront line. The Mississippi River is now easy to view along the riverfront.

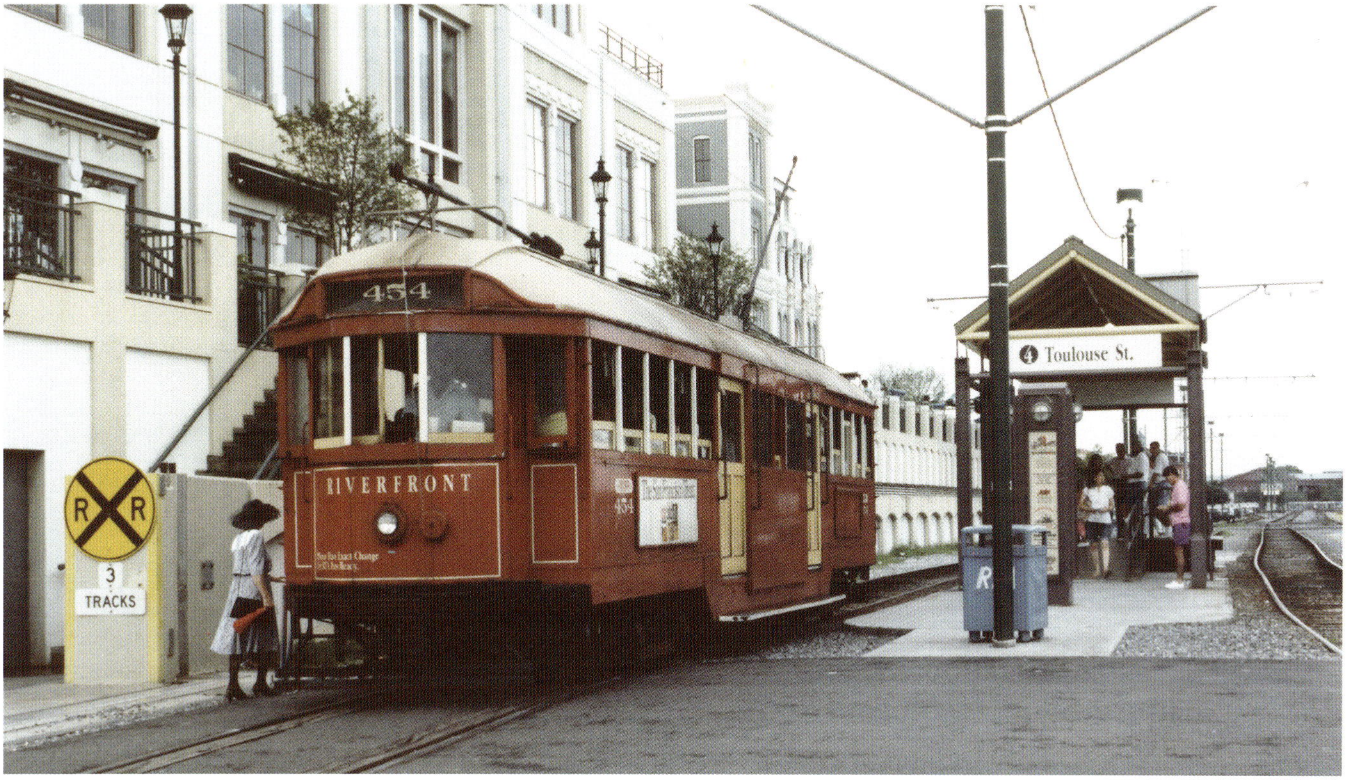

At the Toulouse Street station, on July 21, 1991, RTA streetcar No. 454 is making a passenger stop on a westbound trip on the Riverfront line. On the left side of the streetcar is the multi-level Jackson Brewery Marketplace.

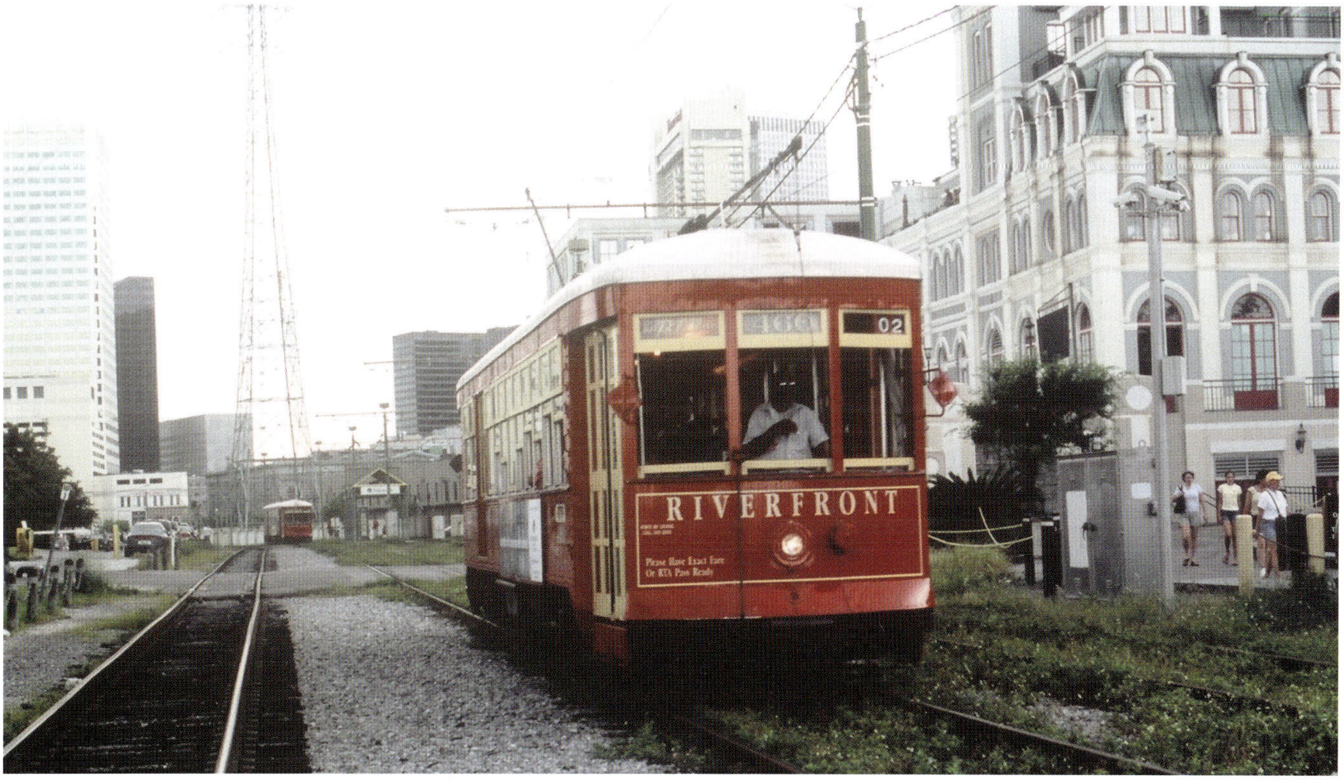

East of the Toulouse Street station, RTA streetcar No. 460 is on the Riverfront line, on July 3, 2004. On September 7, 1997, the Riverfront line was closed, and the track gauge was changed from the 4 foot 8.5 inch standard gauge to the 5 foot 2.5 inch broad gauge of the St. Charles line to access the Carrollton Station shop. The line reopened on December 7, 1997 with broad gauge track and new cars Nos. 457 to 463 built at the Carrollton Station shop in New Orleans.

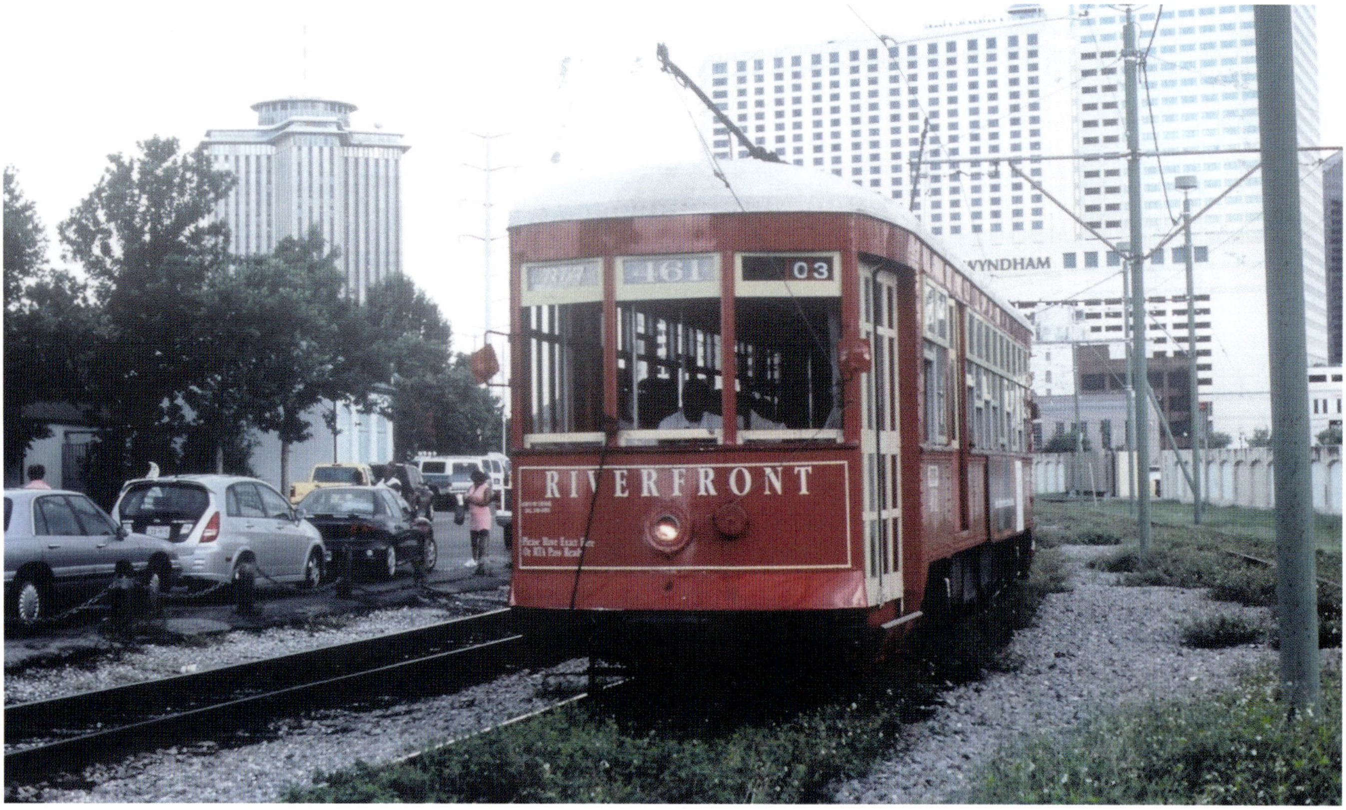

RTA streetcar No. 461 is eastbound on the Riverfront line on July 3, 2004. The Riverfront streetcar is officially route 2, but that number is not displayed on the streetcar.

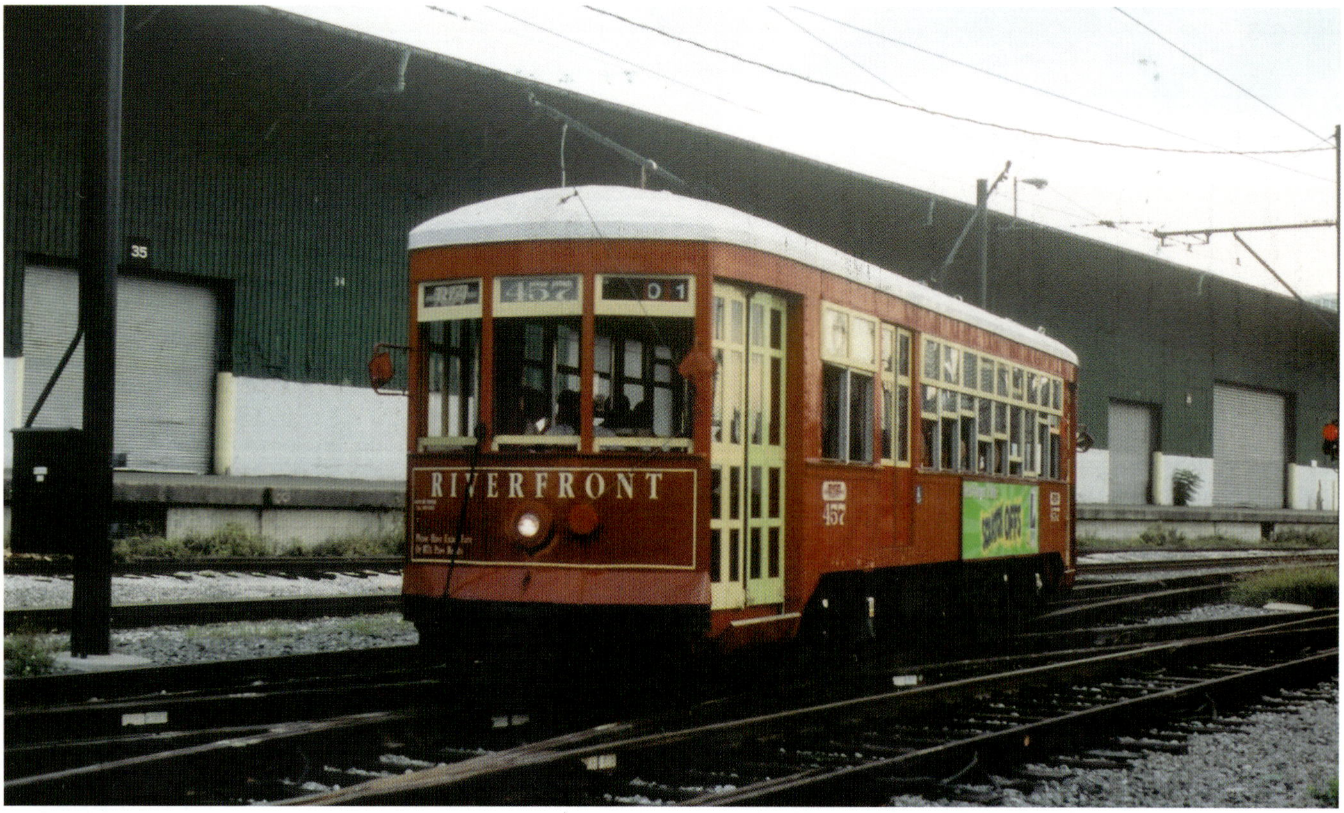

On July 3, 2004, RTA streetcar No. 457 (formerly New Orleans Public Service Inc. car No. 957 from the McKinney Avenue Transit Authority in Dallas, Texas) is coming to the eastern terminus of the Riverfront line at Esplanade Avenue.

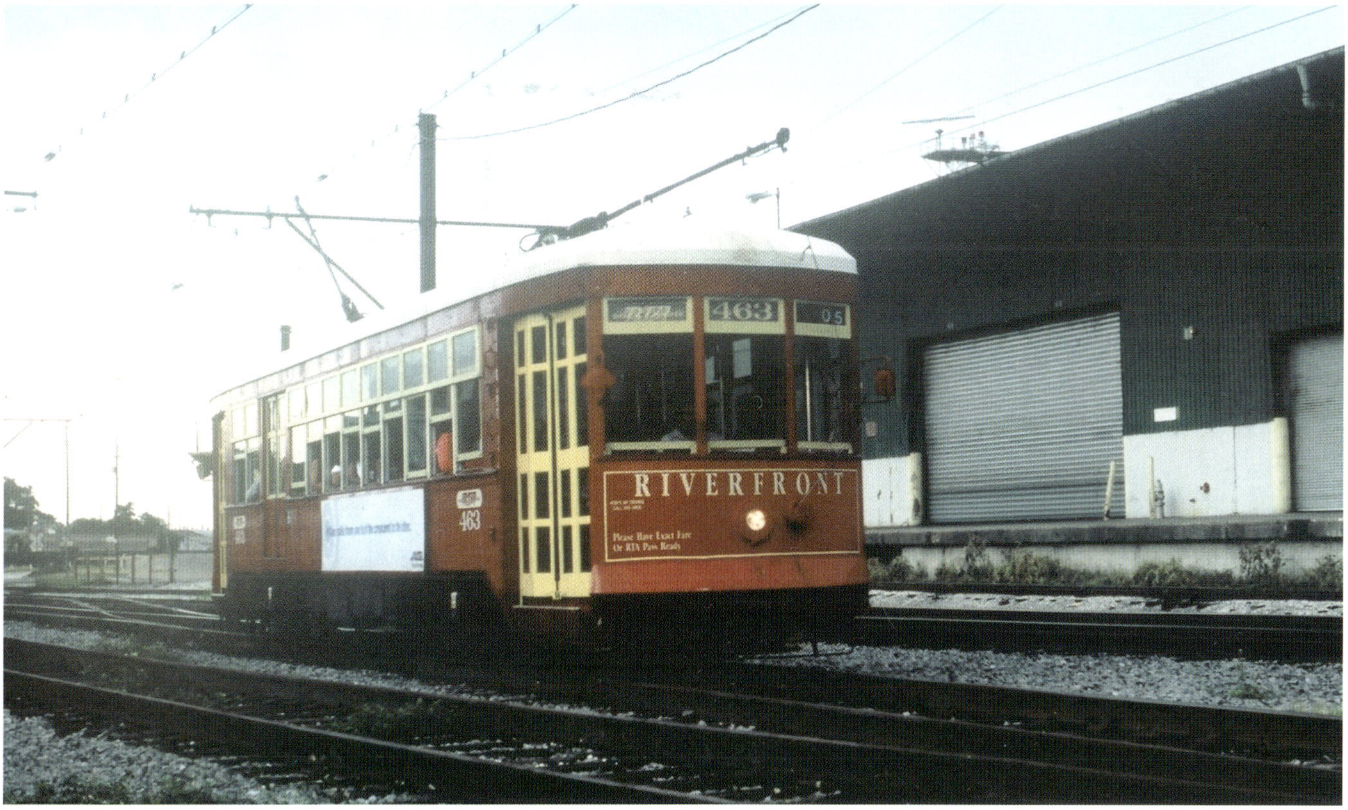

Near the eastern end of the Riverfront line at Esplanade Avenue, RTA streetcar No. 463 is carrying a seated load of passengers on July 3, 2004.

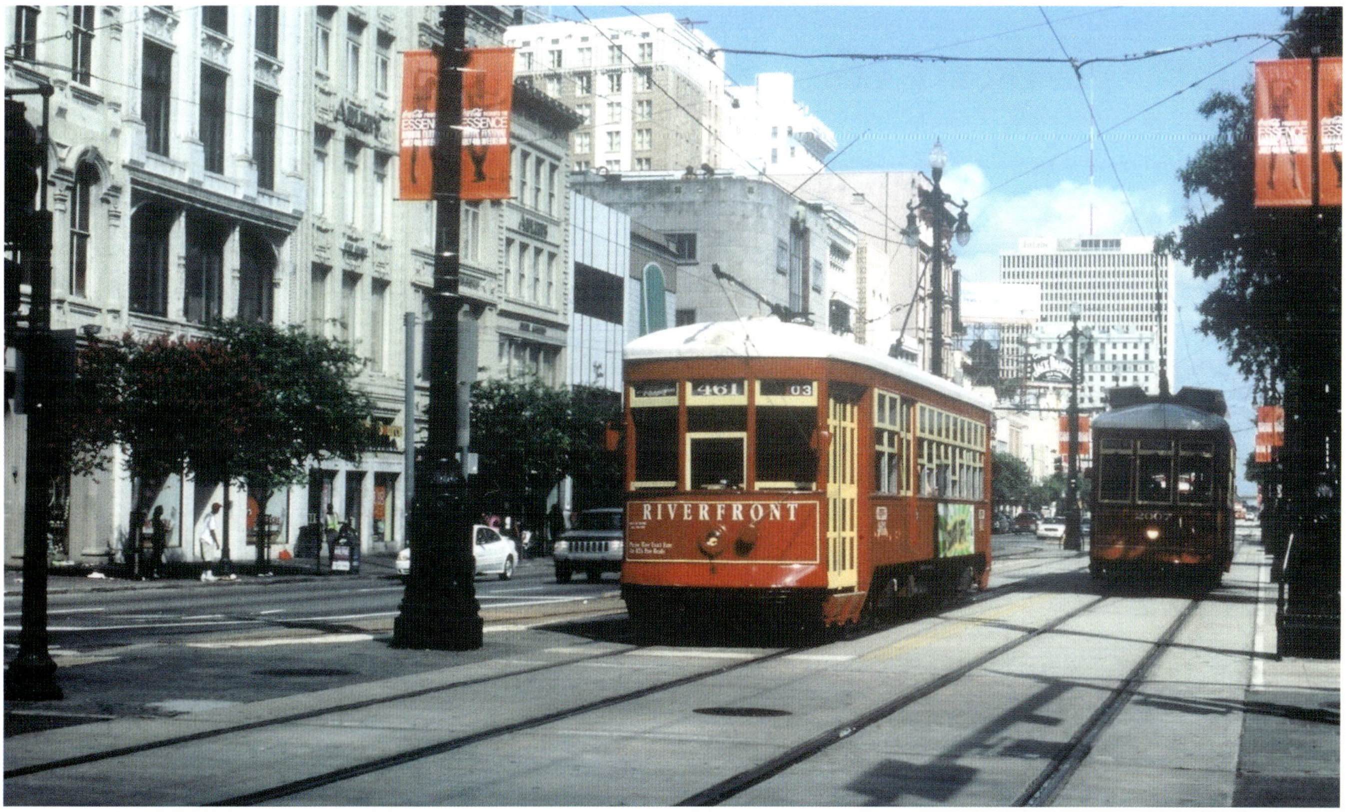

RTA streetcar No. 461 is on Canal Street at St. Charles Avenue heading for the Riverfront line, where it will go into service on July 4, 2003.

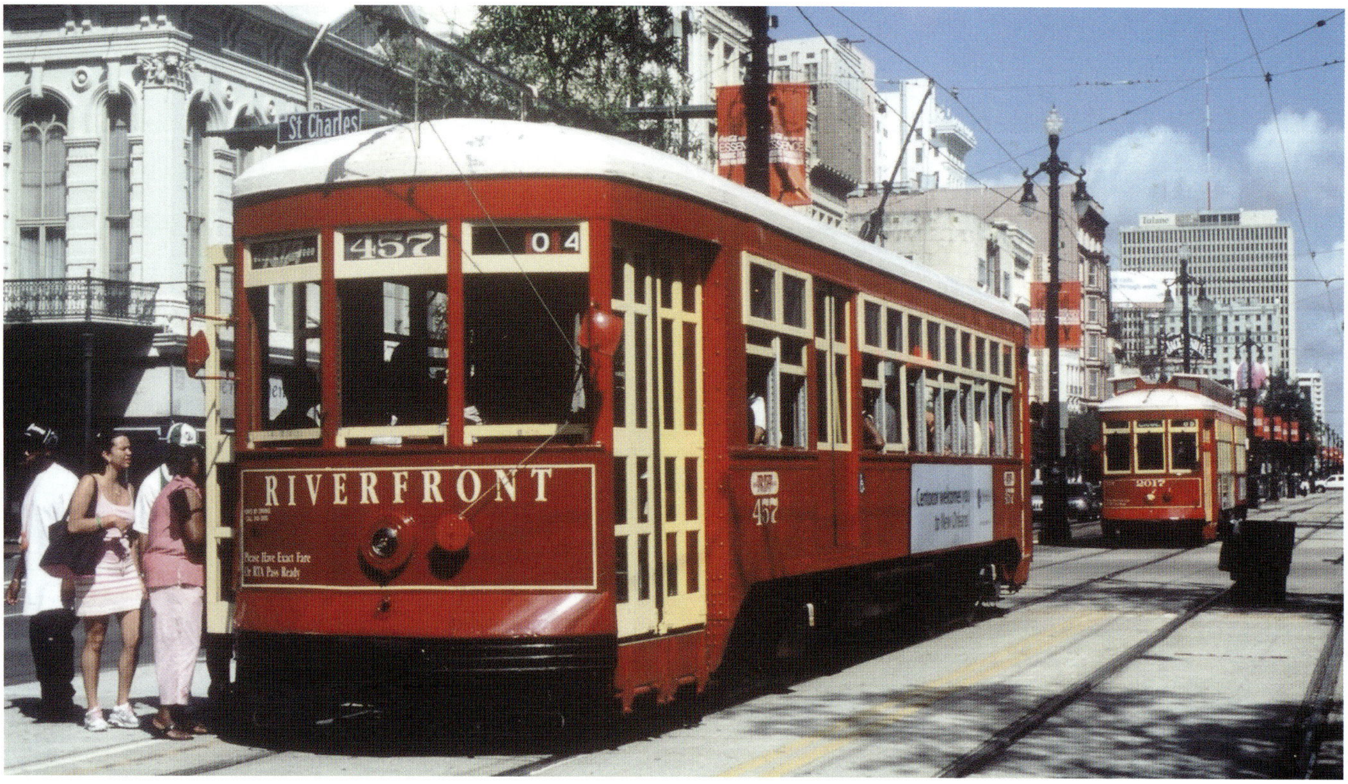

On July 4, 2004, RTA streetcar No. 457 is at a passenger stop on Canal Street at St. Charles Avenue, and will go in service on the Riverfront line at the foot of Canal Street. Not far behind is Canal streetcar No. 2017. It was on October 17, 2003 that streetcar No. 2017 made the first test run, checking clearances, overhead wires, and track work on the new Canal streetcar line from Baronne Street to the terminus on Canal Street at City Park Avenue.

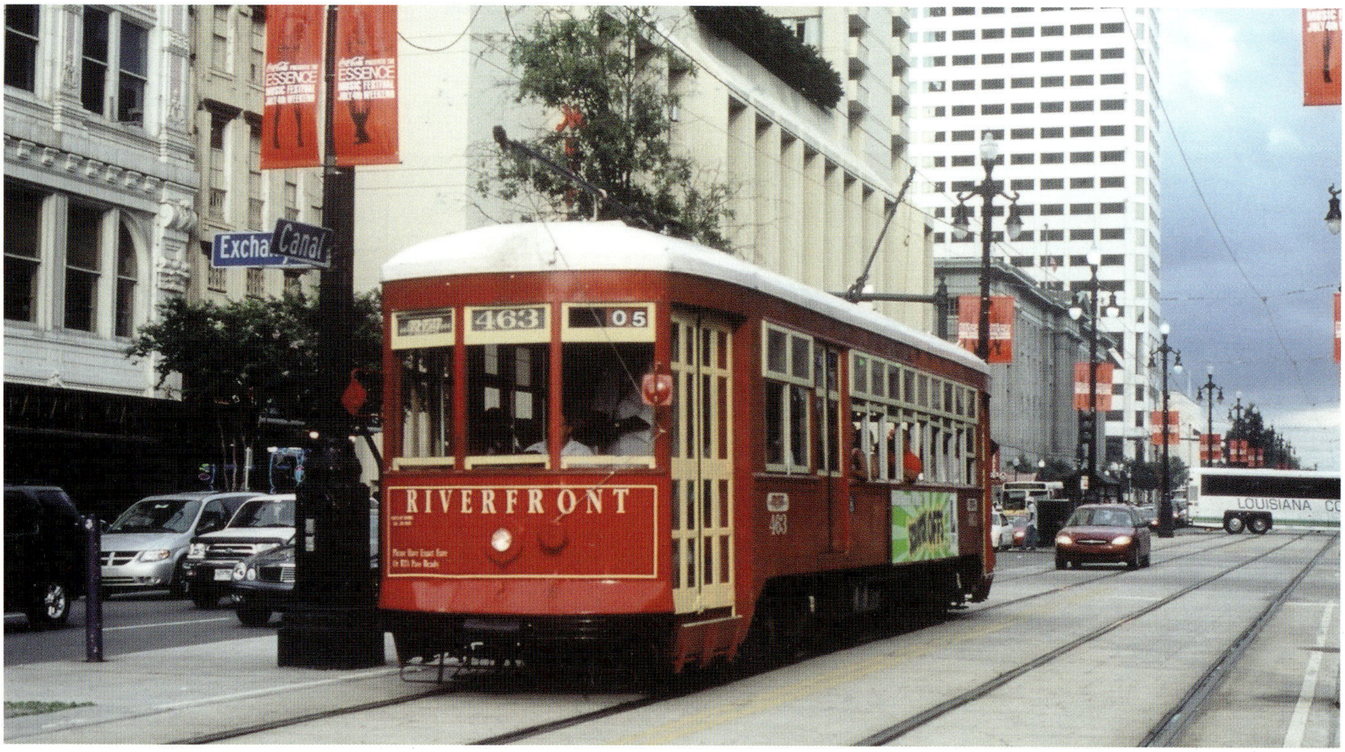

Canal Street at Exchange Place is the scene for RTA streetcar No. 463, which will go in service on the Riverfront line at the foot of Canal Street on July 3, 2004.

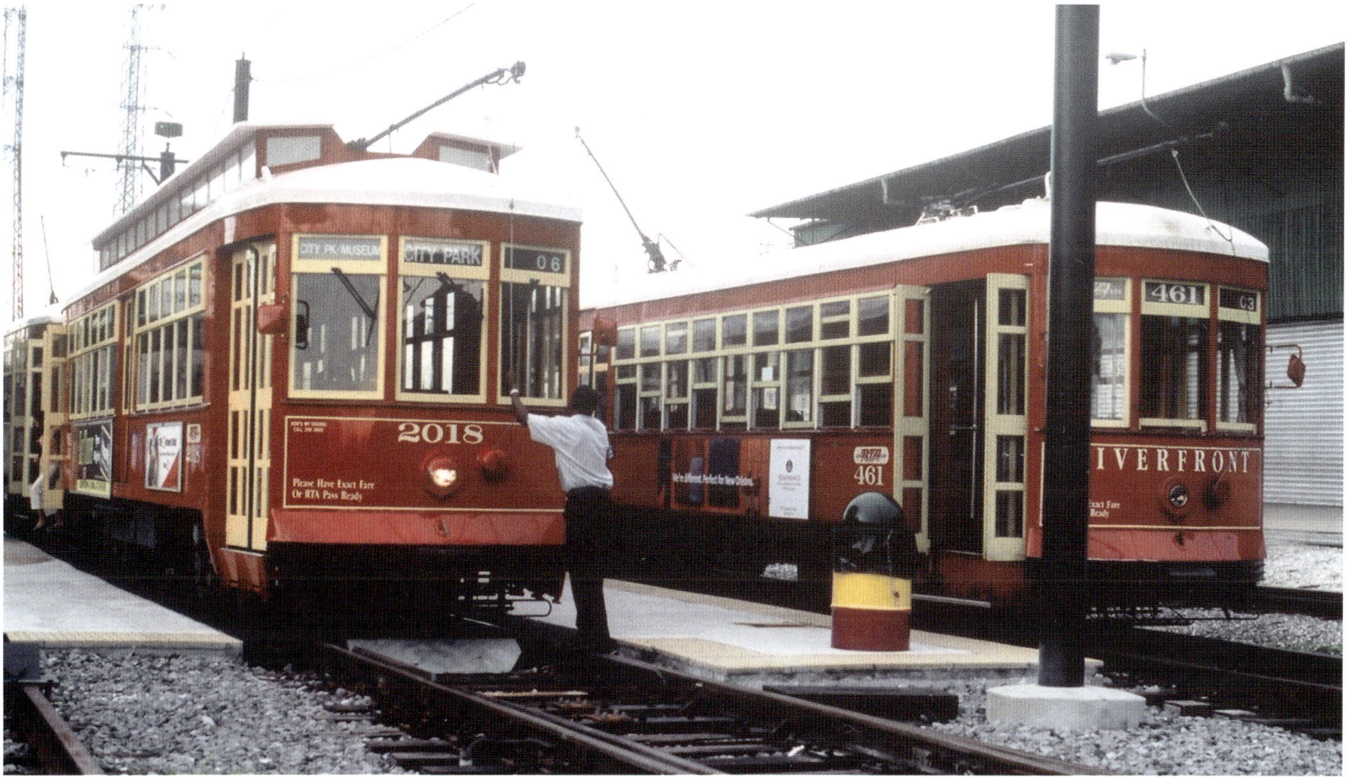

At the eastern terminus of the Riverfront line on Esplanade Avenue, RTA streetcar No. 2018 is destined for City Park via Canal Street while No. 461 is assigned to the Riverfront line on July 4, 2004.

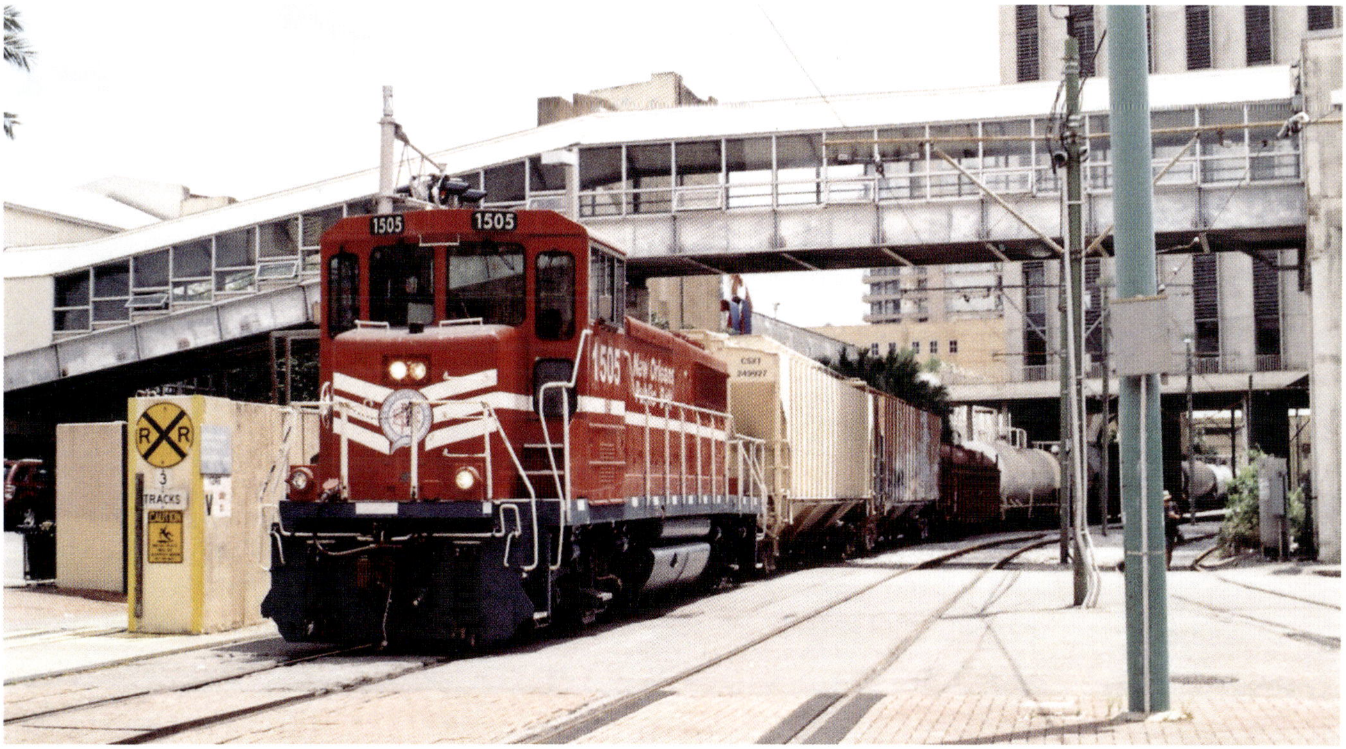

New Orleans Public Belt Railroad 1,400 horsepower type MP1500D diesel locomotive No. 1505, built by Motive Power Industries, is crossing Canal Street parallel to the Riverfront streetcar line on April 23, 2013. This locomotive has a Caterpillar engine type 3512A (4/ EPA Tier 2), Westinghouse type 26L air brake, and weighs 256,000 pounds.

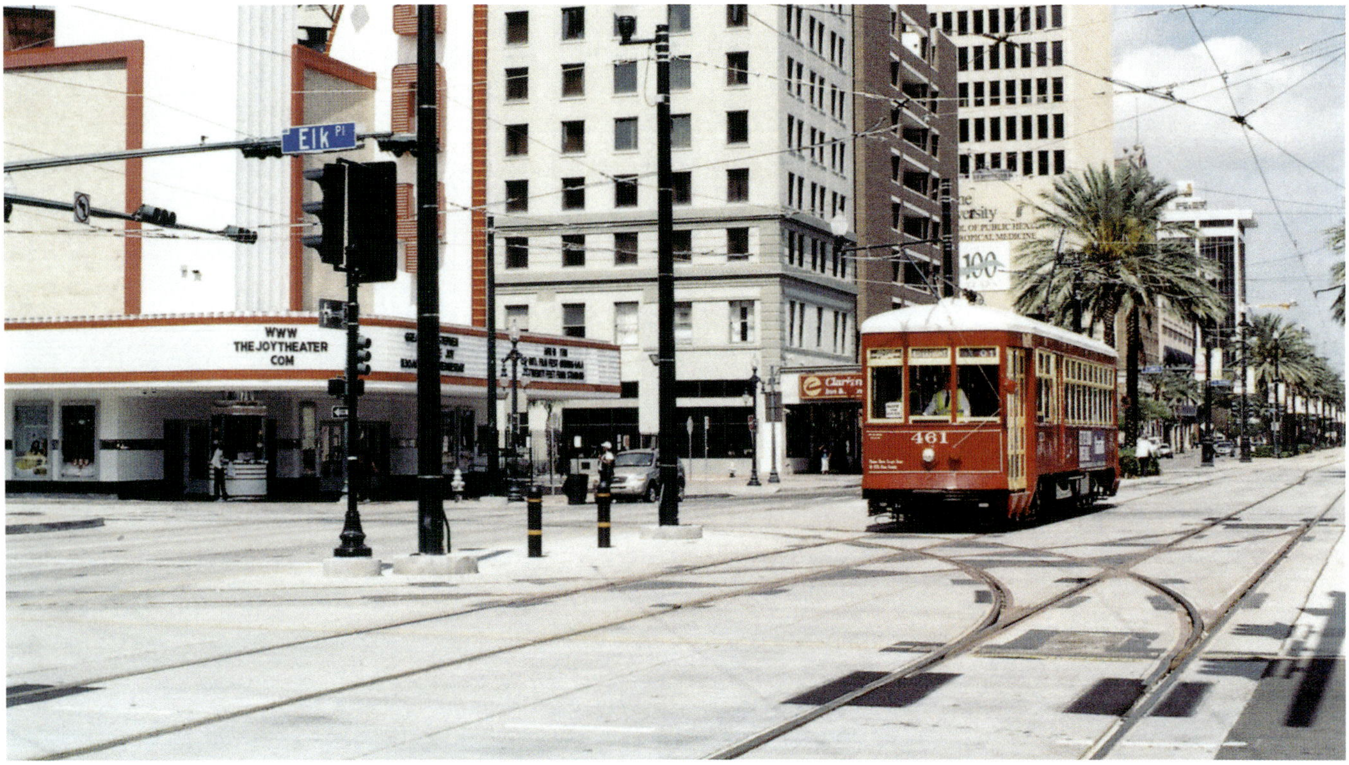

Canal Street at Elk Place finds RTA streetcar No. 461 coming up to the intersection heading to the foot of Canal Street where it will go into service on the Riverfront line on April 23, 2013. The building at the intersection on the left is the historic movie palace, Joy Theater, which opened on February 7, 1947. It closed in 2003, and was damaged in 2005 by the flooding caused by Hurricane Katrina. On December 29, 2011, the renovated theater seating 900 reopened.

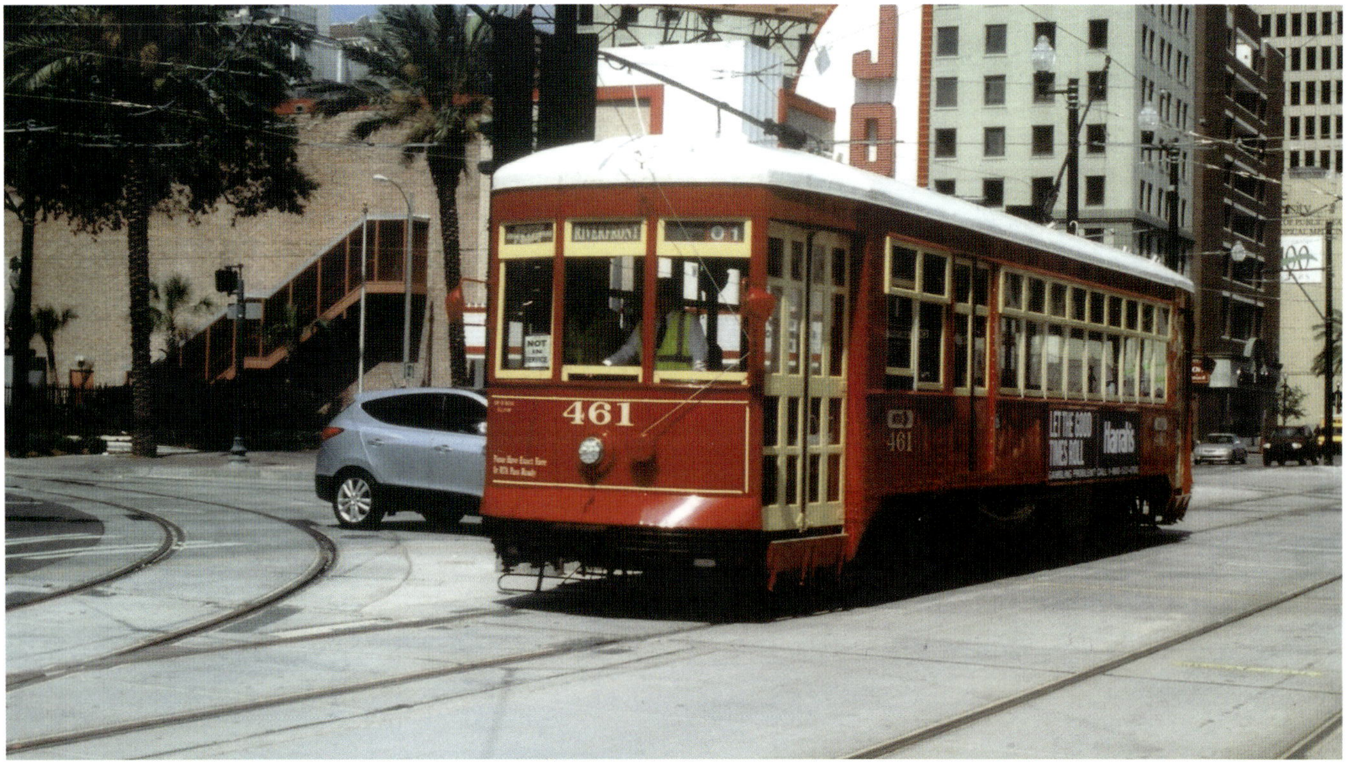

On April 23, 2013, RTA streetcar No. 461 on Canal Street has crossed Elk Place, and the track that curves to the left is the streetcar line that serves Loyola Avenue. Streetcar No. 461 was the only Riverfront car to survive the flooding caused by Hurricane Katrina, because it was at the Carrollton Station shop for repainting.

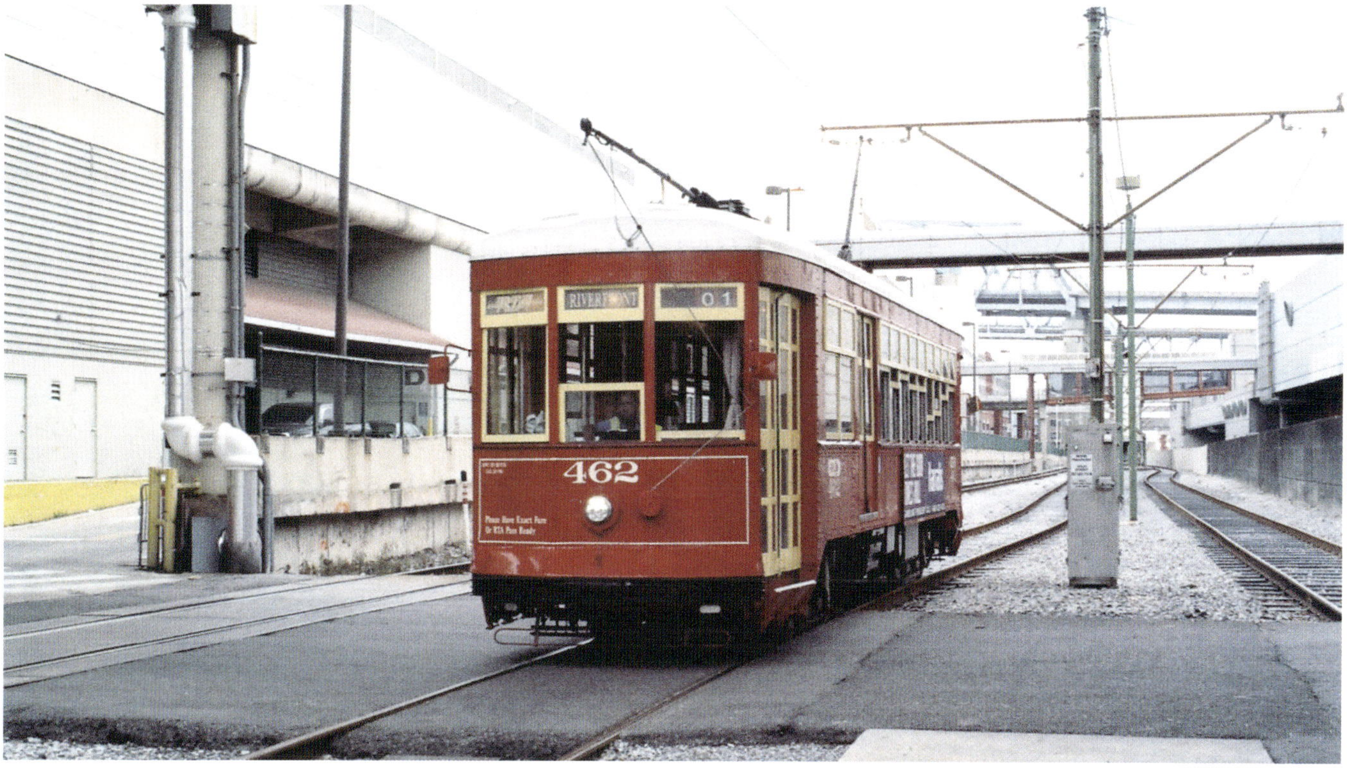

On April 23, 2013, RTA streetcar No. 462 is at Julia Street on the Riverfront line. The New Orleans Public Belt Railroad track is on the left.

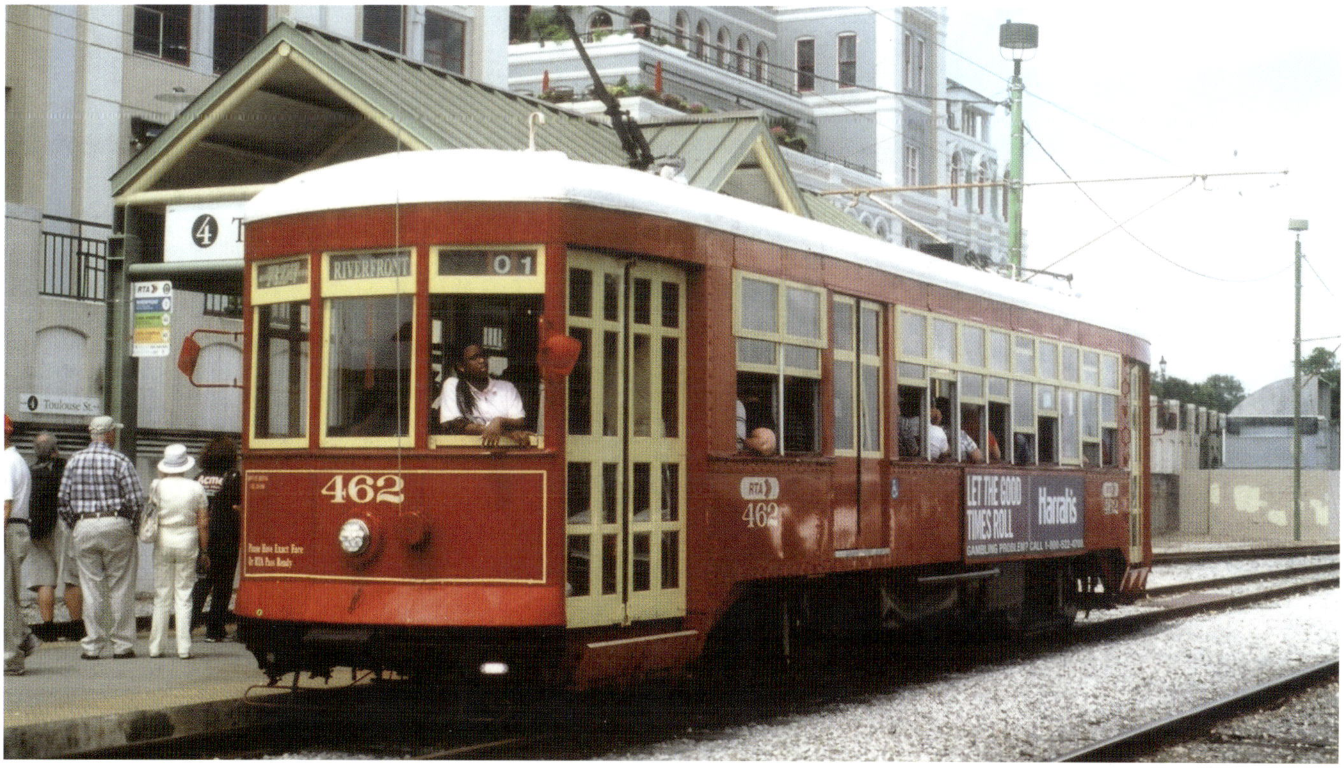

Eastbound RTA streetcar No. 462 is pausing for a passenger stop at Toulouse Street, which is close to Woldenberg Park, on the Riverfront line on April 23, 2013.

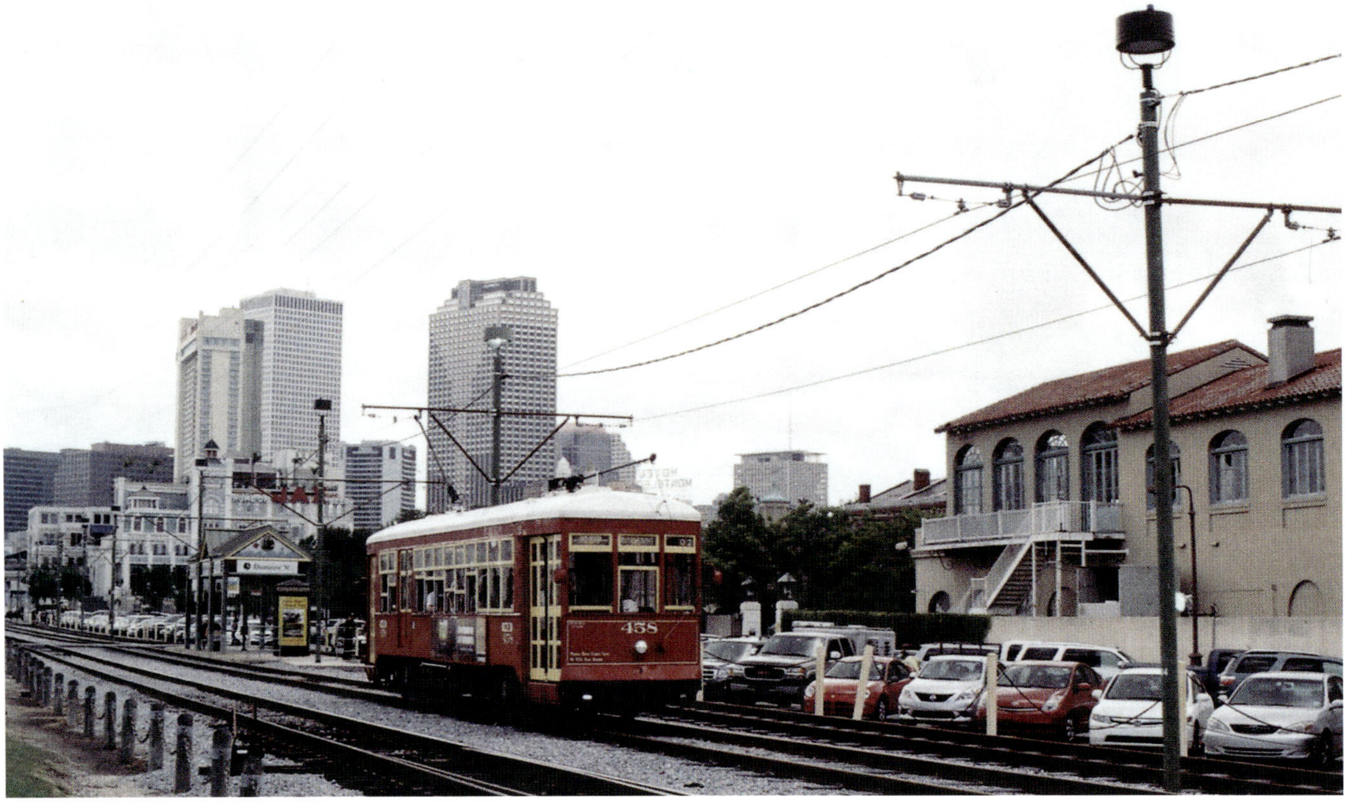

Having passed the Dumaine Street station, RTA streetcar No. 458 is eastbound on the Riverfront line on April 23, 2013, with the New Orleans skyline in the background.

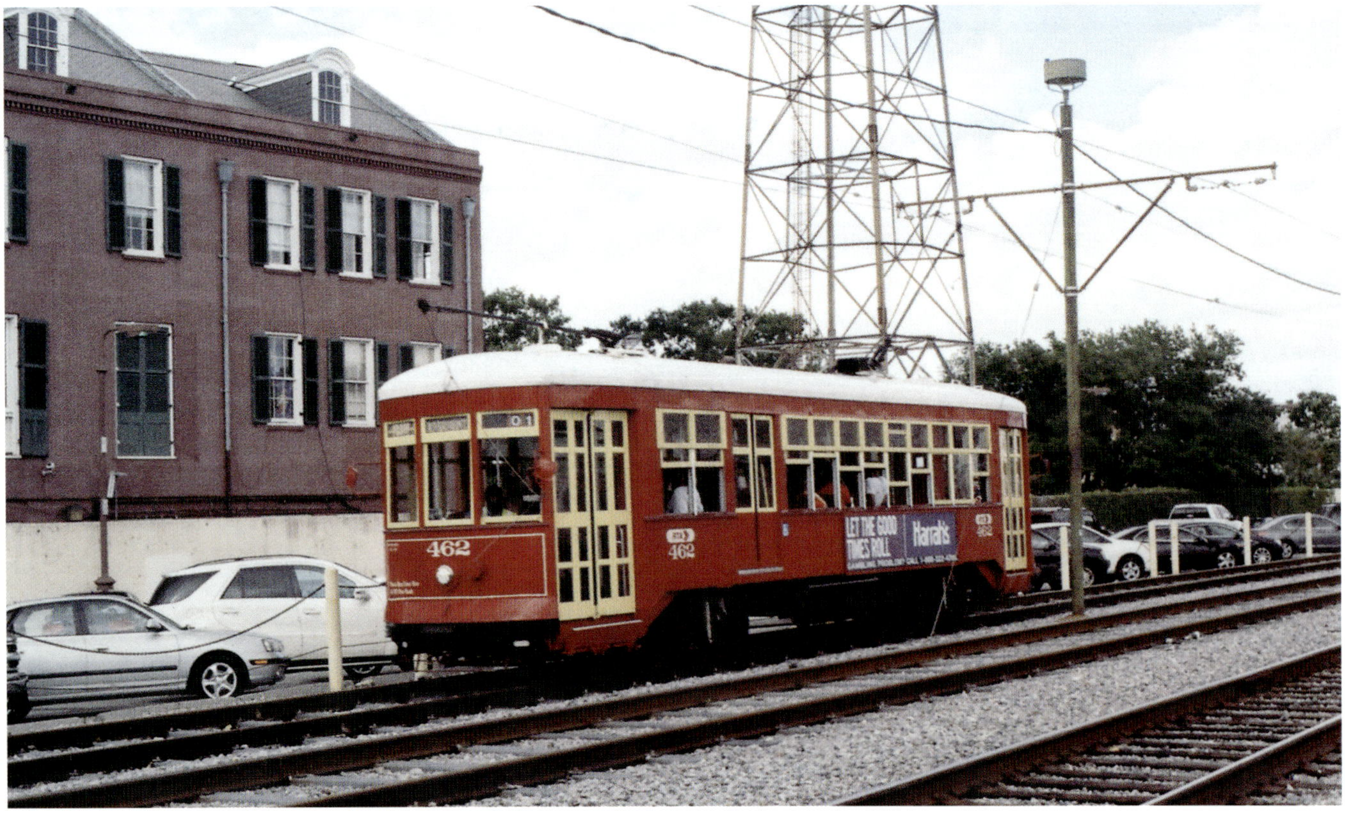

On April 23, 2013, westbound RTA streetcar No. 462 is west of Ursulines Avenue station and will shortly be at Dumaine Street station on the Riverfront line. At the bottom right of the picture is the New Orleans Public Belt Railroad track.

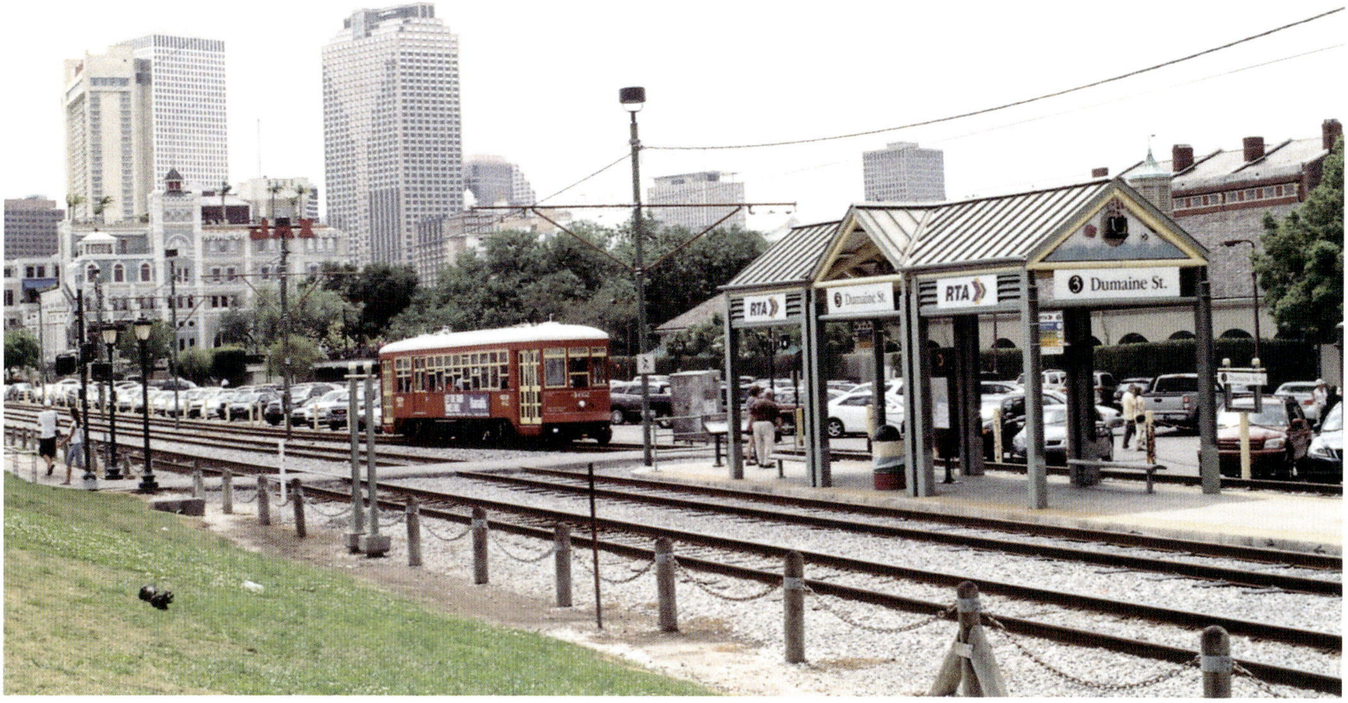

Westbound RTA streetcar No. 462 is west of Dumaine Street station on the Riverfront line, on April 23, 2013. This location is close to the retail shops along Decatur Street.

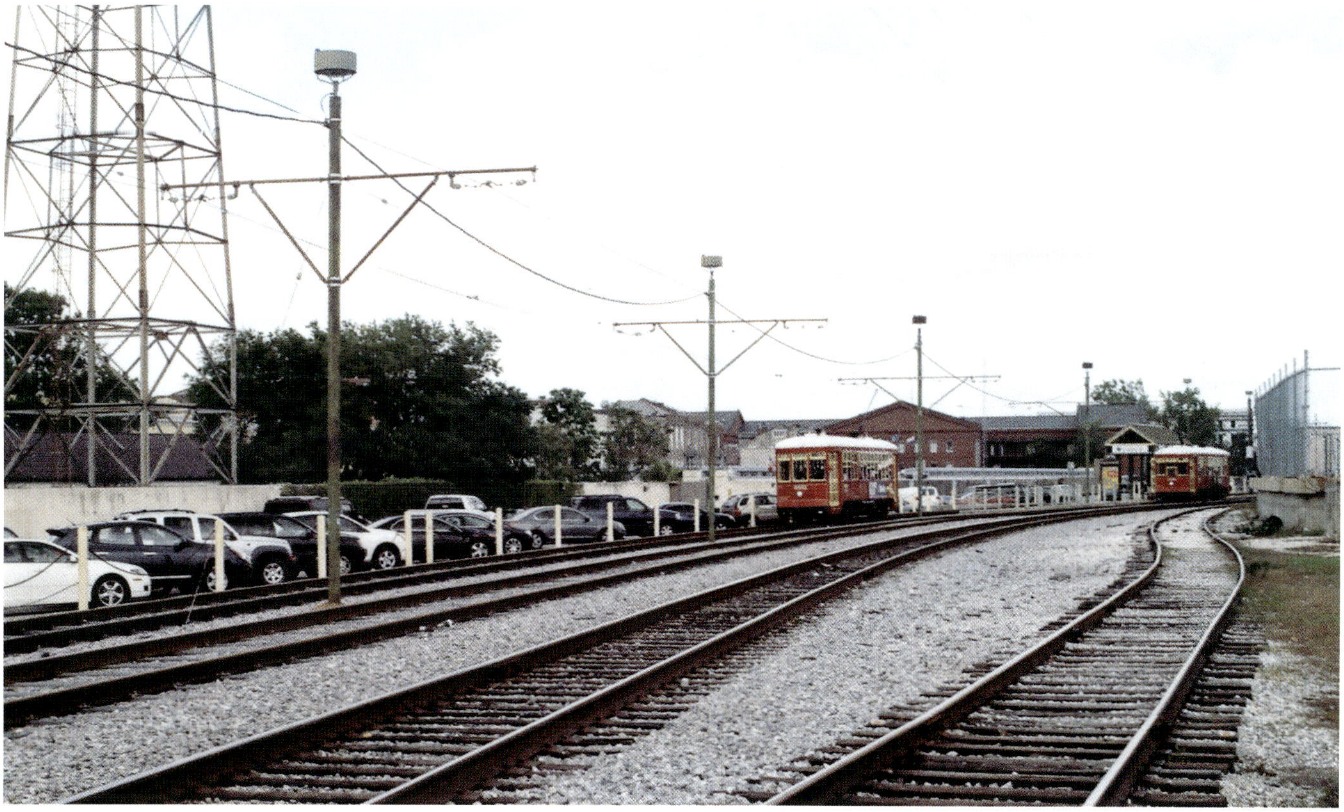

RTA streetcar No. 462 is west of Ursulines Avenue on its westbound trip on the Riverfront line, while the eastbound streetcar is at the Ursulines Avenue station on April 23, 2013. The two tracks on the right are for the New Orleans Public Belt Railroad.

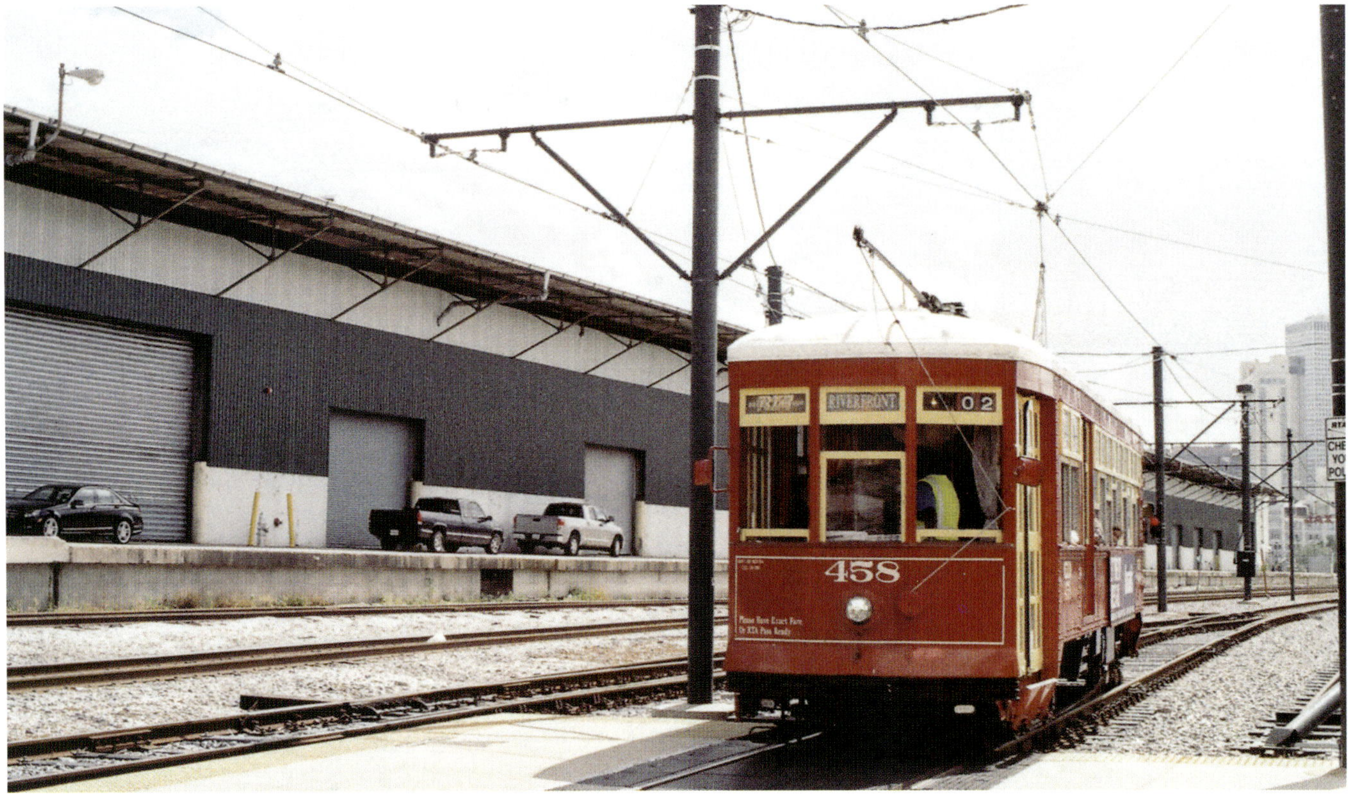

RTA streetcar No. 458 is coming into the French Market Station (formerly Esplanade Avenue Station) on the Riverfront line on April 23, 2013.

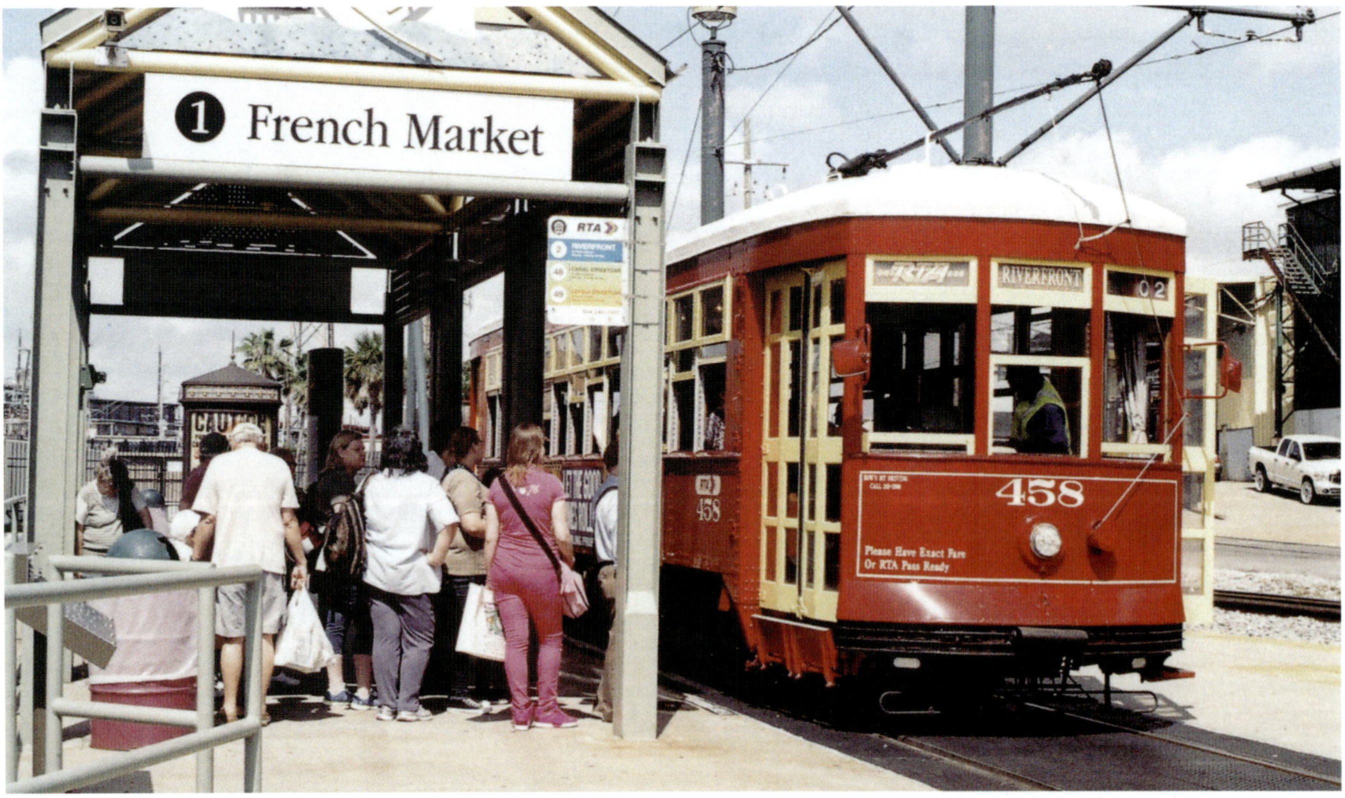

Passengers are lining up at French Market station ready to board RTA streetcar No. 458 for a westbound trip on the Riverfront line on April 23, 2013. The Esplanade Avenue terminal of the Riverfront streetcar line was renamed "French Market" and was rebuilt with three stub tracks around 2005.

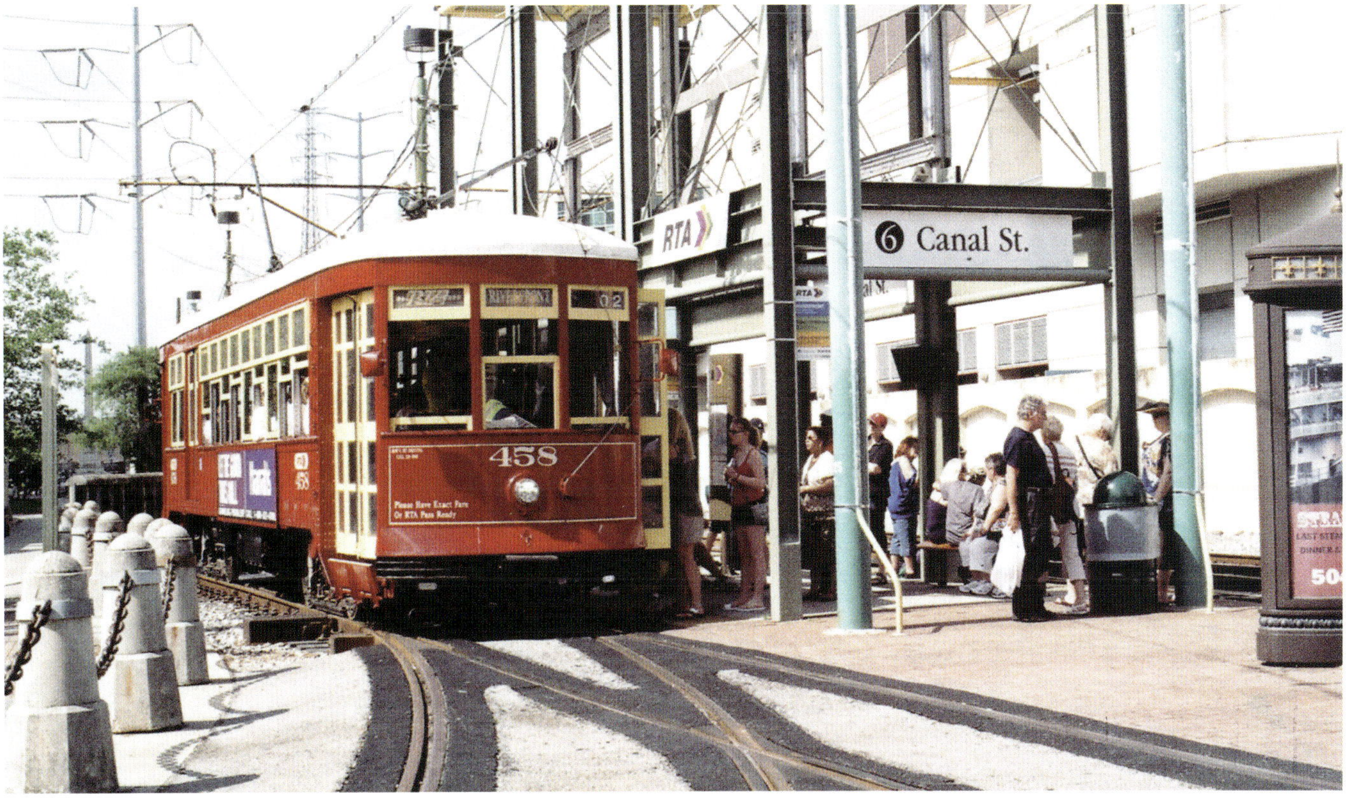

Canal Street station on the Riverfront line is a busy stop on April 23, 2013, as evidenced by people boarding RTA streetcar No. 458.

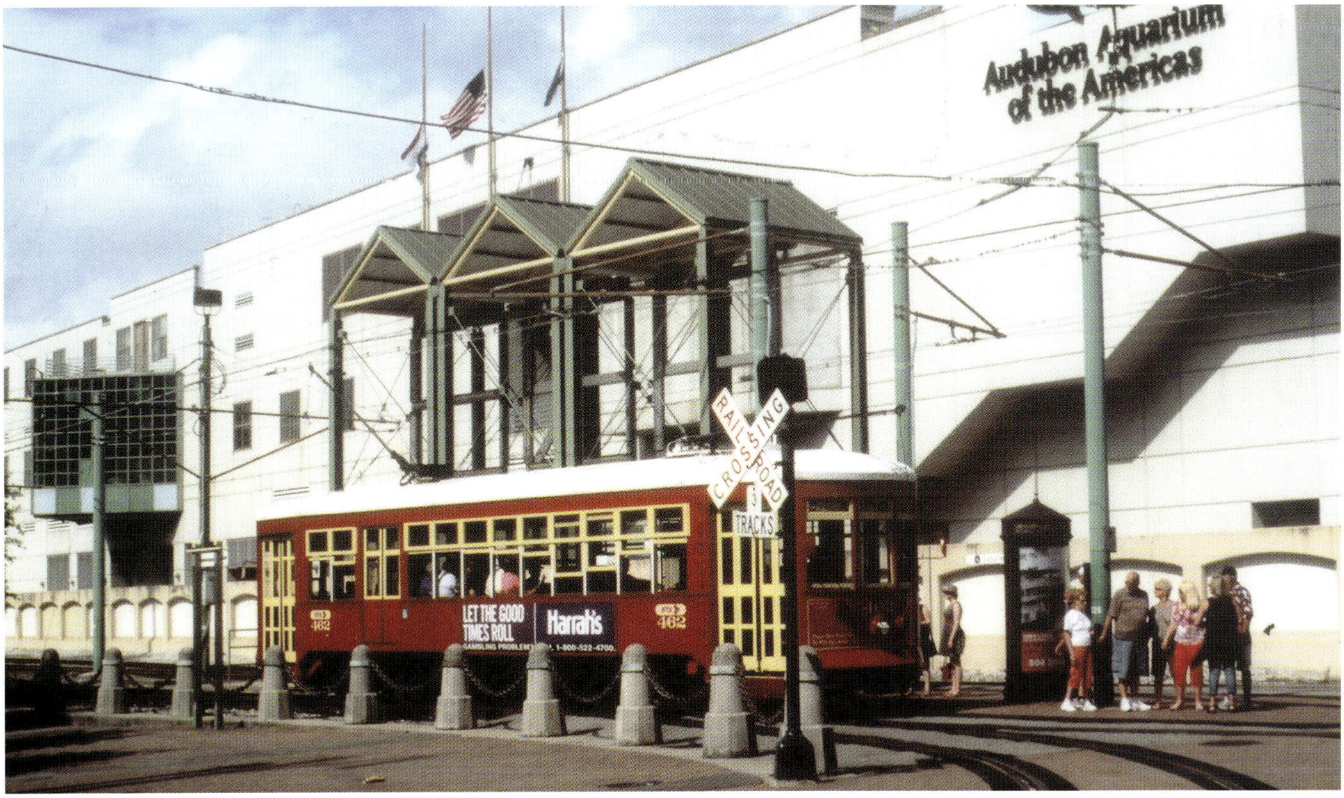

RTA streetcar #462 is at Canal Street station of the Riverfront line on April 23, 2013. The track curving off to the right was used by Canal cars operating from the French Market via Riverfront, Canal Street, and South Carrollton Avenue to the City Park and Museum. It was also used on weekends by Loyola streetcars that were extended to the French Market, on the schedule that was effective on January 27, 2013. This is the access track to the Canal Station carbarn for Riverfront streetcars.

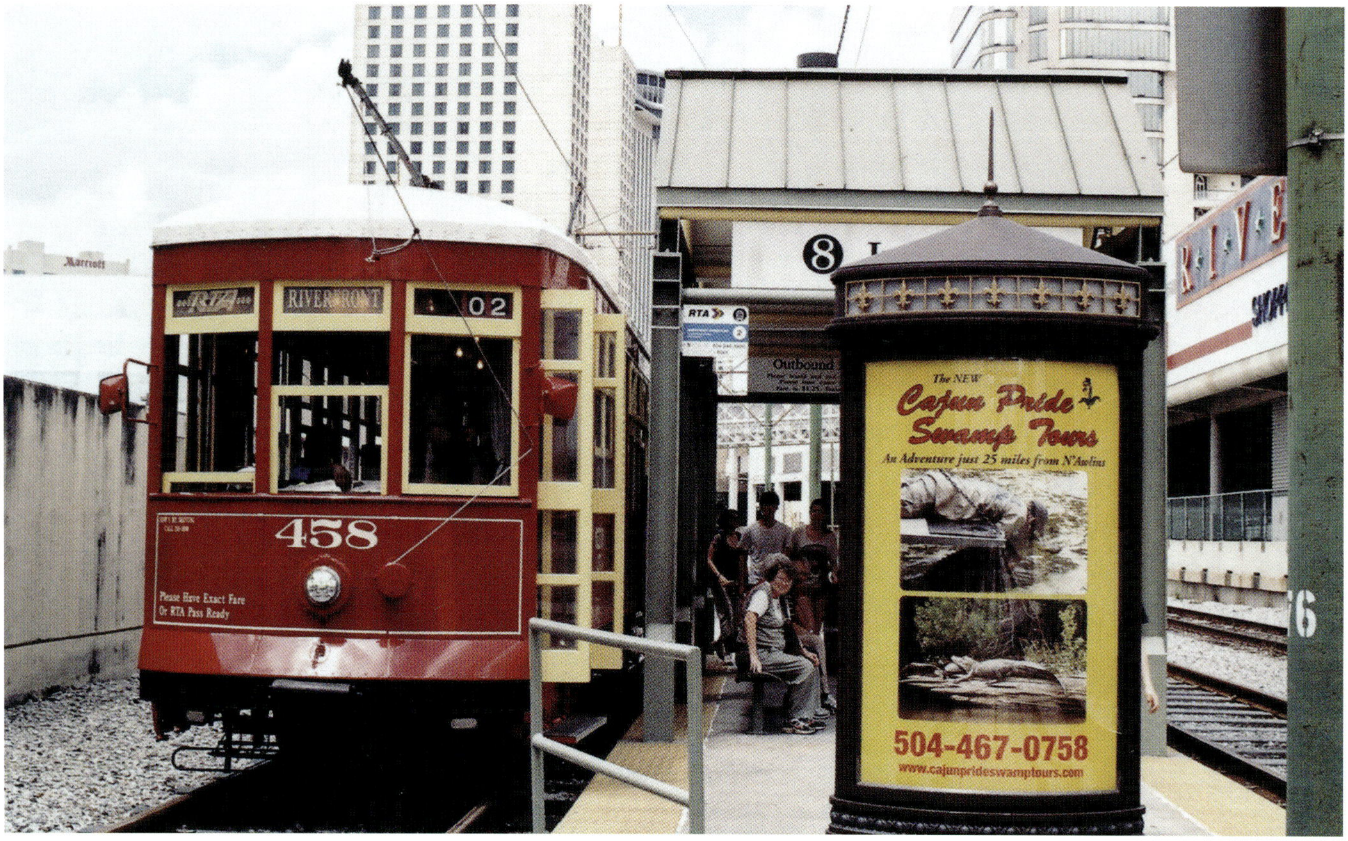

RTA streetcar No. 458 is on the Riverfront line at Julia Street station on April 23, 2013.

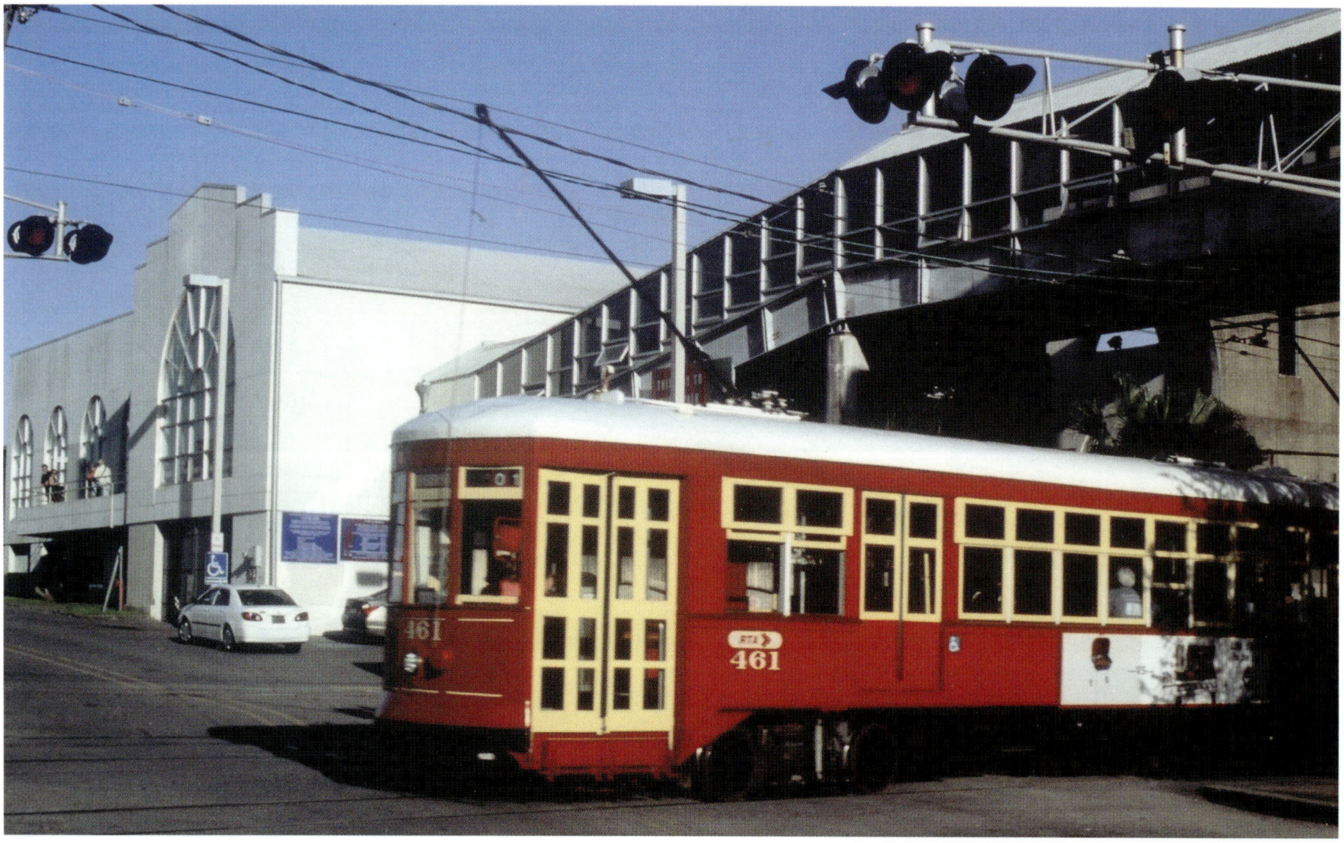

In the late afternoon of April 21, 2013, westbound RTA streetcar No. 461 is crossing Canal Street on the Riverfront line.

Chapter 4

Loyola Streetcar Line

The official groundbreaking ceremony for the 0.8 mile double track Loyola line, connecting the Union Passenger Terminal (used by Amtrak and buses) to Canal Street, was held on June 7, 2011. By August 2011, construction workers began cutting the pavement along Loyola Avenue for the tracks. Portions of Loyola Avenue had to be shut down for the streetcar project. At times, downtown New Orleans had the look of a big construction site, and residents were faced with traffic detours. Funding for the $53 million project was by a $45 million United States Federal Transportation Administration "Transportation Investment Generating Economic Recovery" program, $5 million representing the local government share, and the remainder by RTA Series 2010 Sales Tax Bonds. In addition to the track and special switches at Canal Street and the terminus at the Union Passenger terminal, the project included relocation and replacement of underground utilities, road paving, transit shelters, and landscaping.

On January 28, 2013 at 11 a.m., festivities began for the opening of the Loyola line with federal, state, and local officials in attendance at the New Orleans Union Passenger Station, which featured entertainment by local school children. United States Secretary of Transportation Ray LaHood noted that the streetcar line "has become an important catalyst for revitalizing the downtown business and tourist districts." United States Congressman (Second Congressional District which includes most of New Orleans) Representative Cedric Richmond commented, "Our streetcars are an integral part of this city's rich culture and history so today truly is a day for celebration." At noon, dignitaries were given an inaugural ride. The line opened for the general public at 1 p.m. on January 28, 2013, one week before New Orleans hosted the 2013 Super Bowl. Using surplus streetcars from the Canal line, this route serves the Medical District and New Orleans Public Library at Tulane Avenue, the New Orleans City Hall and Financial District at Poydras Street, and the Main Post Office at Julia Street.

The RTA and Veolia Transportation entered into a delegated management contract in 2009. Under the contract, Veolia Transportation manages and takes care of all aspects of public transit in New Orleans including: operations, maintenance, safety, customer relations, vehicle scheduling, safety, capital planning, and grant administration. The RTA Board of Commissioners sets the policy for fares, service, operations, and is also responsible for the approval of each year's annual transportation development plan, which covers major initiatives, capital purchases, and the operating budget. Building the Loyola streetcar line required team effort by the RTA Board of Commissioners, Veolia Transportation, the United States Federal Transportation Administration, city departments and utilities, plus engineering, and construction companies. Under the delegated management contract, Veolia Transportation (the contractor) was a full partner in the process and implemented the policy set by the RTA. Veolia Transportation secured the funding, developed the specifications, hired the engineering and construction firms, and oversaw the Loyola streetcar project with subcontractors to meet Federal Transportation Administration requirements.

Having ridden and walked the Loyola line, it looks like it was made to be there and blends well with the urban landscape. The line has a nice Monday-to-Friday daytime ridership. Weekend ridership is lighter, but when the Amtrak train arrives, the passenger shelter near the Union Passenger Terminal attracts numerous riders for the convenient ride to the business district and hotels along Canal Street. There are visible signs of a renaissance taking place along Loyola Avenue with the opening of the streetcar line. New Orleans has made significant progress since the devastating Hurricane Katrina, and the streetcar is another tool in the toolbox for economic development.

The streetcar that almost went out of existence in New Orleans and in the United States is back on track. When there is widespread support from the public, business, and government, the streetcar can make a difference by channeling people into the business district and making the city more attractive and vibrant.

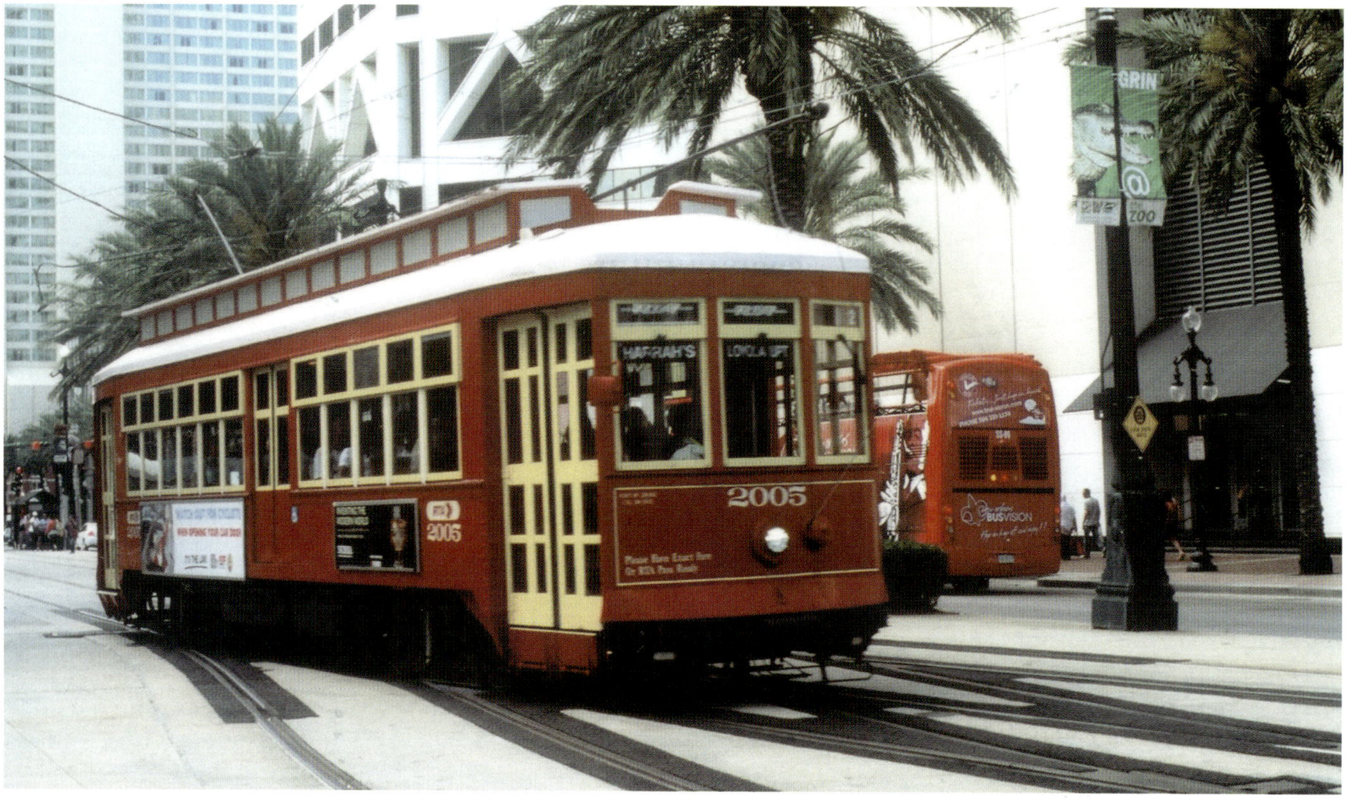

RTA streetcar No. 2005 is at the Canal Street terminus showing Loyola UPT on the destination sign in the front middle window on April 23, 2013. UPT stands for Union Passenger terminal, the main passenger train station in New Orleans, which is served by the Loyola streetcar line.

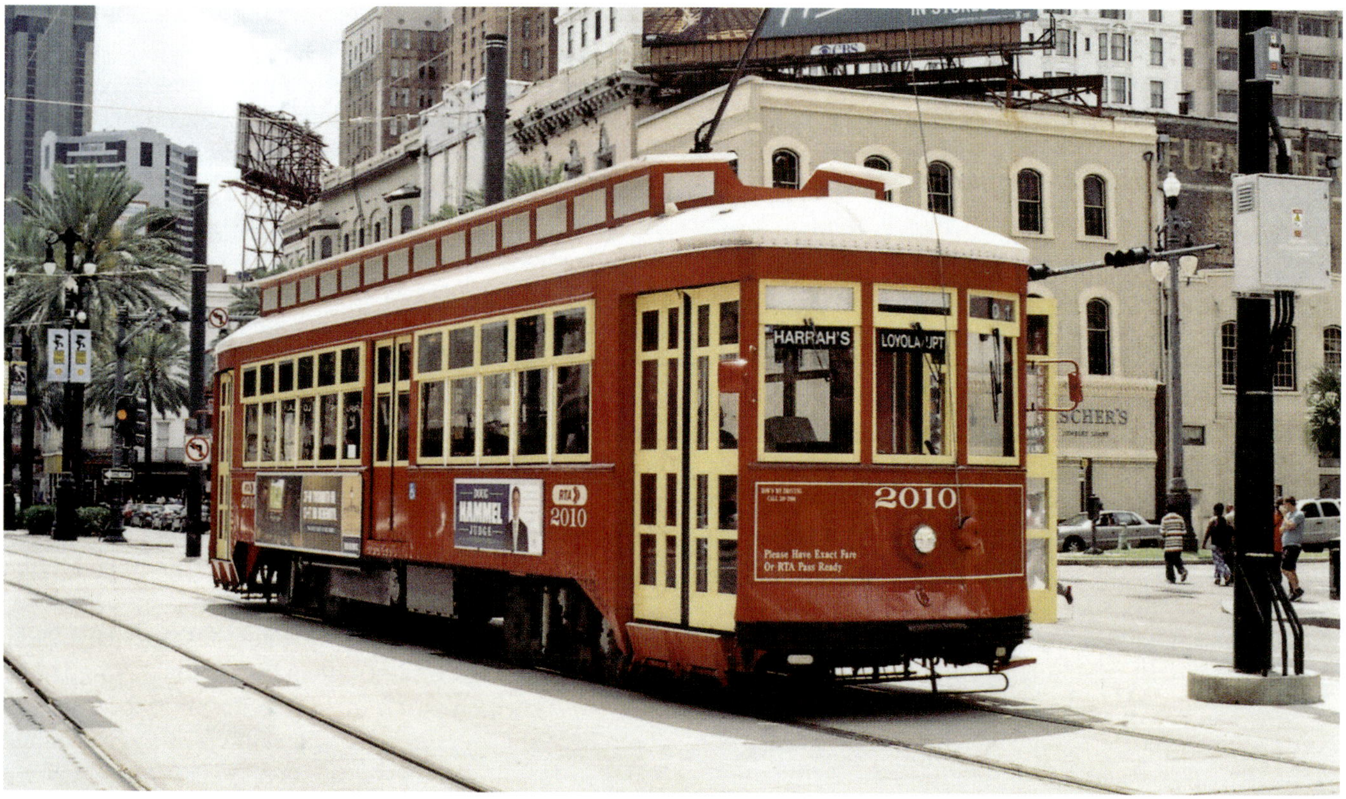

On Canal Street at Rampart Street, on April 23, 2013, RTA streetcar No. 2010 is handling a run for the Loyola Avenue line, connecting the Union Passenger Terminal with the Canal Street commercial district.

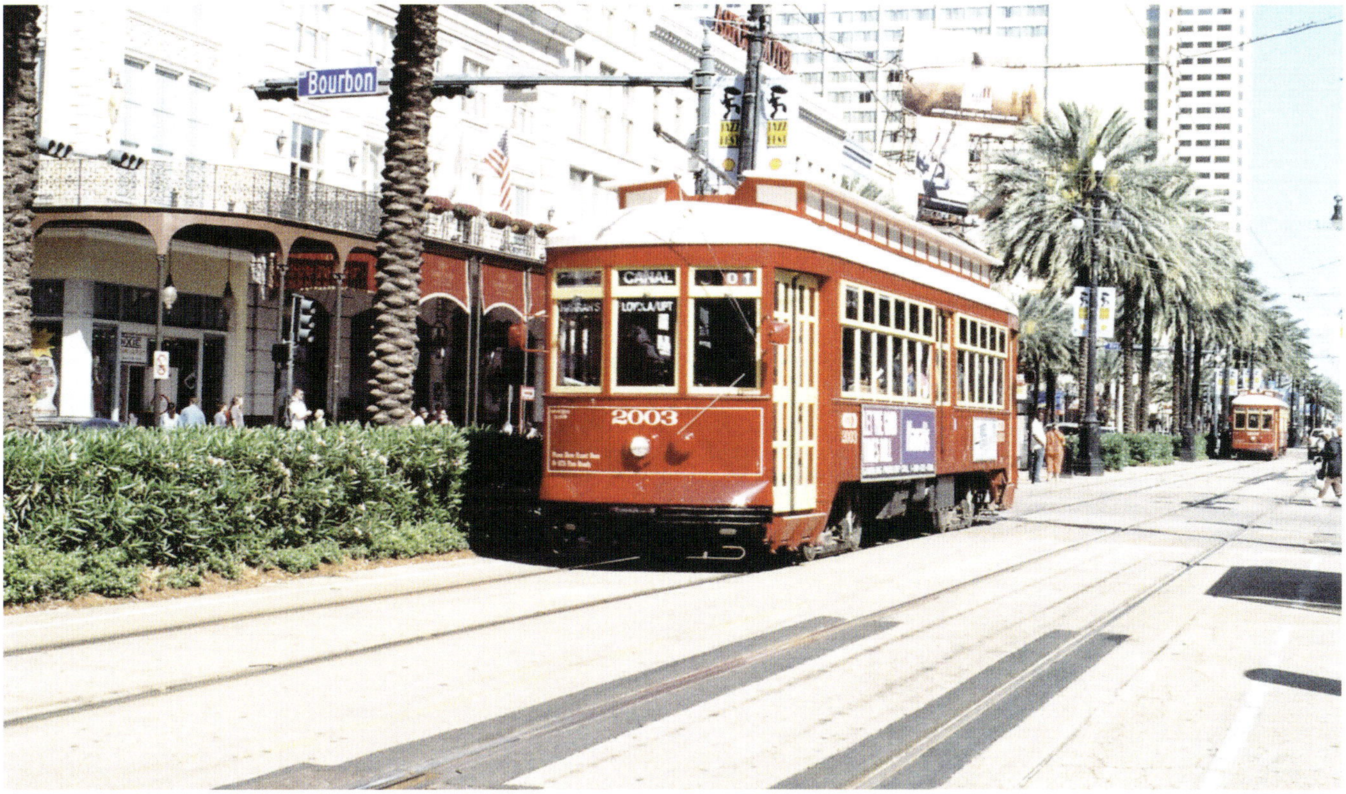

On April 21, 2013, RTA streetcar No. 2003 is at Canal Street at Bourbon Street, heading for the Union Passenger Terminal via the Loyola Avenue line.

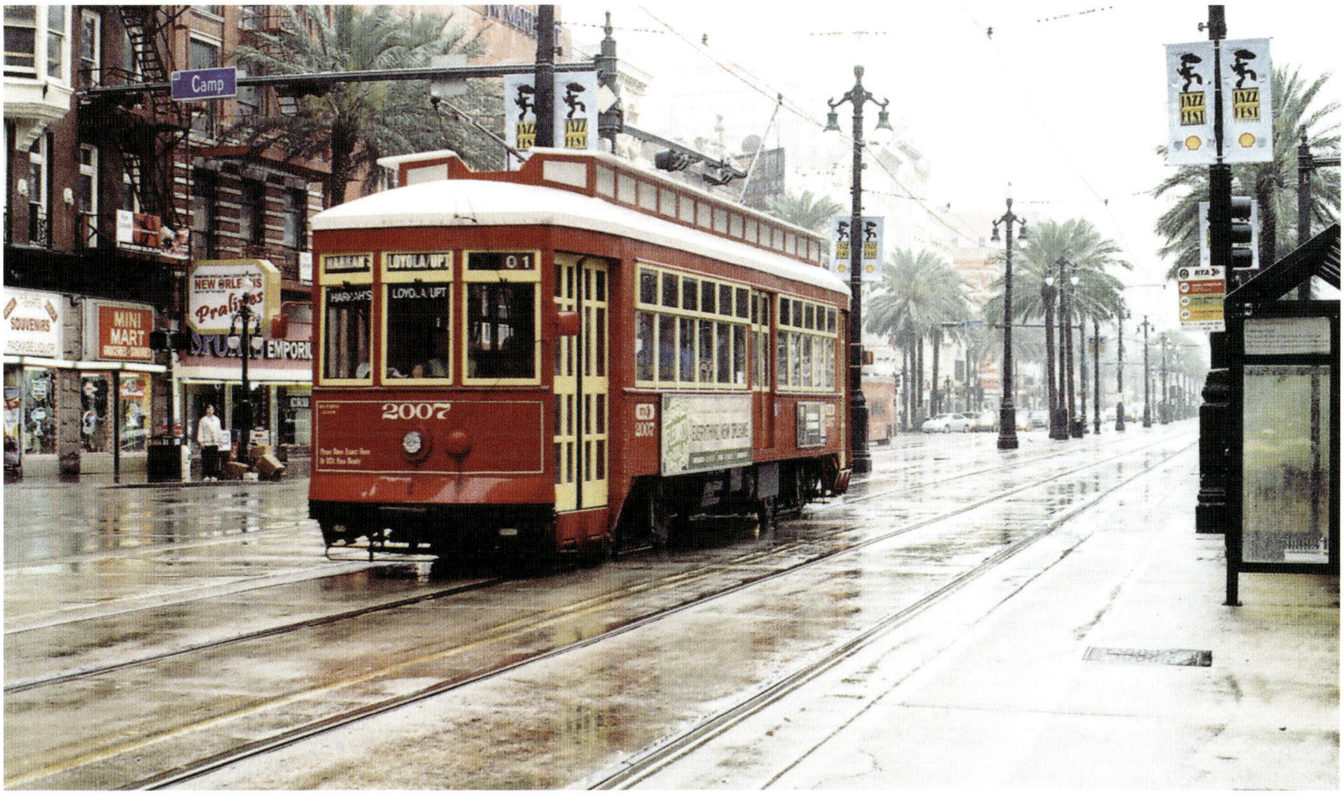

Canal Street at Camp Street is the location of RTA streetcar No. 2007, operating a trip from the Union Passenger Terminal via Loyola Avenue to the foot of Canal Street on a rainy April 24, 2013.

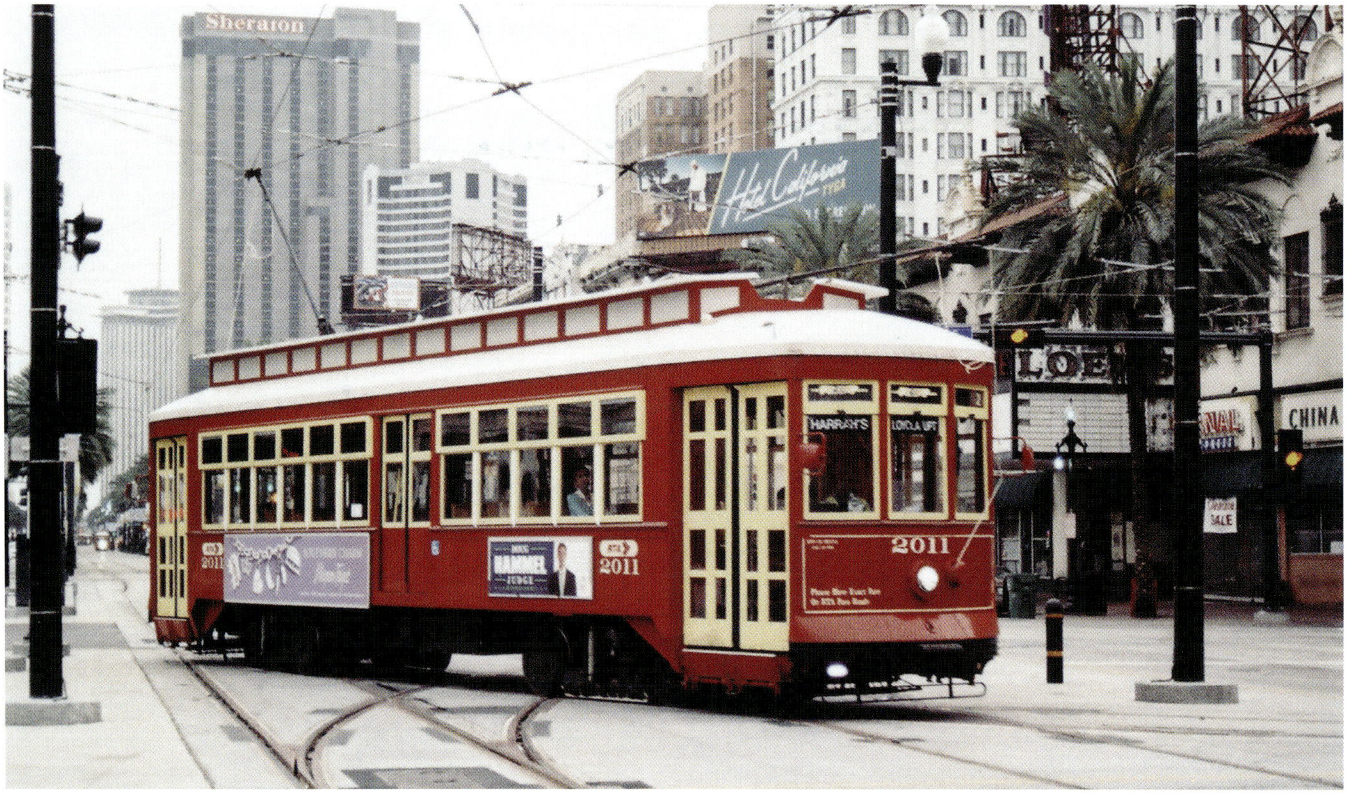

On April 24, 2013, RTA streetcar No. 2011 is turning from Canal Street onto Elk Place, heading for the Union Passenger Terminal, which becomes Loyola Avenue beyond Tulane Avenue. Elk Place begins at Canal Street, and, after two blocks, becomes Loyola Avenue.

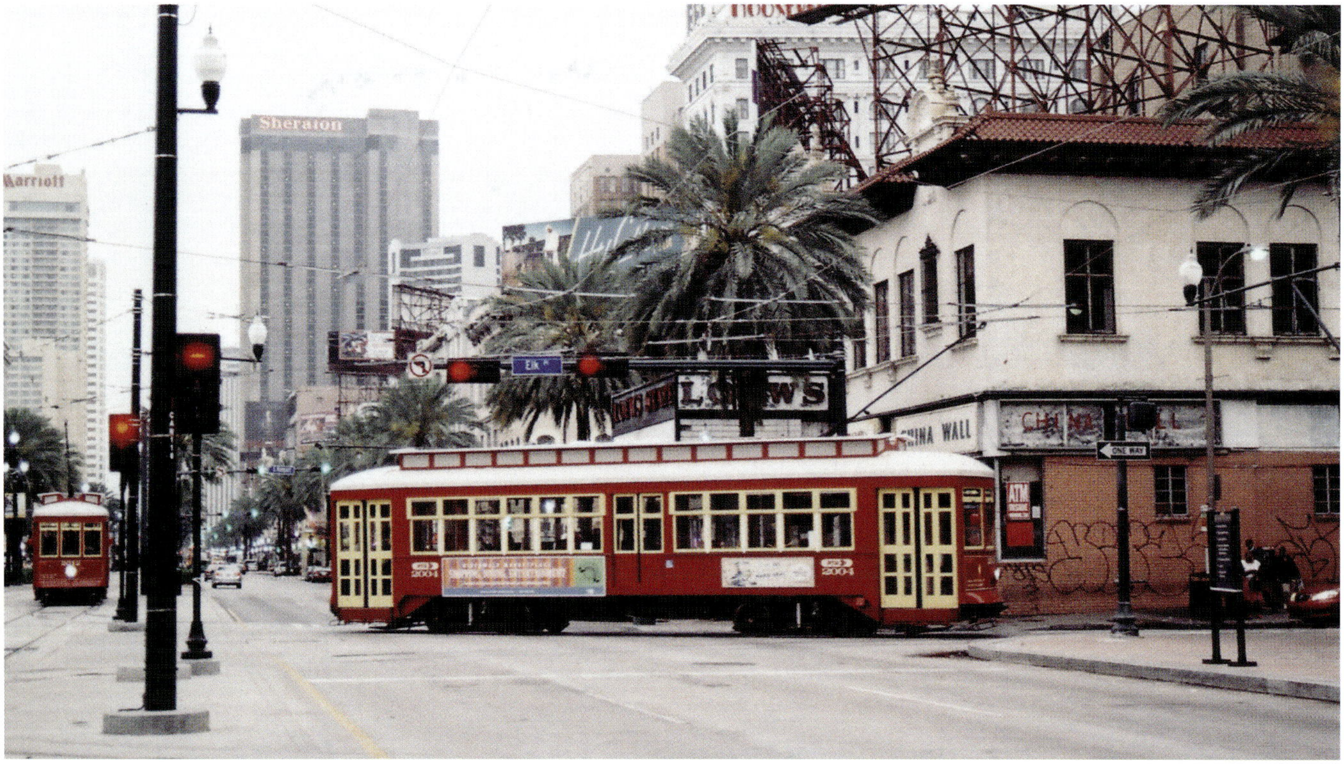

RTA streetcar No. 2004, returning from the Union Passenger terminal via Loyola Avenue, is turning from Elk Place onto Canal Street on April 24, 2013. Elk Place was named in honor of the Elks Home, located in the first block off of Canal Street, directly behind what is now the Joy Theatre.

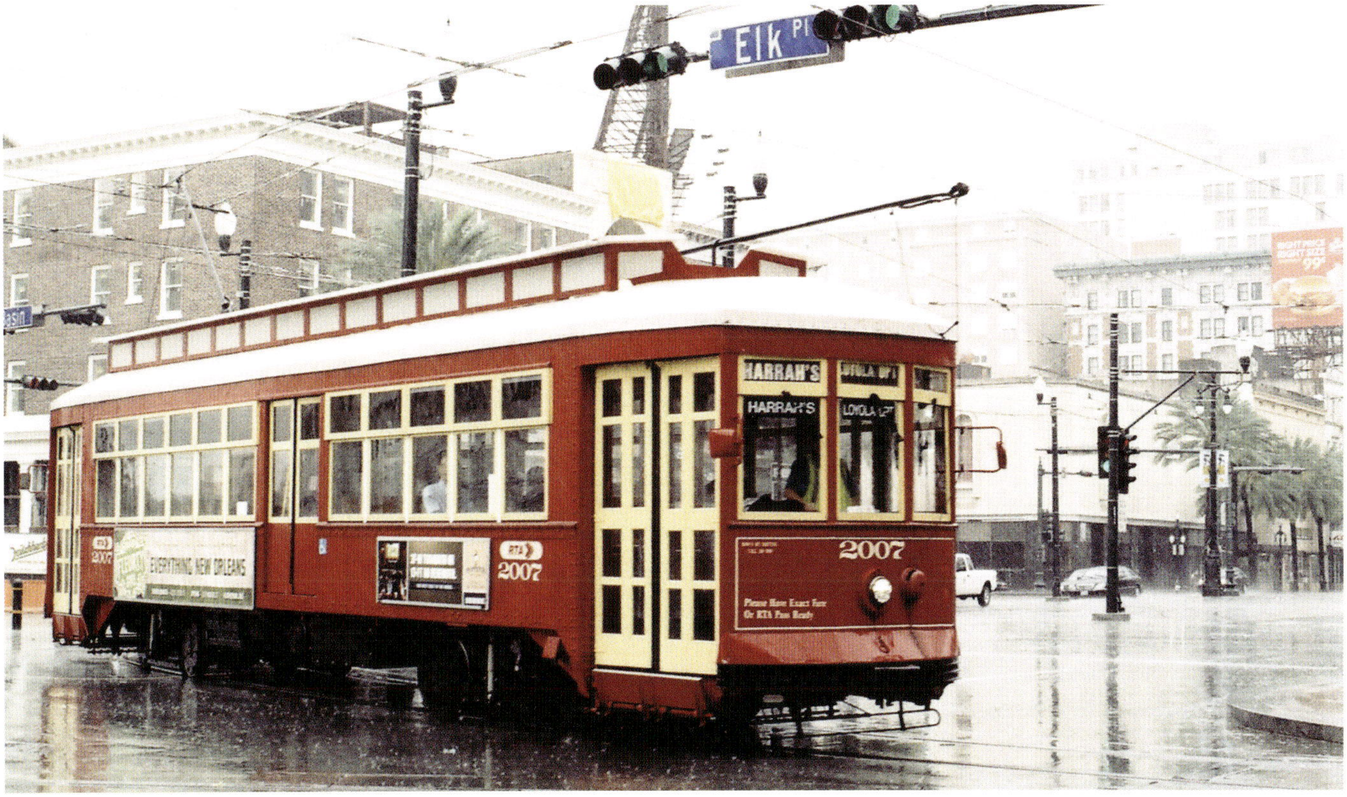

Carefully turning from Canal Street onto Elk Place in the steady rain of April 24, 2013, RTA streetcar No. 2007 is heading for the Union Passenger Terminal. The restored Saenger Theatre that suffered significant damage from Hurricane Katrina is on the left. This theater features the approximately 2,000 pipe Robert Morton theater organ.

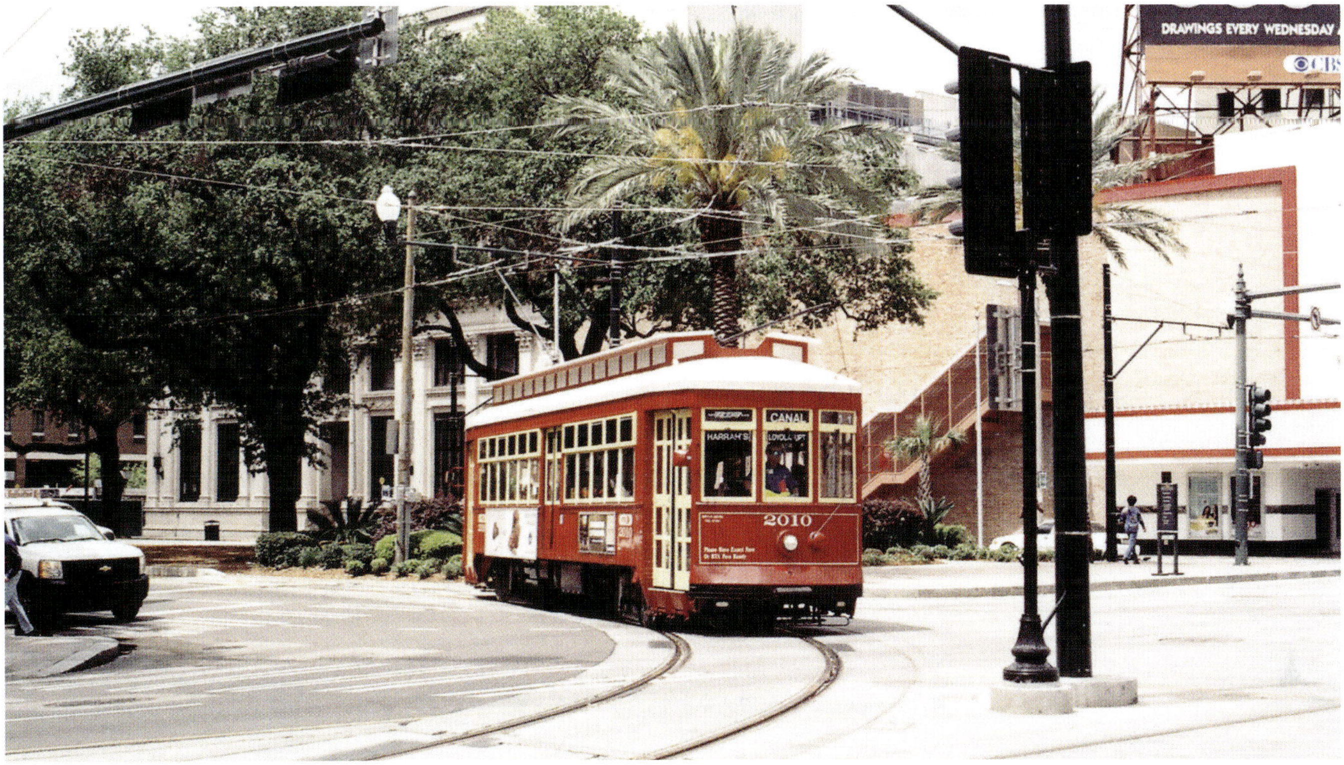

On April 23, 2013, RTA streetcar No. 2010 is turning from Elk Place onto Canal Street on its trip from the Union Passenger Terminal to the foot of Canal Street.

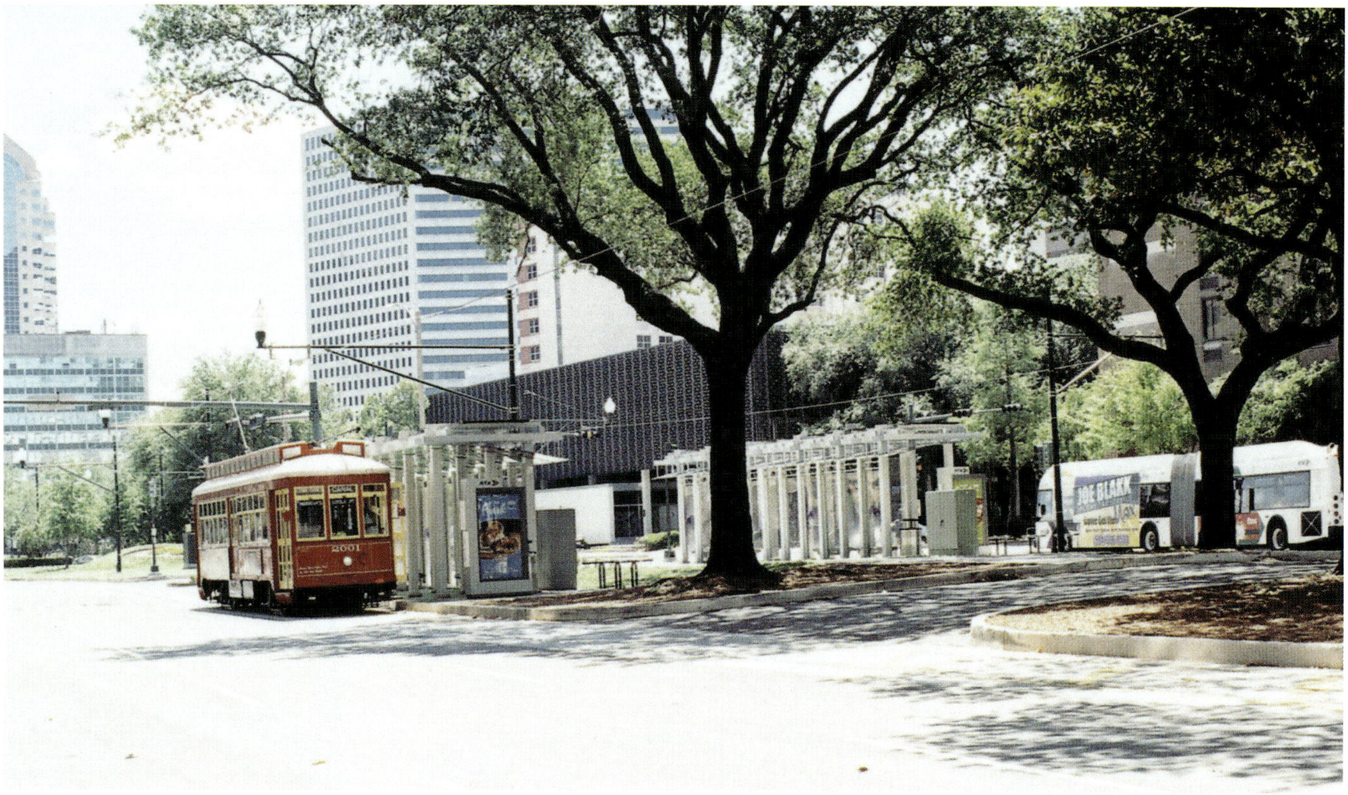

Loyola Avenue line RTA streetcar No. 2001 is on Elk Place at Cleveland Avenue on April 21, 2013, passing the modern style passenger shelter.

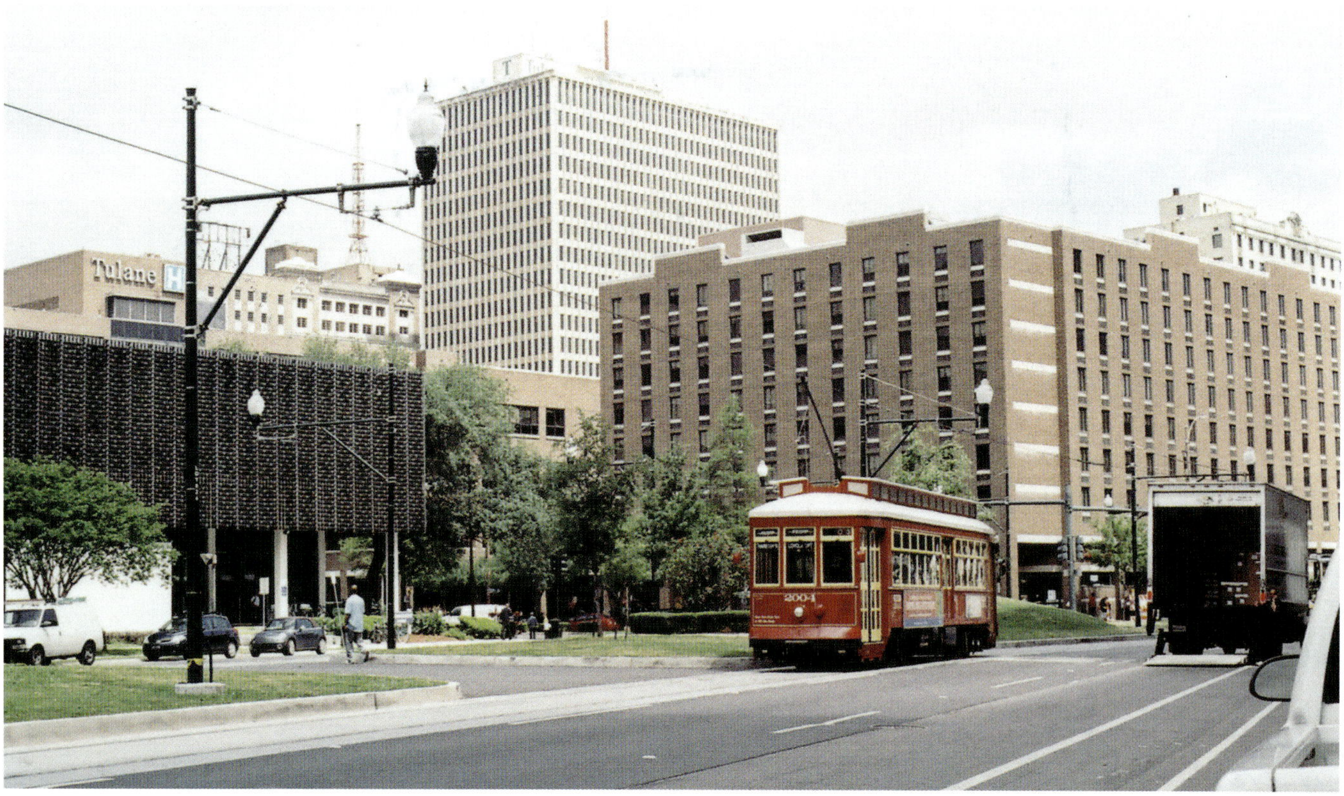

The New Orleans Public library, located at Loyola Avenue at Tulane Avenue, sets the scene for RTA streetcar No. 2004 on April 23, 2013. The three-story New Orleans Public Library building, which opened in December 1958, is the main library location providing a large collection of research material, along with all types of books.

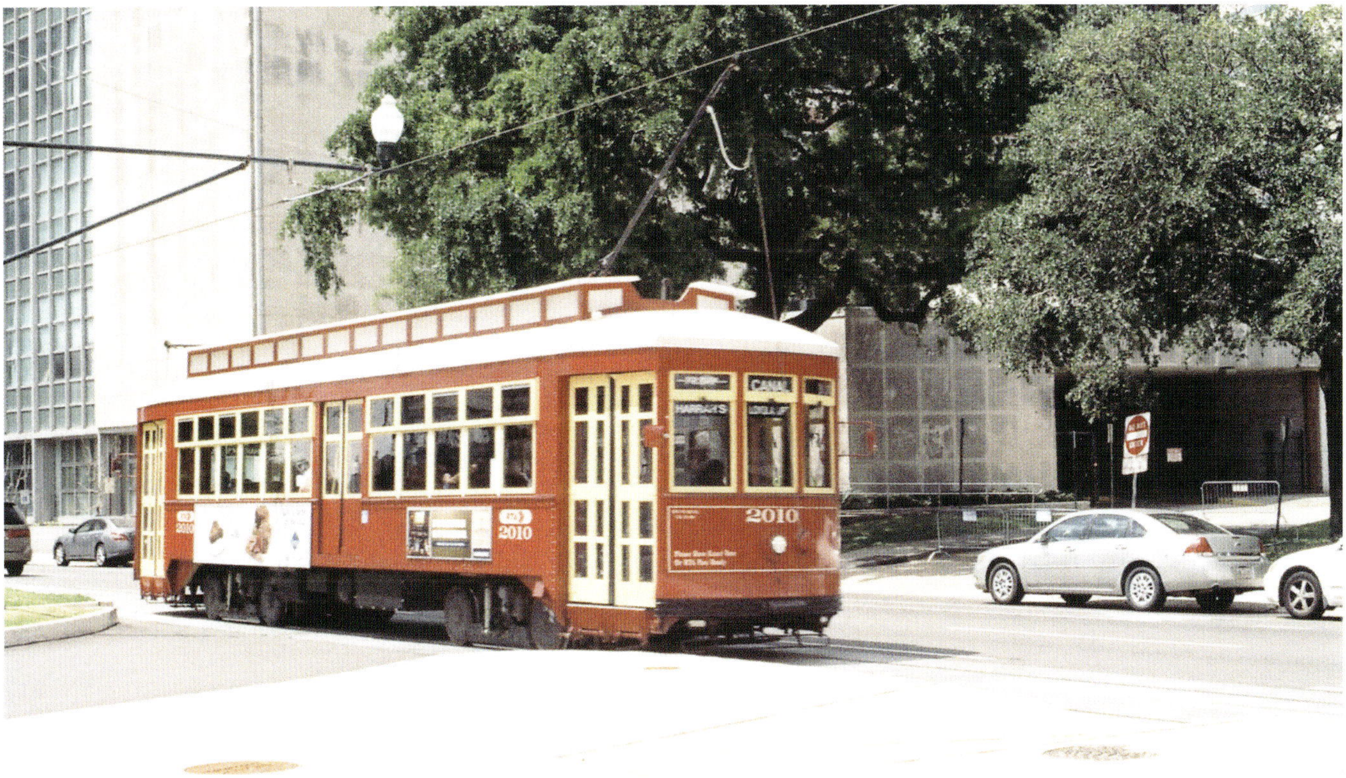

RTA streetcar No. 2010 is on Loyola Avenue on April 23, 2013, with the track on each side of the median on this carefully planned line.

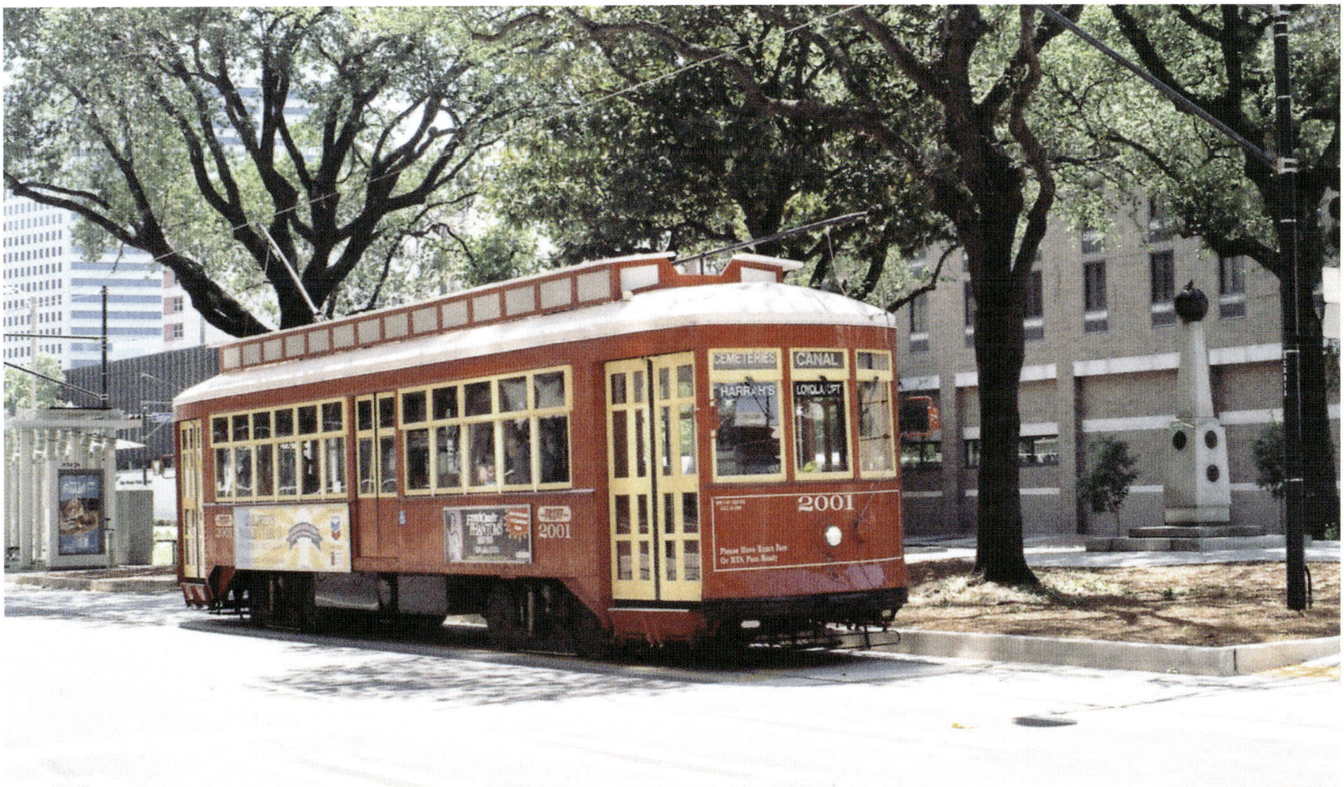

Loyola Avenue at Gravier Street is the location of RTA streetcar No. 2001 on April 21, 2013. Trackage for this line was built on each side of the landscaped median (neutral ground).

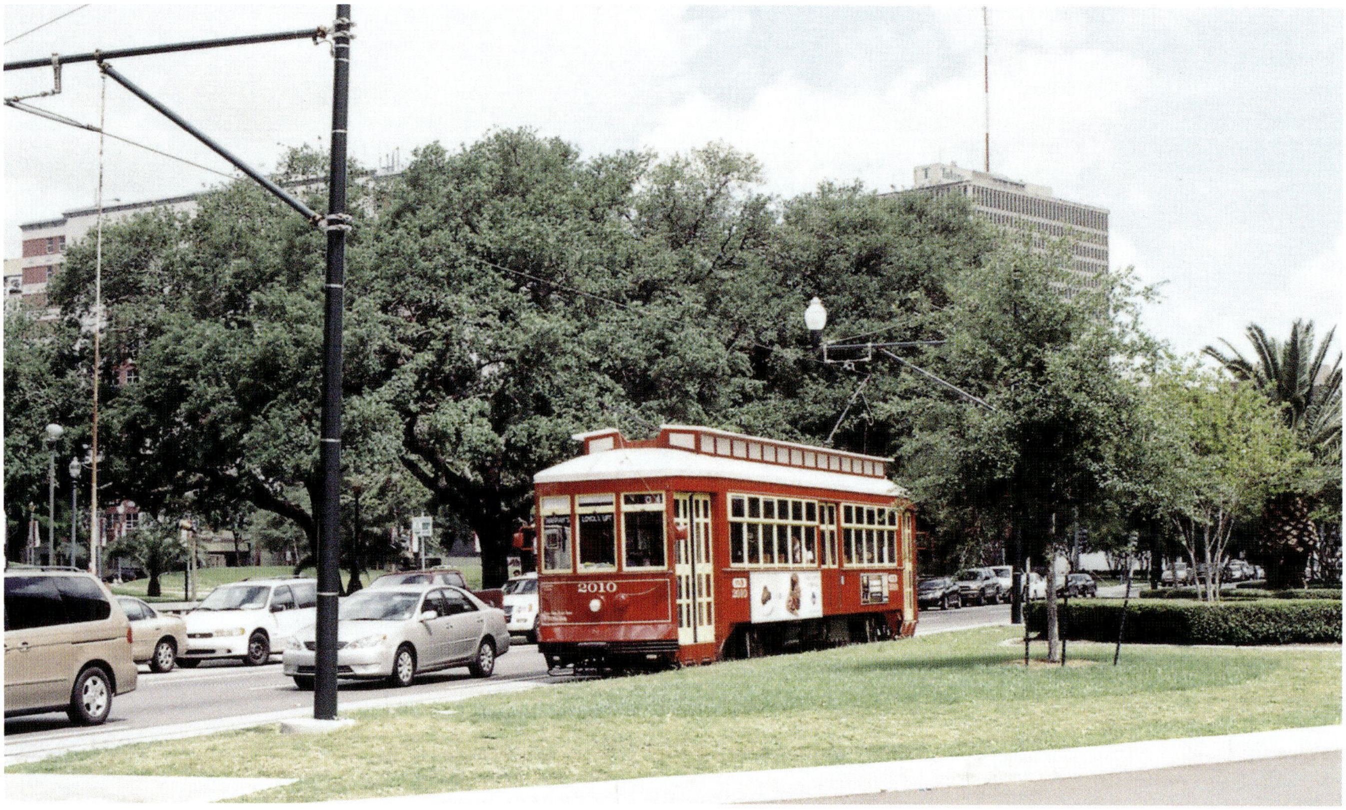

On Loyola Avenue, RTA streetcar No. 2010 fits right in alongside the picturesque, grass-covered center strip on April 23, 2013.

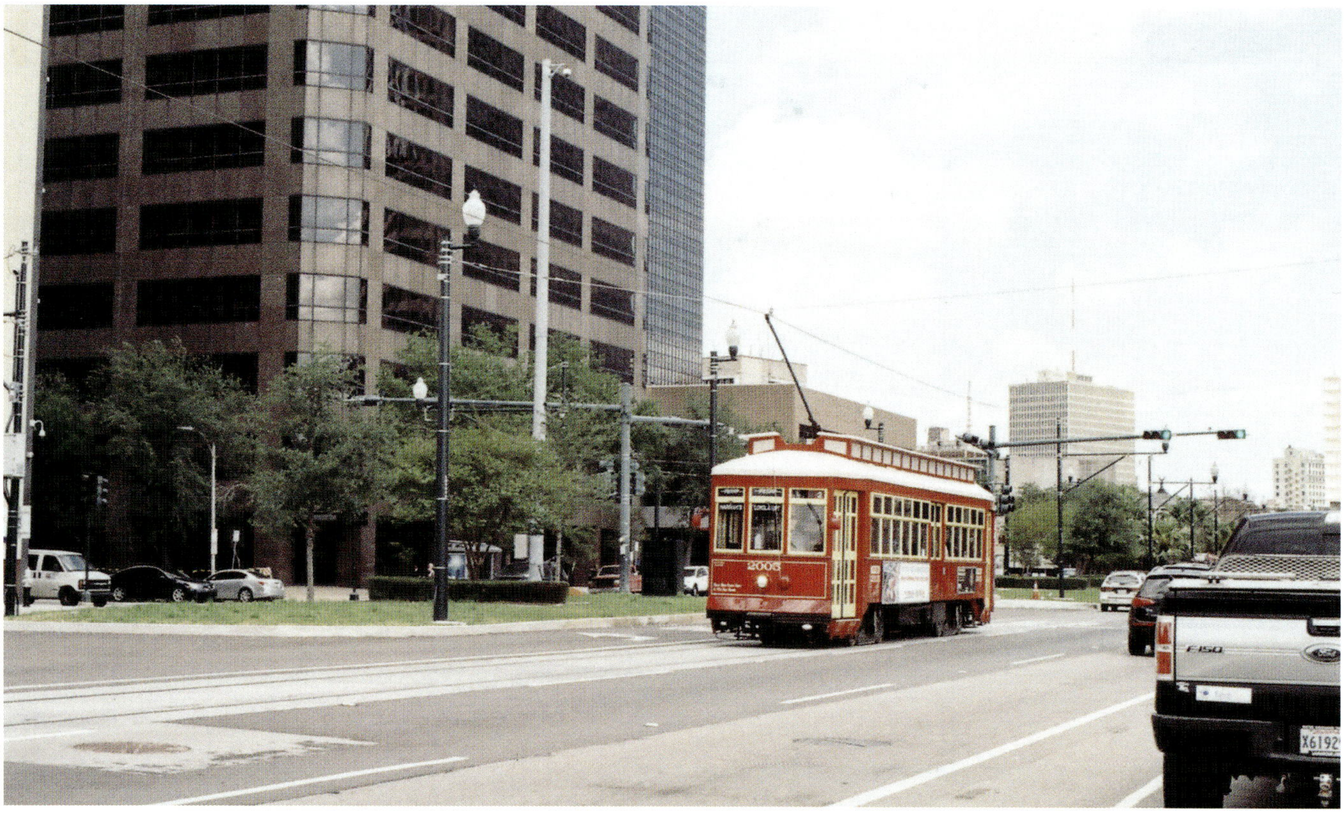

RTA streetcar No. 2005 is on Loyola Avenue on April 23, 2013. In addition to the Union Passenger Terminal, the Loyola line serves the Medical District and New Orleans Public Library at Tulane Avenue, New Orleans City Hall and the Financial District at Poydras Street, and the Main Post Office at Julia Street.

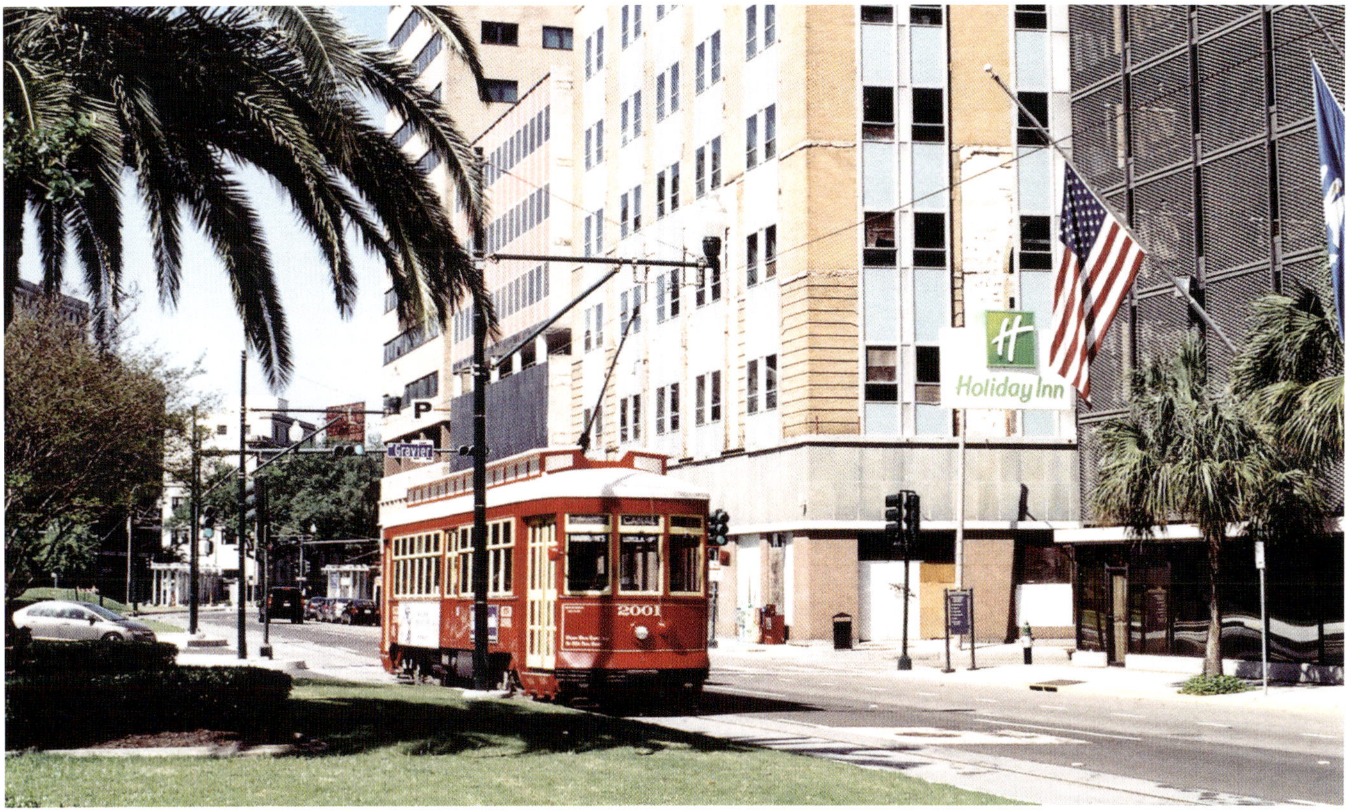

On April 21, 2013, RTA streetcar No. 2001 is on Loyola Avenue between Gravier Street and Perdido Street.

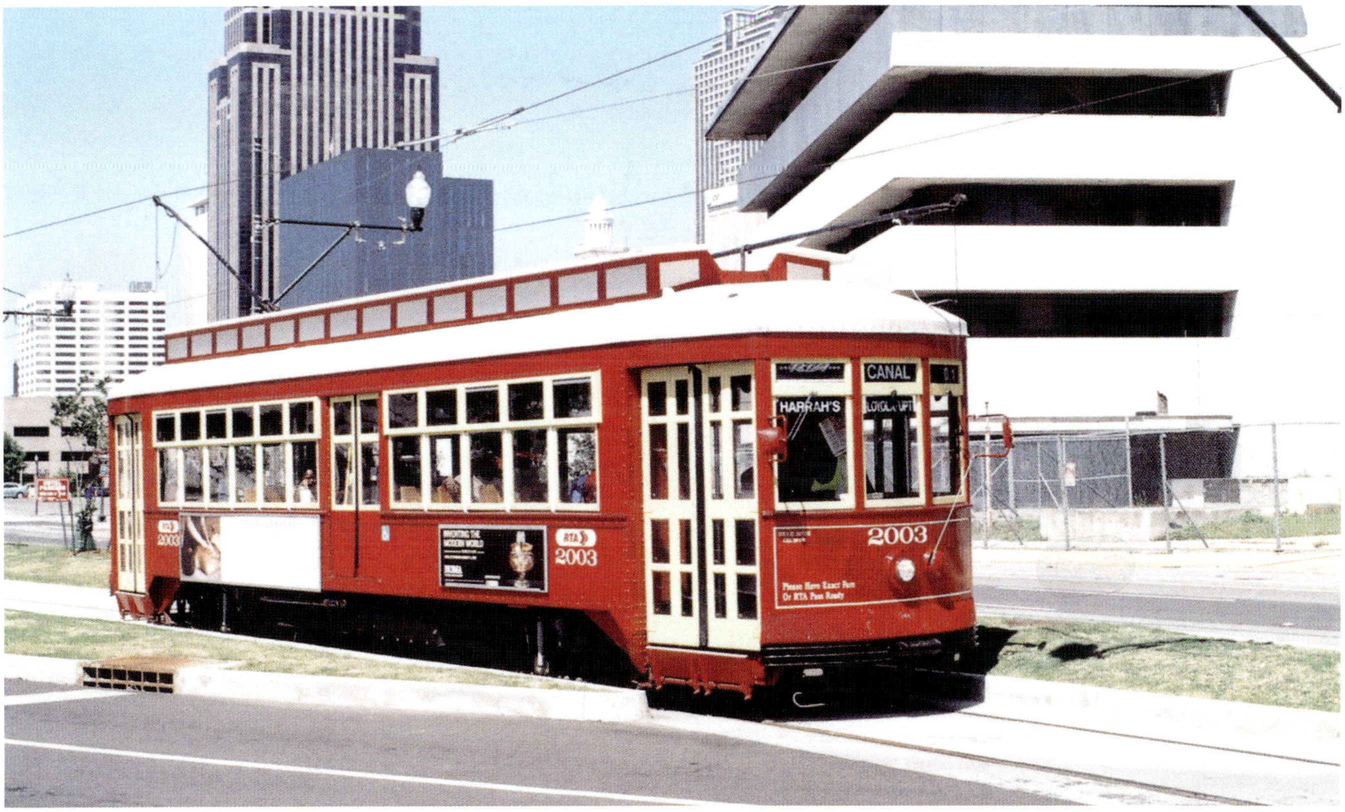

With the New Orleans skyline in the background, RTA streetcar No. 2003 is on Loyola Avenue near the Union Passenger Terminal on April 21, 2013. The white dome in the center is the Hibernia National Bank tower. Founded in 1870, the Hibernia National Bank became a wholly owned subsidiary of Capital One Financial Corporation in November 2005.

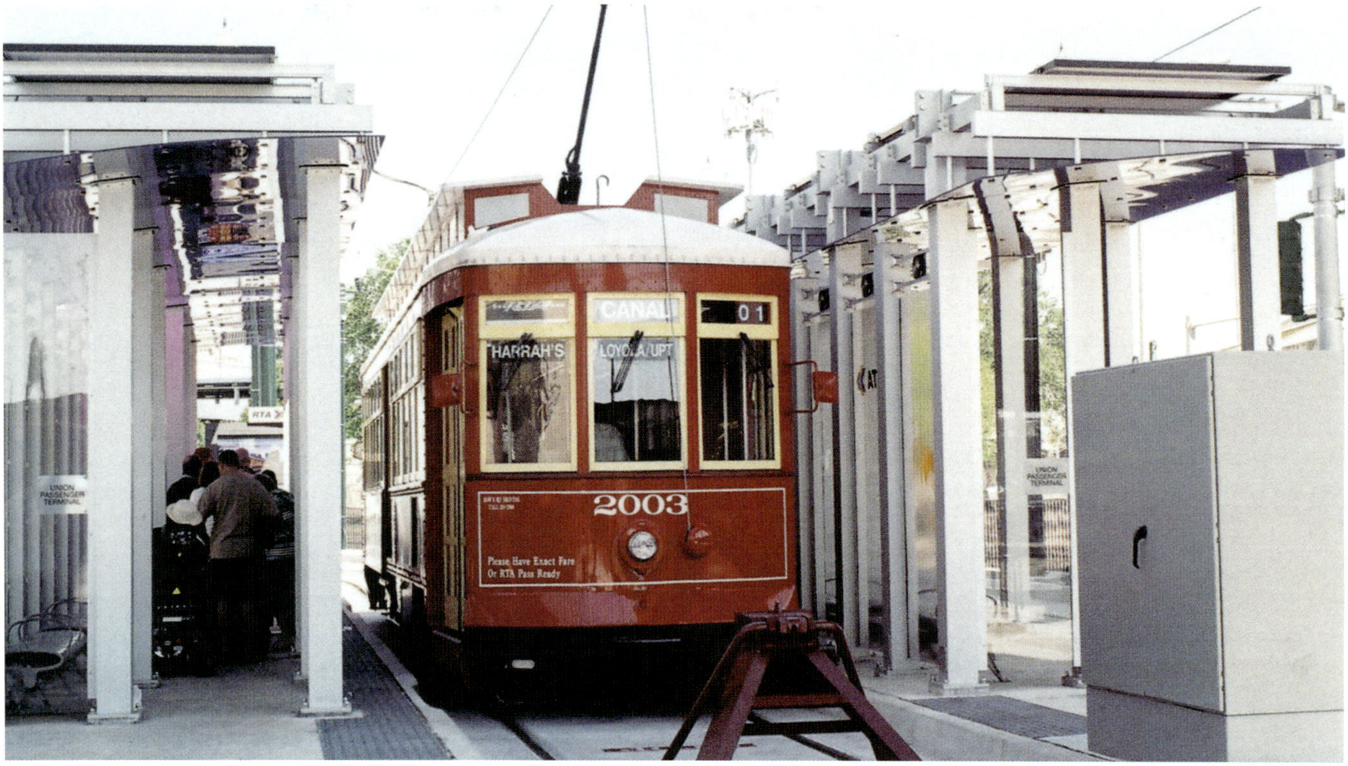

On April 21, 2013, RTA streetcar No. 2003 is at the station, on the Loyola Avenue line, which opened on January 28, 2013, serving the Union Passenger Terminal. The streetcar station is a short distance from the Union Passenger Terminal which opened in 1954, and, in January 2013, serves three Amtrak passenger trains: *Crescent* (New York City to New Orleans), *City of New Orleans* (Chicago to New Orleans), and *Sunset Limited* (Los Angeles to New Orleans).

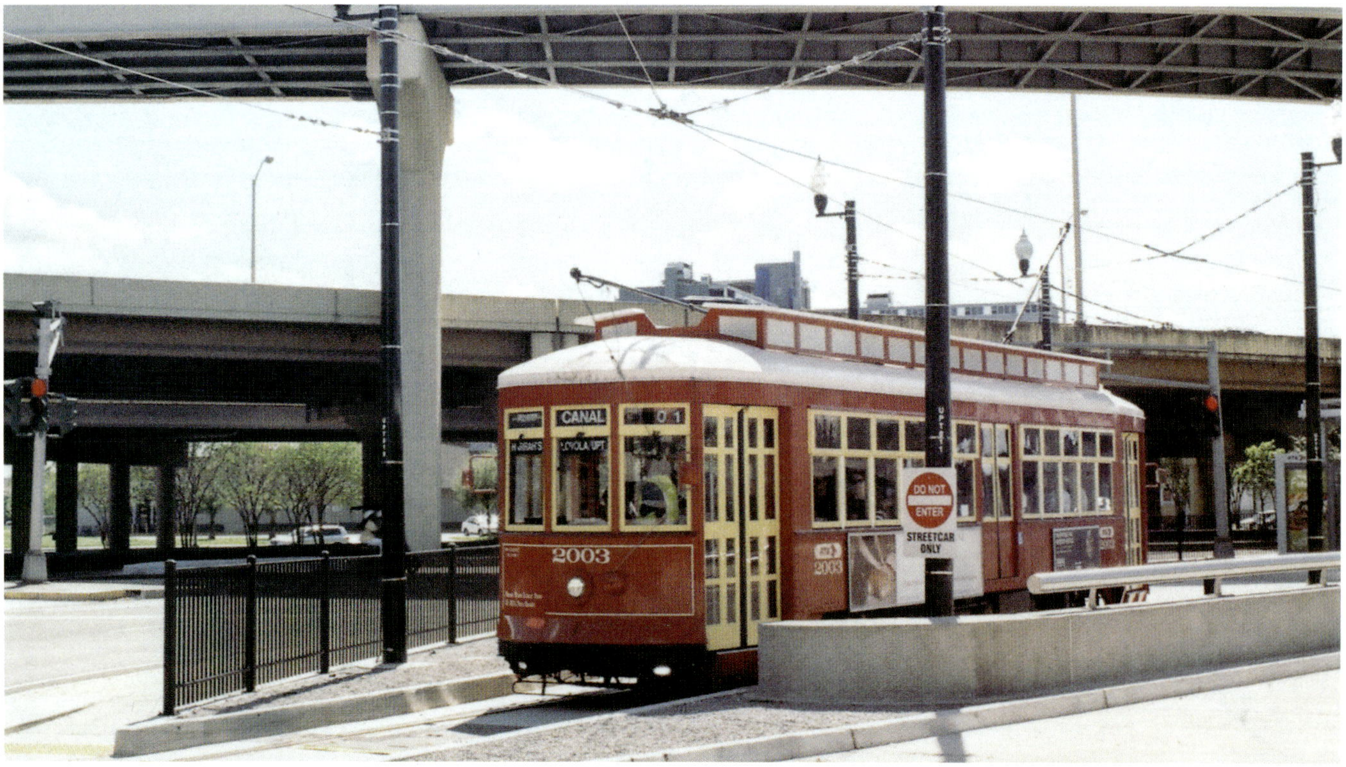

RTA streetcar No. 2003 is leaving the station serving the Union Passenger Terminal on April 21, 2013 for the trip via Loyola Avenue to the foot of Canal Street. The Loyola line added connectivity to New Orleans by making it possible for a traveler to go to the downtown business district, to the riverfront, to the cemeteries, and to City Park by streetcar.